Personality Dimensions and Arousal

PERSPECTIVES ON INDIVIDUAL DIFFERENCES

CECIL R. REYNOLDS, *Texas A&M University, College Station*
ROBERT T. BROWN, *University of North Carolina, Wilmington*

DETERMINANTS OF SUBSTANCE ABUSE
Biological, Psychological, and Environmental Factors
Edited by Mark Galizio and Stephen A. Maisto

HISTORICAL FOUNDATIONS OF EDUCATIONAL PSYCHOLOGY
Edited by John A. Glover and Royce R. Ronning

THE INDIVIDUAL SUBJECT AND SCIENTIFIC PSYCHOLOGY
Edited by Jaan Valsiner

THE NEUROPSYCHOLOGY OF INDIVIDUAL DIFFERENCES
A Developmental Perspective
Edited by Lawrence C. Hartlage and Cathy F. Telzrow

PERSONALITY AND INDIVIDUAL DIFFERENCES
A Natural Science Approach
Hans J. Eysenck and Michael W. Eysenck

PERSONALITY DIMENSIONS AND AROUSAL
Edited by Jan Strelau and Hans J. Eysenck

PERSPECTIVES ON BIAS IN MENTAL TESTING
Edited by Cecil R. Reynolds and Robert T. Brown

THEORETICAL FOUNDATIONS OF BEHAVIOR THERAPY
Edited by Hans J. Eysenck and Irene Martin

A Continuation Order Plan is available for this series. A continuation order will bring delivery of each new volume immediately upon publication. Volumes are billed only upon actual shipment. For further information please contact the publisher.

Personality Dimensions and Arousal

Edited by

JAN STRELAU

University of Warsaw
Warsaw, Poland

and

HANS J. EYSENCK

Institute of Psychiatry
University of London
London, England

Plenum Press • *New York and London*

Library of Congress Cataloging in Publication Data

Personality dimensions and arousal.

(Perspectives on individual differences)
Includes bibliographies and index.
1. Personality—Physiological aspects. 2. Arousal (Physiology) I. Strelau, Jan. II.
Eysenck, H. J. (Hans Jurgen), 1916–   . III. Series.
QP402.P47   1987   155.2'34   87-10808
ISBN 0-306-42437-1

© 1987 Plenum Press, New York
A Division of Plenum Publishing Corporation
233 Spring Street, New York, N.Y. 10013

Printed in the United States of America

Contributors

Kristen Joan Anderson, Department of Psychology, Colgate University, Hamilton, New York

John Brebner, Department of Psychology, University of Adelaide, Adelaide, South Australia

Monte S. Buchsbaum, Department of Psychiatry and Human Behavior, University of California, Irvine, California

Gordon Claridge, Department of Experimental Psychology, University of Oxford, Oxford, England

Christopher Cooper, Department of Psychology, University of Adelaide, Adelaide, South Australia

Andrzej Eliasz, Department of Psychology, Polish Academy of Sciences, Warsaw, Poland

Hans J. Eysenck, Institute of Psychiatry, University of London, London, England

Michael W. Eysenck, Department of Psychology, Birkbeck College, University of London, London, England

Jochen Fahrenberg, Institute of Psychology, University of Freiburg, Freiburg, Federal Republic of Germany

Anthony Gale, Department of Psychology, University of Southampton, Southampton, England

Richard J. Haier, Department of Psychiatry and Human Behavior, University of California, Irvine, California

Michael S. Humphreys, Department of Psychology, University of Queensland, Brisbane, Australia

Mark Katz, Department of Psychiatry and Human Behavior, University of California, Irvine, California

Tatiana Klonowicz, Faculty of Psychology, University of Warsaw, Warsaw, Poland

Paul M. Kohn, Department of Psychology, York University, Downsview, Ontario, Canada

Luciano Mecacci, Institute of Psychology, CNR, Roma, Italy

William Revelle, Department of Psychology, Northwestern University, Evanston, Illinois

David L. Robinson, Department of Psychology, University of Sydney, Sydney, Australia

Pavel V. Simonov, Institute of Higher Nervous Activity and Neurophysiology, U.S.S.R. Academy of Sciences, Moscow, Union of Soviet Socialist Republics

Ken Sokolski, Department of Psychiatry and Human Behavior, University of California, Irvine, California

Jan Strelau, Faculty of Psychology, University of Warsaw, Warsaw, Poland

Peter F. Werre, Psychiatric Centre Rosenburg, The Hague, The Netherlands

Marvin Zuckerman, Department of Psychology, University of Delaware, Newark, Delaware

Preface

At the beginning of this century, Pavlov developed a plan to explain individual differences in temperament by means of some features of the central nervous system (CNS). This attempt to seek explanations for individual differences in personality in physiological, especially in neurological mechanisms, led later on to research on several personality/temperament dimensions, such as, extraversion, strength of the nervous system, sensation seeking, and so on. Concepts like excitation, inhibition (especially transmarginal or protective inhibition), and, after Moruzzi and Magoun's discovery of the arousing role of the reticular formation, the concept of arousal/activation gained great popularity among biologically oriented personality researchers interested in the biological basis of personality.

Facts collected during the last decades by neurophysiologists as well as by other specialists made it clear that there exist many anatomical-physiological mechanisms responsible for the organism's level of arousal/activation—the endocrine system, the autonomic nervous system, and the CNS with all of its levels and structures. It also became evident that arousal refers to different phenomena at the introspective, behavioral, psychophysiological, and electrophysiological levels.

The very fact that the theoretical construct of arousal does not refer to a unidimensional phenomenon and that it is concerned with individual stimulus- and response-specific factors led personality researchers interested in the concept of arousal to refer, indeed, to different sets of phenomena. This state of affairs makes contacts more difficult among scientists who apply "arousal" or the notions of excitation-inhibition as key concepts in their personality/temperament theories.

A deeper analysis of the separate personality dimensions based on the concept of arousal/activation shows that they often refer to the same phenomena, such as, for example, speed of conditioning, sensory threshold, amplitude of AEP, and so forth. The dimensions of extraversion, impulsivity, sensation seeking, or strength or the nervous system may serve as examples here. The evidence that the different personality concepts have often to do with the same variables or indicators produced a growing tendency to find a common language or at least some mutual understanding among biologically oriented personality psychologists.

This tendency is expressed, among other things, in the fact that since the 1960s several meetings have taken place where experts in arousal-oriented personality dimensions had the opportunity to present their theories and to discuss possible links between them. As an example, the symposia that took place during the International Congresses of Psychology held in Moscow (1966), in Leipzig (1980), and in Acapulco (1984) may be mentioned.

The trend to exchange ideas among experts in extraversion, neuroticism, anxiety, psychoticism, impulsivity, strength of the nervous system, sensation seeking, reactivity, and augmenting-reducing (all of these dimensions referring to the theoretical construct of arousal) is also observable in publications, the number of which has increased in the last decade. This is evident when one follows the tables of contents of the international journal *Personality and Individual Differences* as well as of several other published works. Let us mention as well a few books, such as *Biological Bases of Individual Behavior*, edited by Nebylitsyn and Gray (1972), *Biological Bases of Sensation Seeking, Impulsivity, and Anxiety*, edited by Zuckerman (1983), or the two volume set of *The Biological Bases of Personality and Behavior*, edited by Strelau, Farley, and Gale (1985, 1986).

One of the common denominators of almost all the publications just mentioned is that authors representing different approaches to the study of personality dimensions present their own concepts and theories without paying much attention (although with some exceptions) to the connections existing between the separate dimensions under discussion. Emphasis on similarities and differences among the biologically oriented personality dimensions, with special attention to the theoretical construct of *arousal* to which all of them refer, constitutes the specific concern of this volume.

Personality Dimensions and Arousal, the authors of which are widely recognized experts representing different approaches and interests in a variety of biologically based personality dimensions, consists of four parts preceded by an Introduction and completed by a Postscript.

In the Introduction, Hans J. Eysenck gives a general overview, including a historical account, of the interrelations between personality and the theoretical construct of arousal. Many arguments for the usefulness of the concept of arousal in studies on personality may be found in this introductory chapter.

Part I (Different Perspectives in Research on Extraversion- Introversion) includes chapters that present research on extraversion-introversion conducted in different laboratories and pays attention to various aspects of arousal. Revelle, Anderson, and Humphreys, referring to their own data, argue, among other things, that it is impulsivity rather than E-I regarded as a high order factor that is related to individual differences in the level of arousal. The authors have shown that the study of individual differences in impulsivity combined with studies of human cognitive performance under different levels of arousal leads to interesting results. Cooper and Brebner, taking as a point of departure their stimulus-analysis and response-organization model of extraversion-introversion, postulate that the amalgamation of the constructs of excitation-inhibition and arousal should be considered as an explanatory concept of this personality dimension. In the last chapter of Part I, Werre, using the contingent negative variation as an indicator of the level of arousal, demonstrates the interrelations between level of arousal in task performance situations described as stressful and the level of E-I.

In Part II (Studies of Emotionality and Psychoticism), the reader will find a variety of views on the interrelations between the level of arousal/activation and such dimensions as anxiety, neuroticism, emotionality (all three terms often are used interchangeably), and psychoticism. Michael W. Eysenck advances strong arguments that support his view that individual differences in trait anxiety (neuroticism) can be reasonably explained only when both the biological mechanism (limbic arousal) and human cognitive systems are taken into account. A detailed analysis of the concept of arousal within the framework of research in emotionality (neuroticism) is presented by Fahrenberg, who stresses the methodological aspects of studies in arousal/ activation. The only study on animals presented in this book and conducted by Simonov supports the hypothesis that the interaction of the frontal neocortex–hypothalamus and the hippocampus–amygdala systems are responsible for the neuroticism (emotionality) dimension in dogs. Claridge's contribution regarding the concept of arousal as related to the psychoticism dimension closes Part II. One of the interesting conclusions by this author states "that the inherent disregulation of the 'psychotic' nervous system can potentially lead to extreme levels (in either direction) of different components of 'arousal.'"

The concepts that refer directly to the Pavlovian properties of the conceptual nervous system or for which the neo-Pavlovian typology was a starting point are presented in Part III (Neo-Pavlovian Concepts of Temperament). Robinson develops the idea that the diffuse thalamocortical system (DTS), which has specific psychological correlates, serves as the mediator of Pavlovian excitation. Individual differences in arousability are considered as a result of the sensitivity of the DTS neurons. Mecacci, too, discusses the neo-Pavlovian features of the CNS within the framework of modern neurophysiology. He pays attention to the so-called general and partial CNS properties that, in his opinion, underlie the different specific patterns of arousal discovered in contemporary research. Both remaining chapters deal with the reactivity dimension, a construct developed on the basis of the theory of strength of the CNS and popular among Warsaw psychologists. The empirical evidence presented by Klonowicz relates to facets of the control of reactivity over various forms of arousal. Eliasz, considering the role of temperament in a system of stimulation control, points out that reactivity has an impact on the formation of cognitive orientation toward various aspects of reality.

Part IV (Attempts at Integration Based on the Arousability Concept) includes chapters aimed directly at searching for interrelations among the separate arousal-oriented personality/temperament dimensions. It starts with Zuckerman's chapter in which he discusses the interrelations between strength of excitation, extraversion, anxiety, impulsivity, and sensation seeking, regarding arousal as a key concept of his considerations. The author also presents a multimodal and multiresponse psychophysiological model of sensation seeking. On the basis of psychometric evidence that reflects the link between such dimensions as extraversion, reactivity, neuroticism, augmenting-reducing dimension, and strength of excitation Kohn concludes in his chapter that highly arousable individuals tend to avoid strong stimulation and the reverse. He also discusses important issues regarding the inappropriateness of validating psychometric tests against experimental indexes. The chapter written by Haier, Sokolski, Katz, and Buchsbaum presents a new way of searching for integration among biologically oriented personality dimensions. This is the first time that the technology of Positron Emission Tomography (PET) has been applied in an attempt to see whether the activity of specific brain areas correlates with measures of personality. In the last chapter, Strelau compares eight arousal-oriented personality/temperament dimensions from the point of view of five indexes: inventory data, sensory threshold, amplitude of AEP, efficiency of conditioning, and general behavioral activity. The similarities and differences among the personality dimensions under discussion are enumerated there.

The volume also contains a general overview written by Gale. His chapter is presented as a postscript and has been prepared on the basis of all the other papers included here. The main results of his analysis can be found in Table 2 that deals with explanatory constructs, examples of scales, manipulations, and independent and dependent variables presented in the separate chapters. Short comments are included also. The author introduces in his systems approach analysis of the arousal-oriented personality dimensions the idea of an energic system, a control system, and an evaluation system.

Judgments as to the degree to which this volume contains new ideas and whether it can be regarded as a "refreshing breath" in the studies of biologically oriented personality dimensions must be left to the reader. If, after getting acquainted with the content of the book, he or she agrees that reading it was not a waste of time, our expectations will be fulfilled.

Much of the editorial work was supported by the Polish Ministry of Science and Higher Education (Grant RP. III. 25).

Jan Strelau
Hans J. Eysenck

Contents

INTRODUCTION

Arousal and Personality: The Origins of a Theory 1

HANS J. EYSENCK

Historical Anticipations 2
The Beginnings of Experimental Testing 4
Pavlovian Theories 6
The Concept of Arousal 7
The Place of Theory in a World of Facts 9
"There is Nothing as Useful as a Good Theory"—Lewin 11
References 12

PART I.   DIFFERENT PERSPECTIVES IN RESEARCH ON
          EXTRAVERSION–INTROVERSION

1. *Empirical Tests and Theoretical Extensions of Arousal-Based Theories
   of Personality* 17

WILLIAM REVELLE, KRISTEN JOAN ANDERSON, and MICHAEL S.
HUMPHREYS

Introversion–Extraversion and Performance 18
Impulsivity, Time of Day, and Task Variables 20
Theories of Arousal and Performance 28
Summary and Conclusions 32
References 33

2. *Excitation–Inhibition and Arousal as Explanatory Concepts for Extraversion* 37

CHRISTOPHER COOPER and JOHN BREBNER

A Unified Model of Extraversion 37
Some Behavioral Evidence for the Unified Model 39
Electrophysiological Studies: Some Evidence and Some
    Conclusions 45
References 55

3. *Extraversion–Introversion, Contingent Negative Variation and Arousal* 59

PETER F. WERRE

Introduction 59
Relationship between Contingent Negative Variation,
    Extraversion– Introversion and Neuroticism–Stability ... 61
Interaction between Extraversion–Introversion and Condition
    as Indicated by Contingent Negative Variation 63
Usefulness of the Inverted-U Model 65
Design of a New Testable Model 69
Limitations of the Model 72
Concluding Remarks 74
References 75

PART II. STUDIES OF EMOTIONALITY AND PSYCHOTICISM

4. *Trait Theories of Anxiety* 79

MICHAEL W. EYSENCK

Introduction 79
The Physiological Basis 80
The Cognitive System 83
Future Trends 93
References 94

5. *Concepts of Activation and Arousal in the Theory of Emotionality (Neuroticism): A Multivariate Conceptualization* 99

JOCHEN FAHRENBERG

Introduction 99
Emotionality (Neuroticism) as Assessed by Questionnaire ... 100
Activation (Autonomic Arousal) in Eysenck's Theory 102
Evaluation of Psychophysiological Research on
    Emotionality 102
Multivariate Activation Theory 109
Some Perspectives/Alternatives in Psychophysiological
    Research on Emotionality 111
Conclusions.. 117
References 118

6. *Individual Characteristics of Brain Limbic Structures Interactions as the Basis of Pavlovian/Eysenckian Typology* 121

PAVEL V. SIMONOV

Specific Features of Escape Responses in Rats after Damaging
    Limbic Brain Structures 123
Hippocampal Theta Rhythm and Conditioned Reflexes
    Transswitching in Dogs 127
Conclusion 131
References 131

7. *Psychoticism and Arousal* 133

GORDON CLARIDGE

References 147

PART III.   NEO-PAVLOVIAN CONCEPTS OF TEMPERAMENT

8. *A Neuropsychological Model of Personality and Individual Differences* 153

DAVID L. ROBINSON

Introduction 153
Pavlov's Theory 154

The Neural Bases of Introversion–Extraversion and
   Neuroticism 155
The Neural Bases of Group Intelligence Factors 159
The Neural Bases of Psychoticism and Cognitive Style 162
Pavlovian Concepts, Systems Theory, and Arousability 163
An Integrated Neuropsychological Model 164
Conclusion 169
References 169

9. *Basic Properties of the Nervous System and Arousal Model in the*
   Light of Current Neuropsychophysiology 171

   LUCIANO MECACCI

   The Notion of Basic Properties 171
   Arousal, Cognition, and Personality 175
   Conclusion 180
   References 180

10. *Reactivity and the Control of Arousal* 183

   TATIANA KLONOWICZ

   Introduction 183
   Reactivity and the Resting Level of Arousal 185
   Reactivity and the Impact of Stimulation 186
   Reactivity and Self-Regulation 189
   Reactivity and Anticipation 194
   Concluding Observations 194
   References 196

11. *Temperament-Contingent Cognitive Orientation toward Various*
   Aspects of Reality 197

   ANDRZEJ ELIASZ

   Introduction 197
   General and Selective Sensitivity to Stimuli 198
   Studies on Cognitive Orientation toward Various Aspects of
     Reality 203
   Studies on Cognitive Differentiation (CD) of People, Things,
     and Inner States 208

Final Remarks 211
References 212

PART IV.   ATTEMPTS AT INTEGRATION BASED ON THE
            AROUSABILITY CONCEPT

12. *A Critical Look at Three Arousal Constructs in Personality Theories:
    Optimal Levels of Arousal, Strength of the Nervous System, and
    Sensitivities to Signals of Reward and Punishment* 217

    MARVIN ZUCKERMAN

    Pavlov: Strength of the Nervous System 218
    Neo-Pavlovian Concepts 218
    Eysenck: Extraversion and the Optimal Level of Arousal 220
    Gray: Sensitivities to Signals of Reward and Punishment 221
    Zuckerman: Sensation Seeking, Optimal Level of Arousal of
        Catecholamine Systems 223
    A Multimodal Multiresponse Psychophysiological Study of
        Sensation Seeking 225
    References 230

13. *Issues in the Measurement of Arousability* 233

    PAUL M. KOHN

    Arousability and Sensation Seeking 233
    General versus Partial Properties Revisited 246
    Conclusions 247
    References 247

14. *The Study of Personality with Positron Emission
    Tomography* 251

    RICHARD J. HAIER, KEN SOKOLSKI, MARK KATZ, and MONTE S.
    BUCHSBAUM

    Introduction 251
    Method 252
    Results 256
    Discussion 264
    References 266

15. *Personality Dimensions Based on Arousal Theories: Search for Integration* 269

JAN STRELAU

Introduction 269
Arousal Mechanisms as a Physiological Basis of Different
Personality Dimensions 271
Different Components of Arousal Used as Measures of
Interrelations among Personality Dimensions 274
Biologically Based Personality Dimensions Measured by
Psychometric Data 278
Conclusions and Methodological Remarks 281
References 283

POSTSCRIPT

Arousal, Control, Energetics and Values—An Attempt at Review and Appraisal 287

ANTHONY GALE

Introduction 287
Common Features of Biological Theories of Personality 288
The Concept of Systems 289
Implications of a Systems Approach for Individual
Differences 291
Problems with the Concept of Arousal 294
Arousal and Contemporary Studies of the Expression of
Emotion 297
Bioenergetics and Individual Difference Theory 299
The Relevance of Family Process Theory to Individual
Differences Research 303
Why Have Psychophysiological Approaches to Personality
Failed? 312
Conclusion 313
References 314

Author Index 317

Subject Index 323

INTRODUCTION

Arousal and Personality
The Origins of a Theory

HANS J. EYSENCK

In my first book, *Dimensions of Personality* (Eysenck, 1947), I "took under my wing, tra la la, a most unattractive old thing, tra la la, with a caricature of a face"—to wit, the concept of extraversion-introversion. In the long story of the development of the notions that finally crystallized into this conception, there never had been a time when it had reached a lower point than in the war years that constituted a nadir from which most psychologists felt it would never rise again. To many, if not most psychologists interested in personality, it seemed as if I had attempted to resurrect a corpse, equivalent, perhaps, to trying to reintroduce into physics the notions of phlogiston, or aether, or a geocentric planetary system. Since then, of course, large-scale factor analytic studies in many parts of the world, using many different instruments and methods of analysis, have demonstrated that, descriptively, a dimension of personality closely resembling extraversion-introversion can be found universally and is of considerable help in the description of personality (Eysenck & Eysenck, 1985).

To this descriptive theory, I added a causal one (Eysenck, 1957, 1967, 1981). This theory attempted to explain the typical behavior patterns of extraverts and introverts in terms of lower cortical arousal in the former and greater cortical arousal in the latter. Both, in turn, were produced by differential thresholds and reactions in the reticular activating system and its reciprocal relations with the cortex. In fact, the theory of arousal put forward was a dual one, not unlike that postulated some-

HANS J. EYSENCK • Institute of Psychiatry, University of London, Denmark Hill, London, England.

1

what later by Routenberg (1968). Cortical arousal, which was responsible for extraversion–introversion differences, was contrasted with limbic activation; it was related to the activities of the sympathetic and parasympathetic systems and was responsible for differences in neuroticism–stability. It was also suggested that a high degree of limbic arousal would inevitably lead to a high degree of cortical arousal, so that the postulated independence of the two could be disturbed under these conditions.

HISTORICAL ANTICIPATIONS

The degree to which later work has verified predictions from this theory and its present status have been discussed elsewhere (Eysenck, 1981; Eysenck & Eysenck, 1985), and this is not the place for a survey of this evidence. What is of interest in the discussion concerning the interrelation between personality and arousal is, rather, a historical look at the way in which the concept originated and became associated with extraversion-introversion as well as a philosopy of science discussion of the usefulness of concepts of this kind in science generally. I am speaking of concepts that at the time of their origin had very little experimental backing, were defined differently by different scientists, and were certainly far from presenting a uniform, agreed-upon paradigm. It will be argued that in this, the concept of *arousal* resembles, in its early history, the development of atomic theories in physics and chemistry. These suffered from exactly the same kinds of difficulties, anomalies, and quarrels that are characteristic of the development of arousal theories in physiology and psychology.

The concept of extraversion-introversion has a very long history in psychology, going back to Hippocrates and Galen (Roback, 1927). These early theories of the "four temperamental types" of the melancholic, choleric, phlegmatic, and sanguine were vigourously defended, expounded, and put in the center of European psychology by Kant some 300 years ago (1912–1918). Wundt (1903) was the first to take these four categorical "types" and reduce them to two independent dimensions. The choleric and sanguine types constituted the extraverted, and the melancholic and phlegmatic types the introverted ends of one continuum, whereas the melancholic and choleric types constituted the unstable (high N), and the phlegmatic and sanguine types the stable (low N) ends of the other continuum (Eysenck, 1964). The history of the concept from then on has been traced by Eysenck (1973) and will not concern us here.

Instead, we will turn to certain interesting anticipations of the arousal hypothesis. What seems to have happened here, as also what happened early in the history of the theory of the atom, is that, well in advance of any scientific substantiation, the facts to be explained suggested concepts that later on could be and were discovered to have a true physical or biological basis. The first to put forward such an "arousal" view of the causal factors in extraverted and introverted behaviors was the Austrian psychiatrist Otto Gross, whose two books, *Die Cerebrale Sekundärfunktion* (1902) and *Über Psychopathologische Minderwertigkeiten* (1909), introduced the concepts of "primary" and "secondary" functions. These concepts are basically physiological and refer to the activity of the brain cells during the production of any form of mental content that leads on to the hypothetical perseveration of the nervous processes involved in this production. Thus the nervous process that succeeded in arousing an idea in the mind was supposed to perseverate, although not at a conscious level, and to determine the subsequent associations formed by the mind. Gross also postulated a correlation between the intensity of any experience and the tendency of that experience to persist secondarily and to determine the subsequent cause of mental associations. What was most intense and energy consuming in his view were highly affective and emotionally arousing experiences and ideas. These would therefore be followed by a long secondary function, during which the mental content would still be influenced and in part determined by the perseverative effect of the primary function.

Gross goes on to distinguish two "types." One is the deep/narrow; the other is the shallow/broad type. In the former, we characteristically find a primary function that is highly charged with emotion and loaded with affect, involving the expenditure of great nervous energy and requiring a lengthened period of restitution during which the ideas involved in the primary function go on reverberating and perseverating (long secondary function). In the shallow/broad type, on the other hand, a much less intense primary function, necessitating the expenditure of comparative little energy, is followed by a short period of restitution (short secondary function).

Certain personality characteristics follow from the hypothesis briefly described here. In the broad/shallow person, the short secondary function enables a much greater frequency of primary functions to take place within a given time. This constant readiness for brief actions and reactions suggests a certain superficiality, a distractability, as well as the prompt reaction to external events and quite generally the "changeability" that, according to Wundt (1903), was the essential feature of the extraverted type of person. In the deep/narrow person, the long perseverative secondary function makes the integration of different sets of what Gross calls *themes* (sets of emotions, associations, determining tendencies, complexes, and sentiments centered around one idea that is the object of a "primary function") more difficult and leads to a sejunctive or disassociated type of personality. Disassociation leads to a damming up of the available libido, to inhibition, on the behavioral level, and to absorption in thought and social shyness.

Jung (1921) readily identified the broad/shallow type with the extravert, the deep/narrow type with the introvert. His main difference from Gross lies in the stress he places on the intensity of the primary function. Gross, on the other hand, stresses the length of the secondary function.

> Introversion is characterised by general tension, and intensive primary function and the correspondingly long secondary function. . . . Gross deserves considerable praise for being the first to put forward a simple and unified hypothesis concerning the origin of these types. (Jung, 1921, p. 103)

THE BEGINNINGS OF EXPERIMENTAL TESTING

One great advantage of the formulation given by Gross is that it lends itself extremely well to experimental verification. The first to attempt such a verification was a Dutch philosopher, Heymans (1929), whose early contributions (Heymans, 1908; Heymans & Wiersma, 1906, 1907, 1908, 1909) constitute the first combined descriptive (correlational) and causal (experimental) analysis of a personality dimension. A detailed account of his work has been given by Eysenck (1970).

In essence, Gross's theory introduces a biological concept (primary function) that has many similarities with our modern views of cortical arousal. Obviously the relationship is not perfect, but the essential features of Gross's conception find a ready similarity in cortical arousal. Many of the deductions made by Heymans from Gross's theory are similar to deductions that I have made from arousal theory. Nothing could more clearly demonstrate the similarity of the concepts, although Gross, of course, was working entirely within the confines of a rather abstruse, "conceptual nervous system," whereas my own efforts were directed toward finding a causal basis for extraversion-introversion in a less conceptual and more "real" central nervous system.

Another early proponent of a form of arousal theory for the explanation of extraverted and introverted behaviors was McDougall (1929). He criticized Jung for giving "too rich a content" to the terms extraversion and introversion, which he otherwise agreed "point to some deeplying and very important pecularities of personality" (pp. 294–295).

McDougall goes on to suggest that it is possible to single out, of the complexes of traits to which Jung applies the terms extraversion and introversion, a simple personality factor that is purely one of temperament, and the possession of which, in various degrees of intensity, is an important constitutional factor in every personality. He then proposes that all personalities can be ranged in a single linear scale, according to the degree to which this factor is present in their constitutions. Such a distribution of a temperamental trait is most naturally explained, according to him, by the influence of some one chemical factor generated in the body that exerts a specific influence upon all the nervous system in proportion to the quantity that is produced and liberated into the bloodstream.

McDougall suggests that extraversion may be the positive state, which is characterized in its various degrees as a consequence of correspondingly large quantities or rapid rates of secretion of the postulated substance (which he calls X). Introversion, then, is a negative state, which is characterized by a lack of X. For McDougall, the introvert is a person in whom the lower levels of the nervous system are constantly subject to a high degree of inhibition by the higher cortical activities, so that he or she, by reason of the free dominant activity of the cortex and in virtue of its restraining or inhibitory effect on the outflow of thalamic excitation in its normal or direct channels of emotional expression, is a person in whom thought seems to flourish at the expense of emotion. "Introversion seems then to be the natural consequence of the great development and free activity of the cortex" (McDougall, 1929, p. 300).

To guard against the danger of excessive introversion,

> nature has provided an antidote against such increasing and such excessive introversion. . . . [This antidote is] an extraverting hormone or endocrine substance X, generated in the tissues, the function of which is to prevent, to diminish in some measure, this inhibiting paralysing influence of the cortex upon the more primitive lower-level functions of the nervous system. (McDougall, 1929, p. 300)

McDougall does not claim to be able to identify this substance, but he regards alcohol as a very suitable analog, due to its action of diminishing cortical control over the lower brain levels.

McDougall goes on to advance a theory of the action of alcohol, and his extraverting Substance X, namely that this "acts directly upon all synapses raising their resistance to the passage of the nervous current or discharge from neurone to neurone" (McDougall, 1929, p. 293). This is surely a very meaningful anticipation of the concept of arousal (in introverts) and lack of arousal (in extraverts). McDougall adds an appendix to explain in more detail his theory of inhibition, but there is no need to go into it here. Readers will find a full account in his paper. In my own development of the theory of extraversion-introversion, I found that McDougall had adumbrated many hypotheses that later research was to substantiate—very much as Gross had done.

PAVLOVIAN THEORIES

Apart from Gross and McDougall, the most notable proponent of a form of arousal theory, although, of course, not so named, was Pavlov (Gray, 1964). His theories and their interpretations and improvements by men like Teplow, Nebylitsyn, Strelau, and others have been well documented in a whole series of books (Claridge, 1985; Mangan, 1982; Nebylitsyn, 1972; Nebylitsyn & Gray, 1972; Strelau, 1983), and only the briefest of summaries will be attempted here.

Pavlov was interested in the "nervous types" observed during the course of his famous experiments on the conditioned reflex in dogs. He noted that dogs differed markedly in the rate at which they acquired and lost conditioned responses, and he attempted to account for the observed differences in terms of the variations in the kind of nervous system each animal possessed. In turn, this "nervous type" corresponded to the observed temperament and behavior of the dog. In the last years of his life, Pavlov applied this theory to human personality and to the explanation of abnormal mental states, on the assumption that these represented ways in which some fundamental properties of the nervous system could, in combination, produce differences in behavioral and psychological tendencies.

Pavlov suggested that brains differ in certain basic properties. One of the most important was that of *strength,* which he defined as a capacity of the nervous system to endure and tolerate very strong stimulation. He thought that some nervous systems can maintain a high level of responding over a relatively long period of time and tolerate the effects of very strong stimuli (strong nervous system). The weak nervous system, on the other hand, responded much more strongly even to mild or to moderately intense stimuli, but these strong reactions quickly led to exhaustion. It is this property of the *strength of the nervous system* that has obvious similarities to the notion of arousal. It is the weak nervous system that is quickly aroused, and the strong nervous system that requires much stronger stimulation for such arousal to occur. This led Gray (1970) and others to suggest that the strong nervous system was related to extraversion, the weak nervous system to introversion. The literature has been surveyed in great detail by Mangan (1982) and Strelau (1983). Many of the published data support the hypothesis, but there are also some that go counter to it, although it seems possible to account for these vagaries satisfactorily while retaining the general hypothesis that it is the weak nervous system that is characterized by high states of arousal.

Pavlov posited other properties of the central nervous system, in particular, *equilibrium.* This was based on his view that *inhibition* played as important a role as *excitation* in the nervous system and that the strength of inhibition varied independently of the strength of excitation. Thus nervous systems go through different combinations of weakness or strength of *both* excitation and inhibition, giving rise to this concept of equilbrium or balance between the two opposing processes. Eysenck's (1957) first attempt to account for the biological basis of personality also emphasized the balance between excitatory and inhibitory processes, and it is clear that the preponderance of excitatory or inhibitory processes is also related to the concept of arousal. The situation is made difficult for experimental studies by the undoubted existence of what Pavlov called *transmarginal inhibition,* or *protective inhibition* (Pavlov, 1928). According to his theory, weak nervous systems, when strongly stimulated, will show a paradoxical reduction in the size of the response, an effect Pavlov considered to be due to the intervention of an active inhibitory process that protects the nervous system against further stimulation.

The third and last major property of the nervous system that Pavlov recognized was mobility. This was "the ability to give way—according to external conditions—to give priority to one impulse before the other, excitation before inhibition and conversely" (1952, cited by Strelau, 1983, p. 9). Thus mobility manifests itself in the speed with which a reaction to a given stimulus, when required, is inhibited in order to yield to another reaction evoked by other stimuli. This facilitates an adaptive reaction to an environment that is continously changing, so that the individual, in order to adapt to these conditions, must modify his or her nervous processes in line with these changes. It will be seen that Pavlov's theory, although complex, is ultimately based on some form of arousal in a conceptual nervous system.

THE CONCEPT OF AROUSAL

Given this long development of the concept of arousal as a property of a conceptual nervous system, can we now say that it has "a proper habitation and a name"? Would it be true to say that we now have a complete understanding of the psychophysiolgical basis of arousal? The answer surely must be in the negative, but this pessimistic reply must be qualified by saying that we are certainly much nearer to such an understanding of the concept and that, like all scientific concepts, that of arousal has to be approached along a long and difficult road where every advance has to be paid for in terms of effort and time. The objections raised by physiologists to the concept of arousal are well known, and they have been itemized by Venables (1984), Claridge (1985), and M. W.

Eysenck (1982). Although it might appear at first sight that physiological measures provide a straightforward way of assessing many of the contentions of arousal theory, there are many difficulties. In the first place, the various physiological measures of arousal, such as heart rate, EEG, and skin conductance, typically produced only modest intercorrelations of between +.2 and +.3. In the second place, there are some situations in which one measure indicates increased arousal, whereas the second measure suggests the opposite—a state of affairs termed *directional fractionation* by Lacey (1967). And in the third place, account has to be taken of autonomic response specificity (Lacey, 1950, 1967). Stress typically produces a pattern of great activation in some autonomic measure and a much smaller activation in other measures. This pattern remains fairly constant for any given individual from one stressor to another, but there are pronounced individual differences in the precise pattern of autonomic activation. Eysenck and Eysenck (1985) have discussed the problems raised by these factors, and they will be discussed in detail in other chapters in this book.

Another difficulty derives from the law of transmarginal inhibition. If we look at the literature on the relationship between EEG measures of arousal and individual differences and extraversion-introversion, we find a considerable degree of heterogeneity in the outcomes. As Gale (1973) has shown, however, this arises largely from the fact that the conditions of measurement have varied from "very boring" through "slightly arousing" to "very arousing." As he also points out, one would expect positive results only in conditions that are mildly arousing, and his survey shows that, indeed, the ongoing studies that point counter to prediction are those involving too little or too much in the way of stress. The difficulty in this line of reasoning, of course, is that it is impossible *a priori* to specify what degree of stress is reasonable and adequate for eliciting the predicted relationship with extraversion. This is a typical task for "ordinary science," and no doubt a solution will be found to this problem in due course by carrying out suitable parameter studies.

What, it may be asked, is the use of such a weak and incomplete theory? I have discussed elsewhere the place of theory in a world of facts (Eysenck, 1985) and will not repeat the points made there in detail. The main point here that is relevant is that psychologists tend to have a curiously ambivalent attitude to theory. They either reject it outright, in favor of some form of Baconian inductive methodology that ceased to be tenable 300 years ago, or else they demand a perfection of theories, right from the beginning, that would rule out most of the theories now current in the hard sciences.

THE PLACE OF THEORY IN A WORLD OF FACTS

Consider, as an example, the history of atomic theory in physics and chemistry. Right from its beginning, as Bernal (1969) points out, the arguments about atomism were closely related to philosophical and sociopolitical problems. The materialism of Democritus, the founder of atomic theory, was later opposed by Plato and the doctrines of idealism that denied the physical existence of atoms. Democritus imagined the universe to be made out of innumerable small, uncuttable (A-Tomos) particles, moving in the void of empty space. The atoms were unalterable; they were of various geometric forms, to explain their capacity for combining to form all the different things in the world; and their movement accounted for all visible change. The doctrine became widely known through Lucretius and his book *On the Nature of Things*. He also popularized the philosophy of Epicurus, who in turn based his thought on the atomism of Democritus. These ideas were taken up during the Renaissance by Gassendi, a Provencal priest and contemporary of Descartes. Gassendi's atoms were massive particles with inertia, and they moved in the vacuum that Galileo's successors had proved to exist. His definition of atoms was adopted by Newton in his *Optics* 50 years later and became widely accepted. Newton, in turn, evolved a picture of the atom composed of shells within shells that were held together successively more firmly. This was a striking logical anticipation of the modern atom with its electrons and nuclei, but like much of his chemistry, at which he worked much longer than at physics, but without any great success, it was forgotten until recently.

The crucial part in making atomism the foundation of chemistry was John Dalton's contribution. He was interested in gasses as elastic fluids and tried to explain their properties on Newtonian principles by the mutual repulsions of the atoms. This caused him to consider the possible proportions of atoms in different kinds of gases and thus to see how to explain the laws of combination of elements in multiples of definite weights, which had gradually emerged from the analyses of the new gases, such as nitrous oxide, nitric oxide, and nitrogen peroxide. He introduced the modern way of denoting these gases in atomic terms, that is, N_2O, NO, and NO_2. This way of writing followed from the assumption that all chemical compounds were made up atom by atom, the atoms of different kinds arranging themselves in pairs, threes, or fours (Singer, 1959).

All that Dalton said about atoms—apart from the bare fact of their existence, which was not novel—was wrong. They are not indivisible nor of unique weight; they need not obey the laws of definite or multiple proportions, and, anyway, Dalton's values for relative atomic weights and molecular constitutions were for the most part incorrect. Why then is his contribution so important? It was he, more than any other single individual, who set modern chemistry on its feet. For, in devising a general scientific theory, the important thing is not to be right—such a thing in any final and absolute sense is beyond the bounds of mortal ambition. The important thing is to have the right idea (Greenaway, 1966). This is what Lakatos (Lakatos, 1968; Lakatos & Musgrave, 1970; Suppe, 1974) means by contrasting a *progressive* research program with a *regressive* one. It is not that theories are true or false, right or wrong; they are to be judged as to whether they give rise to a research program that is constantly discovering new facts, verifying deductions from the theory, and extending it to new fields. This may be contrasted with a regressive research program, such as the Freudian, where all effort is devoted to explaining away negative results, anomalies, and contradictions.

The next step in the history of the atom was, of course, the periodic table of Mendeleev, which was put forward in 1869. Even this tremendous achievement did not pacify the physicists who disliked the notion of a physical world being made of particles, and leading physicists like Mach, Ostwald, and Dumas continued to deny the existence of atoms until the beginning of the century, when Rutherford actually split the atom and J. J. Thomson discovered the electron. Since then, of course, the decomposition of the atom has progressed apace, so that now we have to deal with mysterious entities like quarks. Yet, in its essence, the Rutherford–Bohr atom is conceptually similar to Newton's, although quantum theory has introduced many strange features into this concept, and the end is obviously not yet in sight. During the development of these theories, hundreds of different models of the atom were advanced, furnishing it with hooks and eyes, to link one with another, or suggesting different geometric shapes that, like Lego pieces, would allow atoms to hang together. Thus we do not here have, at any time, a coherent theoretical picture but a great quarrel between physicists and chemists about the very existence of atoms and within the physical domain many different conceptions of atoms. There was far less agreement, even between atomic physicists, about the theory than there is now in respect to arousal, yet the theory marched forward triumphantly and is still the foundation stone of all modern efforts to understand the nature of matter.

What is suggested, therefore, is not that the theory with which this book is concerned is logically consistent, worked out in every detail, and gives rise to testable predictions that are verified in every instance. Such theories do not exist in science, and to search for them, other than as far-distant ideals, is to be plain ignorant of the nature of science. What we have, instead, is a progressive research program in which certain general notions, such as cortical arousal, transmarginal inhibition, and excitation-inhibition are like Pirandello's six characters in search of a play—they are concepts in search of biological identification and definition. The question is not whether cortical arousal *exists*. By their very nature, concepts in science do not exist in the sense that pigs and philosophers and planets exist. Scientific concepts are always inventions of the human mind, created to reduce the blooming, buzzing confusion of the great, wide world to some kind of order, and their justification is their success in doing so.

"THERE IS NOTHING AS USEFUL AS A GOOD THEORY"—LEWIN

The question of whether the theory linking extraversion with cortical arousal is indeed a progressive research program has been dealt with elsewhere (Eysenck & Eysenck, 1985) and so has the important question of the relevance of a proper theory of individual differences to the development of a scientific psychology (Eysenck, 1984). We shall here take it for granted that an experimental, social, industrial, clinical, educational, or any other kind of psychology that does not take individual differences into account relegates a major part of the variance to the error term and hence disobeys the fundamental law of scientific research, which is that no relevant variables may be omitted from theoretical formulation and methodological investigation of scientific problems. Such integration of what Cronbach (1957) called "the two disciplines of scientific psychology" is clearly dependent on the existence of proper theories that can be used to further such integration, and it is suggested that the "cortical arousal" theory, with all its weaknesses, successfully serves such a function. Many examples of how this can be done have been given elsewhere (Eysenck, 1976), and many more will be mentioned in the course of this book. What is so notable is that in spite of the acknowledged weakness of the "cortical arousal" theory of personality, nevertheless, many new and exciting discoveries and verifications have been achieved since its inauguration. Such applications of the theory include perception and learning, memory and conditioning, vigilance and pain research, repression and sensitization, achievement and aspiration, perceptual defense and time judgments, augmenting-reducing and figural aftereffects, sensory deprivation and sensory thresholds. The list is almost endless and covers practically all the phenomena studied by experimental psychologists. In addition, areas of concern to social psychologists, such as altruism and antisocial behavior, sexual attitudes and behaviors, group interactions and social skills, affiliations and personal space, speech patterns and expressive behaviors, field dependence and suggestibility, conflict handling and personal attraction, attitudes and values, recreational interests and industrial performance, occupational choice and aptitude, academic aptitude and achievement as well as mental health and drug use and abuse have been investigated along lines suggested by the theory (Wilson, 1981) with very positive results. It would be very difficult to say that the model has not been a *progressive* one, in the sense intended by Lakatos. This does not mean, of course, that the model is correct or the theory inviolable. It does mean that what Kuhn (1970) has called the "ordinary business of science", that is, its puzzle-solving activity, can now with advantage be brought to bear on the many problems remaining, in the hope that they will in due course be resolved. There is, of course, the alternative of an improved theory being put forward, but until such a theory makes an appearance, it would seem reasonable to try and improve the existing one and discover just how far it can be said to account for the phenomena in its domain. No final answers are likely to be forthcoming in the near future, but continued work along these lines should enable us to come to a more certain judgment of the value of the theory.

REFERENCES

Bernal, J. D. *Science in history*. 4 vols. London: C. A. Watts, 1969.

Claridge, G. *Origins of mental illness*. Oxford: Basil Blackwell, 1985.

Cronbach, L. J. The two disciplines of scientific psychology. *American Psychologist*, 1957, *12*, 671–684.

Eysenck, H. J. *Dimensions of personality*. London: Routledge & Kegan Paul, 1947.

Eysenck, H. J. *The dynamics of anxiety and hysteria*. London: Routledge & Kegan Paul, 1957.

Eysenck, H. J. Principles and methods of personality description, classification and diagnosis. *British Journal of Psychology*, 1964, *55*, 284–294.

Eysenck, H. J. *The biological basis of personality*. Springfield, Il.: Charles C. Thomas, 1967.

Eysenck, H. J. *The structure of human personality* (3rd ed.). London: Methuen, 1970.

Eysenck, H. J. *Eysenck on extraversion*. London: Crosby Lockwood Staples, 1973.

Eysenck, H. J. (Ed.). *The measurement of personality*. Lancaster: MTP, 1976.

Eysenck, H. J. (Ed.). *A model for personality*. New York: Springer, 1981.

Eysenck, H. J. The place of individual differences in a scientific psychology. *Annals of Theoretical Psychology*, 1984, *1*, 232–285.

Eysenck, H. J. The place of theory in a world of facts. *Annals of Theoretical Psychology*, 3, 17–72. (New York: Plenum Press, 1985).

Eysenck, H. J., & Eysenck, M. W. *Personality and individual differences: A natural science approach*. New York: Plenum Press, 1985.

Eysenck, M. W. *Attention and arousal: Cognition and performance*. New York: Springer, 1982.

Gale, A. The psychophysiology of individual differences: Studies of extraversion and the EEG. In P. Kline (Ed.), *New approaches in psychological measurement*. New York: Wiley, 1973.

Gray, J. A. (Ed.). *Pavlov's typology*. London: Pergamon Press, 1964.

Gray, J. A. The psychophysiological basis of introversion-extraversion. *Behaviour Research and Therapy*, 1970, *8*, 249–266.

Greenaway, F. *John Dalton and the atom*. London: Heinemann, 1966.

Gross, O. *Die Cerebrale Sekundärfunktion*. Leipzig: 1902.

Gross, O. *Über Psychpathologische Mindervertigkeiten*. Leipzig: 1909.

Heymans, G. Über einige psychische Korrelationen. *Zeitschrift für angewandte Psychologie*, 1908, *1*, 313–381.

Heymans, G. *Inbiding tot de Speciale Psychologie*. Harlem: Bohn, 1929.

Heymans, G., ' Wiersma, E. Beitrage zur speziellen Psychologie auf Grund einer Massenuntersuchung. *Zeitscrift für Psychologie*, 1906, *42*, 81–127; 1906, *43*, 321–373; 1907, *45*, 1–42; 1908, *46*, 321–333; 1908, *49*, 414–439; 1909, *51*, 1–72.

Jung, C. G. *Psychologische Typen*. Zürich: Raschen, 1921.

Kant, I. *Anthropologie in Pragmatischere Hinsicht* (Vol. 4). Berlin: Bruno Cassiner, 1912–1918.

Kuhn, T. S. *The structure of scientific revolution*. Chicago: University of Chicago Press, 1970.

Lacey, J. I. Individual differences in somatic response patterns. *Journal of Comparative and Physiological Psychology*, 1950, *43*, 338–356.

Lacey, J. I. Somatic response patterning and stress: Some revisions of activation theory. In M. H. Appley & R. Turnbull (Eds.), *Psychological stress*. New York: Appleton-Century-Crofts, 1967.

Lakatos, T. Criticism and the methodology of scientific research programmes. *Proceedings of the Aristoletian Society*, 1968, *69*, 149–186.

Lakatos, T., & Musgrave, A. (Eds.). *Criticism and the growth of knowledge*. Cambridge: Cambridge University Press, 1970.

McDougall, W. The chemical theory of temperament applied to introversion and extraversion. *Journal of Abnormal and Social Psychology*, 1929, *24*, 293–309.

Mangan, G. *The biology of human conduct: East–West models of temperament and personality*. London: Pergamon Press, 1982.

Nebylitsyn, V. D. *Fundamental properties of the human nervous system*. London: Plenum Press, 1972.

Nebylitsyn, V. D., & Gray, J. A. (Eds.). *Biological bases of individual behavior*. London: Academic Press, 1972.

Pavlov, I. P. *Lectures on conditioned reflexes*. New York: Liveright, 1928.

Roback, A. A. *The psychology of character*. London: Kegan Paul, 1927.

Routenberg, A. The two-arousal hypothesis: Reticular formation and limbic system. *Psychological Review*, 1968, *75*, 51–80.

Singer, C. *A short history of scientific ideas to 1900*. Oxford: Claredon Press, 1959.

Strelau, J. *Temperament, personality, activity*. London: Academic Press, 1983.

Suppe, F. (Ed.). *The structure of scientific theories*. Urbana: University of Illinois Press, 1974.

Venables, P. *Psychophysiological perspectives*. In M. G. H. Coles, J. R. Jennings, & J. P. Stern (Eds.). New York: Van Nostrand, 1984.

Wilson, G. D. Personality and social behaviour. In H. J. Eysenck (Ed.), *A model for personality*. New York: Springer, 1981.

Wundt, W. *Grundzüge der physiologischen Psychologie* (5th ed., Vol. 3). Leipzig: W. Engelmann, 1903.

PART I

Different Perspectives in Research on Extraversion-Introversion

Empirical Tests and Theoretical Extensions of Arousal-Based Theories of Personality

WILLIAM REVELLE, KRISTEN JOAN ANDERSON, and
MICHAEL S. HUMPHREYS

It has recently become increasingly popular to claim that individual differences in personality are not very important sources of variation in human behavior. It has been suggested that the noncognitive traits that can be identified show very little consistency across situations, and that although the search for consistent dimensions of personality was reasonable, it has not proved to be very useful and should be abandoned.

One of the alternative approaches that has been offered to replace the trait approach to personality is that of the "interactionists," who argue that the interaction between situations and traits accounts for more variance than simple main effects (Endler & Magnusson, 1976).

WILLIAM REVELLE • Department of Psychology, Northwestern University, Evanston, Illinois, _KRISTEN JOAN ANDERSON_ • Department of Psychology, Colgate University, Hamilton, New York, and _MICHAEL S. HUMPHREYS_ • Department of Psychology, University of Queensland, Brisbane, Australia. The research reported in this chapter was supported in part by Grant MH29209 (01-04) from the National Institutes of Mental Health to William Revelle and Michael Humphreys, by Grant MH 29209 (05-07) to William Revelle, by faculty research grants from Colgate University and Haverford College to Kristen Joan Anderson, and by a grant from the University of Queensland to Michael Humphreys. Preparation of an earlier draft of this chapter done at Oxford University was supported in part by Fogarty Senior International Fellowship TW00580 from the National Institutes of Health to William Revelle.

Unfortunately, this approach does not specify when interactions will occur.

This question of what personality variables should interact with what situational variables is an underlying theme of this book. By studying dimensions of temperament and how individual differences in temperament relate to behavior, it is possible to show how personality variables interact with environmental variables to have systematic effects upon behavior.

One such personality dimension is introversion-extraversion (I-E). It has long been suggested (Claridge, 1967; Eysenck, 1967, 1981; Eysenck & Eysenck, 1985; Gray, 1964, 1981) that I-E may be related to individual differences in physiological arousal and to the neo-Pavlovian dimension of strength of the nervous system. Additionally, the theory of I-E specifies when and why I-E should interact with environmental and task conditions. Our research has been concerned with the relationship of I-E to cognitive performance. In this chapter, we will review the expected relationship between I-E and performance, summarize some of our recent findings, and suggest how we believe further studies should proceed. Our purpose is twofold: (a) to report some recent developments in the relationship between a dimension of temperament and cognitive performance; and (b) to suggest that the general approach of combining experimental psychology with the study of individual differences is a fruitful one.

INTROVERSION–EXTRAVERSION AND PERFORMANCE

Hans Eysenck's theory of I-E as it relates to cognitive performance may be summarized in two postulates: (a) Introverts are more aroused physiologically than extraverts; and (b) performance is curvilinearly related to arousal (an inverted U). Evidence for the first postulate was put forward by Claridge (1967) and Eysenck (1967) and has been reviewed by Eysenck and Eysenck (1985), and Stelmack (1981). Eysenck's second postulate is based on the "Yerkes–Dodson law", which has received substantial empirical support (Broadhurst, 1959; Duffy, 1972; Hebb, 1955; Yerkes & Dodson, 1908), although it is not accepted unequivocally.

In combination, these two postulates predict that on tasks of moderate difficulty, in comparison to extraverts, introverts will perform better in nonstimulating situations, as well in moderately stimulating situations, and less well when under high stimulation or stress. Thus superficially inconsistent relationships between personality and performance across situations are seen not as evidence for the lack of utility of personality traits but rather as evidence for their usefulness. This model predicts, then, that there should be a consistent (albeit complex) pattern of differences in cognitive performance as a function of individual differences in I-E in combination with variations in situationally induced stress.

We have conducted several experiments that test these predictions. The first of these was by Revelle, Amaral, and Turriff (1976). The dependent variable was performance on verbal ability items similar to those of the Graduate Record Examination (GRE). Three conditions were used in a within-subjects design: (a) A relaxed condition; (b) a time pressure condition; and (c) a time pressure condition in which subjects were given 200 mg of caffeine. The results were quite clear: The scores of introverts fell by about .6 standard deviations from the relaxed to the most stressed condition, whereas those of extraverts rose by about the same amount. Although these results are compatible with the curvilinearity assumption (if introverts were at their optimal arousal level in the relaxed condition, whereas extraverts were underaroused in that condition), they did not show curvilinearity *per se.*

Three studies that have shown curvilinearity are those of Gilliland (1976), Gupta (1977), and Anderson (1985). Gilliland studied the effects of three levels of caffeine (0, 2, and 4 mg/kg body weight) on the GRE performance of introverts and extraverts. Using change scores in a pre-post design, Gilliland found that there was a curvilinear relationship between caffeine and performance for introverts, but there was a monotonically increasing one for extraverts. Using an IQ test, Gupta found that performance decreased for introverts with increasing doses of amphetamine, but performance of extraverts showed an inverted-U relationship. Although both of these studies provided reliable evidence for curvilinearity and demonstrated that introverts are more susceptible to performance deficits than extraverts, both used between-subjects designs, and thus neither showed curvilinearity within subjects.

Anderson (1985) has documented curvilinear effects within subjects. Using a Latin-square design, Anderson tested 100 subjects on easy (letter cancelation) and difficult (GRE verbal items) tasks at each of five different levels of caffeine (0, 1, 2, 3, and 4 mg/kg). Subjects were classified as low or high impulsive on the basis of the Eysenck Personality Inventory (EPI, Eysenck & Eysenck, 1964) impulsivity scale (Revelle, Humphreys, Simon, & Gilliland, 1980). Performance on the letter cancellation task (cancelling one letter from a page of randomly ordered capital letters) showed a significant linear increase with caffeine across all subjects. For the GRE items, however, there was a significant interaction of impulsivity with the quadratic trend of caffeine dose: The performance of low impulsives showed an inverted-U relationship to dose, whereas that of high impulsives improved with increases in caffeine dosage.

The results of these studies, as well as those of other investigators, are generally compatible with Eysenck's predictions, and the convergence of results from research using a wide variety of different experimental procedures and arousal manipulations is noteworthy. It is quite clear that under certain circumstances, the performance of introverts is hurt and that of extraverts is helped by increases in arousal.

IMPULSIVITY, TIME OF DAY, AND TASK VARIABLES

In our recent research, we have been concerned with two questions: (a) What are the personality, situational, and task characteristics that interact with arousal manipulations; and (b) how can we explain the presumed curvilinear relationship between arousal and performance? In this section, we will address the first question; in the next, we will consider several models that might help to answer the second.

IMPULSIVITY AND TIME OF DAY

After our initial success in showing that cognitive performance is an interactive function of I-E, time pressure, and caffeine (Revelle *et al.*, 1976), we attempted to specify the conditions governing this relationship. As reported previously (Revelle *et al.*, 1980), we found that although the relationship between personality and caffeine was quite consistent, it was not as compatible with Eysenck's theory as we reported earlier (Revelle *et al.*, 1976). In a series of six follow-up studies, we found that the most consistent relationships were with a subscale of I-E, impulsivity, and that these relationships were moderated by time of day.

The first follow-up study was Gilliland's, which has already been briefly described. In his dissertation, Gilliland (1976) reports that I-E as assessed by the EPI (Eysenck & Eysenck, 1964) had the expected interactive relationship with caffeine in its effect on performance, but when I-E was measured by the Eysenck Personality Questionnaire (EPQ; Eysenck & Eysenck, 1976), it did not have the expected effects. The chief difference between these two scales is in the saturation of impulsivity (Rocklin & Revelle, 1981): The EPI I-E scale has two subscales, impulsivity and sociability, whereas the EPQ I-E scale has only sociability content. A *post hoc* examination of the results, which Gilliland did not report in the published version of his dissertation (Gilliland, 1980), showed that the interaction of I-E with caffeine was due to the impulsivity subscale.

The remaining five studies reported by Revelle *et al.* (1980) examined these impulsivity findings more closely. A similar paradigm was used in each study: College students were recruited for a study involving caffeine. They refrained from consuming stimulants for 6 hours preceding the study. After signing a consent form that screened for medical contraindications, they were given 200 to 300 mg of caffeine (roughly equivalent to 2 to 3 cups of coffee) or placebo using double-blind procedures. Subjects filled out personality inventories for 30 to 40 min and then completed a cognitive performance task, usually the practice GRE used by Revelle *et al.* (1976), although in one study it was a simple verbal analogies test and in another, the verbal, quantitative, and abstract reasoning portions of the Differential Aptitude Test (DAT). The tests were given under time pressure. In several studies, subjects came for multiple day sessions, but we will discuss only the first day results.

In each of the five studies run in the morning, the same pattern was found: With placebo, nonimpulsives (introverts) outscored impulsives (extraverts) by an average (median) of .45 standard deviations. With caffeine, however, this result was reversed: Impulsives did better than nonimpulsives by .36 standard deviations. In fact, in every study done in the morning, caffeine hindered the performance of nonimpulsives and facilitated that of impulsives.

These results were in contrast to those for the other component of I-E, sociability, which did not show such a consistent pattern. I-E, which is a combination of impulsivity and sociability, showed slightly more consistent interactions, as expected, given the impulsivity results.

Self-reports of caffeine consumption indicated no reliable differences between the *ad lib* caffeine consumption of high and low impulsives, rendering explanation in terms of differential familiarity with caffeine implausible.

Further evidence that the performance changes in response to caffeine were not due to idiosyncratic sensitivity to caffeine but instead involved some more central process came from the results of the four studies conducted in the evening. In striking contrast to results from the morning sessions, in each of the evening studies the performance of high impulsives was hindered by caffeine. Low impulsives were helped by caffeine in three of these studies; in the fourth, there was a slight decrease in performance with caffeine for nonimpulsives and a very large decrease for impulsives. The median improvement for low impulsives given caffeine was .18 standard deviations and the median loss for high impulsives was .15 standard deviations.

To summarize, in the morning caffeine helped impulsives and hindered nonimpulsives, but in the evening these effects reversed: Caffeine hindered impulsives and helped nonimpulsives. Thus two subjects who performed equally well in the morning without caffeine could be made to differ by .8 standard deviations by the administration of caffeine or by .6 standard deviations by having them take the test in the evening.

The significance of these findings is twofold. First, they are consistent with the earlier findings of Blake (1967, 1971) that introverts differ from extraverts not in their basal arousal level but in the phase of their diurnal arousal rhythm: Extraverts are less aroused than introverts (in terms of body temperature) during the morning but are more aroused than introverts during the evening. Second, they show that the impulsivity component of I-E is probably responsible for previously reported relationships between I-E and arousal. This finding is congruent with other studies that have shown that many findings attributed to I-E are actually impulsivity effects (Eysenck & Levey, 1972; Eysenck & Folkard, 1980; Gray, 1972; Loo, 1980).

The interaction of impulsivity, caffeine, and time of day requires a reconsideration of the concept of stable (trait) differences in basal arousal. As noted by Gray (1981), much of Eysenck's theory of I-E hinges on the assumption of stable differences in arousal between introverts and extraverts. But if these differences reverse in the evening, why are not introverts extraverts at night? We suspect that impulsivity is a stable individual difference that does not change with diurnal variations in arousal and that there is some characteristic that leads to both impulsivity and a later diurnal arousal rhythm. This characteristic could be the speed of buildup of arousal or the speed of decay of arousal (habituation). If so, then nonimpulsives would build up arousal faster than impulsives, becoming alert sooner in the morning. After several hours, high and low impulsives would achieve the same arousal level, but impulsives would seek new stimulation constantly to maintain the arousal. By evening, nonimpulsives, who have been highly aroused for much of the day, would be fatigued and cease to seek arousal. Arousal would decay, and the nonimpulsive would retire for the evening. Impulsives would not have been as highly aroused for as long and would not be fatigued yet. Thus impulsives would still want to maintain a high arousal level and continue to seek stimulation. Eventually fatigue would set in and even impulsives would call it a night.

This interpretation introduces yet another concept, fatigue, into an already complex theory. Its advantage, however, is that it avoids the nonsensical prediction that introverts should prefer lively parties late in the evening, whereas extraverts should seek sex orgies in the morning.

An alternative way to fit our findings into the traditional I-E theory would be to assume that performance measures reflect within-subject differences in arousal, rather than absolute arousal levels. (Stimulation seeking would indicate between-subject differences.) Perhaps nonimpulsives are always more aroused than impulsives but are closer to their optimal level in the morning than in the evening. In contrast, high impulsives may have a lower optimal arousal level, to which they are closer in the evening. Both groups perform at their best when optimally aroused. This explanation assumes that performance is affected by within-subject arousal and that when subjects are optimally aroused absolute differences between them do not affect performance efficiency. This argument saves the assumption that introverts are always more aroused (in absolute, between-subject terms) than extraverts. But to do so, we added two postulates (low impulsives have higher optimal levels, and absolute level has no effect on performance), making any test of Eysenck's model using performance measures virtually impossible.

We prefer to believe that performance does reflect basal arousal differences and conclude that although nonimpulsives are more aroused than impulsives in the morning, they are less aroused in the evening. We feel that although these results are in conflict with the conventional formulation of I-E, they are strong enough to require a revision of that theory.

Even more important than our time-of-day results is the distinction between impulsivity and extraversion. Although psychometrically an inferior scale, the 9-item impulsivity subscale of the EPI has given us much more stable interactions with caffeine than either the sociability scale or the entire EPI extraversion scale.[1]

AROUSAL AND TASK VARIABLES

The Revelle *et al.* (1980) studies examined very complex performance tasks. Once we specified those conditions that reliably led to impulsivity by caffeine interactions, however, we began to analyze the task parameters of this effect in terms of current cognitive theory.

Our primary concern in addressing task variables was to clarify the determinants of task difficulty, which as noted by Broadhurst (1959) and Yerkes and Dodson (1908), is a critical factor in the relationship between arousal and performance. One of our efforts involved an attempt to decompose the inverted-U relationship into two complementary monotonic functions, one increasing and one decreasing with arousal. The

[1]In some of our more recent studies we have used alternative measures of impulsivity, including items taken from experimental measures of impulsivity developed by S. B. G. Eysenck. We have not found any more consistent results with these measures than with the original nine items derived from the EPI.

logic behind this approach has been spelled out in more detail in Humphreys, Revelle, Simon and Gilliland (1980) and Humphreys and Revelle (1984).

Based on the work of Folkard (1975), Hamilton, Hockey, and Rejman (1977), and Hockey (1979), we (Humphreys *et al.*, 1980; Humphreys & Revelle, 1984) suggested that arousal facilitates tasks that require rapid and sustained information transfer (SIT) but hinders tasks that require storage or retrieval of information in short-term memory (STM).

We have recently completed five experiments with results compatible with the Humphreys and Revelle model. The first examined the effect of impulsivity and caffeine on a proofreading task in which we assessed the detection of two types of errors (Anderson & Revelle, 1982). The detection of intraword (noncontextual) errors, such as misspellings or typographical errors, was assumed to require fewer STM resources than that of interword (contextual) errors, such as faulty grammar or incorrect word usage.

Weinstein (1974, 1977) had found that although noise had no effect on the detection of intraword errors, fewer interword errors were detected in noise than in quiet. Although these results are consistent with our hypotheses, noise may affect performance through either its arousing or its distracting effects. We therefore conceptually replicated Weinstein's studies using our standard caffeine × impulsivity design. We presented 60 subjects with three forms of the proofreading task in a within-subjects design. The first task was given with instructions to mark all incorrect words; the second two tasks were given with instructions to mark either inter- or intraword errors only. All subjects were tested at 9:00 A.M. A significant interaction between impulsivity, drug, and type of error indicated that for the interword errors, caffeine reduced the sensitivity of nonimpulsives and slightly increased the sensitivity of impulsives, but for the intraword errors, caffeine had a detrimental effect for both high and low impulsives. For all three instruction conditions, caffeine reduced the number of words read by low impulsives and increased it for high impulsives.

These results suggested that tasks with a higher memory load are more sensitive to arousal-induced decrements than tasks with a lower memory load. The decreased sensitivity of high impulsives with caffeine to intraword errors is impossible to interpret because this group also read more rapidly: Their decreased sensitivity could have resulted from a speed–accuracy trade-off.

In a second experiment, we examined the effects of impulsivity and caffeine on a visual scanning task (Anderson & Revelle, 1983). This task involves searching through strings of 20 letters looking for those strings that contain all of a set of target stimuli. The target set consisted of either 2 letters (low memory load) or 6 letters (high memory load). Folkard, Knauth, Monk, and Rutenfranz (1976) have shown that these two tasks are differentially affected by arousal as indexed by body temperature: Performance on the two-letter task is a direct function of arousal, whereas performance on the six-letter task is an inverse function of arousal.

We conceptually replicated the Folkard *et al.* study using caffeine and impulsivity as indexes of arousal. At 9:00 A.M. using our standard procedures 84 subjects were tested. As expected, there was a reliable interaction between drug and target size, indicating that caffeine was associated with greater accuracy and more rapid performance on the 2-letter task, but decreased accuracy at about the same pace on the six-letter task. If caffeine and impulsivity affect a similar activational state (arousal), then there should have been a parallel interaction between impulsivity and task. This interaction did not occur, but there was a reliable interaction between impulsivity, target size, and task sequence. (Target size was counterbalanced using two task sequences.) The proportion of targets correctly detected by low impulsives did not vary with target size or sequence. High impulsives, in contrast, were more accurate on the version of the task that was in the first and last of four positions.

These results indicate that high and low impulsives differ from each other in more than just arousal—otherwise, caffeine and impulsivity would have had similar effects. It could be that high impulsives adopted a strategy that was appropriate for the first task they did but did not switch to a strategy appropriate for the second task. An alternative explanation is that in comparison to nonimpulsives, impulsives expended more effort at the beginning (when the stimuli were novel) and end (in anticipation of finishing the task) than during the middle of the experiment.

Our third study (Anderson, Revelle, & Lynch, 1985) examined the effect of arousal on a modified Sternberg (1966) memory scanning task similar to that used by M. W. Eysenck and M. C. Eysenck (1979). A memory set of one to four words was presented by an APPLE II computer, followed by a single probe word that either did or did not come from the memory set. Probe words varied in semantic similarity to the memory set: Some were exact matches of a memory set word, and some were exemplars of a category named in the memory set. At 9:00 A.M. 79 subjects were given either caffeine or placebo. Latencies to correct responses were analyzed. Besides the obvious main effects, caffeine reduced the time needed to prepare to respond (the intercept) but increased the time to scan STM for each additional item (the slope).

The fourth study examined the effect of caffeine and impulsivity on complex analogies (Revelle & Benzuly, 1985). An APPLE II computer using a program developed by Onken and Revelle (1984) presented 48 geometric analogies. These analogies differed in difficulty along two dimensions: the number of elements in each term of the analogy and the number of transformations applied to each element. Following Mulholland, Pellegrino, and Glaser (1980), the number of elements was thought to reflect information transfer load; the number of transformations was assumed to be related to memory load. At 10:00 A.M. 61 subjects were given either 0 or 4 mg/kg of caffeine. Potential speed–accuracy trade-offs were controlled by presenting each item for a fixed period of time before it was removed and the response requested. Caffeine interacted significantly with the number of transformations, facilitating performance for analogies with one transformation (independent of the number of elements) but hindering performance on analogies with three transformations.

The fifth study in this series (Anderson, 1985) has been described earlier; it compared the effects of five levels of caffeine and two levels of impulsivity on performance on two tasks. For the low memory load task (letter canceling), the performance of both high and low impulsives improved across the five levels of caffeine. For the high memory load task (GREs), however, the performance of high impulsives was facilitated, whereas that of low impulsives was an inverted-U function of caffeine dose.

In summary, the studies by Gilliland (1976), Gupta (1977), and Anderson (1985) lend strong support to the hypothesis that performance is a curvilinear function of arousal and that this relationship is moderated by individual differences in impulsivity (Gilliland and Anderson) or extraversion (Gupta). In addition, the studies by Blake (1967) and Revelle et al. (1980) suggest that the arousal differences between high and low impulsives reflect temporary state differences rather than stable trait differences. Finally, the Anderson (1985), Anderson and Revelle (1982, 1983), Anderson et al. (1985), Folkard et al. (1976), and Revelle and Benzuly (1985) studies suggest what some of the task parameters that moderate the arousal–performance relationship might be.

It should be noted that in several studies, caffeine and impulsivity did not interact, and only caffeine showed statistically reliable effects, thus suggesting that high and low impulsives differ from each other in more than just arousal. This conclusion is understandable in light of our time-of-day effects, for although impulsivity can be thought of as a stable dimension of individual differences, the arousal differences between high and low impulsives reverse as a function of time of day.

It is clear from these experiments that the impulsivity by caffeine

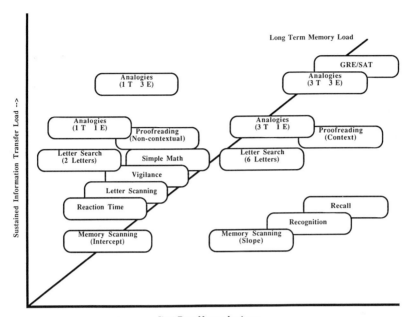

Figure 1. A conceptual organization of cognitive performance tasks along three dimensions of information processing (short-term memory, sustained information transfer, and long-term memory). Tasks further to the right require more short-term memory resources than those to the left. Tasks further up require more sustained information transfer resources than those nearer the bottom. Tasks shown behind other tasks are thought to require more long-term memory components than those drawn closer to the front of the figure. In general, our research has shown that performance on those tasks to the left of the center are facilitated by caffeine or other arousal manipulations, whereas performance on those tasks to the right of the figure is either hindered or shows an interactive effect of caffeine and impulsivity.

interaction can be moderated by task variables. We have thus gone beyond mere demonstrations of curvilinearity and are now able to study what determines the task difficulty parameter of the Yerkes–Dodson law. We can summarize our research results (as well as that of others) by classifying tasks along three dimensions of cognitive resources: SIT, STM, and long-term memory (see Figure 1). In general, those tasks with low STM requirements are facilitated by caffeine or other stimulants, whereas those with high STM but low SIT requirements are hindered by caffeine. Finally, those tasks with both high STM and SIT requirements (and perhaps a large long-term memory component) show interactive effects of caffeine and impulsivity.

THEORIES OF AROUSAL AND PERFORMANCE

Many theories have been proposed to explain the inverted-U relationship between arousal and performance. Several are unable to account for all the findings we have discussed, whereas several others are compatible with most of this evidence.

TRANSMARGINAL INHIBITION

One explanation for inverted-U phenomena is that performance is a monotonic function of arousal but that arousal is an inverted-U function of "arousal potential," which is the sum of all of those properties of the environment that stimulate the person. Arousal increases with increases in arousal potential up to the point at which further increases in stimulation instigate an inhibitory mechanism that protects the organism from too much excitation. Further increases in arousal potential lead to even higher levels of inhibition and hence greater decreases in arousal level.

While this model is likely to be true at extremely high levels of stimulation, it is unlikely that our subjects have been exposed to such extreme levels of arousal potential. Our task variable effects also argue against this explanation. For example, if the poor performance of highly aroused subjects on the six-letter search task is due to the effects of transmarginal inhibition (TMI), why do the same subjects do better on the two-letter task (Anderson & Revelle, 1983; Folkard *et al.*, 1976)? It is possible that different tasks change arousal potential, with the six-letter search task raising the arousal potential enough to induce TMI but the two-letter task not producing TMI. But this view cannot easily account for task effects in the proofreading study (Anderson & Revelle, 1982), in which subjects simultaneously scanned for both types of errors.

RESPONSE COMPETITION

Perhaps the best known theory relating motivation to performance is Hull's drive theory (1952). There are several different explanations that have been derived from drive theory, all of which assume that the probability of making a response is a function of the difference in excitation of two or more competing response potentials.

Spence and Spence (1966) assumed that drive and incentive motivation have a multiplicative effect on habit strength. Thus well-learned responses are facilitated more by increases in drive than less well-learned responses. This theory can explain increases in performance with increases in arousal for dominant or well-learned habits and decreases in performance with increases in arousal for difficult or poorly learned tasks. With additional assumptions about thresholds for excitation, it is even possible to explain inverted-U phenomena. As M. W. Eysenck (1981) has made clear, however, the theory is better at postdicting than at predicting results.

Broen and Storms (1961) proposed that there is a ceiling to excitatory potential: Increases in drive lead to increases in excitatory potential up to this ceiling, but increases in drive beyond that point do not increase the excitatory potential. Thus at low initial drive levels, easy or well-learned tasks would be facilitated by increases in drive, but once the excitatory ceiling has been reached, further increases in drive would increase the likelihood of subdominant responses. Although this model does predict inverted-U phenomena, it predicts that well-learned habits should achieve their maximum probability of response at lower drive levels than less well-learned habits. This prediction is, however, opposite to the initial Yerkes and Dodson (1908) findings, as well as to our own results (Anderson & Revelle, 1983; Anderson, 1985).

Broadbent (1971) modified drive theory to take into account the subject's criteria for responding. Applying a signal detection analysis to the problem of response competition, Broadbent showed that if a response threshold remains constant while drive increases, the probability of making the dominant response will be an inverted-U function of drive. This model also predicts that at low drive levels, subjects should make errors of omission, but at high drive levels, they should make errors of commission. Although this interpretation is consistent with some of our results, it is difficult to see how it could be applied to the pattern of results from the geometric analogies task (Revelle & Benzuly, 1985).

Range of Cue Utilization

The other well-known explanation for inverted-U phenomena is that of Easterbrook (1959), who proposed that increases in arousal lead to decreases in the range of cues that an organism can use. This model can account for the Yerkes–Dodson effect by making the additional assumptions that (a) simultaneous use of relevant and irrelevant cues reduces response efficiency; (b) irrelevant cues are eliminated before relevant ones as the range of cue utilization decreases; and (c) complex tasks require a broader range of cue utilization than less complex tasks.

A serious problem with many tests of Easterbrook's hypothesis is in their operational definitions of arousal. As we have argued previously (Anderson, 1981; Anderson & Revelle, 1982; Humphreys & Revelle, 1984; Humphreys et al., 1980; Revelle et al., 1980), arousal should be construed as a conceptual dimension ranging from extreme drowsiness at one end to extreme excitement at the other. It may be manipulated, physiologically indexed, or behaviorally observed. Any particular measure or manipulation will, however, introduce some irrelevancies. To strengthen the conclusion that observed effects are in fact due to arousal, research on the effects of arousal should therefore include several types of arousal variables to test for convergence between the alternative indexes. Unfortunately, most tests of Easterbrook's hypothesis have used indexes of arousal that have powerful but nonarousal-related effects on the allocation of cognitive resources (Anderson, 1981). For example, although inducing anxiety may increase arousal and consequently narrow the range of cue utilization, it may also lead to an increase in off-task thoughts (Wine, 1971). Thus performance decrements with increased anxiety may be due to arousal, off-task thoughts, or both. Many of our findings are consistent with Easterbrook's model, although it is not clear that it can explain the results of our memory-scanning study (Anderson *et al.*, 1985).

INFORMATION TRANSFER AND MEMORY

An alternative model, which is hard to distinguish empirically from Easterbrook's, is that arousal has different effects on the rate of information transfer and memory availability (Folkard, 1975; Hockey, 1979; Humphreys & Revelle, 1984; Humphreys *et al.*, 1980). In a review of the performance literature (Humphreys & Revelle, 1984), we concluded that arousal facilitates those tasks that require sustained information transfer (SIT)—staying prepared to process incoming stimuli, transmit information, or rapidly execute responses. We also proposed that arousal is monotonically and negatively related to short-term memory (STM) processes such as those involved in digit span, paired associate, or incidental recall after short intervals.

We assume that efficient cognitive performance generally requires both information transfer and memory. The combination of a monotonically increasing function (SIT) with a monotonically decreasing function (STM) can lead to an inverted-U function. Performance at low arousal is limited by the SIT component; performance at high arousal is limited by the STM component.

We also suggested (Humphreys *et al.*, 1980; Humphreys & Revelle, 1984) that incentive motivation, rather than affecting arousal, has a monotonically increasing effect on SIT but no direct effect on STM. Thus, manipulations such as competition, monetary incentives, or ego-involving instructions (e.g., Revelle, 1973) should improve the rate of information transfer but not memory. Because we assume a data-limited

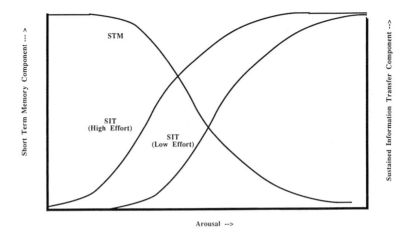

Figure 2. The effects of effort and arousal on two components of information processing. Sustained information transfer is a monotonically increasing function of arousal; availability in short-term memory is a monotonically decreasing function of arousal. Curvilinearity is a result of tasks being limited by a lack of resources for sustained information transfer at low levels of arousal and a lack of memory resources at high levels of arousal. Effort is thought to increase information transfer but not to hinder memory availability. Thus increased effort facilitates performance at low to middle levels of arousal but has little to no benefit at high levels of arousal.

ceiling for both components, incentives would thus lead to improved performance at low arousal levels but have no effect at high arousal.

Although the complete theory (Humphreys & Revelle, 1984) is too complicated to present here, some of these effects can be summarized figurally. In Figure 2, we show the hypothesized effects of two levels of effort for tasks involving both a STM and a SIT component.

This two-component model of performance predicts what variables should interact rather than just describing the interactions. We should note, however, that much of the evidence consistent with this model also supports Easterbrook's hypothesis, as most tasks with a high memory load (which are thus more susceptible to arousal-based deficits) also require a broad range of cue utilization.

GENERAL THEORETICAL ISSUES

When discussing theories of performance decrements, it is important to remember that the link between theory and data is sometimes quite complex. Many assumptions are necessary to relate our theory (Humphreys & Revelle, 1984) to the results of any particular study, including assumptions about the construct validity of measures of both arousal and task parameters. Implicit in our tests of arousal predictions are assumptions about the nature of tasks and vice versa. What is missing is a direct way to test both a theory of motivational effects and a theory of tasks.

Moreover, we assume that arousal facilitates information transfer processes and hinders memory processes, but we are as yet unable to specify exactly how these processes combine to affect performance. This inability is partly due to incomplete understanding of the determinants of task performance and partly due to the ambiguity of such terms as SIT and STM.

To a large extent, SIT and "attention" are similar constructs. Attention, however, has many different meanings that have been used in a variety of different ways. We believe that the concept of sustained attention is related to sustained information transfer and arousal. For example, we have shown (Bowyer, Humphreys, & Revelle, 1983) that on a recognition memory test, high impulsives experienced a vigilancelike decrement over trials, and this effect was reduced by caffeine. The similarity of this result to earlier studies of vigilance suggests that a common explanation should be applied to tasks that require staying prepared to process incoming stimuli, transmit information, or execute responses rapidly.

We are faced with a similar definitional problem with respect to the presumed detrimental effect of arousal on STM. There are several different theories of the processes involved in STM (specifically, capacity and strength); without a specification of the effects of arousal on these processes, we can make only very general predictions (cf. Humphreys, Lynch, Revelle, & Hall, 1983). Is STM hurt by arousal because the size of a memory buffer has been reduced or because the strength of the codes decays faster? Is an inability to recover appropriate memory codes due to their weakness or to increased strength of competing codes? Once again, what is needed is a theory of tasks as well as a theory of motivation.

SUMMARY AND CONCLUSIONS

Finally, we again note our use of impulsivity rather than the higher order construct of I-E. We have studied impulsivity because our results have shown that it has more consistent interactions with arousal manipulations than does I-E, suggesting that it is impulsivity rather than introversion–extraversion that is related to individual differences in arousal. We have persisted in studying impulsivity (rather than trying to develop a scale that assesses phase differences in diurnal rhythm or responsivity to caffeine) because we are not interested in just any individual differences but those that have been found to be influential in the domain of interpersonal behavior. H. J. Eysenck's three dimensional description of personality (1967, 1976, 1981; H. J. Eysenck and M. W. Eysenck, 1985), in which individual differences in impulsivity are presumably captured (Gray, 1981), is a well-developed theoretical structure. This theory may be wrong, but we feel that it is more beneficial to work within that framework, even as critics, than it is to explore individual differences that lack such a theoretical foundation.[2]

In this chapter, we have reviewed evidence relating the personality dimension of introversion–extraversion, or at least the lower order factor of impulsivity, to cognitive performance, and we have discussed various theoretical explanations for the observed results. We have suggested that seeming inconsistencies in behavior may be understood with an appropriate theory of personality, arousal, and performance. We hope we have shown that the combination of the study of individual differences with the study of human performance is a fruitful and worthwhile area.

REFERENCES

Anderson, K. J. *The current status of the Easterbrook hypothesis.* Unpublished manuscript, Northwestern University, 1981.

Anderson, K. J. *Impulsivity, caffeine, and task difficulty: A within-subjects test of the Yerkes–Dodson Law.* Unpublished manuscript, Colgate University, 1985.

Anderson, K. J., & Revelle, W. Impulsivity, caffeine, and proofreading: A test of the Easterbrook hypothesis. *Journal of Experimental Psychology: Human Perception and Performance*, 1982, *8*, 614–624.

Anderson, K. J., & Revelle. W. The interactive effects of caffeine, impulsivity, and task demands on a visual search task. *Personality and Individual Differences*, 1983, *4*, 127–134.

Anderson, K. J., Revelle, W., & Lynch, M. J. *Arousal and memory scanning: A comparison of two explanations for the Yerkes–Dodson effect.* Unpublished manuscript, Colgate University, 1985.

Blake, M. J. F. Relationship between circadian rhythm of body temperature and introversion-extraversion. *Nature*, 1967, *215*, 896–897.

Blake, M. J. F. Temperament and time of day. In W. P. Colquhoun (Ed.), *Biological rhythms and human performance*. London: Academic Press, 1971.

---

[2]We do not have the space to analyze the claim (H. J. Eysenck & M. W. Eysenck, 1985) that impulsivity is best thought of as a combination of E and P, nor the claim that impulsivity is quite adequately measured by the P scale. In terms of consistent effects upon performance, we find that impulsivity produces a clearer pattern of results than do P, E, or N. Much of our recent work has been devoted to a description of the components of tasks that are affected by arousal rather than a detailed examination of the place of impulsivity in a dimensional taxonomy of personality.

Bowyer, P. A., Humphreys, M. S., & Revelle, W. Arousal and recognition memory: The effects of impulsivity, caffeine, and time on task. *Personality and Individual Differences*, 1983, *4*, 41–49.

Broadbent, D. E. *Decision and stress*. London: Academic Press, 1971.

Broadhurst, P. L. The interaction of task difficulty and motivation: The Yerkes–Dodson law revived. *Acta Psychologica*, 1959, *16*, 321–338.

Broen, W. E., Jr., & Storms, L. H. A reaction potential ceiling and response decrements in complex situations. *Psychological Review*, 1961, *68*, 405–415.

Claridge, G. *Personality and Arousal*. Oxford: Pergamon Press, 1967.

Duffy, E. Activation. In N. S. Greenfield & R. A. Sternbach (Eds.), *Handbook of psychophysiology*. New York: Holt, Reinhart & Winston, 1972.

Easterbrook, J. A. The effect of emotion on cue utilization and the organization of behavior. *Psychological Review*, 1959, *66*, 183–201.

Endler, N., & Magnusson, D. (Eds.). *Interactional psychology and personality*. New York: Wiley, 1976.

Eysenck, H. J. *The biological basis of personality*. Springfield, Il.: Charles C Thomas, 1967.

Eysenck, H. J. *The measurement of personality*. Baltimore: University Parks Press, 1976.

Eysenck, H. J. *A model for personality*. Berlin: Springer, 1981.

Eysenck, H. J., & Eysenck, M. W. *Personality and individual differences: A natural science approach*. New York: Plenum Press, 1985.

Eysenck, H. J., & Eysenck, S. B. G. *Eysenck Personality Inventory*. San Diego: Educational and Industrial Testing Service, 1964.

Eysenck, H. J., & Eysenck, S. B. G. *Eysenck Personality Questionnaire*. San Diego: Educational and Industrial Testing Service, 1976.

Eysenck, H. J., & Levey, A. Conditioning, introversion–extraversion and the strength of the nervous system. In V. D. Nebylitsyn & J. A. Gray (Eds.), *Biological bases of individual behavior*. New York: Academic Press, 1972.

Eysenck, M. W. Learning, memory and personality. In H. J. Eysenck (Ed.), *A model for personality*. Berlin: Springer, 1981.

Eysenck, M. W., & Eysenck, M. C. Memory scanning, introversion–extraversion, and levels of processing. *Journal of Research in Personality*, 1979, *13*, 305–315.

Eysenck, M. W., & Folkard, S. Personality, time of day and caffeine: Some theoretical and conceptual problems in Revelle *et al*. *Journal of Experimental Psychology: General*, 1980, *109*, 32–41.

Folkard, S. Diurnal variation in logical reasoning. *British Journal of Psychology*, 1975, *66*, 1–8.

Folkard, S., Knauth, P., Monk, T. H., & Rutenfranz, J. The effect of memory load on the circadian variation in performance efficiency under a rapidly rotating shift system. *Ergonomics*, 1976, *19*, 479–488.

Gilliland, K. *The interactive effect of introversion–extraversion with caffeine induced arousal on verbal performance*. Unpublished doctoral dissertation, Evanston, Northwestern University, 1976.

Gilliland, K. The interactive effect of introversion–extraversion with caffeine induced arousal on verbal performance. *Journal of Research in Personality*, 1980, *14*, 482–492.

Gray, J. A. (Ed.). *Pavlov's typology*. Oxford: Pergamon Press, 1964.

Gray, J. A. The psychophysiological basis of introversion-extraversion: Modification of Eysenck's theory. In V. D. Nebylitsyn & J. A. Gray (Eds.), *The biological bases of individual behavior*. New York: Academic Press, 1972.

Gray, J. A. A critique of Eysenck's theory of personality. In H. J. Eysenck (Ed.), *A model for personality*. Berlin: Springer, 1981.

Gupta, B. S. Dextroamphetamine and measures of intelligence. *Intelligence*, 1977, *1*, 274–280.

Hamilton, P., Hockey, G. R. J., & Rejman, M. The place of the concept of activation in human information processing theory. In S. Dornic (Ed.), *Attention and performance* (Vol. 6). New York: Academic Press, 1977.

Hebb, D. O. Drives and the CNS (conceptual nervous system). *Psychological Review*, 1955, *62*, 243–254.

Hockey, R. Stress and cognitive components of skilled performance. In V. Hamilton & D. M. Warburton (Eds.), *Human stress and cognition*. Chichester: Wiley, 1979.

Hull, C. L. *A behavior system*. New Haven: Yale University Press, 1952.

Humphreys, M. S., & Revelle, W. Personality, motivation, and performance: A theory of the relationship between individual differences and information processing. *Psychological Review*, 1984, *91*, 153–184.

Humphreys, M. S., Lynch, M. J., Revelle, W., & Hall, J. W. Individual differences in Short-Term Memory. In R. F. Dillon & R. R. Schmeck (Eds.), *Individual differences in cognition*. New York: Academic Press, 1983.

Humphreys, M. S., Revelle, W., Simon, L., & Gilliland, K. Individual differences in diurnal rhythms and multiple activation states: A reply to M. W. Eysenck and Folkard. *Journal of Experimental Psychology: General*, 1980, *109*, 42–48.

London, H., & Exner, J. (Eds.). *Dimensions of personality*. London: Wiley, 1978.

Loo, R. Role of primary personality factors in the perception of traffic signs and driver violations and accidents. *Accident analysis and prevention*, 1980, *11*, 125–127.

McLaughlin, R. J., & Eysenck, H. J. Extraversion, neuroticism, and paired associates learning. *Journal of Experimental Research in Personality*, 1967, *2*, 128–132.

Mulholland, T. M., Pellegrino, J. W., & Glaser, R. Components of geometric analogy solution. *Cognitive Psychology*, 1980, *12*, 252–284.

Onken, J., & Revelle, W. ANATEST: A program to generate geometric analogy problems varying in number of elements and number of transformations. *Behavior research methods instruments and computers*, 1984, *16*, 333–334.

Revelle, W. *Introversion/extraversion, skin conductance, and performance under stress*. Unpublished doctoral dissertation, University of Michigan, 1973.

Revelle, W., & Benzuly, M. *Caffeine and memory load: Their effect on analogical reasoning*. Unpublished manuscript, Northwestern University, 1985.

Revelle, W., Amaral, P., & Turriff, S. Introversion-extroversion, time stress, and caffeine: Effect on verbal performance. *Science*, 1976, *192*, 149–150.

Revelle, W., Humphreys, M. S., Simon, L., & Gilliland, K. The interactive effect of personality, time of day, and caffeine: A test of the arousal model. *Journal of Experimental Psychology: General*, 1980, *109*, 1–31.

Rocklin, T., & Revelle, W. The measurement of extraversion: A comparison of the Eysenck Personality Inventory and the Eysenck Personality Questionnaire. *British Journal of Social Psychology*, 1981, *20*, 279–284.

Spence, J. T., & Spence, K. W. The motivational components of manifest anxiety: Drive and drive stimuli. In C. D. Spielberger (Ed.), *Anxiety and behavior*. London: Academic Press, 1966.

Stelmack, R. M. The psychophysiology of extraversion and neuroticism. In H. J. Eysenck (Ed.), *A model for personality*. Berlin: Springer, 1981.

Sternberg, S. High-speed memory scanning in human memory. *Science*, 1966, *153*, 652–654.

Weinstein, N. D. Effect of noise on intellectual performance. *Journal of Applied Psychology*, 1974, *59*, 548–554.

Weinstein, N. D. Noise and intellectual performance: A confirmation and extension. *Journal of Applied Psychology,* 1977, *62,* 104–107.

Wine, J. Test anxiety and direction of attention. *Psychological Bulletin,* 1971, *76,* 92–104.

Yerkes, R. M., & Dodson, J. D. The relation of strength of stimuli to rapidity of habit-formation. *Journal of Comparative Neurology and Psychology,* 1908, *18,* 459–482.

CHAPTER 2

Excitation-Inhibition and Arousal as Explanatory Concepts for Extraversion

CHRISTOPHER COOPER and JOHN BREBNER

A UNIFIED MODEL OF EXTRAVERSION

The proposals that excitatory-inhibitory processes and arousal levels underlie human behavior that we characterize as introvert (I) or extravert (E) and regard as an inherent part of a person's individuality were both originally made by Hans Eysenck (Eysenck, 1957, 1967). Both theories are too well known to need more than a brief reminder that, in the earlier theory, differences in reactive inhibition were suggested to underlie the I-E dimension of personality. Reactive inhibition was a Hullian concept (Hull, 1943) that was defined as a negative drive, that is, a drive not to respond, accumulating centrally as a function of the amount of work done in responding to some specific stimulus pattern. When this inhibitory potential equalled or was stronger than the excitatory potential, that is, the strength of the tendency to respond, then responding ceased. Reactive inhibition dissipated spontaneously as a function of time in Hull's model, and when the excitatory potential became the stronger, responding would recommence. To simplify measuring the amount of work done, many experimenters used tasks in which the same response was repeated so that the strength of reactive inhibition

CHRISTOPHER COOPER and JOHN BREBNER • Department of Psychology, University of Adelaide, Adelaide, South Australia.

was a function of the number of responses made and the time interval between them.

A large body of experimental evidence grew up around the reactive inhibition theory of extraversion, so much so that when Eysenck proposed his arousal level theory of extraversion in 1967, in which introverts tend to be overaroused and extraverts underaroused, it did not supplant the reactive inhibition explanation, and both appeared in the research literature concurrently for some years. Because there was experimental support for both theories, it seemed reasonable to try to amalgamate them into one unified explanation, and this is what we did more than 10 years ago (Brebner & Cooper, 1974).

As explained in several articles, for example, Brebner (1983) and Brebner and Cooper (1985b), the amalgamation of the separate views was achieved by distinguishing central processes concerned with the analysis of stimuli from those involved in response organization. It was then allowed that these processes could, independently, be in either an inhibitory or an excitatory state. The two states show themselves behaviorially in the respective tendencies to cease or attenuate an activity or to continue or augment it. Individuals at the I end of the dimension were characterized by deriving excitation from stimulus (S) analysis but inhibition from response (R) organization. Es showed converse tendencies to generate inhibition from tasks high on demands for S-analysis but excitation if the R-organization demands were high. The original reactive inhibition explanation was incorporated into the unified model through the proposition that the feedback from responding created S-analysis and, therefore, an inhibitory state in Es but an excitatory one in Is.

Some questions are raised by this simple new model. For example, are excitatory and inhibitory states independent of one another? Many tasks will be unbalanced in separate directions for Is and Es, but the question is whether S-analysis produces only excitation in Is and inhibition in Es, or whether relatively more of one state is created than the other. The assumption that if they are separate processes, then inhibition and excitation will oppose one another where they affect the same S-analysis or R-organization process means that the balance of inhibition and excitation will be the same whether they are separate states or the ends of a dimension of inhibition-excitation. Strelau (1970) has pointed out that, although Pavlov believed inhibition and excitation were separate processes, more recent theorists, for example Eysenck (1967), have regarded them as opposite ends of a continuum. The working assumption here leans in this direction but leaves open the possibility that inhibition and excitation may be identified as separate processes.

More central to this chapter, however, is the fact that Eysenck's formulation has been deliberately organized to be compatible with physiological arousal formulations with the explicit intention of obtaining for it a causal basis not available from the limited psychological correlational techniques (e.g., Eysenck, 1967, p. xxi; 1981, p. 14). Although continued psychological efforts within the paradigm (Eysenck, 1983) have offered refinements to his formulation and may be bringing it closer to being consistent with an understanding of the principles of the relevant aspects of brain function, it can be seen that there are such difficulties associated with achieving the latter that are inherent in the nature of neuroscience that the ultimate goal of establishing a causal explanation for the model may continue to prove somewhat elusive. In fact, a case can be made for the psychological model's being of greater value to neuroscience than the reverse.

SOME BEHAVIORAL EVIDENCE FOR THE UNIFIED MODEL

Returning to the unified model, Eysenck's arousal-level theory is dealt with through the overall balance of inhibition-excitation so that the Es' greater tendency to respond can be seen as consistent with increasing arousal levels. Some support for the view that Es require either intense and varied stimulation or the opportunity to respond in order to maintain their arousal was evident in the Brebner and Cooper (1974) study that required the subject to respond to a signal that occurred regularly once every 18 sec. At the conclusion of this task that made very low response demands on those carrying it out, Is remained alert and did not report adversely on the task, but Es reported the task was boring, and most admitted that they found themselves dozing off during the experiment.

In a later study (Brebner & Cooper, 1978), subjects looked at slides of various types for as long as they wished before pressing a hand-held microswitch to try to move to the next slide. Whether the slide changed or not was controlled by a computer program that needed 2, 8, or 16 responses to be made before activating the projector, or that 50 sec had elapsed. After three successive 50-sec periods, during which no amount of responding was effective, one E subject decided that it must be necessary to view each slide for at least 1 minute before responding. Operating under this self-imposed regime of high S-analysis and very low R-organization demands, this subject's alertness steadily decreased until she fell asleep—a convincing demonstration of decreased arousal in the virtual absence of response organization. Also, we have shown that E subjects tended to return to a "baseline" of alpha activity faster than Is did after listening to arousing music (Carr, 1976).

Table 1. Mean RT (msec) and Number of
Commissive Errors (n) Made on Catch Trials
by Is and Es

	Catch trial proportion					
	10%		40%		70%	
	RT	n	RT	n	RT	n
Is	313	0	321	0	337	0
Es	289	42	328	44	344	11

It can, no doubt, be recognized that we have retained the psychological concept of excitation in the model because using excitation defined operationally to mean the tendency to continue in or augment an ongoing activity and inhibition as the tendency to discontinue or attenuate a current activity permits development of the model. Since the model's inception (Brebner & Cooper, 1974) behavioral and performance data have offered greater support to it than electrophysiological attempts to measure arousal in I and E subjects while they are carrying out some experimental task.

Thus, for example, the degree of excitation for Is and Es as measured by the tendency to make commissive errors on catch trials in a simple reaction time (RT) task was tested by Brebner and Flavel (1978). Table 1 shows the mean RT for both groups with the number of commissive errors.

It is noteworthy that Es' mean RT was slowed considerably more than that of Is as the demands for R-organization diminished with the increase in the proportion of catch trials, even though Es continued to make more errors. This result does not lend itself to explanation in terms of Es trading accuracy for speed; rather it shows Es' excitation level is a positive function of the demands for response organization. An explanation in terms of reactive inhibition does not fit this result because an inhibitory effect due to responding would have been expected to lengthen Es' RT as a function of the number of responses made instead of shortening RT, as was found. Any explanation in terms of arousal level that does not distinguish the process of R-organization from S-analysis likewise is difficult to apply to the results, because, if it is argued that RT is negatively related to arousal levels that are determined by the amount of stimulation, then Is should be faster than Es where catch trials are fewest and this is not the case.

Further evidence supporting the new model's unification of Eysenck's theories comes from experiments on performance under crowded and uncrowded conditions (Katsikitis & Brebner, 1981; Khew & Brebner, 1985). In the first of these studies, I and E subjects were given the task of canceling letters found in a standard set of pages of English prose. Two levels of difficulty were employed for the cancelation task—easy, which required one letter only, the letter *a*, to be canceled, and—difficult, where the four letters *w*, *m*, *n*, and *c* had to be canceled. The task was performed under uncrowded conditions by half the subjects, but the remaining eight subjects carried out the task seated in a small room 2.68 m × 1.26 m. In the crowded condition, each individual made physical contact with at least two others. The effects of invading the personal space of other people have been studied since the first description of the norms for interpersonal distances (Hall, 1966). In the present context, among the most relevant are studies that indicate that infringements of personal space create arousal, for example, Saegart's (1974) demonstration that being crowded increases palmar sweating; the finding by Aiello, DeRisi, Epstein, and Karlin (1975) that GSR responses are increased when a person is approached closely by others; and the fact that heart rate and blood pressure (Evans, 1975) and cortisol levels (Heshka & Pylypuk, 1975) increase with crowding. These results all point to being more affected under crowding (which creates arousal, or, in our terms, creates further S-analysis demands) that affects Es' performance more than that of Is. If the crowded condition created emotional effects in high N subjects, then what would be predicted is a fourway interaction, I-E × N × Crowding × Difficulty. Although it is somewhat unusual to use complex interactions to test psychological theories, it has been possible to do so in some of the studies suggested by the amalgamated model.

If N and emotional responses do not enter into the interaction but only an increase in S-analysis demands, the prediction is for a threeway interaction, I-E × Crowding × Difficulty. This is what was found (see Figure 1). Es' performance became much worse than Is' on the difficult task when crowded. The Khew and Brebner (1985) experiment confirmed the earlier Katsikitis and Brebner result that crowding affected Es more than Is at a letter cancelation task and added the new result that disconfirming subjects' expectancies of whether they would or would not be crowded also had more effect on Es.

The Brebner and Cooper (1985a) study extended the model's prediction into the area of individual differences in inspection time (IT). *IT* is defined as the shortest exposure duration at which performance at a discrimination task is virtually errorless (Nettelbeck & Lally, 1976). Some writers, for example, Brand and Deary (1982), have hailed IT as a culture-free measure of intelligence because significant correlations between IT and intelligence test scores have been obtained. However, problems with IT can arise if the nature of the perceived event changes

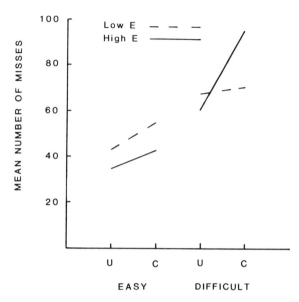

Figure 1. The interaction of E with task difficulty and being uncrowded (u) or crowded (c).

as the limits of discrimination are reached. Mackenzie and Bingham (1985), for example, report that, when using two lines of different length at varying exposure durations, some subjects make use of apparent movement cues rather than discriminating between the lines in terms of their length. On the grounds that Es will tend to reduce S-analysis if they can, an experiment was carried out using a computer-controlled series of presentations of two lines of different length presented on a video monitor at six different exposures. The experiment was carried out under a "fast" and "slow" rate of stimulus presentation in an effort to manipulate the degree of S-analysis involved in the task. The performance of Is and Es at this IT task was compared. What emerged from this experiment was:

1. Es had significantly shorter ITs than Is did—118 msec versus 163 msec for Is.
2. Four of the eight I subjects stated that they used the apparent movement strategy to perform the task, and five of the eight Es claimed to have used that strategy. Those who used the strategy had significantly shorter ITs (126 msec) than those who did not (160 msec).
3. There was a significant interaction between whether strategies were used or not and the fast and slow conditions. Strategy users obtained much shorter ITs in the fast condition, 118 msec against 177 msec.

Table 2. Mean IT Msec for I and E Subjects Who Did or Did Not Adopt the Apparent Movement Strategy for the Fast and Slow Conditions of the Experiment

	I		E	
Conditions	Strategy used	Not used	Strategy used	Not used
Fast	180	160	68	200
Slow	170	150	104	133

4. What is most important is that the threeway interaction between I-E × Strategy users/Not users × Fast/Slow condition was significant. The mean ITs are shown in Table 2; it can be seen that although the Es' use of the apparent movement strategy was reflected in their performance, this was not so for I subjects.

Again, this finding is difficult to relate to arousal levels, but it does seem to implicate differences in the process of S-analysis as the basis of the different ITs obtained by the two personality groups. Too much should not be built upon a single result, but it is conceivable that, because of the inherent excitatory effect the central process of S-analysis has in Is, even by using the apparent movement strategy, those subjects were unable to shorten that process sufficiently to match the shortest exposure durations.

Another test of the amalgamated model (Khew, 1984) also showed differences in the performance of Is and Es that distinguish between S-analysis and R-organization. Subjects were given a visual discrimination task of deciding whether the outline of a triangle or a square was embedded in a random pattern of dots generated on a computer-controlled video monitor. Varying the density of the dots made the task more or less difficult, and two conditions differing in the difficulty of the discrimination were used. Khew also varied response complexity using both a simple response of pressing one of two keys to note whether the figure was a triangle or a square and a more complex response that began as the simple response but was then followed by key-pressing responses with the other three fingers in the order of middle, ring, and little finger.

The aim in Khew's experiment was to manipulate the degree of S-analysis and R-organization demands. Using the simple discrimination, Es were shown to respond more quickly than Is. When the more difficult discrimination was used, however, both groups took longer to initiate the more complex response, and I-E interacted with response complexity as can be seen in Table 3. It shows that although Is were faster than Es in making the simple response to the more difficult discrimination, when the more complex response was required, their response time increased by more than 1 sec, whereas that of Es rose by only 374 msec.

Table 3. Mean Reaction Times and Standard Deviations (msec) of Responses to Discrimination Tasks

	Simple discrimination			
	Simple response		Complex response	
Es	487	16.7	477	15.4
Is	530	22.4	518	28.0
	Difficult discrimination			
	Simple response		Complex response	
Es	2215	233.9	2589	172.1
Is	1883	131.6	2893	441.4

This is in line with a relatively inhibitory effect for Es of the S-analysis demands of the more difficult discrimination being offset by an excitatory effect when the R-organization demands are increased with the more complex response. For Is, the postulated excitatory effect of S-analysis with the difficult discrimination is countered by an inhibitory effect when the more complex response increases the inhibitory effect R-organization has for these subjects. The standard deviations also follow this pattern. They are greater for both groups where a greater inhibitory effect is postulated.

Khew also recorded the time to complete the complex response as well as the time to initiate it. Because this aspect of the complex response involves making the response as well as organizing it and because feedback from multiple responses emitted rapidly were involved, it was anticipated that the effect of this increased S-analysis would be inhibitory for Es but excitatory for Is. Table 4 shows the times from initiation to completion of the complex response. Although Es take slightly longer to complete the response than Is when the discrimination is difficult and very slightly shorter times than Is when the discrimination is simple, the interaction falls just short of statistical significance ($p = .053$). Nev-

Table 4. Mean Movement Times and Standard Deviations (msec) of Complex Responses

	Complex response			
	Simple discrimination		Difficult discrimination	
Es	1109	102.8	1306	112.8
Is	1135	117.7	1226	59.3

ertheless, again the standard deviations are of interest in that a much lower value is obtained by Is than Es when the more difficult discrimination and complex response are employed.

ELECTROPHYSIOLOGICAL STUDIES: SOME EVIDENCE AND SOME CONCLUSIONS

Fine grain effects such as Khew showed even within the same total action made by Is and Es do seem to testify to the importance of distinguishing between S-analysis and R-organization processes and their effects. To relate these behavioral effects to a physiological level of arousal might eventually be possible if the electrophysiological techniques that have developed since Berger's (1929) original scalp recording method allow us to distinguish between the neural activity underlying S-analysis and that associated with R-organization. But despite the stimulus-response history of psychology, this is still not possible, although there are some interesting possibilities, including the slowly rising negative shift, the so-called "readiness potential," and other deflections of the movement-related potential on the one hand, and the medium latency waves (between 50–150 msec poststimulus), on the other. The medium latency wave that they term the *P1–N1 deflection* has been used by Haier, Robinson, Braden, and Williams (1984) to divide individuals into groups of "augmenters" for whom increased stimulus intensity is linked to increased ERP amplitude and "reducers" who show reduced ERP amplitude when stimulus intensity is increased. Haier *et al.*'s reducers were extraverted with a mean score of 18.8 on the Eysenck Personality Questionnaire compared to their augmenters' average of 13.6. However, although the E scores of Haier *et al.*'s two groups differed significantly, the mean score of 13.6 for augmenters locates them in the middle of the range rather than at the I end of it. Furthermore, one of the reducers who was regarded as an outlier and excluded from the results had an E score that was almost seven standard deviations below the group mean. It might turn out that the relationship is a curvilinear one if that one outlier is representative of Is.

There has also been an explicit attempt to evaluate the present theory using electrophysiological techniques—on the supposition that aspects of brain activity related to sensorimotor function should reveal individual differences that might be interpreted to be consistent with the theory. Campbell and Noldy-Cullum (1985) referred to a study that used the auditory-evoked potential in an effort to discriminate between Is and Es in terms of the theory's claims for differences in S-analysis and R-organization. They paid particular attention to the so-called N1–P2 and the P3 waves that occur with peak latencies of about 80, 160, and 450 msec after the stimulus. The stimuli were tone pips, and the procedures used were based on the "oddball" technique—occasional "target" pips occur at random among a stream of "standard" stimuli. Task difficulty was adjusted in terms of the differences in frequency between the standard and the target tone pips; attention was modulated by having participants either count the targets, signal them with a key press, or ignore them (they were to read a book instead); and the remaining parameter to be varied was stimulus intensity—"loud" stimuli were presented at 90 dB SPL (sound pressure level) and "soft" at 60 dB.

No differences were found in the amplitude of the N1–P2 deflection evoked by the standard and target stimuli between Is and Es in either the easy or difficult task or with either the loud or soft stimuli. On the other hand, differences in RT measures were claimed (no details were provided). These authors follow the interpretation of the N1–P2 excursions established by Campbell (1985) as representing primarily physical qualities of the stimulus but with possibly a longer lasting negativity that relates to internal, psychological events. They conclude that when these internal events (attention, for example) are strictly controlled the lack of group effects contradicts the suggestion that Is are more sensitive than Es.

With respect to the N1–P2 excursion, two comments might be made: First, it is not entirely clear that the present model necessarily sees Is as more sensitive to sensory stimulation than Es, although the older literature sometimes shows that this is so. Second, it is not clear that Campbell and Noldy-Cullum (1985) have chosen the most sensitive ranges for their various parameters: The "easy"/"difficult" discrimination manipulation was not successful in that both were associated with error-free trials, and the stimulus intensities selected, 60 and 90 dB SPL, had been shown in earlier studies to be just beyond the range at which sensitivity to manipulation of attention was apparent in those components (Schwent, Hillyard, & Galambos, 1976, Figure 2)—particularly at the long interstimulus intervals that Campbell and Noldy-Cullum apparently used. In their discussion of the possible reasons for the lack of sensitivity of these deflections to attentional factors at intensities beyond 60 dB SPL, Schwent et al. (1976) raise the possibility of a "saturation" effect at about that level, so that stimuli more intense will not result in a larger N1 wave, no matter what the intensity of attentional conditions might be. The study is reported in relation to the "catch-trial" study of Brebner and Flavel (1978) as if it might be meant to be some replication of that study. The extent to which it might be so is a moot point.

In any case, it is difficult to understand what these waves might represent in terms of brain function, given that they are at their maximum amplitudes over the frontocentral scalp regions, with a latency of 80 msec or more, and further that, although the primary auditory cortex response to sound stimuli may not be visible in the scalp potentials, it probably occurs with latencies less than 30 msec (Picton, Hillyard, Krausz, & Galambos, 1974).

Interpretation of the P3 data is even more complex, and no more will be attempted here than to make one or two minor observations. It has a very late peak (well in excess of 300 msec), and it is positive running, which, according to an analysis by Creutzfeldt, Watanabe, and Lux (1966), might reflect deeper lying inhibitory synaptic events. It is seen to reflect entirely endogenous events and is not related to stimulus parameters (Campbell, 1985). It is a wide wave, which may reflect temporal variability in the trials used in the summation process. The earlier interpretation of Hillyard's group was that it reflected a "response set," selecting particular stimuli out of those passed through the stimulus filter. This is the attentional process that is referred to as "stimulus set" and is seen to be reflected in N1-P2 (Picton & Hillyard, 1974). The relationship between the peak of P3 and reaction time is variable, depending, for example, on the relative demands for accuracy or speed (an interesting demonstration of which is provided by Campbell, 1985, Figure 6.6). Campbell and Noldy-Cullum (1985) regard the constancy of P3 latency in comparison to the group differences in RT as indicating that the former represents "stimulus evaluation" time, whereas the RT differences represent a difference in response bias.

In these studies, measurement of brain events was undertaken, but they were seen in relation to psychological considerations; the drawing of implications in physiological terms was not attempted. One can easily guess at the reasons for that; of course, the main one is that there is very little information about the brain events that the components of the evoked response represent. The problems of volume conduction and uncertainty of cortical and other brain mechanisms prevent the drawing of any clear conclusions about the brain events. This is part of a larger problem of relating behavioral events to brain function.

There are difficulties that face authors from disciplines outside neuroscience who are not party to the assumptive framework of those working within neuroscience: They may be neither clearly aware of the assumptions (not often made explicit for the benefit of other readers) that color the experimental approaches used to promote brain understanding and the interpretation of the material these produce. Nor may they be aware of the limitations of the technology available to neuroscientists and the consequent qualifications that must attend its use. Technological capacity in neuroscience is generally capable of studying brain elements and events on a microscopic scale: Although it can "see" be-

yond the level of individual cells and parts of cells, it is limited to the
study of function at that level. In other words, although groups and
systems of cells can be traced histologically, the function of such group-
ings and systems cannot be established. Nor, as it happens, can physiology seem to make much sense of data collected over an extended time
scale that is beyond a range measured in msec.

These limitations seem to have generated a "bottom-up" development of a notion of the brain's functional organization: Impressions are
generated by single cell approaches of function in structures studied
individually. Brain understanding is thus developing by a process of
rather haphazard, not to say opportunistic, accretion of impressions of
function of individual parts. And there is very little to indicate how the
function of the parts might coordinate. This, in turn, produces another
generally hidden assumption about whole-brain function—as a bag of
parts, so to speak. Such an impression cannot be experimentally dis-
qualified yet, but it may prove to be misleading in the long run.

The lack of a concept of whole-brain function to provide coherence
and context in which to locate the information produced about individual structures renders interpretation of such information vulnerable
to alternative biases. Experiments are often cast in terms of behavioral
preconceptions. (The term *"behavioral"* is used here to connote either
"lay" formulations or those refined by the psychological process.) An
illustration of the point can be seen in the context in which the information provided by Hubel and Wiesel (1962, 1965, and 1968, in particular)
is set about cellular activity in the visual cortex: It is much more often
seen in the behavioral context of "form vision" than in the context of
relevance to whole-brain function. Seen in the latter context, it may be
that the trigger-feature aspects they have documented are, in effect,
irrelevant (Uttal, 1975).

This tendency, essentially by default, to study the function of brain
structures individually, within preconceived behavioral contexts, rein-
forces the notion of the brain as a set of structures by implying a "function" localized in each. The "mechanism" implied by psychological
study is thus seen to "map" onto—or correlate with—mechanisms elaborated by physiological approaches in the "spatial" sense to the extent
that the former are described in relation to individual structures. It may
not be too much of an exaggeration to claim that the coherence lacking
from the viewpoint of the brain's functional organization can be said to
be provided by the *behavioral* context. This general state of affairs weak-
ens the contribution that the material "borrowed" from neuroscience
can make to behavioral understanding in that the strongest claim for a
given behavioral function is probably no more than that it is "consistent
with" the correlated aspect of brain function. Whether "explanation" for

behavioral functions can ever be seen to be provided solely from brain mechanisms elucidated by physiological methods depends on one's position in the philosophical debate on reductionism (see, for example, Churchland, 1982). But this situation, resting as it does on imposed correlations, does not seem to escape a certain circularity. One might also recall in this general context the remarks made by Bannister (1966), who argued that physiological and psychological constructs, coming from such different universes of discourse, cannot be related—that any belief that such can be done, rests, among other confusions, upon "a 'critical flicker fusion effect' whereby the simple repeated juxtaposing of psychological and physiological constructs convinces reader and writer that they have been integrated" (Bannister, 1966, p. A15).

These various interpretational problems can be viewed in relation to the concept of arousal as seen both as a behavioral and as a physiological mechanism, which is often known as the Ascending Reticular Arousal System (ARAS). This latter concept has had a long history, having had a strong early impetus from the experiments by Moruzzi and Magoun (1949) that involved the stimulation of the so-called "reticular formation" of the cat at various levels of the brain stem with electrical stimulation delivered through a needle electrode. "Arousal" was assessed mainly on the basis of brain wave pattern. Numerous other experiments of this type were performed within the assumptions of the concept (reviewed by Moruzzi, 1972). Another use of it was made by Singer (1979) who made a case for the nonspecific projections being seen to contribute to the modulation of the excitability of cells of the visual cortex in sensory processing in addition to the more generally accepted more global function of the system in regulating the state of alertness of the animal as a whole.

These experiments were cast explicitly in an attempt to find mechanisms for the switching of the arousal state between sleep and wakefulness, in the case of Moruzzi and Magoun, and for the modulation of the functional state of the visual cortex in relation to visual processing, in Singer's case. They were also cast in the general assumptive framework that has existed from the early days of microanatomy, that is, that a dichotomy can be discerned between "specific" and "nonspecific" projections. In the case of some projections, particularly those in relation to connections between the brain and the environmental interfaces (sensory and motor systems), precise, discriminating representations of the interfaces can be demonstrated in various brain structures. There is correspondence in such demonstrations between the physiological and the microanatomical arrangements. In the case of other projections, such precision of representation is not recognized, functionally or structurally. This has been the case with the reticular formation that is there-

fore characterized as "nonspecific." (The lack of appearance of differentiation in patterns of interneuronal connectivity to histological
examination of such structures does not necessarily mean that some sort
of differentiation does not exist—only that the pattern has not been
recognized.)

In the experimental procedure commonly used to study the system
(such as was used by Moruzzi and Magoun [1949] and Singer [1979], for
example), the stimulating current introduced by the needle electrode
would be conducted away from the point of the needle and presumably
would stimulate neuronal elements over a wide area synchronously.
Before the results of such experiments were taken as informative, it
would be useful to have a demonstration that the activity evoked in such
a manner did not deviate far from natural patterns of activity—that it
was not merely demonstrating how the cellular mechanism responds to
artifactual stimulation. The cytoarchitectonic arrangements in a structure seem as if they are "designed to receive" as input particular spatiotemporal patterns of activity. Clark (1969) demonstrated, in the anaesthetized cat, that cells in one of the auditory relay nuclei did not
respond to electrical stimulation of the auditory nerve with frequencies
greater than 200 Hz, whereas they responded in characteristic ways to
stimulation at the same frequencies when applied through the natural
transduction mechanism involving natural sound stimulation of the
organ of Corti. He attributed this to the probability that the electrical
stimulation produced synchronous activation of all, or large blocks of,
the fibers in the auditory nerve and that this abnormal spatiotemporal
pattern was blocked by inhibitory mechanisms preceding the target
structure (from which the recordings were being taken) in a manner that
does not obtain when the more natural form of stimulation is provided.
In other words, we are speaking of forcing the various structures into an
abnormal function and thus providing results that are irrelevant. In any
case, if, in normal function, these more diffuse-looking pathways were
conveying differentiated patterns of activity, this fact would be obscured
by this sort of methodological approach, thus tending to perpetuate the
notion of the "nonspecific" contribution of such projections.

It is true that Scheibel and Scheibel (1958) demonstrated that the
isodendritic core, a term preferred by Ramon-Moliner and Nauta (1966),
had a cytoarchitectonic organization that suggested self-stimulating
properties of a kind consistent with the functional properties proposed
for the ARAS. However, from the anatomical demonstrations by Brodal
(1957), the connections of the brain stem and its various constituent
structures could also be considered to be differentiated. In fact, if one
were to consider species of animals without a cerebral cortex (e.g., the
sharks), it is clear that the brain stem connections are sufficiently differ-

entiated to allow appropriately differentiated behaviors in order to insure their long survival. The demonstration of Kuypers and Lawrence (1967) of the systematic pattern of connection from the neocortex to brain stem wherein the connections are made between structures with similar function (visual cortex to superior colliculus, for example, or motor cortex to brain stem motor structures) further suggests that it might not be altogether appropriate simply to regard the brain stem's complement of structures as providing undifferentiated support. To do so, in fact, would need the assumption that continued evolution of the brain stem into corticated species has been moving back to less differentiated patterns of connectivity. An alternative is to see the neocortex as an extensive elaboration of the existing brain stem organization that, in its abundant cellularity, provides for more differentiated behavioral capacities.

The firing response of a neurone to the influence conveyed through a given synaptic projection is dependent upon the existing level of its membrane potential. In this sense, there is a place for a system that adjusts the level of excitation of neurones, but it is not so clear that it needs to be a system that is dedicated simply to adjusting the membrane potential levels of relevant neurones in a nonspecific manner, such as is seen to be the (somewhat exclusive) function of the "reticular formation." Similarly, another set of structures has been explored, separately, that is seen to provide the opposite effect of "inhibition"; it includes midline thalamic nuclei and (in the cat, at least) the orbitofrontal cortex (Skinner & Lindsley, 1967). Again, in line with some of the preceding remarks, the link between these two systems seems to be established rather more strongly in the behavioral context—insofar as they are seen to correspond to the postulated mechanisms for "excitation" and "inhibition"—than in the physiological account of their interrelationships.

There is no intention here to review the material available concerning these mechanisms. We merely want to illustrate the difficulties in establishing a biological account of the mechanisms postulated in this general line of psychological enquiry. Three general problems can be seen to be associated with the current "arousal" concept. In the first place, it is usually seen by the physiologists principally as a system governing sleep/wakefulness cycles—not fluctuation of arousal within the wakeful state. More recent research into the system draws attention to an oscillating, reciprocal interaction between a set of three brain stem nuclei, one releasing acetylcholine, another, serotonin, and the third, catecholamine, as their transmitters. The model has been reviewed in Hobson and Scheibel (1980). Second, and related to this, it is essentially a "static" impression. Time is not easily handled in neurophysiological modeling: There can be no impression of the operation of the brain during a behavioral sequence, nor of the way in which an arousal system, as envisaged, might influence it. Third, it is generally (but not always; see the concluding remarks by Hobson, in Hobson & Scheibel, 1980, pp. 137–141) conceived as a dedicated, nonspecific system—an "arousal" mechanism is "spatially" mapped on to the ARAS system—but a claim can be made that the anatomy suggests a different impression.

An alternative "brain view" would be to consider the implications of a "top-down" approach. The point can, perhaps, be made by a conservative view of the brain: Microscopically and macroscopically, it can be seen as a neuronal machine where the constituent neurones are collected together in groups seen as the named nuclei, laminated structures, and so on, that are interconnected in a highly complex meshwork of one-to-many and many-to-one patterns. This view of the brain is not entirely consistent with the view discussed earlier, but it may be rather more so with another: that is, that the "matching" between brain and behavioral functions may be more realistically sought in the "temporal" dimension—in the temporal fluctuation of spatiotemporal patterns of activity through the brain. One can choose, as a starting point, the making of a response—some brief action in tasks such as are common in the studies used in this area. What is physiologically evident is that a brain action has "selected" a spatiotemporal sequence of activation of motor units in the various responding muscles. This means that a patterned recruitment of the corresponding motoneurones has been effected by the subtly balanced influences from the various axonal projection systems converging upon the motor nuclei housing the synaptic receiving surfaces of those motoneurones. It seems inappropriate to ignore the anatomical complexities: The number of nuclei in the spinal cord and the brain stem, cortical areas, and sensory input fiber systems that project upon motor nuclei is considerable. Each of these contributing structures has also received inputs from various other structures (including the input sensory systems) so that in them, too, one can envisage the development of spatiotemporal patterns of activity. They will also interconnect, directly and indirectly. To contemplate, then, how a brief action emerges, it may be more productive to imagine the progressive evolution in an interconnected population of brain structures of a spatiotemporal pattern of activity, part of which is a particular pattern in the motor nuclei housing the motoneurones, rather than a patterned volley of activity delivered down a particular pathway to those nuclei. The latter impression would lead backward to trying to envisage volleys of activity being delivered through sequences of brain structures each endowed with some notional, "localized" function.

In passing, it can be seen that one consequence of the meshwork idea is that *if* the influence of a particular projection is focused on, the coordinated activity of all the other inputs might be seen as "nonspecific" sensitivity adjustment—an "ARAS"-like influence, so to speak. Although it matters little from the psychological point of view—either impression will serve to correspond with the impression from the behavioral studies—there is likely to be some advantage in trying to understand the actual working of the mechanism, rather than in accepting a convenient simplification. It is not yet possible to assert the superior likelihood of either model, but the preceding considerations and the differential appearance of the microanatomical connection patterns favor the meshwork idea, although one could argue that the two are not necessarily mutually exclusive and might involve only a shift in emphasis.

There is no attempt to localize function explicitly, but in this discussion, the process of responding to a stimulus in a perceptuomotor psychological task can, perhaps, be seen in two aspects. The second aspect can be taken, *arbitrarily*, to commence at structures such as the "motor" cortex and corresponding brain stem areas, when the "executive" (to coin a term) spatiotemporal pattern of activity has finally evolved in the brain. This includes the patterns in these "motor" structures that ultimately generate the response. The first aspect, then, will be the evolving of that pattern among the brain structures. This will include patterns in the structures receiving the sensory inputs.

Even choosing to focus upon the motor cortex is a very considerable simplification, as a glance at a review of the connections and activity of the corticospinal neurones will confirm (Phillips & Porter, 1977). Nevertheless, confining attention to the pyramidal tract emerging from the motor cortex, some initial impressions can be achieved. Evarts (1966) raised the problem that, although pyramidal tract neurones in the motor cortex of monkeys seem to receive influence from visual stimulation after a short latency (30 msec or so) in the anaesthetized animal, activity does not appear to change in motor cortical cells for at least 100 msec when such change precedes a behavioral response (which appears with a minimal reaction time of 180 msec). There can be no description of what is happening in the intervening period, but the suggestion here is that a spatiotemporal pattern is evolving through the brain structures, each contributing to the total pattern according to its other connections and the nature of its own cytoarchitectonic arrangements. In other words, the impression is that the behavioral progression is mapped in brain function, not "spatially" as a progression of activity moving through a sequence of brain structures so much as a "temporal" development of the spatiotemporal pattern in a more global set of brain structures. These include those leading to the motor nuclei, and the 70 msec not otherwise accounted for are taken up by the evolution of the spatiotemporal pattern of activity within the meshwork that at some later stage includes the production in the motor cortex of the "executive" patterns.

Although it might be considered that there is not necessarily an isomorphism between the constructs conceived in behavioral science and those developed within brain science, one might sustain, as an article of faith, that there must be some equivalence in the formulations developed in the two. For example, this process of the evolution of "executive" spatiotemporal patterns could, in brain terms, be seen as a similar sort of process as is envisaged in the concept of "stimulus analysis" in the psychological framework. And, as such, specifically, in the context of the present personality model, it might take longer to evolve in introverts. What the process might involve, in brain terms, might be analogous to the TOTE process in behavioral terms in which the mechanism is perceived as taking information, operating on it, taking more information, operating on it, taking more information, if needed, and so on, until there is enough to execute the action (Miller, Galanter, & Pribram, 1960). It is interesting, in this context, that similarly to the quite long sequence of brain waves evoked by a punctate or very short sensory stimulus (such as those reviewed previously), quite long sequences of action potentials have been found, again using an averaging technique, in response to light flashes (e.g., Sasaki, Saito, Bear, & Ervin, 1971). Presumably these later effects are functionally relevant.

There is an obvious problem in this approach: There is no clear-cut way of distinguishing "stimulus-analysis" processes from those that might be related to "response-organization." In fact, they seem to be two ways of looking at the same process as there is no apparent boundary between structures with what might be called "sensory" functions and those with "motor" functions that can be taken to be in sequence. When the whole structure is seen as a meshwork of gray matter structures, encouragement to perceive any "localization" of function is very much reduced. As the process of "stimulus-analysis" was arbitrarily, for the sake of discussion, taken to lead to the genesis of the executive spatiotemporal patterns of brain activity, including the patterns associated with muscular activation, so the spatiotemporal patterns initiated by the stimulus can be taken, again arbitrarily, to begin the process of "response-organization." Perhaps the newer technology might be able to find individual differences to correspond with the behavioral distinctions by averaging with respect to stimulus, for the former, and with respect to the motor action, for the latter.

Perhaps. So far, the results are not encouraging; the earlier result of Stelmack, Achorn, and Michaud (1977), in which N1–P2 amplitude was seen to be greater in Is (which was seen to be consistent with their proposed higher level of cortical excitation), has been contradicted by the later study of Campbell and Noldy-Cullum (1985) discussed before. The meshwork view of the brain developed here erodes the identification of behavioral functions with various brain structures. As just expressed, it also loses identification with postulated psychological processes: For example, it cannot contribute to the debate about the relevance of "additive" models of information processing as reviewed in this context by Campbell (1985). At the same time, however, the lack of effect in the various components of the evoked potentials so far derived, contrary to the understanding of the relevance of those components in relation to postulated theory, does not necessarily mean that the theory is wrong, any more than it means that the components of the evoked waveforms may still be incorrectly interpreted. If the behavioral data are confirmed and shown to be robust, then insofar as this suggests individual differences in brain function, the eventual expectation would be that this would be reflected in differences in brain electrical patterns. Further work in this direction, perhaps by seeking a more sensitive range of parameters (decades of experience in this whole area has amply demonstrated that individual effects are very sensitive to establishing the appropriate levels of parametric values), if successful will, of course, have benefits in both directions.

We would wish to reiterate that behavioral evidence is needed first to lead to the interpretation of physiological evidence.

REFERENCES

Aiello, J. R., DeRisi, D. T., Epstein, Y. M., & Karlin, R. A. Crowding and the role of interpersonal difference preference. *Sociometry*, 1975, *40*, 271–282.

Bannister, D. The myth of physiological. *Bulletin of the British Psychological Society*, 1966, 19/63, A15.

Berger, H. Über das Elektroenkephalogramm des Menchen. *Archives für Psychiatrie und Nervenkrankheiten*, 1929, *87*, 527–570.

Brand, C. R., & Deary, I. J. Intelligence and inspection time. In H. J. Eysenck (Ed.), *A model for intelligence*. Berlin: Springer, 1982.

Brebner, J. A model of extraversion. *Australian Journal of Psychology*, 1983, *35*, 349–359.

Brebner, J., & Cooper, C. The effect of a low rate of regular signals upon the reaction times of introverts and extraverts. *Journal of Research in Personality*, 1974, *8*, 263–276.

Brebner, J., & Cooper, C. Stimulus- or response-induced excitation. *Journal of Research in Personality*, 1978, *12*, 306–311.

Brebner, J., & Cooper, C. *Personality factors and inspection time*. Paper presented at the meeting of the International Society for the Study of Individual Differences, St. Felieu, Spain, 1985. (a)

Brebner, J., & Cooper, C. A proposed unified model of extraversion. In J. T. Spence, & C. E. Izard (Eds.), *Motivation, emotion and personality*. Amsterdam: North-Holland, 1985. (b)

Brebner, J., & Flavel, R. The effect of catch-trials on speed and accuracy among introverts and extraverts in a simple RT task. *British Journal of Psychology*, 1978, *69*, 9–15.

Brodal, A. *The reticular formation of the brain stem. Anatomical aspect and functional correlations.* Edinburgh: Oliver & Boyd, 1957.

Campbell, K. B. Mental chronometry. I. Behavioural and physiological techniques. In B. D. Kirkcaldy (Ed.), *Individual differences in movement.* Lancaster: MTP Press, 1985.

Campbell, K. B., & Noldy-Cullum, N. Mental chronometry. II. Individual differences. In B. D. Kirkcaldy (Ed.), *Individual differences in movement.* Lancaster: MTP Press, 1985.

Carr, S. M. *Speed of habituation of the EEG and GSR components of the orienting and startle reaction(s) to auditory stimulation, as a function of personality dimensions.* Unpublished B.Sc. thesis, University of Adelaide, 1976.

Churchland, P. S. Mind–brain reduction: New light from the philosophy of science. *Neuroscience*, 1982, *7*, 1041–1047.

Clark, G. M. Responses of cells in the superior olivary complex of the cat to electrical stimulation of the auditory nerve. *Experimental Neurology*, 1969, *24*, 124–136.

Creutzfeldt, O. D., Watanabe, S., & Lux, H. D. Relations between EEG phenomena and potentials of single cortical cells. I. Evoked responses after thalamic and epicortical stimulation. *Electroencephalography and Clinical Neurophysiology*, 1966, *20*, 1–18.

Evans, G. W. *Behavioural and physiological consequences of crowding in humans.* Unpublished Ph.D. dissertation, University of Massachusetts, 1975.

Evarts, E. V. Pyramidal tract activity associated with a conditioned movement in the monkey. *Journal of Neurophysiology*, 1966, *29*, 1011–1027.

Eysenck, H. J. *Dynamics of anxiety and hysteria.* New York: Praeger, 1957.

Eysenck, H. J. *The biological basis of personality.* Springfield, Il.: Charles C Thomas, 1967.

Eysenck, H. J. (Ed.). *A model for personality* Berlin: Springer, 1981.

Eysenck, H. J. Is there a paradigm in personality research? *Journal of Research in Personality*, 1983, *17*, 369–397.

Haier, R. J., Robinson, D. L., Braden, W., & Williams, D. Evoked potential augmenting-reducing and personality differences. *Personality and Individual Differences*, 1984, *5*, 293–301.

Hall, E. T. *The hidden dimension.* New York: Doubleday, 1966.

Heshka, S., & Pylypuk, A. *Human crowding and adrenocortical activity.* Paper presented at the meeting of the Canadian Psychological Association, Quebec, 1975.

Hobson, J. A., & Scheibel, A. B. The brainstem core: Sensorimotor intergration and behavioural state control. *Neuroscience Research Program Bulletin*, 1980, 18(1).

Hubel, D. H., & Wiesel, T. N. Receptive fields, interaction and functional architecture in the cat's visual cortex. *Journal of Physiology*, 1962, *160*, 106–154.

Hubel, D. H., & Wiesel, T. N. Receptive fields and functional architecture in two nonstriate visual areas (18 and 19) of the cat. *Journal of Neurophysiology*, 1965, *28*, 229–289.

Hubel, D. H., & Wiesel, T. N. Receptive field and functional architecture of monkey striate cortex. *Journal of Physiology*, 1968, *195*, 215–243.

Hull, C. I. *Principles of behavior.* New York: Appleton-Century-Crofts, 1943.

Katsikitis, M., & Brebner, J. Individual differences in the effects of personal space invasion: A test of the Brebner–Cooper model of extraversion. *Personality and Individual Differences*, 1981, *2*, 5–10.

Khew, K. *The effects of discrimination-response-complexity on introverts' and extraverts' performance.* Unpublished B.Sc. thesis, University of Adelaide, 1984.

Khew, K., & Brebner, J. The role of personality in crowding research. *Personality and Individual Differences*, 1985, *6*, 641–643.

Kuypers, H. G. J. M., & Lawrence, D. G. Cortical projections to the red nucleus and the brain stem in the rhesus monkey. *Brain Research*, 1967, *4*, 151–188.

Mackenzie, B., & Bingham, E. Intelligence, inspection time, and response strategies in a university population. *Australian Journal of Psychology*, 1985, *37*.

Miller, G. A., Galanter, E., & Pribram, K. H. *Plans and the structure of behavior.* New York: Holt, 1960.

Moruzzi, G. The sleep-waking cycle. *Ergebnisse der Physiologie, biologischen Chemie und experimentellen Pharmakologie*, 1972, *64*, 1–165.

Moruzzi, G., & Magoun, H. W. Brain stem reticular formation and activation of the EEG. *Electroencephalography and Clinical Neurophysiology*, 1949, *1*, 455–473.

Nettelbeck, T., & Lally, M. Inspection time and measured intelligence. *British Journal of Psychology*, 1976, *67*, 17–22.

Phillips, C. G., & Porter, R. *Corticospinal neurones. Their role in movement.* London: Academic Press, 1977.

Picton, T. W., & Hillyard, S. A. Human auditory evoked potentials. II: Effects of attention. *Electroencephalography and Clinical Neurophysiology*, 1974, *36*, 191–199.

Picton, T. W., Hillyard, S. A., Krausz, H. I., & Galambos, R. Human auditory evoked potentials. I: Evaluation of components. *Electroencephalography and Clinical Neurophysiology*, 1974, *36*, 179–190.

Ramon-Moliner, E., & Nauta, W. H. J. The isodendritic core of the brain stem. *Journal of Comparative Neurology*, 1966, *126*, 311–336.

Saegart, S. *Effects of spatial and social density on arousal, mood, and social orientation.* Unpublished Ph.D. dissertation, University of Michigan, 1974.

Sasaki, H., Saito, Y., Bear, D. M., & Ervin, F. R. Quantitive variation in striate receptive fields of cats as a function of light and dark adaption. *Experimental Brain Research*, 1971, *13*, 273–293.

Scheibel, M. E., & Scheibel, A. B. Structural substrates for intergrative patterns in the brain stem reticular core. In H. H. Jasper, L. D. Proctor, R. S. Knighton, W. C. Noshay, & R. T. Costello (Eds.), *Reticular formation of the brain.* Boston: Little and Brown, 1958.

Schwent, Y. L., Hillyard, S. A., & Galambos, R. Selective attention and the auditory vertex potential. II. Effects of signal intensity and masking noise. *Electroencephalography and Clinical Neurophysiology*, 1976, *40*, 615–622.

Singer, W. Central-core control of visual-cortex functions. In F. O. Schmitt & F. G. Worden (Eds.), *The Neurosciences: Fourth Study Program.* Cambridge, MA: M.I.T. Press, 1979.

Skinner, J. E., & Lindsley, D. B. Electrophysiological and behavioral effects of blockage of the nonspecific thalamo-cortical system. *Brain Research*, 1967, *6*, 95–118.

Stelmack, R. M., Achorn, E., & Michaud, A. Extraversion and individual differences in auditory evoked response. *Psychophysiology*. 1977, *14*, 368–374.

Strelau, J. Nervous system and extraversion-introversion: A comparison of Eysenck's theory with Pavlov's typolog   *Polish Psychological Bulletin*, 1970, *1*, 17–24.

Uttal, W. R. *An autocorrelation theory of form detection.* Hillsdale, NJ: Erlbaum, 1975.

CHAPTER 3

Extraversion-Introversion, Contingent Negative Variation, and Arousal

PETER F. WERRE

INTRODUCTION

In order to gain more insight into the relationship between electroencephalographic (EEG) and psychological variables, normal and psychiatric subjects have been examined in a series of experiments. Because Eysenck's (1967) personality theory relates neurophysiological and psychological observations, this theory was chosen as theoretical framework. The design of the experiments was such that hypotheses could be tested in a way that brought the subjects under appreciable stimulus control of the experimenter. As arousal is an important concept of the theory, results are reviewed here because they might give more insight into and delimitation of this concept. Its importance stands out in Gale's (1981) summing-up of the essential constructs of the theory: (a) extraverts are less aroused than introverts; (b) there is an optimum level of arousal; and (c) individuals develop strategies designed to make their inherent level of arousal compatible with the optimum level.

The desirability to bring the subject under stimulus control and the demonstration by McCallum and Walter (1968) that a specific event-related brain potential differentiates normal and neurotic subjects and

---

PETER F. WERRE • Psychiatric Centre Rosenburg, Oude Haagweg 377, The Hague, The Netherlands.

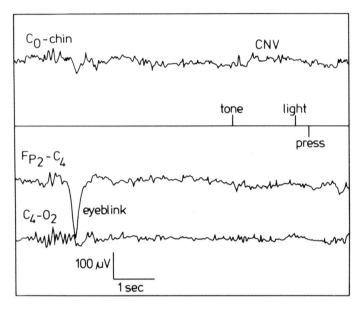

Figure 1. The contingent negative variation is the slow upward wave, marked CNV (upper trace, vertex-to-chin derivation), contingent with the constant foreperiod reaction time task: "After the tone there will be a light that has to be extinguished as quickly as possible by pressing the button." The right frontal-to-central derivation was used to control for eye movements, the right central-to-occipital derivation to monitor alpha rhythm. *Note.* From P. F. Werre, in J. Strelau, F. H. Farley, & A. Gale (Eds.) *The biological bases of personality and behavior.* Copyright 1986 by Hemisphere Publishing Corporation, Washington, D.C. Reprinted by permission.

decreases in amplitude by arousal augmenting events led, among others, to the selection of this potential as an EEG variable. This slow brain wave, called contingent negative variation (CNV), can be generated by a constant foreperiod reaction time task. It occurs between warning and imperative stimuli, maximally over the central and frontal cortex (see Figure 1). In the two experiments that will be described, foreperiods of 2 sec in the first and 1.5 sec in the second were used. Because only in the case of longer, that is, 4 sec and more, foreperiods do CNV components become discernable, these are not taken into consideration. For more general CNV information, the reader is referred to, for example, Kornhuber and Deecke (1980) and Tecce and Cattanach (1982). The choice of the psychological variables was, of course, dictated by the theory: Extraversion (E) and neuroticism (N) scores were obtained with the Amsterdamse Biografische Vragenlijst (ABV), a questionnaire that is the Dutch counterpart of Eysenck's MPI (Wilde, 1962). As extraverts are characterized by relatively low levels of arousal and relatively high levels of inhibition as compared with introverts, and vice versa, a positive correlation was expected between extraversion and CNV amplitude. As mentioned before, CNV amplitude was reported at that time to decrease under arousal-augmenting conditions. Thus, of the most plausible CNV measures, amplitude was choosen as the CNV parameter. Because test–retest reliability was better for maximal amplitude than for amplitude at a fixed time before the imperative stimulus (Werre, Faverey, & Janssen, 1973), mean maximal amplitude was used throughout the studies.

RELATIONSHIP BETWEEN CONTINGENT NEGATIVE VARIATION, EXTRAVERSION-INTROVERSION, AND NEUROTICISM-STABILITY

Some results of the first experiment (Werre, Faverey, & Janssen, 1973, 1975; see also Werre, 1986), based on the examination of 118 naive healthy students (mean age about 23 years, mainly males), can be summarized with the aid of a modification of Gale's (1981) schematic description of Eysenck's theory (see Figure 2). For clarity, it is necessary to consider experimental procedures first. CNV measures were obtained by examining the subjects separately in the morning for about 2 hours. After the electrodes had been applied, the subject was seated in a comfortable chair in a sound-dampened cubicle. Opposite the subject there was a screen with a fixation point for the eyes, to limit eye movements. The subject was required to perform five series of irregularly spaced constant foreperiod reaction time trials (a short tone was followed after 2 sec by a light that had to be extinguished as quickly as possible by pressing a button), first in the standard way, next under three stressful conditions. Then the experiment ended with a condition that was identical to the first (conditions were not varied mainly because of technical reasons). The stressful conditions were (a) double task (counting numbers presented by a loudspeaker in addition to the reaction time task); (b) equivocation (the second stimulus was randomly omitted in 50% of the trials); and (c) a condition in which the subject was required to initiate the trial himself or herself by pressing another button. Mean maximal CNV amplitude was obtained by averaging 20 CNVs, recorded with a vertex-to-chin lead, per condition. Only CNVs not contaminated by eye movements or other artifacts were included.

The psychological testing took place prior to the day of the CNV experiment and yielded as main psychological variables E and N scores. In addition, habitual action preparedness (Dirken's 1970 questionnaire) and intelligence (Snijders and Verhage's 1962 Groninger Intelligence Test [GIT]) were determined. The habitual-action-preparedness (HAB) questionnaire, which gives an indication of task orientation, energy, and

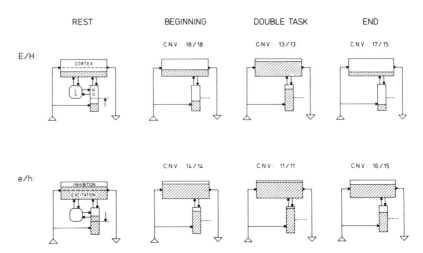

Figure 2. Diagrammatic summary of results of an experiment into the relationship between extraversion-introversion and CNV, using a modification of Gale's (1981) schematic description of Eysenck's theory of the neurophysiological basis of extraversion-introversion. The diagrams show the cortex and brain stem reticular system (RS), forming a functional system mediating arousal. Input and output are indicated on the left and on the right, respectively. It is explained in the text why the limbic system (LS), underlying neuroticism, is not further taken into account. There are various reciprocal connections.

For extraverts (E) and habitual-action-prepared individuals (H) (upper row) and for introverts (e) and not-habitual-action-inclined individuals (h) (lower row), the diagrams represent four different conditions. First, the hypothetical "rest" condition is shown, and then come three experimental conditions. Mean CNV amplitudes, first for extraverts and introverts and after the slanting line for individuals who are and who are not action prepared, are indicated above the diagrams (rounded off to the nearest μV). The different inhibition/excitation ratios are shown by the white and striped areas of the quadrangles. Because recordings that were contaminated by artifacts were eliminated, the number of subjects varied between 30 and 40 for the different categories. For further explanation see text.

eagerness to work, has a positive correlation with extraversion and a negative one with neuroticism.

Only data obtained during beginning, double task, and end conditions are shown in Figure 2. The upper row concerns extraverts and habitual-action-prepared subjects; the lower row, introverts and subjects who are not action inclined. Above the diagrams, the mean maximal CNV amplitudes, rounded off to the nearest μV, are given, first for extraverts and introverts, and after the slanting line, for high and low habitual-action-prepared subjects. The two diagrams to the left, marked *rest*, illustrate the hypothetical inherent organization of extraverts as opposed to introverts. These diagrams depict momentary passages because extraverts as well as introverts are always maneuvering to attain their optimum level of arousal (which may be different for different kinds of task; see, e.g., Gale, 1981). Because it was found that neuroticism (emotional instability-emotional stability) did not correlate with CNV, this personality dimension and the limbic system, which presumably underlies neuroticism, are not taken into consideration here. To the right are the three experimental conditions. In terms of arousal for extraverts, these conditions could be characterized by intermediate arousal (beginning condition), high arousal (double task), and low arousal (end). For introverts, the characterizations high arousal (beginning), very high arousal (double task), and intermediate arousal (end) seem applicable. These characterizations were then not introspectively verified. CNV values indicated that in the case of the introverts, the relation between CNV and arousal could be linear. However, this was not so in the case of the extraverts: The end condition producing presumably the lowest arousal of the six situations generated a CNV that is *lower* than the CNV of the higher arousal-producing beginning condition. That is why at the time an inverted–U relation between CNV and the inhibition-excitation balance that underlies manifest personality was proposed (see Figure 3). Accordingly, the cortical inhibition/excitation ratios, on which the different levels of arousal might be based, are indicated in the diagrams of Figure 2: For high CNV values the inhibition/excitation ratio is about 1 (e.g., the extraverts during the beginning condition); for low CNV values, there is either a prevalence of inhibition (e.g., the extraverts during the end condition) or a prevalence of excitation (e.g., the introverts during the double task condition).

INTERACTION BETWEEN EXTRAVERSION-INTROVERSION AND CONDITION AS INDICATED BY CONTINGENT NEGATIVE VARIATION

Apparently, at least two conditional factors are of importance, that is, input and time. Moreover, it is demonstrated that the outcome is dependent on personality. The result of a subsequent experiment (Janssen, Mattie, Plooij-van Gorsel, & Werre, 1978; Werre, 1986) supported this finding. Twenty-four naive, healthy males (mean age about 24 years) were examined twice, 1 week apart. During each session, CNV was recorded five times, first, prior to the administration of a drug, then in four postdrug measurements. Each of these measurements was distinguished in a condition without and with white noise. CNV computation was comparable to that described before. Before the first session, the extraversion score was determined with the ABV.

The data obtained prior to drug administration were used to test the

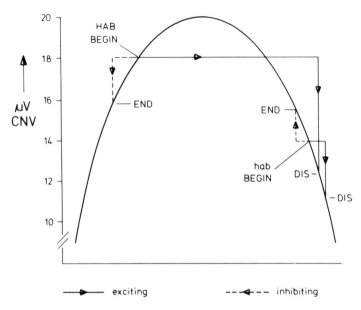

Figure 3. Hypothetical relation between observed (mean) contingent negative variation (CNV) amplitudes (vertical axis) of high (HAB) and low (hab) action-prepared subjects and the inhibition-excitation balance of the central nervous system (horizontal axis). As the HAB questionnaire measures approximately stable extraversion versus unstable introversion, the HAB subjects are thought to occupy the left, inhibition leg of the inverted-U, whereas the hab subjects are presumably situated on the right, excitation leg of the curve. During an excitatory condition (marked DIS; in this case a distracting counting task was added to the standard constant foreperiod reaction time task) and during an inhibitory condition (marked END; repetition of the standard task at the end of the experiment), subjects are thought to move in opposite directions away from the position they occupied during the beginning condition (marked BEGIN). *Note.* From P. F. Werre, H. A. Faverey, & R. H. C. Janssen, in *Nederlands Tijdschrift voor de Psychologie en haar Grensgebieden.* Copyright 1975 by Van Loghum Slaterus, Deventer. Reprinted by permission. See also P. F. Werre, H. A. Faverey, & R. H. C. Janssen, 1973.

idea that input change and time are influential. In other words, an interaction between noise condition and extraversion and an interaction between session and extraversion were expected. Figure 4 illustrates the outcome of an analysis of variance. With respect to the interaction between extraversion and white noise (Figure 4A), the significance found ($p < .05$) indicates that both personality groups responded differently to the noise condition. An *a priori* test showed introverts to have a significantly lower mean value during exposure to white noise than without white noise ($t = 3.07$, $p < .05$, $df = 14$), whereas for extraverts the difference was minimal and not statistically significant (Tukey's t ratio, one-tailed test). The interaction between extraversion and session is

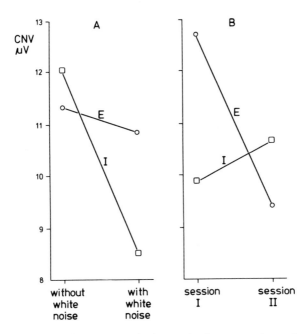

Figure 4. The left side (A) demonstrates the interaction between extraversion and condition. The results of an analysis of variance (R. H. C. Janssen, H. Mattie, P. C. Plooij-van Gorsel, & P. F. Werre, 1978) indicated that extraverts (E) and introverts (I) responded differently to the noise condition. An *a priori* test showed introverts (n = 8; squares) to have a significantly lower mean value during exposure to white noise than without white noise, whereas for extraverts (n = 16; circles), the difference was not significant. The interaction between extraversion and session is shown in B. The effect of sessions proved to be highly significant. An *a posteriori* test did not show a significant difference between sessions for introverts, but it did for extraverts. *Note.* From P. F. Werre in J. Strelau, F. H. Farley, & A. Gale (Eds.), *The biological bases of personality and behavior.* Copyright 1986 by Hemisphere Publishing Corporation, Washington, D.C. Reprinted by permission.

shown in Figure 4B. The effect of sessions proved to be highly significant. An *a posteriori* test did not show a significant difference between sessions for introverts (F = .52; however, note the tendency for CNV increase over time), but for extraverts a significant F ratio was obtained (F = 18.46, $p < .01$, df = 1.22). Clearly, there is a consensus between the results of the two experiments.

USEFULNESS OF THE INVERTED-U MODEL

Several other investigators have contributed substantially to our knowledge of the relation between CNV and psychological functions by condensing various results into general ideas or theoretical models. For instance, Tecce (1972) proposed two psychological functions for CNV findings. This two-process model consists of an attention hypothesis, in which the magnitude of CNV bears a positive monotonic relation to attention, and an arousal hypothesis, in which the magnitude of CNV bears a nonmonotonic (inverted–U) relation to arousal level.

As there are still controversies over the cortical and subcortical origins of CNV components, over the exact psychological genesis of their event-related nature, and so on, all models stem from a selected number of data, and further research is required to test their validity. A good example is the study by Eysenck and O'Connor (Eysenck & O'Connor, 1979; O'Connor, 1980a) on CNV, smoking, arousal, and personality. They based the hypothesis that the effects of uniform amounts of nicotine intake would have differential effects on extraverts and introverts (arousal increase in extraverts, arousal reduction in introverts) on the inverted–U relation often observed between drive and performance. They describe how Pavlov originally assumed a linear relation between drive and performance, to account for the ascending limb, and the emergence of protective inhibition, or transmarginal inhibition, to account for the descending limb. The idea that smoking has a dual action comes from the general observation that, on the one hand, people smoke because they are bored and (presumably) wish to increase their level of arousal, whereas, on the other hand, people smoke because they are tense and (presumably) overaroused and wish to reduce their level of arousal. In testing this theory, Eysenck and O'Connor also found significant personality-group-by-session interaction effects for CNV. As expected, the peak CNV amplitude was found to be greater in extraverts during real smoking sessions and greater in introverts during sham smoking sessions. They interpreted the results as supporting findings relating to the biphasic arousing properties of smoking mentioned in the literature: In animals, small amounts of nicotine produce increases in arousal, whereas larger doses sometimes have the opposite effect.

The following could be added to the extensive discussion of their results in relation to those of other investigators. As described, the left-hand side of the inverted-U is in Eysenck and O'Connor's as well as in our view that section of the curve where extraverts are located under neutral or rest conditions and on which they will rise under (moderately) stimulating circumstances. The right leg, however, is, according to Eysenck and O'Connor, the section where the introverts descend from a relatively high to a lowered arousal position that is "afforded to introverts by smoking, [which] minimizes cognitive distractions and, under low task demand, diminishes excess attentiveness, whilst heightened arousal in the extraverts brings initially greater attentiveness to the environment" (p. 156). This is opposed to the idea advanced in the preceding sections: I prefer to conceive the right-hand side as the section where subjects, especially introverts, descend when they become more and more excited. Obviously, the latter does not fit the general observation that certain subjects smoke to calm themselves. A question that emerges here is: Why do introverts smoke if sham smoking brings them near an optimal inhibition/excitation balance and real smoking leads to overexcitation? Elsewhere (Werre, 1982), I suggested that the answer is contained within the question if the view is taken that the central nervous system (CNS) is an integrating multilevel and multifunctional organization. The stimulant (nicotine) aspect of smoking leading to (over) excitation within the CNV level of the central nervous system, as indicated by CNV amplitude decrease (see Figure 3), and eyeblink increase (O'Connor, 1980a) is taken for granted because the sedating sham aspect of smoking (especially the lip touching/sucking part and perhaps also the social implications of the ritual) leads to inhibition within other, non-CNV-related levels of the CNS. I note that Ashton, Millman, Telford, and Thompson (1974) reported that introverts showed a faster rate of intake than did extraverts. In other words, introverts might smoke in such a way so that the inhibitory lip-touching sham effects prevailed, whereas extraverts smoked differently, mainly to obtain the excitatory drug effect. From another viewpoint, O'Connor (1980b) expressed a similar multilevel/multifunction idea: In general, extraverts tend to smoke more in situations where they need to increase their activity level or need to increase motivation to act (e.g., during boredom), whereas introverts smoke in situations where they wish to enhance their concentration (e.g., as in checking figures or speaking on a telephone in a noisy room).

The preceding implies that the larger dose of nicotine per minute taken by introverts as compared with extraverts (Ashton, Marsh, Millman, Rawlins, Stepney, Telford, & Thompson, 1979) might be an (undesirable) side effect. But another possibility is that introverts aim at two effects: One goal is the sedating effect on the sham smoking levels of the CNS to which CNV is not related; the other goal is the creation of overexcitation within the CNV-related CNS level. Overexcitation within the latter level is created to block strong emotional and intellectual activities, which are related to other levels, that are unacceptable for the individual in question. That is to say, as soon as the introvert feels that these unacceptable feelings and thoughts might be evoked or become conscious, he or she will counteract by smoking and/or by other comparable behavior patterns. This leads to a subjective feeling of calmness.

Of course, there are other explanations. Nelsen (1978), for instance, proposed that the effect of nicotine on arousal may arise from its stimulating action on both the reticular and limbic systems. Arousal mediated by the reticular system is nonspecific, whereas arousal mediated by the limbic system allows for more selective or goal-directed behavior. These two arousal systems are mutually inhibitory, and nicotine could be selectively activating the limbic system, thereby counteracting the hyperactivation mediated by the reticular system. However, because smoking is such a complex event, interpretation of results remains a hazardous enterprise.

If the inverted-U model (Figure 3) is correct, then discrepancies between data mentioned in the literature can be reconciled. For instance, Ashton *et al.* (1974) described a CNV magnitude (a measure that takes into account both amplitude and latency) enhancing effect of caffeine and a reducing effect of nitrazepam. But Janssen *et al.* (1978) predicted, on the basis of Eysenck's (1957) drug postulate (i.e., that depressant drugs increase cortical inhibition and decrease cortical excitation, thus producing extravert behavior; stimulant drugs decrease cortical inhibition and increase cortical excitation, thus producing introvert behavior), that CNV, which is considered here to be a sign of cortical inhibition, would increase after administering chlordiazepoxide (a benzodiazepine like nitrazepam) and decrease after caffeine. They verified this hypothesis significantly by comparing the chlordiazepoxide with the caffeine group. However, in making comparisons within groups, only the decrease between the measurement before taking caffeine and the one a halfhour after administering this drug was significant. The explanation of these dissenting results could lie in the distinction between the experimental conditions. A striking difference is that in the case of the Ashton *et al.* experiment, three subjects and several observers sat together in the subject room. Also, there was some bodily contact between subjects and observers (to count the radial pulse). It is clear that these circumstances could have a different effect on the excitation–inhibition balance as compared with our isolated subject situation. The socially reassuring circumstances could have placed the majority of subjects on the left, inhibition leg of the inverted-U, whereas the more stressful isolation of the Janssen *et al.* experiment probably did the contrary. Thus the opposite points of departure on the inverted-U could explain why the results of the two studies are opposed. Of course, another less likely possibility is that, in addition, the majority of subjects in the Ashton *et al.* study consisted of extraverts, as opposed to an introvert majority in the case of the Janssen *et al.* investigation.

Another enigma is that reported by Tecce and Cole (1974) regarding the effect of amphetamine: 13 out of 20 normal women showed a decrease and the remainder an increase in CNV amplitude. The authors considered a variety of factors that might have accounted for the difference found, but none of them did. However, they did not look at personality differences. Because personality differences appear to be an important factor, it is possible that the women who showed the CNV increase (and felt more alert) were the more extraverted ones of the group, whereas those who showed the decrease (coupled with what the authors called "paradoxical" drowsiness, which is, after all, a reaction form of several overexcited individuals) were the most introverted subjects of the group. This comment applies equally to the Janssen *et al.* experiment. As was mentioned, the within-group results were not impressive. This is possibly a consequence of using the linear instead of the inverted-U model. Had the latter been used, then the effects would have been studied on extraverts and introverts separately. In the case of the extraverts, one could have predicted that the sedative would have caused a CNV decrease and the stimulant some increase or decrease, whereas, in the case of the introverts, opposite effects would have been predicted.

DESIGN OF A NEW TESTABLE MODEL

Notwithstanding the fact that the results of the first and second experiments reviewed support each other, further experimentation is needed to see whether the ideas advanced hold. For that purpose, sharper delineation of a (temporary) model is of value. Although Figure 2 gives a nice overall picture of assumed events, it is too complex to give testing procedures a fair chance because several of the steps cannot be approximated. At present, restriction to the cortex is attractive, not because subcortical structures are not involved but because direct measurement of brain stem reticular system activity, limbic system activity, reciprocal connection activity, and the like, is at the moment impracticable. The model, of which Figure 3 is a sketch, is not logical because it imperfectly fuses trait and state characteristics. The results reported are therefore used next to design a new simple testable model, while keeping as much as possible within the boundaries of the theory.

These results can be interpreted as follows (Figure 5). Individuals have a varying percentage of (fronto-central) cortical neurons that are able to work at their disposal, the remaining percentage being either overinhibited or overexcited. This percentage is dependent on brain structure (underlying personality traits) and condition (input, time, etc.). Some individuals have—on the basis of their specific brain structure—a relatively high percentage of cortical neurons that are overinhibited, that is, that are not immediately available to work whenever necessity or desirability arise. To decrease overinhibition and at the same time to free more cortical neurons, these individuals (have to)

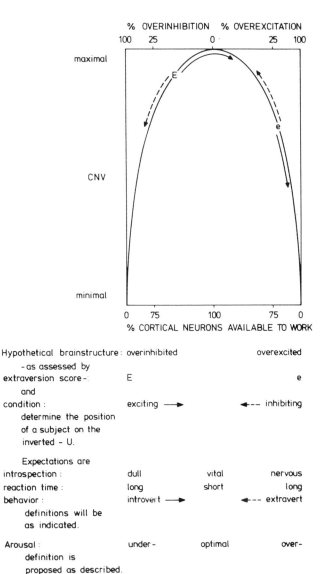

Figure 5. Diagrammatic summary of the hypothetical relation between overinhibited or overexcited cortical neurons and neurons available to work as indicated by CNV. CNV values found for different exciting and inhibiting conditions can be systematized as indicated, if it is taken for granted that (a) extraverts, on the basis of a specific brain structure, are more or less overinhibited during neutral conditions, whereas introverts are more or less overexcited; and (b) that CNV is a sign or measure of cortical synchrony related to momentary inhibition of a large proportion of those cortical neurons that are available for task execution. Thus, it is expected that most extraverts when brought or maneuvering

maneuver for external and/or internal (e.g., evocation of memories) input increase and/or decrease of habituation (monotony), in this manner manifesting introvert behavior—left side of the inverted-U. Maneuvering will usually lead to ascending—to the right. In so doing, these individuals probably feel better. Other individuals have—on the basis of another type of brain structure—a relatively large percentage of cortical neurons that are overexcited, leaving a small proportion capable to work. To increase the latter proportion and at the same time decrease the percentage of overexcited neurons, these individuals maneuver to realize input decrease and/or to take advantage of habituation, in this way manifesting extravert behavior (right side of the inverted-U; maneuvering will usually lead to ascending [to the left]). Probably this is accompanied by hedonic satisfaction, too. In both instances, a larger proportion of cortical neurons becomes available for whatever cerebral activity is wanted.

This cerebration is accompanied by the usual changes over time of the excitation/inhibition ratio of the cortical neurons that (have become available to) work. It is conceivable that at specific moments there will either be an appreciable prevalence of excitation or of inhibition. The latter is thought to occur, for example, during a task that needs, at certain moments of its execution, a relatively small number of active/excitable neurons (for instance, for the detection of the light that is expected and for the preparation to press the button fast in accordance with the reaction time task instruction) and at the same time inactivity/inhibition of all other neurons available to work to prevent interference. CNV is thought to be related to the latter phenomenon, that is, momentary inhibition of a large proportion of cortical neurons available to work during performance. The preceding is rendered in Figure 5.

This model is now in the process of being tested. Psychoactive drugs are administered to define exciting and inhibiting conditions. For excitation, a stimulant drug (or white noise) is preferred to an additional task, like the double-task condition of the first experiment, because the

---

from a monotonous into an exciting condition will report a change from drowsy or dull to alert and vital and show introvert behavior and improved performance (short reaction times). However, for introverts, the same change of condition would lead to (an increase of) nervousness and deterioration of performance (longer reaction times). Inhibiting conditions, on the contrary, would favor most introverts and not extraverts.

As an example, the mean extravert (E) and the mean introvert (e) of the first experiment (beginning condition) are marked. The system is such that for E the chance that a cortical neuron is available to work is about 90%; the chance that it will be overinhibited is about 10%. For e chances are about 70% available to work and about 30% overexcited. Note that reaction times were found to be short for E and long for e. For further explanation see the text, especially with respect to reaction time and automatization.

latter, besides causing decrease of overinhibition and/or increase of overexcitation, uses part of the cortex for information processing next to the cortical neurons dealing with the reaction time task. This information processing might hamper the generation of a full-blown CNV, causing unnecessary complication. Introspective reports obtained during the EEG experiments give an indication of mood, and performance speed is assessed by measuring reaction time. Eysenck's (1957) drug postulate is used for hypotheses formulation.

LIMITATIONS OF THE MODEL

Some limitations of the model will be commented on here. For instance, a remarkable finding of the first experiments was that, only during the beginning and not during the end condition, extraverts had higher CNVs and shorter reaction times than introverts. An explanation could be that, during the end condition, more or less automatization, that is, taking over of certain parts of cortical task execution by subcortical centers, occurred. Robinson (personal communication), within his more refined and extensive theoretical framework, gives automatization an important place whenever one is dealing with experiments that include response sequences like the CNV paradigm. He also found that extraverts do better on certain types of cognitive tasks (introverts, of course, do better on other tasks). His explanation for the superior performance of the extraverted individual is that there is less thalamocortically mediated inhibition of the brain stem reticular formation:

> a system that, despite its association with cortical arousal, is very much involved in the acquisition and elaboration of the automatic motor sequences that underlie skilled performance and which probably also underlie skilled covert cognitive manipulation.

According to him, a greater part of the extravert's total behavior, as compared with the introvert's, is produced by brain stem systems that are responsible for the "unconscious" automatic responses that become available when motor sequences are much repeated in response to particular stimuli. Thus, whenever thalamocortically mediated inhibition of the brain stem is relatively strong, it interrupts the learning of motor skills and probably also the learning of cognitive skills if the latter are associated with efferent systems. Without the help of automatic responses, the demand on conscious processes is very great, and this results in introverted behavior. Whenever inhibition is relatively weak, (social) situations are less demanding because a lesser proportion of total responses needs to be generated and monitored by voluntary conscious processes. To phrase it in the language used before: There is a relatively large proportion of cortical neurons available to work, and this type of individual is therefore capable of more spontaneous, less self-conscious (sociable) behavior, that is, he or she is an extravert. Accordingly, automatization could be responsible for a dissociation of (cortical) CNV and (by now subcortical) reaction (time) over time.

Robinson's (1983) work gives a good example of how subcortical structures can be included in a testable model. His input–output model for the diffuse thalamocortical system includes three elements, representing aggregates of thalamic neurons, cortical neurons, and the general loss or dissipation of energy associated with any real system. Experiments revealed that the model can account for most of the within- and across-subject amplitude variation of EEG evoked responses to sinusoidally modulated diffuse light. Relating the results to Pavlovian/Eysenckian theory, Robinson found that the hypothetical excitatory and inhibitory processes of the central nervous system, which Pavlov associated with differences in human personality, correspond to the transmission properties of, respectively, the cortical and thalamic neuron populations of the diffuse thalamocortical system. Robinson's (personal communication) explanation of CNV generation differs from that advanced before. He claims that CNV is best explained as resulting from the aggregation of negative extracellular potential shifts that accompany intracellular depolarizations or EPSPs that are produced in Cortical Layers I and II by the brain stem reticular activating system. Thus, in his opinion, CNV is an excitation phenomenon, but it is the result of both excitation and inhibition because it must reflect, too, the degree of opposing inhibition of the brain stem mediated by thalamocortical processes.

Apart from drawing attention to Pavlov's notion of protective or transmarginal inhibition, Eysenck and O'Connor's study is of interest because it shows how component measures taken on CNVs under sufficiently long foreperiod intervals (4 sec and longer) probably add valuable information. For example, O'Connor (1980a) reported that in extraverts the early negativity reflecting an orienting response to the warning stimulus (O wave) was more pronounced during sham smoking. However, during real smoking, the latter negativity, indicating expectation of the imperative stimulus (E wave), became more prominent. Introverts, on the other hand, showed a decrease in E-wave amplitude from sham to real smoking sessions. This led to a model, involving personality differences in attentional strategies employed, that suggests that smoking accompanies enhanced stimulus selectivity in introverts but enhanced response preparation in extraverts. This refinement, too, does not have a place in the model, nor do neuroticism, psychoticism, memory, motivation, circadian rhythmicity, and so forth.

CONCLUDING REMARKS

The way in which I have described the model is somewhat dualistic. On the one hand, the anatomical and physiological terms used are suggestive of actual brain structure and function, whereas, on the other hand, the model itself is more abstract in nature.

For a broader anatomical and physiological perspective, the reader is referred to Robinson's (1982) paper on properties of the diffuse thalamocortical system in relation to Pavlovian/Eysenckian personality theory. Robinson quoted Samuels (1959), who pointed out that the diffuse thalamocortical system is

> functionally organized in a manner which would permit it to control the continuum of consciousness and to serve as a selective mechanism for the facilitation of certain perceptions, sensations, and memories, as well as the inhibition of others. (p. 5)

Elsewhere (Werre, Mattie, Fortgens, Berretty, & Vibert-Jouandet, 1985), it has been suggested that CNV might be related to this selective cortical inhibition and to the "strength of the nervous system as regards inhibition" (Strelau, 1983). Thus, besides cortex and brain stem reticular formation, the diffuse thalamocortical system probably contributes to the neurophysiological basis of E too.

The abstracting approach suggests a system formed of organized elements (it does not really matter whether these elements are identical with neurons, with parts of neurons, or with aggregates of neurons) that are either capable or incapable of being active or cooperative. An element contributes to function (information processing, thinking, reacting, etc.) in a wider context by being excited or inhibited at appropriate times. Incapacity to work is caused by overinhibition or overexcitation. In the foregoing, attention was mainly drawn to the two extreme organizational forms (traits) of the system, that is, that with an inherent tendency toward a large proportion of overinhibited elements and the one with an inherent tendency toward a large proportion of overexcited elements. The intermediate position, characterized by a large proportion of elements that (are available to) function and only small proportions of overinhibited or overexcited elements, is probably common and optimal for most tasks at hand, enabling effective deployment of an adequate number of elements without much adjustment. What happens if a task is considerably below or above the capacity of the system, in other words, really stressful, has not been studied here. Perhaps, in the latter situation, protective inhibition manifests itself. Continuous (re) adjustment to the middle position assumes that the system contains a feedback mechanism. The preceding is in need of a descriptive term, and *arousal* might be a candidate—underarousal indicating a state characterized by considerable overinhibition, overarousal meaning a state of considerable overexcitation, and optimal arousal signifying the vital middle state (see Figure 5). However, it is questionable whether such a restrictive definition would be an improvement. At the moment, the operational definition ("arousal level is the inverse probability of falling asleep") given by Corcoran (1981) in a many-sided exploration of the arousal concept provides more flexibility on the path to reaching a better understanding of the subject.

Acknowledgments

The author is indebted to E. W. Berretty, H. Mattie, and H. G. Stassen for their great assistance in the preparation of this chapter.

REFERENCES

Ashton, H., Millman, J. E., Telford, R., & Thompson, J. W. The effect of caffeine, nitrazepam and cigarette smoking on the contingent negative variation in man. *Electroencephalography and Clinical Neurophysiology*, 1974, *37*, 59–71.

Ashton, H., Marsh, V. R., Millman, J. E., Rawlins, M. D., Stepney, R., Telford, R., & Thompson, J. W. Patterns of behavioural, autonomic and electrophysiological response to cigarette smoking and nicotine in man. In A. Rémond & C. Izard (Eds.), *Electrophysiological effects of nicotine*. Amsterdam: Elsevier/North-Holland Biomedical Press, 1979.

Corcoran, D. W. J. Introversion-extraversion, stress and arousal. In R. Lynn (Ed.), *Dimensions of personality*. Oxford: Pergamon Press, 1981.

Dirken, J. M. *De vragenlijst voor habituele aktie bereidheid*. Groningen: Wolters-Noordhof, 1970.

Eysenck, H. J. *Dynamics of anxiety and hysteria*. London: Routledge & Kegan Paul, 1957.

Eysenck, H. J. *The biological basis of personality*. Springfield, IL: Charles C Thomas, 1967.

Eysenck, H. J., & O'Connor, K. P. Smoking, arousal and personality. In A. Rémond & C. Izard (Eds.), *Electrophysiological effects of nicotine*. Amsterdam: Elsevier/North-Holland Biomedical Press, 1979.

Gale, A. EEG studies of extraversion-introversion. In R. Lynn (Ed.), *Dimensions of personality*. Oxford: Pergamon Press, 1981.

Janssen, R. H. C., Mattie, H., Plooij-van Gorsel, P. C., & Werre, P. F. The effects of a depressant and a stimulant drug on the contingent negative variation. *Biological Psychology*, 1978, *6*, 209–218.

Kornhuber, H. H., & Deecke, L. (Eds.). *Motivation, motor and sensory processes of the brain: Electrical potentials, behaviour and clinical use*. Amsterdam: Elsevier/North-Holland Biomedical Press, 1980.

76PETER F. WERRE

McCallum, W. C., & Walter, W. G. The effects of attention and distraction on the contingent negative variation in normal and neurotic subjects. *Electroencephalography and Clinical Neurophysiology*, 1968, 25, 319–329.

Nelsen, J. M. Psychobiological consequences of chronic nicotinization. In K. Battig (Ed.), *Behavioural effects of nicotine*. Basel: Karger, 1978.

O'Connor, K. P. The contingent negative variation and individual differences in smoking behaviour. *Personality and Individual Differences*, 1980, 1, 57–72. (a)

O'Connor, K. P. Individual differences in situational preference amongst smokers. *Personality and Individual Differences*, 1980, 1, 249–257. (b)

Robinson, D. L. Properties of the diffuse thalamocortical system and human personality: A direct test of Pavlovian/Eysenckian theory. *Personality and Individual Differences*, 1982, 3, 1–16.

Robinson, D. L. An analysis of human EEG responses in the alpha range of frequencies. *International Journal of Neuroscience*, 1983, 22, 81–98.

Samuels, I. Reticular mechanisms and behaviour. *Psychological Bulletin*, 1959, 56, 1–25.

Snijders, J. Th., & Verhage, F. *Voorlopige handleiding bij de Groninger intelligentie test.* Amsterdam: Swets en Zeitlinger, 1962.

Strelau, J. *Temperament, personality, activity.* London: Academic Press, 1983.

Tecce, J. J. Contingent negative variation (CNV) and psychological processes in man. *Psychological Bulletin*, 1972, 77, 73–108.

Tecce, J. J., & Cattanach, L. Contingent negative variation. In E. Niedermeyer & F. Lopes da Silva (Eds.), *Electroencephalography*. Baltimore: Urban and Schwarzenberg, 1982.

Tecce, J. J., & Cole, J. O. Amphetamine effects in man: Paradoxical drowsiness and lowered electrical brain activity (CNV). *Science*, 1974, 185, 451–453.

Werre, P. F. Aspects of the relationship between electroencephalographic and psychological variables in normal adults. In R. J. Broughton (Ed.), *Henri Gastaut and the Marseilles school's contribution to the neurosciences*. Amsterdam: Elsevier Biomedical Press, 1982.

Werre, P. F. Contingent negative variation: Relation to personality, and modification by stimulation and sedation. In J. Strelau, F. H. Farley, & A. Gale (Eds.), *The biological bases of personality and behavior: Psychophysiology, performance, and application* (Vol. 2). Washington, D.C.: Hemisphere, 1986.

Werre, P. F., Faverey, H. A., & Janssen, R. H. C. *Contingent negative variation en persoonlijkheid*. Leiden: Psychiatrische Kliniek Rijksuniversiteit Leiden, 1973.

Werre, P. F., Faverey, H. A., & Janssen, R. H. C. Contingent negative variation and personality. *Nederlands Tijdschrift voor de Psychologie*, 1975, 30, 277–299.

Werre, P. F., Mattie, H., Fortgens, C., Berretty, E. W., & Vibert-Jouandet, O. O. M. Interaction between extraversion and condition as indicated by contingent negative variation. In J. Spence & C. Izard (Eds.), *Motivation, emotion, and personality*. Amsterdam: Elsevier/North-Holland Science Publishers, 1985.

Wilde, G. J. S. *Neurotische labiliteit gemeten volgens de vragenlijstmethode*. Amsterdam: Van Rossen, 1962.

PART II

Studies of Emotionality and Psychoticism

CHAPTER 4

Trait Theories of Anxiety

MICHAEL W. EYSENCK

INTRODUCTION

At first glance, the attempts by personality theorists to provide a taxonomy of personality traits seem to have achieved little in the way of consensus. However, as Eysenck and Eysenck (1985) demonstrated, many (or even most) of the disagreements concerning the number and nature of major personality dimensions stem from looking at the same reality from rather different perspectives. Thus, for example, it is relatively straightforward to reconcile Cattell's emphasis on 16 personality factors (PF) with Eysenck's claim that there are only three major dimensions of personality (i.e., extraversion, neuroticism, and psychoticism). Because Cattell's factors are correlated, it is possible to extract second-order factors. When this is done, Cattell's 16 PF yields factors of exvia and anxiety that correspond closely to the Eysenckian dimensions of extraversion and neuroticism, respectively (Barrett & Kline, 1980; Hundleby & Connor, 1968).

There are various ways of interpreting these findings. According to Cattell, Eber, and Tatsouka (1970),

> It is a mistake, generally, to work at the secondary level only, for one certainly loses a lot of valuable information present initially at the primary level. (p. 112)

Although this argument sounds persuasive, it is actually fallacious. The usual finding is that first-order factors add rather little to the information

MICHAEL W. EYSENCK • Department of Psychology, Birkbeck College, University of London, London, England WC1E 7HX.

contained in second-order factors. Saville and Blinkhorn (1981) adminis-tered the Eysenck Personality Inventory (EPI) and the 16 PF to the same group of people. When they removed all of the variance attributable to extraversion and neuroticism from the 16 PF data, there was little left in terms of useful information about personality.

We have established so far that extraversion and neuroticism or anxiety are of special importance within personality descriptions. Are there any sound theoretical reasons for the preeminence of these two orthogonal dimensions? Tellegen (1985) has provided an interesting an-swer to this question based on his discovery that there are two major orthogonal dimensions of mood: Positive affect (running from low to high positive affect) and negative affect (running from low to high nega-tive affect). If, as Tellegen (1985) and others have assumed, there is a close relationship between personality and mood, then two personality dimensions of special importance would involve susceptibility to posi-tive affect and susceptibility to negative affect, respectively. The evi-dence indicates that extraversion (and particularly its sociability compo-nent) is strongly related to susceptibility to positive affect, whereas neuroticism or anxiety is related to susceptibility to negative affect (Wat-son & Clark, 1984).

There are perhaps two major advantages involved in relating trait anxiety to the broad dimension of susceptibility to negative affect. First, it makes it clear that trait anxiety should be regarded as a mood-disposi-tional dimension, with the effects of trait anxiety on behavior being typically rather indirect. Second, it suggests a way of establishing more precisely what is being measured by tests of trait anxiety. For example, the positive and negative items on both the state and trait measures of Spielberger's State–Trait Anxiety Inventory appear to be measuring rather different constructs (cf. Watson & Clark, 1984). It may well be that the positive items (e.g., joyful, content) are measuring positive affect rather than the negative affect assessed by the negative items. As a consequence, the scales are actually measuring a combination of high negative affect and low positive affect that might more appropriately be called *unhappiness* or *unpleasantness* rather than negative affect or a spe-cific anxiety factor.

THE PHYSIOLOGICAL BASIS

Two related but nevertheless distinct hypotheses concerning the physiological basis of individual differences in trait anxiety or neurot-icism have been put forward by Eysenck (1967) and by Gray (1982). Eysenck (1967) proposed that neuroticism depends on the functioning of the visceral brain, which consists of "the hippocampus, amygdala, cingulum, septum, and hypothalamus" (p. 230). More specifically, he claimed that differences between those high and low in neuroticism could be accounted for "in terms of differential thresholds for hypothalamic activity" (p. 237) and to differences in responsivity of the sympathetic nervous system "with high neuroticism scores associated with greater responsivity."

Gray (1982, 1985) argued that the links between personality and physiology were more obvious if one considered the personality dimension of anxiety (an amalgam of neuroticism and introversion) rather than neuroticism *per se*. However, the substantial correlation between measures of anxiety and neuroticism means that they are rather similar constructs. According to Gray (1982), individuals high and low in trait anxiety differ in their susceptibility to signals of punishment, and this susceptibility in turn depends on the behavioral inhibition system (BIS). Indeed, Gray (1985) argued that "*ex hypothesi*, activity in the BIS constitutes anxiety" (p. 6). The behavioral inhibition system is thought to comprise the septohippocampal system, its monoaminergic afferents from the brain stem, and its neocortical projection in the frontal lobe.

Much of the evidence adduced by Gray (1982) involves drug research and is based on the assumption that antianxiety drugs (benodiazepines, barbiturates, and alcohol) all impair the functioning of the behavioral inhibition system and thereby reduce anxiety. The research has followed two main approaches: (a) direct investigation of antianxiety drug action within the brain; and (b) a comparison of the behavioral effects of antianxiety drugs with the effects of other manipulations of the brain.

Gray (1982) considered a number of findings based on the second approach. For example, the behavioral changes produced by antianxiety drugs closely resemble those occurring after there are septal and hippocampal lesions, which suggests the probable involvement of the septohippocampal system in anxiety.

The rationale underlying the first approach was depicted in the following way by Lyons (1982):

> If X (antianxiety drugs) reduce Y (anxiety) by altering region of the brain Z (the septohippocampal system, SHS), Then Y amounts, neurologically, to Z. (p. 490)

He then went on to argue forcefully that the logic of this approach was suspect, demonstrating the point by means of an analogous example where the conclusion manifestly does not follow:

> If X (a potato in the exhaust) reduces or disrupts Y (the functioning of an internal combustion engine) by altering Z (the free outflow of gases along the exhaust system), Then Y amounts, mechanically, to Z. (p. 490)

Lyons (1982) then attempted to demolish the logic of Gray's (1982) second approach along similar lines. There is clearly some force in Lyons's arguments, but he ignored other aspects of Gray's (1982) reasoning. In particular, Gray's (1982) identification of the brain regions involved in anxiety was based on all of the available evidence and did not depend solely on studies using antianxiety drugs.

Before examining other potential limitations with Gray's (1982) theoretical approach, it is worth considering psychophysiological research comparing individuals high and low in trait anxiety or neuroticism. In general, the findings have proved disappointing. Eysenck and Eysenck (1985) concluded their review by arguing that "the psychophysiological data collected so far are not sufficiently sensitive or detailed to permit precise identification of the underlying physiological structures" (p. 235). Part of the problem may be that most of the studies have been conducted under relatively stress-free conditions that minimize individual differences in physiological responding. However, Plouffe and Stelmack (1979) manipulated environmental stress and failed to discover significant differences in pupillary response at any level of stress.

A further difficulty is that the findings obtained appear to depend in mysterious ways on the exact psychophysiological measures taken. For example, high trait anxiety reduced the habituation rate of the orientation reaction in all three studies in which finger-volume responses were measured, but no effects of anxiety appeared when electrodermal responses were measured (O'Gorman, 1977). O'Gorman reviewed 11 other studies dealing with the effects of neuroticism on the habituation rate of the orienting reaction. Significant findings were obtained in five of these studies, two of which found significant differences in both directions between those high and low in neuroticism. A simple headcount reveals that high neuroticism was associated with faster habituation in four cases and with slower habituation in three cases. Although these findings seem very inconclusive, it should be noted that high neuroticism slowed down the rate of habituation in 2 of the best studies (Coles, Gale, & Kline, 1971; Nielsen & Petersen, 1976).

Much stronger evidence that anxiety affects physiological functioning has been obtained when anxious patients are compared with normal controls (e.g., Kelly & Martin, 1969; Lader & Wing, 1966), perhaps because of the substantial differences between the groups in state anxiety. The disappointing results with normals high and low in trait anxiety may be due in part to the fact that individuals vary in terms of which physiological measure is most sensitive—a notion that Lacey and Lacey (1958) expressed in their "principle of autonomic response stereotypy." Furthermore, peripheral measures can provide at best no more than an indirect reflection of central physiological processes.

In spite of the limitations in the data, it seems probable that there are important physiological differences between those high and low in trait anxiety. Even if there are, this does not make a physiological theory of trait anxiety adequate. The reason for this can be seen if we consider Gray's (1982) theory in more detail. He argued that there are four kinds of stimuli that activate the behavioral inhibition system: signals of punishment; signals of nonreward; novel stimuli; and innate fear stimuli. Obviously, these stimuli will activate the behavioral inhibition system only when two conditions are satisfied: (a) the stimuli are thoroughly processed; and (b) they receive potentially threatening interpretations. In other words, Gray's (1982) theory indicates the necessity of accounting for the cognitive system's involvement in trait anxiety but does not provide such an account.

There is a further, very general, limitation with the theories proposed by Eysenck (1967) and by Gray (1982). Both theories emphasize the importance of heredity and fail to provide adequate explanations of the role played by environmental factors in trait anxiety. As Gray (1982) has admitted:

> Studies . . . of the personality traits of neuroticism and extraversion . . . estimate the contribution of heredity to these conditions at about 50 percent of the variance. But that means, of course, that another 50 percent of the variance remains to be accounted for; and it is likely that learning (of as yet unknown kinds) plays a determining role in this respect. (p. 438)

For example, the fact that individuals obtaining the same trait anxiety score on a standard questionnaire may nevertheless differ substantially in terms of the events that make them anxious indicates the importance of considering the life experiences of each individual. It may be that classical conditioning is relevant here, as Eysenck (1979) has argued. However, Gray (1979) claimed that conditioning is of relatively minor importance. It may, therefore, be the case that the impact of the environment on trait anxiety can be understood fully only when more is known of the functioning of the cognitive system.

THE COGNITIVE SYSTEM

LONG-TERM MEMORY

There has been increased interest in recent years in establishing the possible importance of the cognitive system in accounting for individual differences in trait anxiety. A theory of trait anxiety that was almost entirely cognitive in nature was proposed by Hamilton (1983):

> *Anxiety* should be regarded as a particular set or network of connotative data that, on the basis of past experience and autonomous elaboration of their

cognitive structures, provides a store of long-term memories. These are available for retrieval when stimulated, just like other long-term memory data. . . . The greater the predisposition to generate aversive expectancies or behavior outcomes, the greater the appropriate memory store, the lower the retrieval threshold for this type of information, and the greater the response bias toward primary processes of identifying and avoiding real or potential aversiveness. (p. 114)

There is not much evidential support for Hamilton's (1983) theory, but his emphasis on individual differences in the contents of long-term memory is entirely reasonable. In the first place, trait anxiety is usually assessed by questionnaires that require the respondent to retrieve relevant information from long-term memory. Second, there is the important phenomenon of mood–state-dependent retrieval (Bower, 1981), in which information learned in one mood state is more likely to be recalled subsequently if the mood state at recall is similar to that at the time of learning rather than dissimilar. This phenomenon has sometimes proved rather elusive (e.g., Bower & Mayer, 1985) but can be obtained provided that the learner perceives a causal link between the to-be-remembered information and his or her current mood (Bower, 1985). Mood–state-dependent retrieval is relevant here as it indicates that information about current mood state is stored in long-term memory. Because mood states are substantially affected by the level of trait anxiety or neuroticism (Williams, 1981), it follows that high-anxiety and low-anxiety individuals should differ in their long-term memories. The same conclusion follows from another phenomenon—that of mood-congruent learning (e.g., Bower, Gilligan, & Monteiro, 1981)—in which emotionally toned material is learned best when its affective value matches the learner's current mood.

Differences in long-term memory between high-anxiety and low-anxiety individuals can be considered in terms of rather general schemata (i.e., broad memory structures) or of more specific units of information (e.g., worries or concerns). Butler and Mathews (1983) provided evidence that anxious patients may possess "danger schemata." The patients felt themselves to be significantly more at risk from various potential environmental dangers than other people, whereas this self–other discrepancy was not found in the normal control group. At the more specific level of worries, Borkovec, Robinson, Pruzinsky, and De-Pree (1983) obtained a correlation coefficient of +.67 between trait anxiety and the percentage of a typical day that was spent worrying. This finding may be due to the fact that those high in trait anxiety have a greater number of highly organized worries than those low in trait anxiety, or it may reflect differential accessibility of worries as a function of individual differences in anxiety. This issue has not yet been resolved, but the finding that high-anxiety individuals worry more than low-anxiety individuals even when their initial level of state anxiety is comparable (Eysenck, 1984) is consistent with a structural rather than a process interpretation of the association between anxiety and worry.

There are various potential advantages of focusing on differences in long-term memory as a function of trait anxiety. For example, there are gradual changes in trait anxiety that occur over time in nearly all of the longitudinal studies (Conley, 1983), and these changes may reflect the progressive elaboration and refinement of schemata in long-term memory. Of course, other explanations for changing levels of trait anxiety are possible, but none of the theoretical constructs of traditional trait theory provides a natural account of these gradual changes.

The cognitive approach argued for here has implications for the controversial issue of whether trait anxiety should be regarded as a unidimensional or a multidimensional construct. If different schemata are formed for the various major activities and concerns of life, then it seems probable that the tendency to experience anxiety will depend in part on the schemata activated by any given situation. In other words, the cognitive approach implies a multidimensional view of trait anxiety. On the other hand, traditional trait theory implies a unidimensional view. If, for example, some individuals have more responsive physiological systems than others, then it is likely that those with particularly responsive systems should be highly anxious in all stressful situations, whereas those with unresponsive systems should experience little anxiety in any situation.

The evidence is less conclusive than one would like, but it broadly supports the multidimensional view. One of the leading multidimensional theorists is Endler (1983), who has claimed that there are at least five different dimensions or facets of trait anxiety: social evaluation, interpersonal, physical danger, ambiguous situations, and daily routines. The basic prediction of Endler's (1983) theory is that the increase in state anxiety produced by a threatening situation over a neutral situation will be greater among those high in trait anxiety than among those low in trait anxiety only when the nature of the threatening situation is *congruent* with the dimension of trait anxiety that is being investigated. Thus, for example, the social evaluation dimension of trait anxiety should interact with a social evaluation situation to produce increases in state anxiety, but the same dimension of trait anxiety should not interact with a situation involving physical danger. Endler (1983) reviewed 14 studies that provide a total of 18 tests of his multidimensional theory and claimed that 13 of the tests were consistent with prediction.

In spite of these findings, Endler's (1983) theoretical approach has significant problems. It is not clear that there are five clearly distinguishable dimensions of trait anxiety, and it may be preferable to postulate fewer dimensions. The evidence is strongest so far as social evaluation and physical danger are concerned, and these two dimensions were considered in many more studies than the other three dimensions in the 18 tests of his theory reviewed by Endler (1983).

In sum, it is plausible to assume that individuals high and low in trait anxiety differ in predictable ways in the information they have stored in long-term memory. More speculatively, such differences in the content of long-term memory may help to account for the changes in trait anxiety over time and the apparent multidimensionality of trait anxiety. In addition, these differences may affect the perceptual, attentional, and interpretative processes applied to environmental stimulation, possibilities that are considered in detail in the next section.

COGNITIVE PROCESSES: REPRESSION AND SENSITIZATION

When one considers possible differences between high-anxiety and low-anxiety individuals in the functioning of the cognitive system, then one reasonable starting point is to consider the initial processing of threatening stimuli. Broadly speaking, such stimuli may either be approached, in the sense of being thoroughly processed, or they may be avoided (i.e., minimally processed). The first systematic exposition of this point of view was provided by Byrne (1964). He used the term *sensitization* to describe the approach strategy and the term *repression* to refer to the avoidance strategy. Byrne (1964) then went on to argue that there are systematic individual differences in preferred strategy and to devise a test (the Repression–Sensitization Scale) to assess these individual differences. Although Byrne disputed the point, the evidence indicates unequivocally that the Repression–Sensitization Scale is simply a measure of trait anxiety (cf. Watson & Clark, 1984). Thus research based on the Repression Sensitization Scale is of direct relevance to the theme of this chapter.

The published literature concerned with the hypothesized differences between repressors (or low-anxiety individuals) and sensitizers (or high-anxiety individuals) in their processing of threatening stimuli presents a confused and inconsistent picture. There has been most interest in the phenomenon of perceptual defense, which occurs when taboo or emotionally threatening stimuli have higher perceptual recognition thresholds than neutral stimuli (Dixon, 1981). On the assumption that perceptual defense involves partial avoidance of, and reduced processing of, threatening stimuli, then the obvious prediction is that repressors or low-anxiety individuals should show greater perceptual defense than sensitizers or high-anxiety individuals. However, as reviews by Eysenck (in press) and by Eysenck, MacLeod, and Mathews (in press) indicate, many studies have failed to support the prediction. Even in those studies obtaining a greater perceptual defense effect in repressors than in sensitizers, it is not clear whether this reflects genuine perceptual effects or response-bias effects. When perceptual sensitivity uncontaminated by possible response bias has been measured (Van Egeren, 1968; Wagstaff, 1974), no differences have been found between repressors and sensitizers in the perceptual defense paradigm.

Negative findings have also been obtained from studies in which the duration of visual attention to threat-related pictures (e.g., mutilated bodies and corpses) has been measured. The obvious prediction is that repressors should spend less time than sensitizers inspecting such pictures, but the usual finding is that there is no difference between the two groups (Carroll, 1972; Lewinsohn, Berquist, & Brelje, 1972).

It is tempting to conclude that systematic differences between repressors and sensitizers in the initial processing of threat-related stimuli simply do not exist. However, an alternative hypothesis has been examined in a series of recent studies (Eysenck *et al.*, in press; Halkiopoulos, unpublished; MacLeod, Mathews, & Tata, in press). The basic notion is that high-anxiety and low-anxiety individuals differ in their approach/ avoidance strategies toward threat-related stimuli only when at least one threatening and one neutral stimulus are presented concurrently. In other words, individuals differ in terms of a *selective* bias that cannot be used when only one stimulus at a time is present, as was the case in virtually all of the perceptual defense and duration of visual attention studies.

The experimental paradigm that has been used to test this hypothesis was introduced by a student of mine, Christos Halkiopoulos, in unpublished research. He made use of a modified dichotic listening task in which pairs of words were presented concurrently, one to each ear. All of the words on one channel had to be attended to and shadowed (i.e., repeated back aloud), and the words on this attended channel were a mixture of threat-related (e.g., grave, fail) and neutral (e.g., sale, chairs) words. All of the words on the other, unattended channel were affectively neutral. In order to ascertain the allocation of attentional or other processing resources, a tone requiring a rapid response was occasionally presented to one ear shortly after a pair of words had been presented. The assumption was that response latencies to the tone would be faster when processing resources were already being allocated to that channel than when they were not. The subjects were allocated to groups on the basis of their scores on the Facilitation–Inhibition Scale (Ullmann, 1962)—a test that correlates extremely highly with Byrne's Repression–Sensitization Scale.

The data of interest concern the speed of response to the tones, and they were quire dramatic. The crucial finding was a highly significant interaction involving the three factors of facilitation-inhibition, attended word type (threatening vs. nonthreatening), and tone channel (attended vs. unattended). As predicted, facilitators appeared to have allocated processing resources to the channel on which a threatening word had just been presented. This was shown in the data by the very rapid responding to the tone when it followed a threatening word in the same ear, coupled with the very slow responding to the tone when it followed a threatening word in the other ear. Also as predicted, inhibitors had exactly the opposite pattern of response times, as if they actively avoided attending to the channel on which a threatening word had just been presented.

Subsequent research has made use of a visual analog of the paradigm used by Halkiopoulos (unpublished). MacLeod et al. (in press) compared a group of normal controls with a group of patients having a primary diagnosis of generalized anxiety. They discovered that anxious patients responded more rapidly to the visual probe when it replaced a threatening word than when it replaced a neutral one, whereas the control subjects responded more rapidly when the probe replaced a neutral word than a threatening one. Thus the basic pattern of findings reported by Halkiopoulos (unpublished) was replicated, and further successful replications on this visual analog task with high-anxiety and low-anxiety normals have been carried out by Broadbent (personal communication) and myself (research in progress).

What are the implications of these findings? First, there is finally convincing evidence of threat avoidance by low-anxiety individuals and of threat approach by high-anxiety individuals. It thus appears that there is some substance in Byrne's (1964) theoretical conjectures. Second, it is clear that consistent individual differences in approach and avoidance strategies are found only in certain circumstances and are not as prevalent as Byrne (1964) assumed. At the present time, the evidence suggests the existence of selective biases in favor of, or against, threatening stimuli that primarily affect performance when the environment permits selective allocation of processing resources, as occurs when at least one threat-related stimulus and one neutral stimulus are presented concurrently. Mathews and MacLeod (in press) discovered that selective bias was detectable in a dichotic listening task even when there was no conscious awareness of any of the threat-related words. This suggests that the selective biases are probably operating at a preattentive level. Third, these selective biases may well be of significance in everyday life. If high-anxiety individuals usually process threat-related stimuli much more thoroughly than low-anxiety individuals, then this could help to explain why anxious patients regard themselves as more "at risk" than normal controls (Butler & Mathews, 1983) and why high-anxiety individuals are typically higher in state anxiety than low-anxiety individuals even in apparently nonstressful conditions (Watson & Clark, 1984).

Considerations of biological utility indicate strongly that these selective biases are likely to operate only when mildly threatening stimuli are presented. Any major threat to the safety or life of the individual will presumably always preempt the available processing resources. This does not significantly reduce the importance of selective biases because in everyday life minor threats normally outnumber major threats by a wide margin.

The conceptualization presented here can be compared with the one advocated by Krohne and Rogner (1982). There is agreement to the extent that they emphasize that repressors and sensitizers differ in terms of the allocation of attentional resources:

> *Redirection* of attention after threat appraisal is viewed as the mediating process between the R–S (i.e., repression–sensitization) behavioral tendency and interindividual differences in performance. (p. 174)

In addition, the theoretical position presented here and that of Krohne and Rogner (1982) both regard the approach and avoidance strategies as rather inflexible and insufficiently sensitive to situational requirements.

Despite this measure of agreement, there are some major differences between the two theoretical approaches. Krohne and Rogner (1982) do not attempt to delineate the boundary conditions within which repressors and sensitizers differ in their allocation of processing resources, nor do they allow explicitly for the involvement of preattentional processes. In at least one respect, the two approaches seem very different. Our data suggest that repressors or low-anxiety individuals are skilled at distinguishing between mildly threatening and neutral stimuli and can even do this preattentively. In contrast, Krohne and Rogner (1982) proposed an almost diametrically opposed hypothesis:

> Persons at the two poles of the R-S (Repression-Sensitization) continuum are presumably characterized by a low ability to discriminate between dangerous and nondangerous cues. While repressors indiscriminately appraise relatively many situations as nondangerous, sensitizers, on the other hand, experience many situations as threatening. (p. 172)

A theoretical issue of particular interest is whether the schemata stored in long-term memory influence the functioning of selective biases. Evidence that is partially relevant here was obtained by MacLeod *et al.* (in press) in their study of visual attention. Their anxious patients were divided into two groups on the basis of whether they reported worrying primarily about social concerns or about physical concerns (e.g., illness), and the threatening words presented during the experiment were classified as either physically threatening (e.g., injury, agony) or socially threatening (e.g., criticized, ashamed). A schema-based explanation for the operation of the approach or sensitizing bias toward threatening stimuli seems to predict that the bias would be most likely to operate when the nature of the threatening stimulus matches the primary worry domain. In fact, the extent of selective bias in anxious patients was unaffected by whether there was a match or a mismatch, so that there is no definitive evidence that schemata in long-term memory are involved. The reason for this may simply be that schemata influence postattentional rather than preattentional processes.

It has now been established that those high and low in trait anxiety differ in their selective biases when a threatening and a neutral stimulus are presented together. Such biases may also be involved in other situations, as, for example, when someone is interpreting an ambiguous stimulus that has both a threatening and a neutral interpretation. According to the exhaustive access model (Simpson, 1984), every possible interpretation of an ambiguous stimulus is activated automatically, and it may be that preattentive selective biases influence the particular interpretation that reaches conscious awareness.

The obvious prediction is that sensitizers or those high in trait anxiety should be more likely than repressors or those low in trait anxiety to perceive ambiguous stimuli as threatening. This was found in one study by Blaylock (1963) with homographs having aggressive and neutral meanings, but the finding was not replicated in a second study. Rather stronger evidence was obtained by Haney (1973), who found that sensitizers were much more likely than repressors to interpret ambiguous sentences in threatening ways.

The paradigm that Haney (1973) used suffers from the disadvantage of being rather complex, in that each subject had first of all to consider the two alternative interpretations of each sentence that were provided by the experimenter, then had to relate them to his or her own interpretation, and finally had to decide which alternative interpretation was closer to his or her interpretation. As a consequence, Haney's (1973) data may not provide us with direct evidence about the subjects' initial interpretations. A more straightforward paradigm was used by Eysenck et al. (1986). In essence, they presented homophones having a threatening and a neutral meaning (e.g., die, dye; guilt, gilt) on a tape recorder and simply asked the subjects to write down the spelling of each word. As predicted, high-anxiety subjects wrote down more threatening interpretations than did low-anxiety subjects. Additional analysis revealed that the level of state anxiety did not influence homophone interpretation.

The findings of Eysenck *et al.* (in press) can be explained by assuming that automatic activation of the two meanings of the homophones provides information at a preattentive level about the threat or affective value of each meaning and that selective biases operating on this information determine which interpretation is available first to consciousness. However, there is a simpler explanation. Eysenck *et al.* (1986) found that there was a strong tendency for the more familiar or frequent meaning of the homophones to be produced more often than the less familiar one. It might thus be that the high-anxiety subjects produced more threatening interpretations than low-anxiety subjects simply because they are more familiar with such interpretations on the basis of their past experience.

In spite of these interpretative ambiguities, the fact remains that individuals varying in their level of trait anxiety differ systematically in their interpretations of polysemous stimuli. Although the details remain obscure, the data indicate the importance of the cognitive system, which determines how ambiguities are resolved. The particular interpretation selected then undoubtedly affects the subsequent involvement of the other systems implicated in anxiety (e.g., the physiological).

The fact that individuals who are low in trait anxiety systematically avoid threat-related stimuli and threatening interpretations of ambiguous stimuli could be taken to imply that they are very affected by threat and so have developed an avoidance coping strategy. This was certainly the view of Byrne (1964), who argued that individuals who are intermediate on the Repression–Sensitization Scale are on average less maladjusted than those who are either repressors or sensitizers. This can be contrasted with the more traditional view (e.g., Eysenck, 1967) that susceptibility to maladjustment is lowest among those low in trait anxiety (i.e., repressors) and highest among those high in trait anxiety.

Interestingly enough, it appears that there is an element of truth in both theoretical positions. In other words, so-called low-anxiety individuals constitute a heterogeneous group, some of whom are genuinely free from anxiety, whereas others are defensive and much affected by threat and stress. The distinction has usually been drawn by making use of the Marlowe–Crowne Social Desirability Scale, which (in partial contrast to its name) seems to measure defensiveness, protection of self-esteem, and affect inhibition. It is then possible to identify groups of genuinely low-anxious individuals or nondefensive repressors (based on low trait anxiety or repression–sensitization scores and low social desirability scores) and defensive repressors (based on low trait anxiety or repression–sensitization scores and high social desirability scores).

Despite their comparably low scores on trait anxiety or repression-sensitization, nondefensive repressors and defensive repressors have been found to differ behaviorally in various ways. Schill and Althoff

(1968) presented auditorily a series of sentences in which there was a mixture of sexual, aggressive, and neutral contents. The sentences were presented in noise, and the subject's task was to write down each sentence. The most interesting finding was that the nondefensive repressors were significantly better than the defensive repressors at perceiving the sexual sentences and, indeed, did not differ from nondefensive sensitizers. Related findings were obtained by Schill, Emanuel, Pedersen, Schneider, and Wachiowiak (1970). When the experimenter was male, the male subjects produced many more sexual responses in free association to double-entendre words if they were nondefensive repressors than if they were defensive repressors.

It is difficult to interpret the findings of Schill and Althoff (1968) and Schill *et al.* (1970). Although it is possible that preattentive selective biases of the kind discussed earlier were involved, it is entirely possible that response bias was the primary factor. In addition, these studies fail to provide any direct evidence concerning the levels of maladjustment and susceptibility to stress in the two groups. This gap was filled in an important study by Weinberger, Schwartz, and Davidson (1979). They administered Taylor's Manifest Anxiety Scale and the Marlowe–Crowne Social Desirability Scale and distinguished between low-anxious subjects (i.e., those with low scores on both scales) and repressors (i.e., those with low trait anxiety but high scores on the Marlowe-Crowne). These two groups were compared during the performance of a moderately stressful phrase association task. Despite the fact that the repressors scored somewhat lower on trait anxiety than did the low-anxious subjects, six different measures all indicated that the repressors were actually significantly more stressed than the low-anxious subjects. Three of the measures were physiological in nature (i.e., heart rate, spontaneous skin resistance responses, and forehead muscle tension), and the other three measures were based on task performance. On most of these measures, the repressors' performance was more indicative of stress than the performance of a further, high-anxiety group.

Weinberger *et al.* (1979) drew the following conclusion from their findings:

> Repressors as well as high-anxious persons tend to cope ineffectively with psychosocial stress relative to truly low-anxious persons. (p. 379)

This conclusion is supported by clinical evidence. It has been discovered, for example, that repressors tend to avoid seeking help with their personal difficulties, although they actually have the most severe presenting problems (e.g., Pellegrine, 1971).

The notion that there are two kinds of individuals who score low on questionnaire measures of trait anxiety has potential relevance for the earlier discussion of preattentive selective biases. An avoidance selective bias may not be a general characteristic of all low scorers on trait anxiety. Instead, in the terminology used by Weinberger *et al.* (1979), repressors may have a preattentive selective bias against threat-related stimuli, whereas those who are low-anxious may not have a bias toward or against threatening stimulation.

In sum, those high and low in trait anxiety show systematic differences in their cognitive functioning. More specifically, high- and low-anxiety individuals differ in their use of preattentive and attentional processes in the presence of threatening stimuli and in their use of interpretative mechanisms when confronted by ambiguous stimuli that can be regarded as threatening. As a consequence, individual differences in trait anxiety cannot be understood properly until the functioning of the cognitive system has been examined fully.

FUTURE TRENDS

The starting point for the development of a more adequate conceptualization of trait anxiety is the recognition that a number of somewhat separate but nevertheless interdependent systems are involved. Lang (1971) suggested a distinction among behavioral, physiological, and verbal systems, whereas a more useful distinction might be among behavioral, physiological, and cognitive systems. There is plentiful evidence that the various systems often fail to respond concordantly (e.g., Craske & Craig, 1984; Weinberger *et al.*, 1979), which indicates the importance of focusing on the ways in which each system affects the others. It is obvious that this can be done only when experimental studies routinely assess the concurrent functioning of each system—a desirable state of affairs that remains the exception rather than the rule.

Some discordances among the systems involved in anxiety are of rather little importance because they merely indicate that any measure of anxiety can be affected by various factors that are irrelevant to anxiety. Thus, for example, the "natural" behavioral response to anxiety is passive avoidance, but the constraints generally operating in everyday life may prevent this response from occurring. However, some discordances may be of considerable theoretical interest. An illustration of this is the study by Weinberger *et al.* (1979) that was discussed in the previous section. In essence, they discovered that it was possible to predict that some individuals who appeared low in anxiety as assessed verbally would nevertheless appear high in anxiety as measured physiologically and behaviorally.

The potential advantages of considering different anxiety-related systems concurrently can also be seen if we consider physiological concomitants of repressive and sensitizing strategies. Niemelä (1974) placed subjects in a situation in which, on each trial, there was a high probability that they would receive an electric shock. A few of the subjects reported that they tended to discount the possibility of receiving a shock during the anticipation period, and their self-reports about their behavior in everyday stress situations similarly pointed to an avoidance or repressive strategy. The relative effectiveness of this strategy and the more common approach or sensitizing strategy was investigated by recording GSRs throughout the experiment. The repressors typically produced small, or no, GSRs during the anticipation period but very high GSRs in response to shock delivery. In comparison, the other subjects produced larger GSRs during the anticipation period but smaller GSRs consequent upon the shock itself. In other words, an avoidance or repressive coping strategy may delay the onset of anxiety as defined physiologically but may ultimately lead to high levels of stress. In contrast, the approach or sensitizing strategy incurs immediate costs but may reduce anxiety subsequently. It must be borne in mind that the repressive strategy studied by Niemelä (1974) may differ importantly from the preattentive avoidance bias discussed earlier.

In sum, most theories and research on trait anxiety have emphasized one component of anxiety at the expense of other components. What is needed is a two-stage approach along the lines adumbrated in this chapter. The first stage is to increase our understanding of the cognitive, physiological, and behavioral systems involved in anxiety. The second stage, which has hardly started, consists of describing and accounting for the ways in which these systems interact to produce individual differences in trait anxiety.

Acknowledgments

Many thanks to Andrew Mathews for his helpful comments on an earlier draft of this chapter.

REFERENCES

Barrett, P., & Kline, P. The location of superfactors P, E, and N within an unexplored factor space. *Personality and Individual Differences*, 1980, *1*, 239–247.

Blaylock, B. A. H. *Repression-sensitization, word association responses, and incidental recall.* Unpublished master's thesis, University of Texas, Austin, 1963.

Borkovec, T. D., Robinson, E., Pruzinsky, T., & DePree, J. A. Preliminary exploration of worry: Some characteristics and processes. *Behaviour Research and Therapy*, 1983, *21*, 9–16.

Bower, G. H. Mood and memory. *American Psychologist*, 1981, *36*, 129–148.

Bower, G. H. Discussant at Mood and Cognition Symposium, Cognitive Psychology Section, British Psychological Society, Oxford, 1985.

Bower, G. H., Gilligan, S. G., & Monteiro, K. P. Selectivity of learning caused by affective states. *Journal of Experimental Psychology: General*, 1981, *110*, 451–473.

Bower, G. H., & Mayer, J. D. Failure to replicate mood-dependent retrieval. *Bulletin of the Psychonomic Society*, 1985, *23*, 39–42.

Butler, G., & Mathews, A. Cognitive processes in anxiety. *Advances in Behavior Research & Therapy*, 1983, *5*, 51–62.

Byrne, D. Repression-sensitization as a dimension of personality. In B. A. Maher (Ed.), *Progress in experimental personality research*. New York: Academic Press, 1964.

Carroll, D. Repression-sensitization and duration of visual attention. *Perceptual and Motor Skills*, 1972, *34*, 949–950.

Cattell, R. B., Eber, H. W., & Tatsouka, M. M. *Handbook for the Sixteen Factor Personality Questionnaire (16 PF)*. Champaign, Il.: Institute for Personality and Ability Testing, 1970.

Coles, M. G. H., Gale, A., & Kline, P. Personality and habituation of the orienting reaction: Tonic and response measures of electrodermal activity. *Psychophysiology*, 1971, *8*, 54–63.

Conley, J. J. The hierarchy of consistency: A review and model of longitudinal findings on adult individual differences in intelligence, personality and self-opinion. *Personality and Individual Differences*, 1983, *4*, 11–25.

Craske, M. G., & Craig, K. D. Musical performance anxiety: The three-systems model and self-efficacy theory. *Behaviour Research and Therapy*, 1984, *22*, 267–280.

Dixon, N. F. *Preconscious processing*. Chichester: Wiley, 1981.

Endler, N. S. Interactionism: A personality model, but not yet a theory. In M. M. Page (Ed.), *Nebraska Symposium on Motivation: Personality—current theory and research*. London: University of Nebraska Press, 1983.

Eysenck, H. J. *The biological basis of personality*. Springfield, Il.: Charles C Thomas, 1967.

Eysenck, H. J. The conditioning model of neurosis. *The Behavioral and Brain Sciences*, 1979, *2*, 155–166.

Eysenck, H. J., & Eysenck, M. W. *Personality and individual differences*. London: Plenum Press, 1985.

Eysenck, M. W. Anxiety and the worry process. *Bulletin of the Psychonomic Society*, 1984, *22*, 545–548.

Eysenck, M. W. Personality, stress arousal, and cognitive processes in stress transactions. In R. W. J. Neufeld (Ed.), *Advances in investigation of psychological stress*. New York: Wiley, in press.

Eysenck, M. W., MacLeod, C., & Mathews, A. Cognitive functioning and anxiety. *Psychological Research*, in press.

Gray, J. A. Is there any need for conditioning in Eysenck's conditioning model of neurosis? *The Behavioral and Brain Sciences*, 1979, *2*, 169–171.

Gray, J. A. *The neuropsychology of anxiety*. Oxford: Clarendon, 1982.

Gray, J. A. Issues in the neuropsychology of anxiety. In A. H. Tuma & J. Maser (Eds.), *Anxiety and the anxiety disorders*. London: Erlbaum, 1985.

Hamilton, V. *The cognitive structures and processes of human motivation and personality*. Chichester: Wiley, 1983.

Haney, J. N. Approach–avoidance reactions by repressors and sensitizers to ambiguity in a structured free-association. *Psychological Reports*, 1973, *33*, 97–98.

Hundleby, J. D., & Connor, W. H. Interrelationships between personality inventories: The 16 PF, the MMPI and the MPI. *Journal of Consulting and Clinical Psychology*, 1968, *32*, 152–157.

Kelly, D. & Martin, I. Autonomic reactivity, eyelid-conditioning and their relationship to neuroticism and extraversion. *Behaviour Research and Therapy*, 1969, 7, 233–244.

Krohne, H. W., & Rogner, J. Repression-sensitization as a central construct in coping research. In H. W. Krohne & L. Laux (Eds.), *Achievement, stress, and anxiety*. London: McGraw-Hill, 1982.

Lacey, J. I., & Lacey, B. C. Verification and extension of the principle of autonomic response stereotypy. *American Journal of Psychology*, 1958, 71, 50–73.

Lader, M., & Wing, L. *Physiological measures, sedative drugs, and morbid anxiety*. Oxford: Maudsley Monograph, No. 14, 1966.

Lang, P. The application of psychophysiological methods to the study of psychotherapy and behavior modification. In A. Bergin and S. Garfield (Eds.), *Handbook of psychotherapy and behavior change*. New York: Wiley, 1971.

Lewinsohn, P. M., Berquist, W. H., & Brelje, T. The repression–sensitization dimension and emotional response to stimuli. *Psychological Reports*, 1972, 31, 707–716.

Lyons, W. Some questions of strategy in neuropsychological research on anxiety. *The Behavioral and Brain Sciences*, 1982, 5, 490–491.

MacLeod, C., Mathews, A., & Tata, P. Attentional bias in emotional disorders. *Journal of Abnormal Psychology*, in press.

Mathews, A., & MacLeod, C. Discrimination of threat cues without awareness in anxiety state. *Journal of Abnormal Psychology*, in press.

Nielsen, T. C., & Petersen, K. E. Electrodermal correlates of extraversion, trait anxiety and schizophrenia. *Scandinavian Journal of Psychology*, 1976, 17, 73–80.

Niemelä, P. Coping patterns in shock anticipation and in everyday stress. *Scandinavian Journal of Psychology*, 1974, 15, 268–272.

O'Gorman, J. G. Individual differences in habituation of human physiological responses: A review of theory, method, and findings in the study of personality correlates in non-clinical populations. *Biological Psychology*, 1977, 5, 257–318.

Pellegrine, R. J. Repression-sensitization and perceived severity of presenting problems of four hundred and forty-four counseling center clients. *Journal of Counseling Psychology*, 1971, 18, 332–336.

Plouffe, L., & Stelmack, R. M. Neuroticism and the effect of stress on the pupillary light reflex. *Perceptual and Motor Skills*, 1979, 49, 635–642.

Saville, P., & Blinkhorn, S. Reliability, homogeneity, and the construct validity of Cattell's 16PF. *Personality and Individual Differences*, 1981, 2, 325–333.

Schill, T., & Althoff, M. Auditory perceptual thresholds for sensitizers, defensive and nondefensive repressors. *Perceptual and Motor Skills*, 1968, 27, 935–938.

Schill, T., Emanuel, G., Pedersen, V., Schneider, L., & Wachiowiak, D. Sexual reponsivity of defensive and nondefensive sensitizers and repressors. *Journal of Consulting and Clinical Psychology*, 1970, 35, 44–47.

Simpson, G. B. Lexical ambiguity and its role in models of word recognition. *Psychological Bulletin*, 1984, 96, 316–340.

Tellegen, A. Structures of mood and personality and their relevance to assessing anxiety, with an emphasis on self-report. In A. H. Tuma & J. Maser (Eds.), *Anxiety and the anxiety disorders*. London: Erlbaum, 1985.

Ullmann, L. P. An empirically derived MMPI scale which measures facilitation-inhibition of recognition of threatening stimuli. *Journal of Clinical Psychology*, 1962, 18, 127–132.

Van Egeren, L. Repression and sensitization: Sensitivity and recognition criteria. *Journal of Experimental Research in Personality*, 1968, 3, 1–8.

Wagstaff, G. F. The effects of repression-sensitization on a brightness scaling measure of perceptual defence. *British Journal of Psychology*, 1974, 65, 395–401.

Watson, D., & Clark, L. A. Negative affectivity: The disposition to experience aversive emotional states. *Psychological Bulletin*, 1984, 96, 465–490.

Weinberger, D. A., Schwartz, G. E., & Davidson, R. J. Low-anxious, high-anxious, and repressive coping styles: Psychometric patterns and behavioral and physiological responses to stress. *Journal of Abnormal Psychology,* 1979, *88,* 369–380.

Williams, D. G. Personality and mood: State–trait relationships. *Personality and Individual Differences,* 1981, *2,* 303–309.

CHAPTER 5

Concepts of Activation and Arousal in the Theory of Emotionality (Neuroticism)

A Multivariate Conceptualization

JOCHEN FAHRENBERG

INTRODUCTION

Autonomic arousal and cortical arousal are essential concepts in Eysenck's theory of personality because individual differences in these functions are related to the well-known dimensions of emotionality (neuroticism) and extraversion-introversion. Psychophysiological personality research has been strongly influenced by these postulates, although autonomic and cortical arousal are theoretical constructs that still lack consistent operationalizations. Research has not yet produced standard patterns or dimensions of physiological processes specifying the CNS, ANS, and behavioral parameters that define the concepts and those that do not. No standardized assessment has been put forth to reliably measure individual differences and to allow for cross-laboratory comparison and, thus, for possible integration of experimental results. An evaluation of the contradictory research evidence remains extremely difficult.

Research on habitual physiological correlates of emotionality has

JOCHEN FAHRENBERG • Institute of Psychology, University of Freiburg, Freiburg, Federal Republic of Germany.

been particularly frustrating. As soon as the correlation analysis is restricted to the questionnaire level there can, however, be no serious doubt that the empirical data strongly suggest the notion of a second order trait dimension of emotionality (neuroticism). Many investigators have observed positive correlations between an individual's N (neuroticism)-score and the reported frequency as well as subjectively rated intensity of complaints on various autonomic, sensory, and somatic functions, fatigue, stress, and so on. Such findings on a general trait of nervousness or psychosomatic irritability are at variance with findings from psychophysiological research: Correlations between an individual's N-score and objectively assessed measures of physiological reactivity are low and in most cases insignificant. This state of affairs could lead to retaining the null hypothesis or could elicit argumentation leading to conceptual clarification and more advanced research programs.

In this chapter, Eysenck's notion of autonomic arousal (activation) is discussed from several points of view. Neither a complete review of the experimental literature nor a comprehensive historical account of the development of this theory is intended. The discussion is mainly based on a series of psychophysiological experiments and questionnaire studies from the Forschungsgruppe Psychophysiologie, University of Freiburg, conducted during the last 20 years. Subsequently, a number of research perspectives are formulated as well as general heuristics that could be of strategic use to further developing and theoretically refining the important issues and, hopefully, help to solve the puzzling contradiction in research on emotionality.

EMOTIONALITY (NEUROTICISM) AS ASSESSED BY QUESTIONNAIRE

Clinical descriptions of nervousness that date back to Whytt (1765) depict a syndrome of mood fluctuation and irritability associated with sleeplessness and many physical complaints of autonomic, somatic, and sensory dysfunctions. Such items have been used in questionnaires to assess individual differences in emotionality and anxiety. This nervousness syndrome is also obvious in Eysenck's Maudsley Medical Questionnaire (MMQ) and subsequent inventories—MPI, EPI, and EPQ (Eysenck & Eysenck, 1969, 1976). Emotionality is a second-order personality dimension comprising such first-order components as mood fluctuations, sleeplessness, nervousness, irritability, sensitivity, inferiority feelings, and absentmindedness. However, somatic complaints were gradually omitted during test development and the EPQ-N-scale now retains only a few items of this kind: sleeplessness, tiredness, and fidgetiness.

A considerably higher proportion of somatic complaints is included in the item pool of the *Freiburger Persönlichkeitsinventar* (FPI), a personality inventory that is widely used in Germany (Fahrenberg & Selg, 1970). The FPI-1 Nervousness scale represents a broad spectrum of somatic and psychosomatic complaints. An even more extended item pool was used in factor analyses to develop the 10 scales, 6 to 10 items each, of the *Freiburger Beschwerdenliste* (FBL) (Questionnaire for Somatic Complaints, Fahrenberg, 1975): General State of Health, Emotional Reactivity, Cardiovascular, Gastrointestinal, Nose and Throat, Tension, Sensory, Pain, Motoric, Skin, and Somatic Complaint Total Score.

The FPI consists of 10 first-order scales and, additionally, 2 second-order scales—FPI-E and FPI-N. The latter were derived during this test construction to match Eysenck's concepts. At that stage, FPI-N did not contain any somatic complaint items in order to investigate the relationship between Emotionality and FPI-1 Nervousness. Although the content of the items did not overlap, a substantial correlation exists between FPI-N and FPI-1, namely $r = .64$ ($N = 3318$ normal subjects, male and female, with an age range from 15 to 84 years). With respect to particular dimensions of somatic complaints, subsequent investigations revealed consistent relationships between Emotionality (FPI-N) and all of the 10 FBL scales with a correlation between FPI-N and FBL-11 (total score) on the order of $r = .55$ (Fahrenberg, 1975; Hampel & Fahrenberg, 1982; Myrtek, 1984).

The revised FPI-R (brought out in 1984) now reunites emotionality items and somatic complaint items to give an integrated FPI-R-N second-order dimension (Fahrenberg, Hampel, & Selg, 1984). Based on a sample of 2035 adults 16 years and older that are representative of the population of the Federal Republic of Germany, it may be concluded that Emotionality (FPI-R-N) is substantially related to the first-order factors, Life Satisfaction ($r = -.64$), Strain (.61), Irritability (.58), and Somatic Complaints (.55). Consequently, it can be reliably predicted that individuals who report mood fluctuations, irritability, worry, and feelings of inferiority will also report more frequently and more intensely various autonomic, motor, and sensory complaints. Derived by statistical methods, a generalized and rather stable trait of psychosomatic dysregulation is evident, thus giving an empirical basis to Whytt's (1765) original notion of nervousness. Although it is an extremely global concept, it proves to be a highly reproducible trait dimension. Evidence derived from questionnaires continues to be a strong motive to seek for objective psychophysiological correlates that could explain nervousness as a constitutional pattern or trait.

ACTIVATION (AUTONOMIC AROUSAL) IN EYSENCK'S THEORY

The personality dimension *emotionality* (*neuroticism*) derived from Q data is related to individual differences in emotional and autonomic responsiveness. The limbic system of the brain is thought to be the neuroanatomical basis of this trait because it appears to be largely involved in the regulation of emotions. It has been postulated that

> some people are innately predisposed to respond more strongly, more lastingly and more quickly with their autonomic nervous system to strong, painful or sudden stimuli impinging upon the sense organs. (Eysenck & Rachman, 1965, p. 31)

Thus individual differences in emotionality are interpreted in terms of differential thresholds of hypothalamic activity and differences in responsivity of the sympathetic nervous system. Eysenck used the term *activation* to distinguish this autonomic arousal from cortical arousal produced by reticular activity. Various ascending and descending pathways link the reticular activating system with the hypothalamus, thus connecting both arousal systems. Eysenck assumes that reticular activity does not necessarily affect limbic system activity, but postulates that limbic system activity will increase reticular and cortical arousal. Both arousal processes are partially independent, but they may interact. The distinction between these systems tends to break down when a high level of activation/arousal is induced or when highly emotional individuals are involved (Eysenck, 1967; Eysenck & Eysenck, 1985).

A wide range of physiological measures are thought to be indicative of autonomic arousal: skin conductance, muscular tension, heart rate, blood pressure, EEG, and respiration rate. Eysenck states, however, that there usually are no significant differences between high-N and low-N subjects in measures of autonomic arousal obtained in relaxed conditions. Such differences should emerge in stressful conditions or in chronic emotional states in neurotic patients.

EVALUATION OF PSYCHOPHYSIOLOGICAL RESEARCH ON EMOTIONALITY

Eysenck's Conclusions and Suggestions

As mentioned before, Eysenck assumes a partial independence between autonomic arousal and cortical arousal. However, the physiological measures that are considered to be appropriate indicators of autonomic arousal are also discussed as measures of cortical arousal. The habituation paradigm and EEG parameters appear to be more specifically related to the dimension of extraversion-introversion (Eysenck, 1967; Eysenck & Eysenck, 1985). The discriminant validity of these hypothetical indicators is, however, equivocal and consequently so is the operationalization of two arousal processes. The following passages are cited from the Eysencks' recent book to illustrate the conceptual difficulties as well as the frustrating evaluation of empirical findings.

> However, we are still left with various uncertainties, since psychophysiological measures do not reflect directly the activity of either the reticular formation or the visceral brain. For instance, EEG desynchronization occurs as a consequence of either arousal or activation. This means that it is difficult to provide a satisfactory empirical test of the notion that arousal and activation are related but separate. (Eysenck & Eysenck, 1985, p. 218)

> Attempts have been made to discover physiological differences between introverts and extraverts in a variety of experimental paradigms and using a number of psychophysiological measures (e.g., the EEG, electrodermal responses, pupillary responses). It is perhaps reasonable to conclude that introverts usually show greater physiologial responsiveness than extraverts to stimulation, with the most consistent findings being obtained with electrodermal measures. (Eysenck & Eysenck, 1985, p. 231)

> The data are undoubtedly disappointing, and it is hard to disagree with Stelmack's (1981) pessimistic conclusion that correlations between neuroticism and psychophysiological responsiveness have not been reported with sufficient consistency to permit inferences of the physiological determinants (p. 61). The problem may lie in the persistant use of insufficiently stressful conditions. (Eysenck & Eysenck, 1985, p. 234)

A higher degree of physiological responsiveness in EEG-measures *as well as* autonomic responsiveness is, accordingly, related to the introverted personality type. Conceptual clarification seems to be needed. Therefore, in the following discussion several issues are raised to assist theoretical and methodological developments.

INDEPENDENT EMPIRICAL TESTS

A comprehensive review of research literature pertaining to the psychophysiology of emotionality (neuroticism) cannot be given here (see Eysenck, 1967; Eysenck & Eysenck, 1985; Fahrenberg, 1967, 1977; Stelmack, 1981). The discussion will be restricted to a series of psychophysiological experiments conducted in our laboratory at the University of Freiburg. These investigations were large-scale, multiparameter, and multisituation studies that included systematic replications. The term *activation process* is used in the following discussion as a general term for arousal, excitation, stress and strain, and the like.

Myrtek (1984), in his extensive investigations of constitutional psychophysiology conducted with about 700 individuals (healthy subjects and cardiac patients), studied among other trait dimensions the hypothetical constructs *autonomic lability, sympathicotonia-vagotonia,* and *physical fitness.* He used an unusually broad spectrum of physiological measures and a variety of stressor conditions that differed in intensity and quality. Correlational analysis, factor analysis, and cluster analysis revealed that the notion of a relatively consistent dimension or pattern of autonomic lability is not tenable on empirical grounds. Second, in summing up the findings from these extensive and carefully conducted studies, Myrtek (1984) was forced to retain the "null hypothesis of psychophysiological covariation" with respect to emotionality (FPI-N) and measures of autonomic nervous system functions.

The negative results and conclusions of Myrtek's research are in agreement with two other investigations from our laboratory that used a different approach to test Eysenck's hypothesis. In the first study, an individual's Emotionality score was thought to be an important predictor of activation state and activation reaction in a stress situation and should prove so under conditions of a typical activation experiment. Male students ($N = 125$), none from psychology courses, were examined under five conditions (rest, mental arithmetic, interview, anticipation, and blood taking). Criterion variables were self-rating of tenseness, as well as heart rate, finger pulse volume amplitude, electrodermal activity, respiratory irregularity, eye blink activity, forehead and extensor digitorum electromyogram, and relative power of EEG alpha. Statistical analysis by correlation and multiple regression procedures revealed that Emotionality (FPI-N) and Total Score of Somatic Complaints (FBL-11) fail to reliably predict individual differences in state and reaction parameters of activation processes (Fahrenberg, Walschburger, Foerster, Myrtek, & Müller, 1979, 1983).

The second investigation employed data that were obtained from 58 students of physical education under five conditions (rest, mental arithmetic, reaction time, preparing a free speech, cold pressor test). The recordings were repeated at intervals of about 3 weeks, 3 months, and 1 year. Financial rewards were given to increase the challenge imposed by performance tests and the painful cold pressor test. Further recordings were conducted outside the laboratory in prestart conditions and during performance of a 1000-m run in the stadium. These data allowed the test of the predictive validity of questionnaire scores of emotionality and frequency of somatic complaints in a manner nearly identical to the multivariate study just described. Again, the null hypothesis was retained (Fahrenberg, Foerster, Schneider, Müller, & Myrtek, 1984). Concerning the generalizability of results, appropriate reservations certainly should be made. These investigations, however, did take special precautions with respect to subject sample size, broad sampling of physiological measures, intensity of stimulation, reliability estimates, different scoring methods, and use of the jackknife technique as well as a simulated random number model as a reference. Because the extended research reports can be found in the three resulting books, it may suffice here to present the essential conclusion from this research program: Further use of emotionality (neuroticism) supposing a consistent psychophysiological basis would be misleading as this theoretical construct has not been sufficiently substantiated by empirical data.

METHODOLOGICAL ASPECTS

In their evaluation of research on physiological correlates of emotionality, Eysenck and Eysenck (1985) cite only a few experiments, and they do not refer explicitly to methodological developments in psychophysiological assessment. A number of multivariate investigations that deal with the empirical test of the theory have not been mentioned. The general conclusions are still based on univariate experiments, although a multivariate reconceptualization of the activation-arousal theory appears to be inevitable.

In some laboratories, considerable progress has been made in assessing individual differences in activation (arousal) processes. The basic facts of response fractionation and response patterning in physiological data demand methodological consequences. Univariate experiments to test psychophysiological hypotheses have become obsolete in most instances.

Reviews of psychophysiological research usually deal at some length with the covariation issue and inquire into possible explanations of inconsistent, generally low, or negligible correlations between psychological and physiological parameters of activation processes. Many sources of error have been revealed that could threaten the internal validity of psychophysiological experiments (for overviews, see Fahrenberg, 1983, 1986a,b; Gale & Edwards, 1983; Rösler, 1984).

Problems of measurement, sampling, and experimental design cannot be discussed here. Internal validity should, of course, be increased by avoiding or reducing obvious sources of error. However, it appears to be extremely improbable that the frustrating state of affairs with respect to physiological correlates of emotionality could be explained merely by errors of measurement. Such an interpretation ignores recent investigations that carefully analyzed such methodological issues by conducting parameter studies, employing many experimental and statistical controls, and developing more precise assessment strategies.

Evaluating Eysenck's theory has led to another fundamental issue: Precisely under what conditions is an appropriate test to be conducted?

(Eysenck & Eysenck, 1985; Gale, 1983; Myrtek, 1984; Stelmack, 1981). According to Eysenck (1981a), his basic assumptions are valid only if certain "parameters of testing" are adequately selected. He considers two major aspects: (a) arousal-producing characteristics of the experiment itself, that is, strength of stimuli, intensity of stressor conditions, stimulus background, overall setting, and demand characteristics; and (b) interactive effects due to the supposed higher sensitivity of emotional labile subjects who perform under threatening conditions. Operational definitions of appropriate stimulus parameters and experimental settings, however, were not suggested by Eysenck, although such specifications are essential for empirical testing and cross-laboratory comparisons.

CONCEPTUAL ASPECTS

The distinction between *activation (autonomic arousal)* and *arousal (cortical arousal)* still appears to be an essential postulate of Eysenck's theory, although the physiological parameters used, admittedly, lack discriminant validity. In an attempt to solve basic problems of Eysenck's theory, Gray (1981) has proposed a reformulation on both the physiological and the questionnaire levels. He reviewed evidence from animal experiments and postulated that there are (a) a fundamental behavioral inhibition system (BIS), comprising the septohippocampal system, with its monoaminergic afferents from the brain stem and its neocortical projections to the frontal lobe; and (b) a behavioral activation system (BAS) corresponding to Old's reward system. Furthermore, he considers the primary fight/flight system and unspecific arousal functions of reticular structures. Obviously, this approach is based on neurophysiological considerations and thus conforms to Krech's (1950) opinion that psychologists should develop hypothetical constructs that are basically compatible with neurological concepts.

Gray (1983) again addressed the issue concerning where, in the multidimensional personality space, we are likely to find factors reflecting the causal influence of separable subsystems in the brain. He extends his considerations to the octants of Eysenck's three-dimensional PEN system, includes neurotic and psychotic disorders, circadian influences in arousal thresholds, and many other phenomena. These associations and theoretical speculations may be of heuristic value but are at the same time frustrating because nearly everything seems to fit: It is a rotational procedure, so to speak, without simple structure criteria.

Several authors besides Gray have elaborated on such hypothetical neurobiological multicomponent models (e.g., Andresen, 1987; Ehrhardt, 1975; Fowles, 1980; Pribram & McGuiness, 1975). There is little doubt that neurosciences gradually will advance in this respect. However, these suggestions and postulates appear to be of little consequence for research in differential psychophysiology unless the proponents of such "models" and flow charts suggest practical strategies as to how to differentially assess the activity of such neural subsystems, loops, and other brain structures in the intact human individual participating in an experiment. Such specifications and precise topography of arousal processes are extremely desirable but are, unfortunately, not available at present. We can imagine that some aspects of regional CNS activity may be indicated by positron emission tomography or magnetic resonance spectrography in the future, but for the time being peripherally recorded physiological functions and the EEG have to be used in order to differentiate patterns of regulation and to develop valid indicators of theoretically postulated subsystems of CNS activity.

The issue addressed by Amelang and Bartussek (1985) is theoretically important. The questionnaire scales that measure the dimensions E and N were developed to fit into an orthogonal system, although activation and arousal are considered to be dependent on each other. Amelang and Bartussek (1985) assume that this orthogonality serves to distort the functional relationships. Tellegen (1978) raised another theoretical point that deserves attention. Emotionality scales usually consist of items that predominantly describe negative feelings and negative experiences—moodiness, depression, worry, inferiority, lability, and other aspects of neuroticism. Positively toned states are hardly included in this concept. On the other hand, it is a reasonable assumption that the limbic system and parts thereof will be correspondingly active in positive emotional states. The questionnaire scales are designed for clinical groups representing nervousness and obviously do not depict a bipolarity of the hypothetically underlying neurophysiological processes. Andresen (1987) has reviewed the evidence for monopolar or bipolar concepts in research on emotion and emotionality. He concluded that in psychophysiological research a dimension of positively toned activation should be separated from a dimension of negatively toned activation.

Another issue that needs conceptual clarification is the choice of experimental designs that deal with the assumed interaction of E and N. The interaction of these traits introduces further difficulty in interpreting the findings of a given experiment. This issue has not been incorporated into designs that are common to this research but has been eliminated or partialled out by selecting "high-" or "low-" N subjects. Such designs that use extreme groups instead of samples representing the trait continuum are open to methodological criticism. Instead of simple ANOVA designs, multiple regression procedures, or some kind of "dose-dependent" analysis seems to be much more adequate to depict the postulated nonlinear dependency of E and N that is, in turn, modulated by stimulus intensity.

For conceptual clarification, it may be of heuristic value to consider Eysenck's comments on investigations that report negative results. I refer to his reviews on the three respective books from our laboratory for the journal *Personality and Individual Differences* (Eysenck 1981b, 1982, 1985). In these reviews, Eysenck concludes that a contradiction exists between this research and research from other laboratories covered by Stelmack's (1981) review. Stelmack, however, notably excepts emotionality from his positive conclusion concerning the psychophysiology of extraversion-introversion.

Eysenck (1982) considers types of stressors and types of physiological measures as possible reasons for negative results. It would be impossible to maintain that conditions and dependent variables other than those selected in our experiments would have produced the same negative results. The methods used in our study include a number of rather conventional, together with some less familiar, measures, but there exist many more that have not yet been tried. A typology of such stressor conditions as suggested by Eysenck is desirable and would be useful to restrict the fields of validity of the theory. It is conceivable that during this process of conceptual clarification and operationalization criteria for appropriate testing the hypotheses can be established eventually.

A PHILOSOPHY OF SCIENCE APPROACH

An attempt at conceptual clarification was made by Brocke (1985). His argument is based on the premise derived from the philosophy of science that the standard representation made for psychological theories must fulfil some minimum requirement as is common with the physical sciences. Such a basis of representing a theory is needed (a) for the precise evaluation of the present status of the theory; and (b) for the monitoring of the empirical progressivity of theory development.

Brocke (1985) proposes a semantic structuring of subsequent stages of Eysenck's arousal-activation theory and proceeds to a set of theoretical postulates that includes theories of situational arousal and habitual arousal. The essential parameters of testing are systematically stated as "peripheral conditions" that should precede each set of postulates. The fields of validity thus have limitations depending on whether, in an experimental design, a variable or a constant level of *arousal* is produced with or without any confounding influence of *activation*-related processes (see Brocke & Battmann, 1986).

Brocke (1985) does not advance to a similar specification for the semantic content of the theory's terms. This, of course, would be a troublesome task because it would require operationalization of theoretical constructs of activation and arousal and specifications of appropriate levels of stimulus (stress) intensity. Such specifications are necessary for ethical and practical reasons because psychophysiological experiments cannot begin to gradually increase stimulus intensities from the lowest possible level to a very high intensity. Such specifications of "high" or "low" stimulus levels are crucial for theory testing. They cannot, however, be found in the original research publications on emotionality.

Semantic analysis of Eysenck's theory certainly would lead to three fundamental issues: (a) the aforementioned lack of sufficient operationalization and empirical discrimination of activation and arousal; (b) the definition of appropriate levels of stimulus (stress) intensity, ranging from the specific stimulus to the general experimental setting, demand characteristics, and individual coping style; and (c) the recognition of a possible circularity in defining the preceding "peripheral conditions" on empirical grounds by measures that are the dependent variables in hypothesis testing.

Brocke's (1985) discussion helps to remind us that an empirical theory should only be subjected to appropriate tests and that a theory should demonstrate progressivity. To avoid immunization, however, psychological theories, at each stage, must be formulated in such a way that essential deductions could be rejected (falsified) on empirical grounds.

MULTIVARIATE ACTIVATION THEORY

Because activation processes are higher nervous system functions of varying intensity and synergistic patterning, their study requires a complementary and multivariate psychological-physiological approach. However, as an extended discussion of multivariate activation research has already been given elsewhere, a condensed presentation of some basic aspects may suffice here (Fahrenberg, 1983, in press).

Many investigations have demonstrated the well-known psychophysiological reaction to stimulation, that is, the ergotropic, synergistic pattern of increased alertness and tension, decreased synchronization of the EEG, increased cardiac output and respiratory functions, increased muscular tension, increased output of adrenaline, cortisol, and so forth. This frequently observed *average* response profile formerly has been conceived as an indication of a unitary dimension of activation or deactivation shown in a systemic, unidirectional, homogeneous increase/

decrease of many parameters, which depict a synergistic action of the organism as a whole.

An evaluation of such data from a differential perspective, however, has failed to establish an empirical basis for an unidimensional activation theory. This traditional notion is only tenable as a rather restricted concept, that is, only for certain experimental conditions and only to response profiles *averaged across subjects*. An individual's score on a specific activation variable may characterize the functioning of the particular response system, but there is no sufficient empirical support to reliably assume a *corresponding proportional* state score or state change on another autonomic, somatic, or psychological system in that same individual. The striking response fractionation found in psychophysiological data has encouraged many additional hypotheses to explain it and, thus, has stimulated methodological advancements. The patterning of physiological responses consequently has attracted more attention, and in such investigations, important theoretical contributions were achieved. For example, the patterning with respect to stimulus-specific, individual-specific, and motivation-specific responses has been reliably established (Fahrenberg, 1986; Foerster, 1985; Foerster, Schneider, & Walschburger, 1983). In differential psychophysiology, multiparameter-multisituational data sets are needed that are suited for genuine multivariate analysis. Only such data sets can meet the requirements of comprehensive research in general synergisms and in physiological individuality.

Criticism of the general factor model in activation theory has encouraged speculation on two-factor and multiple-factor models. This development resembles the history of factor analytic research on intelligence. It is, however, questionable whether the latent trait model and the concept of unitary factor dimensions, familiar to psychological trait theories, can be readily applied to physiological data. Compared to convergent problem solving and performance data, in physiological functions, synergistic and antagonistic regulatory processes, that is, nonlinear relationships, interactions, and functional fluctuation seem to be more prominent, thus calling for dynamic modeling approaches, time series, and thorough differentiation of patterns.

Although there is little support for global concepts or two-factor models suggested by several authors, the notion of activation as a *multicomponent* process with *various degrees* of coupling between such response systems continues to be a viable concept. Based on the literature, a number of hypothetical components can be derived in each of the domains of subjective state, behavioral activity, central nervous systems, autonomic systems, and neuroendocrine systems. At present, rather heterogeneous perspectives prevail directed at *functional systems* like sympathetic-adrenergic activity or sleep–waking cycle, *dimensional concepts* like mood factors derived from R- and P- technique analyses, and demarcations with respect to specific *organ systems* like neocortex, heart, or skin.

As compared to speculations on arousal systems in reticular and limbic structures, such a multicomponent approach is much more inclined to operationalizations. Physiological measures for such components exist and eventually more valid marker variables that could be employed in the psychophysiological laboratory will be available. The refinement of such construct–operation units (see Fiske 1978) in future research programs would serve to overcome the acknowledged inconsistencies of psychophysiological investigations.

For example, in cardiovascular psychophysiology, there is recently a trend away from the oversimplified use of heart rate, heart rate variability, and blood pressure measures. Psychophysiologists now are more readily following the lead of physiologists in applying more refined methods for differentiating functional systems of alpha- and beta-adrenergic as well as vagal influences on the heart and the arterial system by employing, for example, specific ECG parameters, spectral analysis of heart rate variability, amplitude of sinus arrhythmia to depict respiratory gating of vagal innervation, noninvasive measures of stroke volume, preejection period, left ventricular ejection time, contractility, pulse wave velocity, and other haemodynamic parameters. There is a good chance to learn, especially in cardiovascular psychophysiology, whether by refined measurement and parameter combination the objectives of systemic analysis can be achieved.

Multivariate activation theory should be further developed to give an adequate account of general synergistic patterns and differential aspects, response fractionation and response patterning, assessment strategies, and predictive validity. The scope of such a multivariate approach will provoke criticism concerning its feasability and practical application. However, conventional single-channel physiological measurement approaches are obsolete in most psychophysiological research orientations.

SOME PERSPECTIVES/ALTERNATIVES IN PSYCHOPHYSIOLOGICAL RESEARCH ON EMOTIONALITY

TOP-DOWN AND BOTTOM-UP STRATEGIES

Research on physiological correlates of emotionality appears to have reached a standstill. The null hypothesis has been empirically retained though not provable for logical reasons. To overcome the relative stagnation in this field of research, new heuristics and modified research programs are needed. At any rate, conceptual clarifications as suggested in the preceding paragraphs will result in a recategorization of issues. Science advances by replacing rather global conceptions by a set of more specific propositions, that is, more refined postulates and terms that can be more readily subjected to empirical test.

The Eysenckian theory, from its beginnings, has provided such differentiation by its hierarchical structure, although this perspective of at least four organizational levels (specific response level, habitual response level, primary trait level, and secondary type level) has found less attention during the past years. The structure of personality with respect to this hierarchical organization was investigated predominantly using the questionnaires. It should be noted, however, that even a single item usually represents a complex, subjectively weighted average or aggregate across behavior elements, situations, and replications over the individual's lifetime. Hierarchical analyses that parallel the construction of the N-scales for physiological measures and for behavioral elements of the second-order trait dimension cannot be found in the literature.

In systems theory, two approaches that complement each other are labeled *top down* and *bottom up*. Bottom-up analyses demand conceptual and methodological refinement as well as precise assessment of lower levels (subsystems) that gradually advance to higher levels of organization. Top-down analyses would lead to stepwise decomposition of global systemic properties.

In psychophysiological research, it is obvious that we are dealing with quite different levels of organization and various degrees of abstraction or complexity that require studies of the relationships between somatic data, calling for a hierarchical model (Fahrenberg, 1967, 1977). There have been many attempts to correlate rather crude single physiological measures with personality variables of some kind, often in a very arbitrary manner. An alternative would be to establish physiological patterns first, and then, subsequently, look for correlates or matches with known psychological patterns, dimensions, or types. Probably the latter approach is more promising because it appears to correspond better to the assumption of different levels in the psychobiological organism.

Myrtek (1984) has subjected this proposition to empirical testing. His factor analytic work indicated that the generally low covariation between emotionality (FPI-N) and autonomic lability data cannot be increased by structuring the physiological data to obtain factor scores. This disappointing result may not, however, be the final statement on the issue of adequate matching of functional levels within the hierarchy of subsystems.

Two general heuristics can be conceived: (a) *decomposition* of the global second-order dimension N to systematically consider primary dimensions, items, and even more elementary self-ratings of momentary state; and (b) integration of elementary physiological measures and microprocesses by empirical analysis that relates to known physiological patterns and regulatory mechanisms, and by means of psychometric methods (i.e., developing composite scores by scale construction and aggregation techniques). Another essential aspect would be to further develop behavioral indicators, that is, behavior ratings and objective behavior measures of emotionality. This multimodal conceptualization of neuroticism was more obvious at the beginning of this trait's history in psychological research.

Decomposing Neuroticism

Eysenck and Eysenck (1969) are rather sceptical concerning personality dimensions at the primary level. They suppose that E and N on the secondary level hold far more promise as invariant and theoretically promising factors than do the primary factors they discussed. These primary factors are not, from their point of view, invariant across sex, age, and education, and represent "half arbitrary, half accidental conglomerations of items" (Eysenck & Eysenck, 1969, p. 331). The task of structuring personality at the primary level thus remains unsolved.

Major components of emotionality (neuroticism) assessed by questionnaires have been mentioned already. With respect to the MPI and EPI, findings from different analyses depict some inconsistencies that may possibly be explained by differences in sampling and statistical procedures (Eysenck & Eysenck, 1969; Howarth, 1976; Loo, 1979). Factor analysis of items from existing N-scales is probably not an appropriate strategy for decomposing N into salient primaries because the item pool in the process of scale construction becomes gradually restricted by selecting a small number of relatively homogeneous items. Such components of N could be considered when physiological and behavioral correlates are investigated.

Psychophysiological relationships on the item level have not been systematically investigated so far. The availability of corresponding physiological measures remains the major obstacle in this single-item approach to psychophysiological correlations. This strategy was employed some years ago in a preliminary attempt to validate questionnaire items relating to somatic complaints similar to those in the FBL questionnaire (Fahrenberg, 1967). The results were far from promising. The fact that for the great majority of the questionnaire items no distinct physiological measures were available, at that time discouraged any attempt at validating single somatic complaint items in question-naires.

More research findings are available at an even more elementary level. In many psychophysiological investigations, self-ratings are employed to obtain data on actual state of mood, tenseness, irritation, perceived heart rate, perceived muscular tension, and so forth (e.g., Fahrenberg *et al.*, 1983; Stemmler, 1984). These ratings represent momentary dispositional predicates as compared to habitual dispositional predicates found in answering questionnaire items. However, correlation coefficients (R technique) between state and change ratings of "tense," "alert," "irritated," and various physiological measures generally failed to obtain significance levels, thus suggesting response fractionation (Fahrenberg & Foerster, 1982).

MORE ADEQUATE PHYSIOLOGICAL VARIABLES

Systemic/Hierarchical Aspects of Physiological Processes. Corresponding to the decomposition of N, a bottom-up strategy could be employed for physiological data. It seems trivial, but physiological variables differ widely with respect to functional level, physiological system, and complexity. Psychophysiologists have, in the past, been concerned with only a small segment of this variable domain. Even under this restriction, it remains equivocal what kind of data could be more rewarding in correlational studies: parameters abstracted from the EEG (complicated by topography and intricate spatial folding of the many cortical sources of dipoles) or from the autonomic-neuroendocrine systems (complicated by effector organ properties and mediating variables). Gradually, a more systemic approach that overcomes univariate and often arbitrary variable selection will be necessary.

Another aspect in acquisition of valid physiological data refers to the intensity and generalizability of experimentally induced activation processes. There can be little doubt that psychophysiologists will follow new research options that are provided by development of portable monitoring systems for physiological functions (for a review and an empirical laboratory–field comparison, see Fahrenberg, Foerster, Schneider, Müller, & Myrtek, 1984, 1986).

Aggregation of Physiological Data. The assessment of relevant physiological parameters, systemic properties, and reaction patterns in the laboratory and in field conditions eventually could serve to attain theoretically meaningful integration of the data. An analogous, although basically psychometric approach to higher order properties, is the aggregation strategy that has been much discussed (Paunonen, 1984), although rarely applied, in personality research. For example, Wittmann and Schmidt (1983) employed an aggregate of data from self-reports and tests that were obtained for 16 days over an interval of 8 weeks to predict the individual score on Extraversion. Results were promising, although the small student sample ($N = 20$) requires special reservations.

Composite scores and factor scores that constitute aggregations across different physiological variables are well known in psychophysiological methodology, although the initially postulated superiority of such scores in linking physiological to psychological variables is not yet shown (for further discussion, see Fahrenberg, 1983; Myrtek, 1984). Besides Myrtek's (1984) factor analytic work two large-scale investigations employed psychometric procedures to develop more complex physiological scores (Fahrenberg et al., 1979, 1984; Fahrenberg & Foerster, 1982). Factor analyses and item analyses were applied on physiological data for the construction of scales, for example, a cardiovascular scale and an electrodermal scale. While constructing physiological scales, primary data were aggregated across physiological variables, across experimental conditions, across replications of the entire experiment, and finally, across certain conditions in the laboratory and in the field. It must be said, however, that the results were not encouraging because the composites did not result in more substantial correlation coefficients or superior predictability with respect to FPI-N than did single measures. The evaluation of such analyses constitutes a complex problem so that independent investigations appear to be desirable.

Schweizer (1986) made a new attempt in aggregating physiological data that are obtained under various conditions of observation. This even broader approach calls for a planned replication that is possible with respect to the aforementioned two large-scale data sets. From the findings of this systematic investigation, it may be concluded that psychometric aggregation is not a promising approach in psychophysiological personality research.

CONSEQUENCES FOR THE CONSTITUTIONAL APPROACH

Reviewing a series of empirical investigations that retain the null hypothesis places in doubt the biological-constitutional theory of emotionality (neuroticism). The sceptical conclusion was stated precisely by Averill and Opton (1968, p. 285): "It appears unlikely that normal variations in personality are greatly dependent upon gross constitutional differences in physiological functioning." This point of view has also been found, analogously, in biological psychiatry where research has not yet succeeded in identifying the specific neurophysiological-neurotransmitter basis of endogeneous depression and schizophrenia.

Such scepticism now is very common in psychomorphological research that relates somatic types, derived from anthropometric measures, to temperament traits (e.g., Myrtek, 1984). A small proportion of common variance that may exist could be explained by two hypothetical effects. A large, muscular individual may differ in his or her experience of common challenges and consequently may adapt differently than a leptomorphic individual. The process of shaping one's self-concept may be influenced by social stereotypes that do, indeed, relate somatic types and temperament (Buse & Pawlik, 1984). Thus the constitutional theory of body types would be replaced by a cognitive interpretation of psychomorphological relationships that would emphasize the role of learning and self-attribution processes during an individual's development rather than genetic, neurobiological aspects.

This argument may also hold for emotionality. There is no consistent relationship between self-rated emotionality and *specific* properties of CNS and/or ANS functioning. Mood fluctuations and somatic complaints are due to subjective evaluation of the *milieu interne*, that is, exaggerated concern about perceived somatic functions, ubiquitous autonomic activity, concern about strain and overload, insufficiency, and so forth. These postulates remind one of the traditional concept of hypochondria (see Fahrenberg, 1967; Pennebaker, 1982).

The remarkable homogeneity of test items depicting various aspects of nervousness may be explained by assuming a process by which an individual's information about his or her internal monitoring of bodily functions and interoceptions are interpreted and shaped to conform to a scheme: cognitive consistency instead of a unitary psychobiological trait. The concepts of hypochondria and nervousness both are viable and rival concepts.

Instead of elaborating here on such a cognitive reformulation of the concept of emotionality, it only will be pointed out that the role of cognitive processes appears to be compatible with at least some of the empirical findings, especially with the null hypothesis of psychophysiological covariation discussed by Myrtek (1984). Neurophysiological correlates of individual differences in emotionality need not necessarily be denied by this theory, but these could be represented as an unspecific activity in the associative neocortex and all areas where symbolic-semantic analyses like problem solving, moral and aesthetic evaluations, and its like take place. It probably will depend on the researcher's general attitude toward the neuroscience or the cognitive science whether he or she tends to postulate that relatively consistent and stable personality traits like emotionality, assessed by questionnaires, are based on distinct properties of separable subsystems of neuronal substrate or on diffuse cortical, but essentially semantic, representations.

In psychophysiological activation experiments, we still have no means to assess global properties of the limbic system like "thresholds," "activity," "excitability," or individual differences in such functions. These are very global, neurophysiologically vague concepts; theoretical constructs that entirely lack indicators of established empirical discriminant-convergent validity. We have to acknowledge, furthermore, that psychophysiological research, with the possible exception of electromyographic analyses of facial expression (see Fridlund & Izard, 1983), has not yet attained reliable identification of basic emotional patterns derived from autonomic, endocrine, or EEG measures. Although it appears to be a common conviction that such patterns are represented in and may be elicited from distinct parts of the limbic system, attempts at reliable empirical discrimination have failed so far (for a critical review see Stemmler, 1984). Advances in psychophysiological differentiation of emotional patterns would indicate that properties of limbic system functioning could be assessed with sufficient validity so that psychophysiological theories of individual differences in emotionality may, one day, be subjected to appropriate tests.

CONCLUSIONS

Psychophysiological research on physiological correlates of the established *emotionality (neuroticism)* trait dimension has come to a standstill. Findings of questionnaire studies generally support the postulated psychophysiological relationship, but research that employs objectively measured physiological parameters in large-scale, methodologically well-controlled and replicated investigations has not substantiated these hypotheses. This paradox imposes a challenge to clarify theoretical and methodological issues, some aspects of which may be traced to the traditional concepts of nervousness and hypochondria.

In conclusion, further theoretical clarification appears to be mandatory especially with respect to the vague concept of physiological responsivity, to the empirical distinction of autonomic and cortical arousal, and to the specification of appropriate testing conditions. The methodology to assess individual differences in activation processes can be further improved, although it seems to be extremely improbable that negative results with respect to Eysenck's hypotheses can be explained by unreliability of present psychophysiological measurement. Advanced research programs, however, should be based on a multivariate activation theory as outlined before. There have been essential contributions made to differential psychophysiology by establishing response specificities, by developing multicomponent models of activation processes, and by refining assessment strategies to account for patterning and hierarchical organization as well as including more adequate parameters of physiological systemic functioning. The acknowledgment of various levels of organization in higher nervous system functions may have heuristic value if consequently bottom-up and top-down strategies with respect to emotionality and elementary physiological parameters will be evaluated. The biological basis of distinct personality traits remains a relevant question that has many implications for psychosomatic and psychiatric disorders, psychotherapy, stress–strain research, and many other fields.

REFERENCES

Amelang, M., & Bartussek, D. *Differentielle Psychologie und Persönlichkeitsforschung* (2nd ed.). Stuttgart: Kohlhammer, 1985.

Andresen, B. *Differentielle Psychophysiologie valenzkonträrer Aktivierungs dimensionen.* Frankfurt: Lang, 1987.

Averill, J. R., & Opton, E. M. Psychophysiological assessment: Rationale and problems. In P. McReynolds (Ed.), *Advances in psychological assessment (Vol. 1).* Palo Alto, Calif.: Science and Behavior Books, 1968.

Brocke, B. *The structure of the arousal/activation theory of personality. An analysis in view of the standard representation mode for psychological theories.* Paper presented at the 2nd Conference of the International Society for the Study of Individual Differences, St. Feliu, Spain, 1985.

Brocke, B., & Battmann, W. Die Aktivierungstheorie der Persönlichkeit. Eine systematische Darstellung und partielle Rekonstruktion. *Zeitschrift für Differentielle und Diagnostische Psychologie,* 1985, 6, 189–213.

Buse, L., & Pawlik, K. Kretschmers Konstitutionstypologie als implizite Persönlichkeitstheorie: Selbst-Attribuierungs-Effekte in Abhängigkeit vom Körperbau-Persönlichkeits-Stereotyp. *Zeitschrift für Differentielle und Diagnostische Psychologie,* 1984, 5, 111–129.

Ehrhardt, K. J. *Neuropsychologie "motivierten" Verhaltens.* Stuttgart: Enke, 1975.

Eysenck, H. J. *The biological basis of personality.* Springfield, Il.: Charles C Thomas, 1967.

Eysenck, H. J. (Ed.). *A model for personality.* Berlin: Springer, 1981. (a)

Eysenck, H. J. Book review. *Personality and Individual Differences,* 1981, 2, 173–174. (b)

Eysenck, H. J. Book review. *Personality and Individual Differences,* 1982, 3, 349.

Eysenck, H. J. Book review. *Personality and Individual Differences,* 1985, 6, 411–412.

Eysenck, H. J., & Eysenck, M. W. *Personality and individual differences.* New York: Plenum Press, 1985.

Eysenck, H. J., & Eysenck, S. B. G. *Personality structure and measurement.* London: Routledge & Kegan Paul, 1969.

Eysenck, H. J., & Eysenck, S. B. G. *Psychoticism as a dimension of personality.* London: Hodder & Stoughton, 1976.

Eysenck, H. J., & Rachman, S. *The causes and cures of neurosis.* London: Routledge & Kegan Paul, 1965.

Fahrenberg, J. *Psychophysiologische Persönlichkeitsforschung.* Göttingen: Hogrefe, 1967.

Fahrenberg, J. Die Freiburger Beschwerdenliste FBL. *Zeitschrift für Klinische Psychologie,* 1975, 4, 79–100.

Fahrenberg, J. Physiological concepts in personality research. In R. B. Cattell & R. M. Dreger (Eds.), *Handbook of modern personality theory*. Washington, D.C.: Hemisphere, 1977.

Fahrenberg, J. Psychophysiologische Methodik. In K. J. Groffmann & L. Michel (Eds.), *Enzyklopädie der Psychologie. Psychologische Diagnostik. Bd. 4. Verhaltensdiagnostik*. Göttingen: Hogrefe, 1983.

Fahrenberg, J. Psychophysiological individuality: A pattern analytic approach to personality research and psychosomatic medicine. In S. Rachman & T. Wilson, *Advances in Behaviour Research and Therapy* (Vol. 8, pp. 43–100). London: Pergamon Press, 1986.

Fahrenberg, J. Psychophysiological processes. In F. R. Nesselroade & R. B. Cattell (Eds.), *Handbook of multivariate experimental psychology* (2nd ed.). New York: Plenum Press, in press.

Fahrenberg, J., & Foerster, F. Covariation and consistency of activation parameters. *Biological Psychology*, 1982, *15*, 151–169.

Fahrenberg, J., & Selg, H. *Das Freiburger Persönlichkeitsinventar FPI*. Göttingen: Hogrefe, 1970.

Fahrenberg, J., Foerster, F., Schneider, H. J., Müller, W., & Myrtek, M. *Aktivierungsforschung im Labor-Feld-Vergleich*. München: Minerva, 1984.

Fahrenberg, J., Foerster, F., Schneider, H.-J., Müller, W. & Myrtek, M. Predictability of individual differences in activation processes in a field setting based on laboratory measures. *Psychophysiology*, 1986, *23*, 323–333.

Fahrenberg, J., Hampel, R., & Selg, H. *Das Freiburger Persönlichkeitsinventar FPI*. Revidierte Fassung FPI-R und teilweise geänderte Fassung FPI-A1. (4th ed.). Göttingen: Hogrefe, 1984.

Fahrenberg, J., Walschburger, P., Foerster, F., Myrtek, M., & Müller, W. *Psychophysiologische Aktivierungsforschung. Ein Beitrag zu den Grundlagen der multivariaten Emotions- und Stress-Theorie*. München: Minerva, 1979.

Fahrenberg, J., Walschburger, P., Foerster, F., Myrtek, M., & Müller, W. An evaluation of trait, state, and reaction aspects of activation processes. *Psychophysiology*, 1983, *20*, 188–195.

Fiske, D. W. *Strategies for personality research*. San Francisco: Jossey-Bass, 1978.

Foerster, F. Psychophysiological response specificities: A replication over a 12-month period. *Biological Psychology*, 1985, *21*, 169–182.

Foerster, F., Schneider, H. J., & Walschburger, P. *Psychophysiologische Reaktionsmuster. Zur Theorie und Methodik der Analyse individualspezifischer, stimulusspezifischer und motivationsspezifischer Reaktionsmuster in Aktivierungsprozessen*. München: Minerva, 1983.

Fowles, D. C. The three arousal model: Implications of Gray's two-factor learning theory for heart rate, electrodermal activity, and psychopathy. *Psychophysiology*, 1980, *17*, 87–104.

Fridlund, A. J., & Izard, C. E. Electromyographic studies of facial expressions of emotions and patterns of emotions. In J. T. Cacioppo & R. E. Petty (Eds.), *Social psychophysiology*. New York: Guilford, 1983.

Gale, A. Electroencephalographic studies of extraversion-introversion: A case study in the psychophysiology of individual differences. *Personality and Individual Differences*, 1983, *4*, 371–380.

Gale, A., & Edwards, J. A. A short critique of the psychophysiology of individual differences. *Personality and Individual Differences*, 1983, *4*, 429–435.

Gray, J. A. A critique of Eysenck's theory of personality. In H. J. Eysenck (Ed.), *A model for personality*. New York: Springer, 1981.

Gray, J. A. Where should we search for biologically based dimensions of personality? *Zeitschrift für Differentielle und Diagnostische Psychologie*, 1983, *4*, 165–176.

Hampel, R., & Fahrenberg, J. *Die Freiburger Beschwerdenliste FBL*. Research Report. Psychological Institut, University of Freiburg, 1982, No. 7.

Howarth, E. A psychometric investigation of Eysenck's Personality Inventory. *Journal of Personality Assessment*, 1976, *40*, 173–185.

Krech, D. Dynamic systems, psychological fields, and hypothetical constructs. *Psychological Review*, 1950, *57*, 283–290, 345–361.

Loo, R. A psychometric investigation of the Eysenck Personality Questionnaire. *Journal of Personality Assessment*, 1979, *43*, 54–58.

Myrtek, M. *Constitutional psychophysiology*. New York: Academic Press, 1984.

Paunonen, S. V. The reliability of aggregated measurements: Lesson to be learned from psychometric theory. *Journal of Research in Personality*, 1984, *18*, 383–394.

Pennebaker, J. W. *The psychology of physical symptoms*. New York: Springer, 1982.

Pribram, K. H., & McGuiness, D. Arousal, activation, and effort in the control of attention. *Psychological Review*, 1975, *82*, 116–149.

Rösler, F. Physiologisch orientierte Forschungsstrategien in der differentiellen und diagnostischen Psychologie: II. Zur Systematisierung psychophysiologischer Untersuchungen. *Zeitschrift für Differentielle und Diagnostische Psychologie*, 1984, *5*, 7–36.

Schweizer, K. *Aggregation und Vorhersagbarkeit*. Rheinfelden: Schäuble, 1986.

Stelmack, R. M. The psychophysiology of extraversion and neuroticism. In H. J. Eysenck (Ed.), *A model for personality*. Berlin: Springer, 1981.

Stemmler, G. *Psychophysiologische Emotionsmuster*. Frankfurt: Lang, 1984.

Tellegen, A. Eysenck Personality Inventory. In O. K. Buros (Ed.), *The eighth mental measurements yearbook*. Highland Park, NJ: Gryphon Press, 1978.

Whytt, R. *Observations on the nature, causes and cure of those disorders which are called nervous* (2nd ed.). Edinburgh, 1765.

Wittmann, W. W., & Schmidt, J. *Die Vorhersagbarkeit des Verhaltens aus Trait-Inventaren*. Research Report, Psychological Institute, University of Freiburg, 1983, No 10.

CHAPTER 6

Individual Characteristics of Brain Limbic Structures Interactions as the Basis of Pavlovian/Eysenckian Typology

PAVEL V. SIMONOV

Using the parameters of intensity, mobility, and balance of excitation and inhibition processes as a basis for formulating his classification of higher nervous activity types, Pavlov pointed to the importance of individual features in the interaction of brain macrostructures. For instance, he related an "intellectual type" of person to the functional predomination of the frontal neocortical areas and an "artistic type" to the predomination of other neocortical areas and "emotive" subcortical formations. Elaborating the concepts of Pavlov, Teplov and Nebylitsyn have defined general properties of the nervous system: activity and emotionality. Nebylitsyn (1968) assumed that "activity" depends on the individual features of the functional system, the frontal neocortical regions–activating reticular formation, whereas "emotionality" depends on the interaction of the frontal neocortex with the brain limbic system. According to Eysenck (1972), interaction of the ascending activating system with the frontal neocortical regions lies at the root of the nervous system strength parameter as well as the degree of extraversion–intro-

PAVEL V. SIMONOV • Director, Institute of Higher Nervous Activity and Neurophysiology, U.S.S.R. Academy of Sciences, Moscow, U.S.S.R.

version. Modifying Eysenck's scheme, Gray (1972) added the hippocampus and medial part of the septum to these two structures. Robinson (1982) suggests that the transmission properties of the diffuse thalamocortical system corresponds to the Pavlovian/Eysenckian theory of human personality.

It has been shown that destruction of some limbic structures in animals of different genetic lines leads to substantially different consequences (Isaacson, 1980; Isaacson & McClearn, 1978). On the other hand, mice belonging to the lines with different sizes of hippocampus and neocortex possess characteristic features in the open field test as well as during elaboration of escape conditioned responses (Wimer, Wimer, & Roderick, 1971).

Investigations carried out in our laboratory have led to the conclusion that the four brain structures play a leading role in the genesis of emotional responses and in the organization of goal-directed behavior (Simonov, 1984).

According to the informational theory of emotions (Simonov, 1978, 1984), emotions, as the direct controllers of behavior, are determined by two factors: the presence of actual needs and the probability (possibility) of satisfying these needs in interaction with the environment on the basis of phylo- and ontogenetic experience.

The experimental data obtained in our laboratory showed that the interaction of four brain structures that play the major role in estimation of the signals coming from the environment and the choice of reactions corresponds to these ideas on behavioral organization (Simonov, 1974, 1979).

The "motivational system"—hypothalamus and amygdala— proved to be important in defining the dominant need at the specific moment that is subjected to immediate satisfaction, whereas, at the same time, the amygdala provides for the organization of a hierarchy of coexistent and/or competing motivations. The "informational system," incorporating the frontal neocortical areas and hippocampus, evaluates satisfaction of the needs and the probability of reinforcement for conditioned signals. Due to the frontal neocortical regions in this case, behavior is oriented to the signals of high probability events, and the preservation of the hippocampus is necessary for responses to the signals with low probability of reinforcement. Specialization of the functions of the aforementioned brain structures suggests that individual features of each of them and, even more so, peculiarities of their interaction determine to a large extent the individual (typological) features of animals' behavior (Simonov, 1981). The results of two series of experiments presented next, are consistent, in my opinion, with the hypothesis put forward here.

SPECIFIC FEATURES OF ESCAPE RESPONSES IN RATS AFTER DAMAGING LIMBIC BRAIN STRUCTURES

Studies on escape responses reinforced by incorporation of neutral stimuli (intensification of light and sounding of tone) or biologically specific action (painful cry of the partner) showed that the most effective stimulus for most of the rats (about 60%) was a painful cry of the partner. About 30% of the animals respond more intensely to switching on light and sound, whereas 10% are equally sensitive to both types of aversive stimuli. It is hard to say to what extent these individual features of behavior depend on genetic or environmental factors, though there are data showing that the frequency of pressing the lever, reinforced by switching on the light and lowering the noise, is predetermined genetically to the extent of 71% in laboratory rats (Oakeshott & Glow, 1980). It has been of interest to elucidate to what extent these behavioral features depend on the preservation of limbic brain structures.

MATERIALS AND METHODS

Experiments were conducted on 20 white male rats. The experimental chamber was a wooden box with dimensions of $33 \times 41 \times 34$ cm. The box contained (a) a relatively spacious area 33×23 cm; (b) a plexiglas "house" 16×14 cm with a constantly open door and a pedal floor that when pressed switched on a timer; and (c) a room for a partner with the floor of metal wire located next to the "house" and separated from it by a thin transparent sound-transmitting partition. The whole chamber was illuminated by scattered light of a lamp with a power of 100 W mounted under the ceiling of the room.

The animal under investigation was placed in the large section of the chamber every day for 5 minutes, and its stay in the "house" on the pedal was recorded. For the first 5 days, each appearance of the rat in the house was accompanied by switching on an additional light provided by a 100-W lamp located 45 cm from the chamber floor and a stimulus tone with a frequency of 220 Hz and loudness of 80 dB. In the subsequent 5 days, each entry into the "house" was accompanied by electric shock to the feet of the rat "victim" with a strength of 1 to 2 mA. The shock lasted 3 to 5 sec with 5-sec intervals until the rat under investigation stayed on the pedal. In the last 5 days, the entry into the "house" intensified illumination and switched on the sound.

In order to damage the frontal neocortical areas, Pigareva removed the relevant plate of the cranial bone and performed thermocoagulation of the brain tissue with an electrode of nichrome wire. Coagulation of

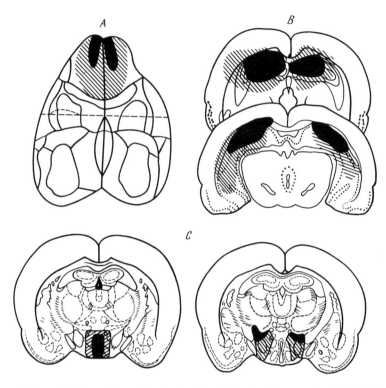

Figure 1. Reconstructive schemes for destruction of the frontal neocortex (A), the hippo-campus (B), and the lateral and ventromedial hypothalamus (C) in rats. The black area indicates the minimal extent of destructions in the given group of animals; hatching indicates the maximum extent.

subcortical formations was performed by means of stereotaxically intro-duced electrodes insulated with lacquer with the exception of the tip that was 300 mcm in diameter (current of 2.5 mA for 25 sec). Stereotaxic coordinates were determined by the atlas of Fifkova and Marshall (1960). The experiments were initiated 10 days after the operation. Upon com-pleting the experiments, Mats subjected the brains of the rats to a histo-logical examination by the Nissel method. Each section 20 to 40 mcm in thickness was stained with cresyl-violet (see Figure 1).

THE RESULTS

In Figure 2, a solid line shows the average time that seven intact rats stayed on the pedal. For these animals, the signals of the partner's defensive excitation (cry, movements, secretion of specific smelling sub-

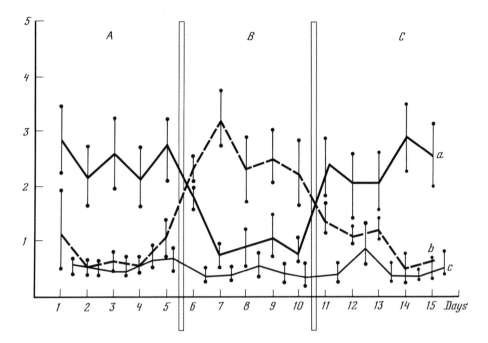

Figure 2. Average time of staying on the pedal under the action of light and tone (A, C) or the partner's cry (B) in intact rats (a), after damage of frontal neocortex and hippocampus (b) and after damage of the frontal neocortex and the hypothalamus (c). Abscissa—days of tests; ordinate—time in min.

stances) appeared to be more effective stimuli than light intensification and tone sounding. Bilateral coagulation of the frontal neocortical regions and hippocampus in these rats resulted in reversing the effects: During the action of sound and light the length of time spent on the pedal decreased, whereas during the "victim's" cry, it increased (broken line in Figure 2).

Nine rats with bilateral damage of the frontal neocortex lateral and ventromedial hypothalamus proved to be equally sensitive to a combination of a sound with intensification of illumination and to the signals of the partner's defensive excitation (see Figure 2). These animals were easily frightened, aggressive, and they responded violently to a touch at the same time as they showed diminishing signs of aversion to open spaces. The rats slowly entered the "house" whenever—rarely—they did so. Then when the light was switched on and with the sound of their partner's cry, they emerged from the "house" 10 to 20 sec later. If something distracted the rat (for instance, if it began cleaning its fur), light, sound, and the "victim's" cry lost their effectiveness.

DISCUSSION

We believe that the results of these experiments are consistent with the data obtained previously with the separate destruction of the frontal neocortex, hippocampus, amygdala, and hypothalamus. Simultaneous damage of the "informational system" structures (frontal neocortex and hippocampus) makes rats highly sensitive to previously low-effective stimuli (light and sound) and at the same time decreases their reactivity to social signals indicating the state of another animal of the same species. As far as damage to the frontal neocortex and the lateral and ventromedial hypothalamus is concerned, the intensified "neurotic" response of a rat to any external stimulus is combined in these animals with an inability to selectively respond to signals of various biological significance.

In assessing the totality of the data available at present, we are inclined to assume that the individual features of relation between the "informational system" (frontal neocortex–hippocampus) and the "motivational system" (amygdala–hypothalamus) lie at the root of the extraversion–introversion dimension (see Figure 3). The relation of the frontal neocortex–hypothalamus and amygdala–hippocampus systems determines the other parameter of individual behavioral features that is comparable in its characteristics to the dimension of neuroticism and emotionality.

From our point of view, Pavlov's concept of the nervous system strength or weakness is more in conformity with that of neuroticism but not with extraversion–introversion as Eysenck (1972) suggests. Garcia-Sevilla (1984) described a series of animal experiments, the aim of which was to test the hypothesis that the personality dimensions of extraversion–introversion and neuroticism–stability could be demonstrated and measured in rats. The activity of the hypothalamus–hippocampus and its relation to the frontal neocortex–amygdala system appears to be of great importance for Pavlov's factor of "mobility" or "inertness."

The bilateral ablation of the hippocampus in rats hinders the occurrence of neurotic reactions in solving difficult tasks, for example, in the elaboration of conditioned transswitching of alimentary and defensive reflexes, according to Asratyan, when one and the same conditioned signal was reinforced in the morning by food and in the evening by painful electrical stimuli. If the procedure of transswitching has already elicited a neurotic breakdown, the subsequent hippocampectomy eliminates this state (Pigareva, 1974). Preobrazhenskaya (1974, 1981) systematically studied the electrical activity of the hippocampus in the process of elaborating conditioned reflex transswitching in dogs.

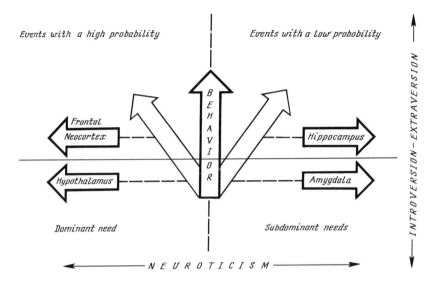

Figure 3. Hypothetical scheme for the dependence of extraversion–introversion and neuroticism dimensions on the individual features in interaction of the four brain structures. Emotional stability is characterized by a relative predominance of the "hypothalamus-frontal neocortex" system whereas in neuroticism the "amygdala-hippocampus" predominates with its symptoms of diffidence, indecisiveness, and inclination to overestimate insignificant events. Individual dominance of the motivational "hypothalamus-amygdala" system is characteristic for introverts; in extraverts, conversely, the informational "frontal neocortex-hippocampus" system is predominantly developed and is turned toward the external environment.

HIPPOCAMPAL THETA RHYTHM AND CONDITIONED REFLEXES TRANSSWITCHING IN DOGS

Materials and Methods

Eight dogs were used to elaborate an instrumental alimentary reflex of pressing, with the right foreleg, a pedal in response to a sound-conditioned signal (tone). Then the same conditioned signal, applied in addition to the action of a signal transswitching (noise and flickering of fan blades), was reinforced with electrical shock by painful stimulation of the hindleg. The dog could terminate and prevent this stimulation entirely by raising the left foreleg to a certain level. The details of elaborating alimentary and defensive instrumental conditioned reflexes have been described previously (Preobrazhenskaya, 1974).

Metal electrodes were implanted under Nembutal narcosis into a dorsal region of the hippocampus, according to the coordinates of Lim's atlas. The electrical activity of the hippocampus was regarded as rhythmic if regular fluctuations lasted at least 1 sec. The number of regular fluctuations was counted in the electrohippocampogramm (EHG) recording in successive 1-sec periods, and this number was compared with fluctuations determined by the analyzer. Each situation (defensive and alimentary) included at least 30 measurements, and the average frequency of fluctuations and its error were calculated.

THE RESULTS

Figure 4 presents histograms for the distribution of each frequency in the rhythmic activity of the hippocampus in four dogs, A, B, C, and D, in alimentary (I) and defensive (II) situations of tests with transswitching of conditioned reflexes.

It can be seen that the transition from the alimentary situation to a defensive one resulted in a more frequent hippocampal theta rhythm in all dogs: Histograms are displaced to the right. At the same time, each animal is characterized by its own range of changes in the frequency spectrum of EHG regular activity, and this range correlates with the dynamics of elaboration of conditioned reflex transswitching (see Figure 5). In dogs B and D, with more frequent theta rhythm, the elaboration of transswitching was comparatively easy and rapid: The dogs started to respond to the conditioned signal in accordance with the given situation after 5 to 6 days. It was different with dogs A and C, where conditioned reflex activity was unstable and had a wavelike character with a tendency to neurotization.

Similar data were obtained in experiments with other dogs. The animals with comparatively slow hippocampal theta rhythm were marked by poor communicability and indifference to the experimenter. They also had difficulties in solving other problems related to changes in the mode of activity.

DISCUSSION

The results obtained are consistent with data available in the literature (cf. Irmis, Radil-Weiss, Lat, & Krekule, 1970) on the correlation between the dominant frequency of hippocampal theta rhythm in rats and the exploratory activity characteristic of every animal. Both indexes are sufficiently stable for the same rat. Thus the range of changes in hippocampal theta rhythm individually typical of a given animal could be said to reflect the parameter that Pavlov designated as "inertness" (or, on the contrary, "mobility") of the nervous system. If we take into consideration the role that, according to modern concepts (Anderson &

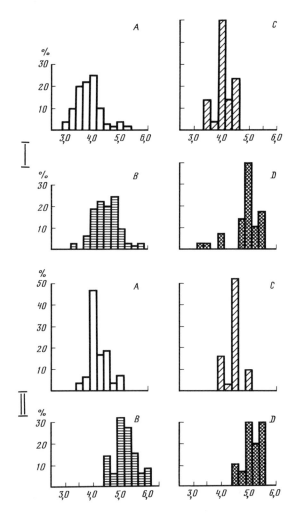

Figure 4. The distribution of frequencies of hippocampal electrical activity in dogs A, B, C, and D in the alimentary (I) and defensive (II) situations. Abscissa–cycles per sec; ordinate—percentage of the total number of measurements.

Eccles, 1962), is played by feedback inhibitory mechanisms in the genesis of biopotential rhythmic fluctuations, then the hypothesis of Pavlov relating to mobility of excitation and inhibition of nervous processes acquires concrete neurophysiological content. On the other hand, the data on participation of the hippocampus in the processes of recording information as well as in the processes of its extraction from memory (Simonov, 1974) make the connection of individual features of hippocampal theta rhythm with individual features of behavior understand-

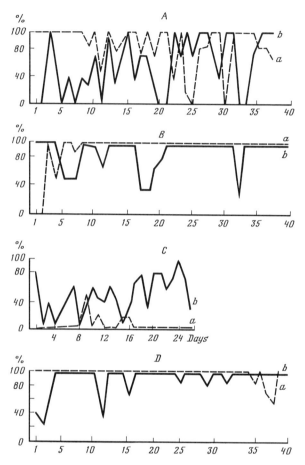

Figure 5. Dynamics of the elaboration of transswitching of alimentary (a) and defensive (b) conditioned reflexes in four dogs. Abscissa—days of tests; ordinate—percentage of conditioned reflexes in relation to the number of conditioned signal applications.

able. Previously we showed that the degree of spatial synchronization in the electrical activity of the hippocampus and hypothalamus increases immediately before realization of the instrumental conditioned reflex; this attests to intensification of the functional interaction of these two structures at the given stage of goal-directed behavior. Our common assumption is reduced to the proposition that the individual features of the four brain structures lie at the root of the individual behavioral features that previously were described in the form of the four temperaments by the ancient Greeks, in Pavlov's types of higher nervous activity and the extraversion–introversion dimension. Various forms of disorders in the normal interaction of the aforementioned structures probably determine the main types of neurosis.

CONCLUSION

The role of brain limbic structures in the individual features of animals' behavior was studied in two series of experiments. It was found that bilateral destruction of frontal regions of the neocortex and hippocampus in rats increases their reactivity to the action of neutral stimuli (light and sound) and simultaneously decreases their sensitivity to the signals of defensive excitation in another animal. Bilateral damage of the frontal neocortex and the lateral and ventromedial hypothalamus equally increases the reactivity of rats to sound, light, and cry of the partner. The dogs with more frequent hippocampal theta rhythm develop transswitching of food and defensive instrumental conditioned reflexes more rapidly and easily.

Correlation of these results with the facts obtained previously and the data available in the literature leads to the conclusion that individual features in the relation of the "informational system" (frontal neocortex and hippocampus) to the "motivational system" (amygdala and hypothalamus) lie at the root of the extraversion–introversion dimension. The relationship of the "frontal neocortex–hypothalamus" and "hippocampus–amygdala" systems is reflected in the neuroticism (emotionality) dimension. The activity of the "hypothalamus–hippocampus system" is very important for mobility or inertness, according to Pavlov. Various forms of disorder in the normal interaction of the four brain structures apparently determine the main types of experimental neurosis.

REFERENCES

Anderson, P., & Eccles, J. Inhibitory phasing of neuronal discharge. *Nature,* 1962, *196,* 645–647.

Eysenck, H. J. Human typology, higher nervous activity and factor analysis. In J. A. Gray & V. D. Nebylitsyn (Eds.), *Biological bases of individual behavior.* New York: Academic Press, 1972.

Fifkova, E., & Marshall, J. Stereotaxic atlas of the rat. In J. Bures, M. Petran, & J. Zachar (Eds.), *Electrophysiological methods in biological research.* Prague: Czechoslovac Academy of Science, 1960.

Garcia-Sevilla, L. Extraversion and neuroticism in rats. *Personality and Individual Differences,* 1984, *5,* 511–532.

Gray, J. A. The psychophysiological nature of introversion-extraversion: A modification of Eysenck's theory. In J. A. Gray & V. D. Nebylitsyn (Eds.), *Biological bases of individual behavior.* New York: Academic Press, 1972.

Irmis, F., Radil-Weiss, T., Lat, J., & Krekule, I. Inter-individual differences in hippocampal theta activity during habituation. *Electroencephalography and Clinical Neurophysiology,* 1970, *28,* 24–31.

Isaacson, R. Limbic system contributions to goal-directed behavior. In R. Thompson & B. Shvyrkov (Eds.), *Neural mechanisms of goal-directed behavior and learning.* New York: Academic Press, 1980.

Isaacson, R., & McClearn, G. The influence of brain damage on locomotor behavior of mice selectively bred for high or low activity in the open field. *Brain Research,* 1978, *150,* 559–567.

Nebylitsyn, V. D. The problem of general and partial properties of the nervous system. *Voprosy Psikhologii,* 1968, *4,* 29–43 (in Russian).

Oakeshott, J., & Glow, P. Genetic and environmental determinants of sensory contingent bar pressing in laboratory rats. *Australian Journal of Psychology,* 1980, *32,* 31–43.

Pigareva, M. L. Elaboration of conditioned alimentary reflexes having different probabilities of reinforcement in rats with hippocampal lesions. *Acta Neurobiologiae Experimentalis,* 1974, *34,* 423–433.

Preobrazhenskaya, L. A. Hippocampal electrical activity and different types of conditioned reflexes in dogs. *Acta Neurobiologiae Experimentalis,* 1974, *34,* 409–422.

Preobrazhenskaya, L. A. Individual differences of hippocampal electrical activity and conditioned reflexes in dogs. *Zhurnal vysshei nervnoi Deyatelnosti,* 1981, *31,* 479–488 (in Russian).

Robinson, D. L. Properties of the diffuse thalamocortical system and human personality: A direct test of Pavlovian/Eysenckian theory. *Personality and Individual Differences,* 1982, *3,* 1–16.

Simonov, P. V. On the role of the hippocampus in the integrative activity of the brain. *Acta Neurobiologiae Experimentalis,* 1974, *34,* 33–41.

Simonov, P. V. Central neural mechanisms of emotional states according to the information theory of emotions. In K. Lissak (Ed.), *Neural and neurochemical organization of motivated behavior.* Budapest: Akademiai Kiado, 1978.

Simonov, P. V. The role of emotions in the formation of instrumental conditioned reflex. *Acta Neurobiologiae Experimentalis,* 1979, *39,* 621–632.

Simonov, P. V. Role of limbic structures in individual characteristics of behavior. *Acta Neurobiologiae Experimentalis,* 1981, *41,* 523–582.

Simonov, P. V. The need-informational theory of emotions. *International Journal of Psychophysiology,* 1984, *1,* 277–289.

Wimer, C. C., Wimer, R. E., & Roderick, T. H. Some behavioral differences associated with relative size of hippocampus in the mouse. *Journal of Comparative Physiology,* 1971, *76,* 57–65.

CHAPTER 7

Psychoticism and Arousal

GORDON CLARIDGE

The title of this chapter contains a conjunction of terms each of which has been the subject of considerable controversy. In order to define the scope of the chapter and before taking up its main theme, it is therefore necessary to make some preliminary remarks about the status of both ideas, starting with psychoticism.

As a *general* concept, the idea that there is some continuity between the normal and the psychotic has appeared in several forms in the literature of abnormal psychology and psychiatry. However, it was Eysenck who first coined the particular term *psychoticism*, originally in his early factor analytic test of Kretschmer's theory of schizothymia-cyclothymia (Eysenck, 1952) and then more recently in his development of psychometric instruments (the P-scales) for measuring psychoticism by questionnaire (Eysenck & Eysenck, 1975, 1976). It might therefore be argued that the contents of the present chapter could be legitimately confined to examining questions about the biological basis of those personality characteristics measured by the Eysenck P-scales. However, the intention is to broaden the discussion somewhat, for two reasons.

First, as just intimated, the development of the concept of psychoticism within Eysenckian theory has formed only one part of a growing interest in trying to define, both descriptively and biologically, those features of normal individuality that might become comprehensible by referring to the psychotic states. Thus several other groups of workers have developed questionnaires intended to measure psychotic traits in

GORDON CLARIDGE • Department of Experimental Psychology, University of Oxford, Oxford, England OX1 3UD.

normal adults (Bentall and Slade, 1985; Chapman, Edell, & Chapman, 1980; Claridge & Broks, 1984; Faily & Venables, personal communication; Neilsen and Petersen, 1976). Admittedly, some of these investigators have been inspired less by a concern, as in Eysenck's case, with normal personality description and more by an attempt to characterize individuals who might be predisposed to psychotic breakdown—an exercise encountered in a different guise in the longitudinal studies of children carried out under the heading of "high-risk" research (Watt, Anthony, Wynne, & Rolf, 1984). But whether the question is formulated as one for differential psychology or as one for research on psychiatric morbidity, it is likely that the answers to be found will be identical. For, as noted elsewhere when discussing the general issue of how personality and mental illnesses are connected, normal individual differences and predispositions to disorder can be construed as one and the same thing (Claridge, 1985).

The second, and to some extent related, reason for widening the discussion beyond Eysenckian psychoticism arises out of doubts that have sometimes been cast on the validity of the latter as a descriptive dimension of truly psychotic traits. Although not wishing to elaborate on the issue at this point—its significance will eventually become evident—it is perhaps worth noting what the consequences for the discussion here would be, should those doubts be justified. If it were indeed the case that Eysenck's third dimension is wrongly named (i.e., it does not actually represent genuine *psychotic* traits), then the answers we get to any questions we ask about its biological basis, though interesting in themselves as observations about the P-scales, may not have much relevance to our understanding of "psychoticism" in the broader sense in which, in the previous paragraph, I chose to define it.

Turning to the second term contained in the title of this chapter, I have often felt that as an explanatory concept in psychology "arousal" has many of the qualities of a difficult but persuasive lover, whom reason tells one to abandon yet who continues to satisfy an inescapable need. There is no doubt that ever since it was first formulated as a psychological construct (and certainly after it was given some physiological "reality" in brain research), the notion of arousal has helped to summarize a useful fact about behavior and the nervous system: That is, that both—often enough in parallel for the purposes of casual observation—appear to vary along a continuum of wakefulness, energetics, irritability, sensitivity, emotionality, readiness to respond, or however individual writers have chosen to characterize changes in organismic excitability. Of course, on close inspection and in detailed usage, the idea has often betrayed those seduced by it, a fact forcibly underlined in a paper by Venables (1984) on the status of the arousal concept in psychology.

One important observation by Venables concerns the failure of different psychophysiological indexes of "arousal" to show high, or even moderate, degrees of correlation. Quoting an example from his own work, Venables notes that there may be a very low degree of association even between variables selected from a relatively homogeneous measurement domain, such as electrodermal activity. He goes on to conclude that it would be a "foolhardy man" who would set out to look in such data for a broad factor of arousal comparable to that of, say, general intelligence. In pursuing the analogy with intelligence, Venables is drawing attention to the fact that the latter is generally conceptualized as a stable characteristic of individual variation, having *trait* qualities. "Arousal," on the other hand, has both trait and *state* connotations. That is to say, in some contexts the term is used to refer to the possibility of permanent differences between individuals: In others, it is perceived as a fluctuating condition of the organism, subject to a wide range of internal and external influences. Many years ago I suggested that these two components might be theoretically separable if a distinction were made between "arousal" and "arousability," each perhaps being measurable—at least in principle—by a different kind of psychophysiological index (Claridge, 1967). Nevertheless, as Venables points out, trait and state concepts of arousal tend frequently to be confused in common psychological usage.

There is another facet to the failure of correlation between different measures of arousal; this is also one to which Venables draws our attention. Even if it were the case that stable, trait measures of individual differences in "arousability" could be established, it is unlikely that these could be collapsed into a single factor that would have detailed explanatory power. In other words, arousal is not a unitary concept. Instead, in physiological terms, it reflects the interaction between several subsystems—motor, autonomic, cortical—which may have only loose functional connections with one another (Lacey, 1967).

To Venables's concerns about arousal and its measurement we can add several others, though the first perhaps has more optimistic overtones. It refers to the possibility that the very failure of measures of arousal to correlate in an entirely predictable way when examined across unselected groups of subjects is itself significant, in pointing to genuine variations in the way different components of arousal are connected or operate in relation to one another in different individuals. In other words, the patterning or profile of different types of arousal measure might be an important parameter of individual variation in its own right, though its discovery will normally be masked in conventional forms of correlational analysis. This perspective on arousal as it relates to individual differences has particular relevance, I believe, to the understanding of the biology of psychoticism, a point to which I will return later.

A second additional observation about arousal that needs to be made—only touched upon obliquely by Venables—concerns the often blurred usage of the term to refer, on the one hand, to an intervening variable that might account for some observed change in performance and, on the other hand, to a hypothetical process that, it is assumed, is somehow being measured directly—"directly" to the extent that the investigator may feel he or she is able to infer the central state of his or her subjects from psychophysiological or electrophysiological evidence. The confusion here is further confounded by the fact that what are strictly measures of *performance* are sometimes employed as "direct" measures of arousal. A good relevant example here is the two-flash threshold, which has commonly been included—as a measure of cortical arousal—alongside, and without distinguishing its different status from, more conventional psychophysiological indexes (e.g., Lykken & Maley, 1968). Evaluation of such data is usually along the lines that cortical and autonomic arousal are not linearly related—for which indeed there is some evidence from studies using a more direct (EEG) measure of the former (Stennett, 1957). But the interpretation is certainly further complicated by the well-known, putative (though admittedly difficult to establish) inverted-U principle relating *performance* to arousal.

Finally, a comment needs to be inserted about the incompleteness of any conceptual nervous system model—however well thought out— that makes reference only to the *excitatory* aspects of brain activity. Many psychologists who make use of the arousal concept often do so ignoring the equally important role of active *inhibitory* processes in the nervous system, processes that almost certainly have status in their own right as sources of individual variation. This means that observed behavior— whether indexed with gross performance measures or with psychophysiological responses—will almost always represent the effect of reciprocally acting excitatory and inhibitory influences in the brain. This notion of a *balance* between excitation (or arousal) and inhibition was, of course, fundamental in the Pavlovian theory of nervous types to which several contemporary biological models of personality can be traced (Claridge, 1985). However, in the West it is only those workers—Eysenck, and others influenced by Pavlovian theory through his writings—who have laid particular stress on the idea (Claridge, 1967; Eysenck, 1957, 1967; Gray, 1981; Robinson, 1982).

Turning, now, to the main theme of this chapter, it is already clear from our foregoing remarks (though there are other reasons to be mentioned in a moment) that the concept of arousal *per se* is unlikely to prove useful in trying to appreciate the biology of psychoticism. Few readers will have had difficulty anticipating that conclusion: After all, the title of this chapter is merely an abbreviation, a shorthand legend under which to discuss a certain body of evidence and set of ideas that have been absorbed, sometimes even by default, into what has come to be regarded as the arousal literature. With this in mind, let us begin by tracing the threads of our discussion to their origins in studies of clinical populations, namely the psychotic states themselves. For it is toward the latter—and mainly schizophrenia because that is where most of the evidence lies—that we can usefully look in order to try and get some first clues about the possible biological basis of psychoticism as a normal trait.

Before considering more recent developments along these lines, it is perhaps worth noting briefly some earlier usages of the arousal concept in the schizophrenia literature. In fact, attempts to explain schizophrenia *solely* as a disorder of arousal had a very short life. This is not surprising. Even if arousal had shown signs of emerging as a well-defined and unitary concept—which, as we have seen, has turned out not to be so—it never had much promise as a complete explanation of the psychotic states or, by the same token, those permanent traits of personality that might predispose to them. For it would have been difficult to explain why it was that many other individuals, also perceived as being highly aroused or highly arousable (the merely anxious, for example), were not psychotic or even remotely likely to become so.

Nevertheless, in the early phases of research on schizophrenia the arousal concept was adopted—and usefully so—as a working construct for trying to understand certain elements in the disorder and to answer some basic questions about it. Exemplary here were the careful studies by Venables and his colleagues, attempting to make sense of what has always been the bane of investigators in the field—namely the great heterogeneity of schizophrenia (Venables & Wing, 1962). They were able to demonstrate systematic differences in measured arousal among precisely defined clinical subgroups as well as interesting relationships with the behavioral state of psychotic patients; for example, the tendency for behaviorally less active and socially more withdrawn individuals to be, paradoxically, more physiologically aroused. This finding, through its point of contact with the Pavlovian notion of "transmarginal inhibition," was important in helping to further the idea that *inhibitory*, as well as excitatory, processes may be malfunctioning in schizophrenia.

Another early use of the arousal concept in schizophrenia research, again owing much to Venables, was its application as a variable that might mediate, or in some other way interact with, the significant cognitive disorders that occur in psychosis, such as the dysfunctions of perception, attention, thought, and language—what in current psychological jargon would be bundled together under the heading *information processing*. In a seminal paper on this topic, Venables (1964) coined the term *input dysfunction* to try to unify the results of a very wide range of studies reviewed, stretching from investigations of schizophrenic thinking, at one end, to psychophysiological experiments, at the other. The paper was important for two reasons. First, it recognized the necessity to integrate ideas about schizophrenia coming from cognitive psychology, on the one hand, and psychophysiology, on the other. Second, it foreshadowed what was to become a significant refinement of the way in which psychophysiological data on schizophrenia were interpreted— away from crude arousal explanations and toward more fine-grain analyses owing as much to ideas about *attention* as to notions about arousal, in its classic sense. Thus Venables himself subsequently shifted the emphasis in his own research, toward one in which electrodermal activity (as part of the orienting response) could be seen as a microcosm of the attentive process. This was a paradigm that was also adopted by others and led to the continuing distinctions that are made between so-called "responder" and "nonresponder" forms of the schizophrenic syndrome (Bernstein, Frith, Gruzelier, Patteson, Straube, Venables, & Zahn, 1982; Dawson & Nuechterlein, 1984; Gruzelier & Venables, 1972; Ohman, 1981). Interpreting such data, Venables was led to suggest that the essential deficit in schizophrenia is a failure in a central "gating-in/gating-out" mechanism implicating the limbic system and probably issuing from an imbalance between excitatory and inhibitory influences on attention (Venables, 1973). Similar thinking lay behind my own early model of schizophrenia in which I proposed a failure of regulation in the nervous system, resulting in a dissociation or uncoupling of brain systems mediating arousal and attention (Claridge, 1967). Several themes are therefore seen here to begin converging: certain ideas from the nonphysiological models of information processing theory; prototypical conceptual nervous system models that are no longer dependent on simplistic notions of arousal and that also contain reference to inhibitory as well as excitatory processes; and the possibility of pointing to real brain mechanisms that may play at least some, if not an exclusive, role in schizophrenia. More recent psychophysiological research on schizophrenia has continued to elaborate this convergence, albeit somewhat haphazardly and even though no truly unifying theory has yet emerged (Spohn & Patterson, 1979). How far has such research offered a point of entry into an understanding of the biological basis of psychoticism?

One set of studies that bear directly on the question—though, as noted earlier, the investigators concerned have not always construed their work in quite the same way as we are doing here—concerns research carried out within the high-risk paradigm. In its most complete form, this involves the examination and follow-up of children considered to be vulnerable to later schizophrenic breakdown; the criterion of risk usually is a genetic one, namely that the children have at least one schizophrenic parent. The pioneer study here is the Danish High Risk Project started by Mednick and Schulsinger in 1962 and described in various progress reports since then (Mednick & Schulsinger, 1973; Mednick, Schulsinger, & Schulsinger, 1975). The pivot of the conclusions drawn from the study was the observation that children at risk for schizophrenia showed abnormalities of electrodermal responding when tested in a noxious classical conditioning situation; notably, slow habituation, resistance to extinction, short latency, and rapid recovery of the GSR. This pattern of apparent central nervous hyperresponsiveness was identical to that which Venables (1973), from his studies of schizophrenics, considered characteristic of the gating-in—or openness to the environment—mode of attentional control to be found in certain responder types of patient. Mednick concluded that it was a unique biological descriptor of vulnerability to schizophrenia that was particularly evident in children who eventually broke down, but was also observable in some high-risk children who did not.

Several other research groups have since investigated this claim, either as part of projects of similar longitudinal design, or using other, convergent high-risk strategies. The results have been mixed. Janes, Hesselbrock, and Stern (1978) found no evidence that schizophrenics' offspring differed in electrodermal activity, whereas other workers have reported them to be more hyperresponsive, though not as reflected in the short latency and fast recovery time indexes emphasized by Mednick (Prentky, Salzman, & Klein, 1981; Van Dyke, Rosenthal, & Rasmussen, 1974). In contrast, reporting from the New York High-Risk Project, an ongoing longitudinal study, Erlenmeyer-Kimling, Marcuse, Cornblatt, Friedman, Rainer, and Rutschmann (1984) describe results quite contrary to Mednick's; namely a tendency for schizophrenics' offspring to be, if anything, *less* responsiveness on all of the electrodermal measures they examined. Similar evidence of hyporeponsiveness has been reported by investigators in the Israeli Project (Kugelmass, Marcus, & Schmueli, 1985).

Other observations that bear on the results just described have come from studies of adult subjects in whom risk is defined, not by relatedness to a schizophrenic proband, but according to one or another questionnaire of psychoticism. In the first such published study, Nielsen and Petersen (1976) selected subjects on the basis of a scale of what they called "schizophrenism" and reported that high score did show patterns of electrodermal responding not dissimilar to those observed in Mednick's high-risk children, including shorter latencies of response and faster recovery times. On the other hand, Simons (1981), using the Chapmans' scales, found no relationship between their measure of perceptual aberration and electrodermal indexes of orienting and habituation, though "physical anhedonia" did correlate; the more anhedonic subjects were more *hypo*responsive.

The varied nature of these findings is not surprising, for the results merely seem to mirror the heterogeneity of electrodermal responding observed in schizophrenics themselves. That fact was perhaps half-recognized by Mednick who, in 1972 and in collaboration with Venables, set up a new high-risk project on the island of Mauritius (Venables, Mednick, Schulsinger, Raman, Bell, Dalais, & Fletcher, 1978). The study is unusual in that the criteria for selecting children at risk were entirely psychophysiological. Several infant cohorts were chosen, including two groups who showed *either* hyporesponsiveness *or* hyperresponsiveness in a test situation similar to that used in the original Danish project. The investigators in the Mauritius project therefore appear implicitly to have left open their options as to which of their two extreme responder groups will ultimately be at risk specifically for *psychotic* breakdown. However, it is interesting to note that Mednick himself has always regarded *hypo*responding GSR patterns as more prognostic of antisocial behavior than schizophrenia, and it is instructive to consider how others, working with criminal populations, have interpreted their own, comparable, electrodermal data. Thus Hare (1978), who was concerned to explain primary psychopathy, has described signs of electrodermal hyporesponsiveness (including slow recovery time to novel stimuli) in psychopaths under certain test conditions. He regards this finding as evidence that psychopaths (presumably in contrast to schizophrenics) *"gate out"* stressful stimuli, thus using Venables's model for electrodermal data in a different context. As further support for his interpretation, Hare quotes additional evidence that psychopaths show *greater* anticipatory heart rate than nonpsychopaths, drawing here on Lacey's rather similar theory—that cardiac acceleration under stress reflects an attentional mode of "sensory rejection" (Lacey & Lacey, 1974).

The body of evidence just discussed—and especially the apparent biological commonality of schizophrenic and antisocial traits—articulates an issue of considerable relevance here. The issue has several facets. In the clinical literature, it is reflected in a number of uncertainties about the nature of the psychotic states; that is, their tendency to vary in form and severity, the kind of traits that predispose to them, their genetic basis, the apparent overlap of schizophrenic and antisocial syndromes, and so on (Claridge, 1985). In the personality sphere, the same questions have been or are being asked, albeit in a slightly different form. There is, for example, increasing interest in what association there is, if any, between the various scales of psychoticism currently in vogue and whether those derived strictly from personality theory (and often including specific reference to antisocial behaviors) tap traits that are similar to, or different from, the characteristics measured by more symptom-based questionnaires. In the existing literature, the debate has focused very much on the validity of the Eysenck P-scales as measures of psychoticism, and it is appropriate at this point to bring that problem to the forefront of our discussion. This will also serve to introduce additional evidence about the possible biological basis of psychoticism as a general concept.

There are actually several quite distinct arguments that bear on the issue of the validity of the Eysenck P-scales, arguments that I have elaborated fully elsewhere (Claridge, 1981, 1983). The most relevant here concerns the extent to which the biology of psychoticism and the biology of schizophrenia can be aligned with each other—and, if they can, what the nature of the correspondence is. This is a problem my colleagues and I have been wrestling with for many years; trying, first, to identify some feature of the clinical syndrome of schizophrenia and then utilizing this as a biological probe for investigating psychoticism as a normal trait of personality. The feature on which we chose to focus was brought to our attention in some early clinical studies in which it became evident that schizophrenics could be best distinguished according to the pattern of *covariation* that existed between psychophysiological measures of different type: The direction of correlation was observed to be opposite to that found in other samples (Claridge, 1967). Our interest in this effect was further strengthened by the similar result of another early study of schizophrenics that was carried out, quite independently of our own, by Venables (1963).

Venables's finding that in schizophrenics the two-flash threshold covaried against skin potential level in an entirely opposite way to that observed in normal subjects led to several further investigations of clinical samples (Gruzelier, Lykken, & Venables, 1972; Gruzelier & Venables, 1975; Lykken & Maley, 1968). These studies, which largely centered on the hypothesis that the results for schizophrenics could be explained as due to an inverted-U effect relating "arousal" (electrodermal level) to performance (two-flash threshold), failed to elucidate the phenomenon. However, a serious deficiency in all of them was the use of medicated subjects and in another more recent experiment from our laboratory, involving drug-free patients, we have been able to establish

the likely form of covariation between the two-flash threshold and electrodermal level (skin conductance) in schizophrenia (Claridge & Clark,
1982).

Because of the exigencies of patient research, this last experiment
was actually completed long after a series of covariation studies of two-
flash threshold and electrodermal activity had been carried out, using
other strategies to investigate significance for understanding schizophrenia. Among these was an investigation of the effect of LSD-25 in
normal subjects (Claridge, 1972) and an accumulation of data on two-
flash threshold and skin conductance variations in subjects selected according to their scores on the Eysenck P-scale (Claridge & Birchall,
1978). All of these studies (including that on drug-free patients) agreed
in demonstrating that schizophrenics, subjects under LSD, and normal
high-P individuals genuinely did show an unusual pattern of covariation between the two experimental measures, not conforming to the
inverted-U principle. Our conclusion at that time was that overall the
function seemed to be U-shaped, with high degrees of perceptual sensitivity (low two-flash threshold) occurring at very low or at very high
levels of skin conductance (or potential). The worst perceptual performance was found in the midrange of electrodermal activity. However, it
should be noted in passing—I will return to the point later—that, in all
of our data, this U function was most clearly defined over the *lower*
range of electrodermal level, where a striking feature was the tendency
for some schizophrenics, high-P individuals, and subjects under LSD to
show very acute perceptual discrimination in association with extremely
low levels of skin conductance or potential.

As far as I am aware, only one other group of workers has attempted a partial replication of these findings, namely Robinson and
Zahn (1979, 1985) in two studies comparing normal subjects with high
and low scores on the Eysenck P-scale. In their first experiment they
found that, although the correlations between two-flash threshold and
skin conductance did differ across the two groups, the pattern of
covariation was diametrically opposite to that which we had observed!
The second study reexamined the question, looking at the effects of
manipulating arousal with postural stress on two-flash threshold, electrodermal activity, and heart rate in high- and low-P scorers. Results for
covariation analysis were again different from our own, and in attempting to explain the discrepancy Robinson and Zahn suggest that the
reason may lie in the fact that all of our results were obtained using an
earlier version of the P-scale, that was contained in the unpublished PEN
inventory; they, on the other hand, selected their subjects on the basis of
the EPQ scale. The observation is, I believe, not trivial. To those who
have closely followed the development of "psychoticism" within Ey-

senckian theory, it will have become abundantly clear that the question-naire measurement of the dimension has gradually shifted more and more toward a reliance on items that have an antisocial, rather than manifestly psychotic, flavor. The PEN inventory version, for example, contained several items of the latter type, which were however discarded in constructing the EPQ scale. And this trend is even more evident in the further revision of the P-scale (Eysenck, Eysenck, & Barrett, 1985).

Further support for the conclusion that current P-scales have been weakened—at least as measures of specifically psychotic traits—comes from evidence about their correlation with other putative questionnaire scales of psychoticism, scales that, because of their greater symptomlike item content, might be said to have better face validity. One such scale (or pair of scales) is the STQ, a questionnaire we have recently developed by mapping onto the characteristics of the borderline states as defined in DSM-III (Claridge and Broks, 1984). Of the two scales, that concerned with the measurement of "schizotypy" has most obvious connections with schizophrenia, and our evidence is that there is little, if any, correlation with the EPQ P-scale: The PEN version did, however, correlate significantly with our measure of schizotypy (Claridge, Robinson, & Birchall, 1983). Even more convincing, as far as the EPQ is concerned, is the result of an unpublished investigation by Muntaner and Garcia-Sevilla (1985). They conducted a large-scale correlational study and factor analysis of several questionnaires, including the EPQ, our own STQ, and the Chapmans' scales. Of the three factors accounting for the data, that having the most obvious "schizophrenic" content consisted of schizotypy, perceptual aberration, and magical ideation. A second factor was made up of physical and social anhedonia as well as introversion. The P- and (inversely) the L-scales from the EPQ, however, formed a separate, third, factor; its only loading on the other measures of psychoticism was for the STQ "borderline personality" scale, which taps temperamental traits somewhat similar to those covered by the Eysenck scale. Unlike the latter, however, our borderline personality scale also loaded on the first (schizotypy) factor.

This separation of EPQ P from other aspects of psychoticism might help to clear away a certain indecision expressed by Robinson and Zahn when offering an interpretation of the psychophysiological data they report in the second of their papers, cited earlier. Their strongest result was that high-P (EPQ) subjects showed all of the signs of physiological *hyporeponsiveness*, including poor two-flash threshold discrimination, lower heart rate, and longer latency and slower recovery of skin conductance response. Quoting the correspondence to similar data in the psychopathy literature, they lean heavily toward the view that the EPQ version of the P-scale is therefore a measure of psychopathic, rather than psychotic, traits. However, noting that their findings would also be consistent with the fact that some schizophrenics and high-risk subjects also show hyporesponsiveness, they consider the alternative possibility that the EPQ P-scale perhaps *is* mapping onto psychosis—but only one form of it. The psychometric analyses referred to before would suggest that their first supposition is the more correct and that the antisocial personality traits that *do* form part of the schizophrenia spectrum might be better captured with tests like our borderline personality scale, which has a firmer base in the clinical description of syndromes that border on the psychoses.

The ambiguity we have just encountered lies, not only in the psychometric properties of psychoticism scales, but also, I believe, in the interpretation of, and lack of specificity in, the psychophysiological data themselves. Thus it is perfectly possible (indeed very likely) that physiological hyporesponsiveness (or its opposite) will be observed in several *different* kinds of pathological state and their normal variants. In this respect, it is interesting to recall the evidence referred to earlier (Simons, 1981) that anhedonia—which in Muntaner's factor analysis formed an identifiable component of psychoticism, independent of the Eysenckian form—may also be associated with hyporesponding. In other words, even without reference to the EPQ P-scale it is possible, within the domain of psychoticism, to encompass the idea of heterogeneity of physiological responsiveness. The point is that the latter is a very nonspecific quality of individual variation. This is why we have consistently argued for research that looks for differences in patterning of response across *several* physiological systems, as is exemplified in our own covariation studies.

More recent research in our laboratory has continued to validate that opinion. The studies in question have used psychophysiological techniques in addition to those employed previously, combined with alternative strategies for investigating psychoticism. One example of the latter is an investigation of the adult relatives of schizophrenics, a group of individuals in whom psychotic traits would be expected, on genetic grounds, to be heavily concentrated. This sample was compared with a control group of neurotics' relatives on several psychophysiological indexes, including skin conductance, forearm EMG, and an EEG visual-evoked measure of augmenting-reducing (Claridge, Robinson, & Birchall, 1983, 1985). The results were highly consistent with those of our earlier two-flash threshold studies. Thus the schizophrenics' relatives sample contained a significantly higher proportion of individuals who, in conjunction with very low skin conductance, showed excessively high forearm EMG and/or marked EEG augmenting, which are indicative of increased cortical responsiveness.

The conclusions we would drew from this and our earlier studies is that the crucial psychophysiological quality of psychoticism is *not* hyper-responsiveness (or hyporesponsiveness) *per se*. It lies rather in an increased tendency toward dissociation of the autonomic, motor, and cortical components of arousal, possibly due to a characteristic, weakened form of excitatory and inhibitory regulation in the nervous system. If this were the case, then it is immediately obvious why the psychophysiology in question cannot be captured in a *single* index: Apparent hyperresponsiveness on one measure might be completely contradicted on another. The idea of CNS dysregulation as the basis of psychoticism might also account, better than alternative formulations, for several other aspects of the experimental data in this field, especially their heterogeneity—both across and within subjects—and the difficulty of establishing a typical psychophysiological status for schizophrenia. For peculiarities in the regulation of central nervous responses to environmental demands might indeed be expected to result in fluctuating psychophysiological profiles that are more than usually state-dependent.

Illustrating this last point are some additional observations made in our study, cited earlier, of two-flash threshold and skin conductance in unmedicated schizophrenics (Claridge & Clark, 1982). The patients, who were tested on several consecutive days, showed considerable change on both measures over the course of the experiment; this was so much the case that the U function we were seeking in the data only became evident when the readings from all testing occasions were combined. Also what was very striking was the fact that on the first occasion almost all of the patients fell in the *low* skin conductance range, where the negative arm of the postulated U function was very clearly defined: Yet by the end of testing they had mostly moved into the high range. Two conclusions were drawn. First, and this refers back to a previous comment about our early covariation studies, the most consistently observable (as well as most unusual) feature of psychoticism was the coexistence of *low* electrodermal level and *high* perceptual discrimination. Second, this effect was identifiable in schizophrenics because, somewhat paradoxically, they seemed to be at their *lowest* level of skin conductance when, as judged by our clinical observation, they were least psychologically accessible, perhaps more "aroused," and certainly not habituated to the experimental situation.

Our current thoughts on these, and later, covariation data we have collected are that the inherent dysregulation of the psychotic nervous system can potentially lead to extreme levels (in either direction) of different components of arousal. However, the response profile most commonly observable, and perhaps that most likely to be seen on single-occasion testing in the laboratory, is that occurring under stress or relatively great environmental demand, which leads to a *fall* in electrodermal level (and perhaps other autonomic activity) but a *rise* in cortical responsiveness. Two facts suggest that another feature may be an increase in muscle tonus—the data from our schizophrenics' relatives study, referred to before (Claridge, Robinson, & Birchall, 1983), and our clinical observation that schizophrenic patients with very low recorded electrodermal levels often appear to show high muscular tension.

Also supporting this analysis are the results of another study, carried out in our laboratory, of the effects of LSD-25 in the monkey (Claridge, Stein, & Wingate, unpublished). The aim of the experiment was to explore further our early use of that drug, in humans, as a pharmacological paradigm for psychoticism. The investigation, which involved repeated daily measurements of skin conductance and EEG visual evoked-potential augmenting-reducing, demonstrated predictable effects of LSD: a gradual decrease over time in skin conductance level; steeper augmenting–reducing slopes on occasions when skin conductance was relatively low; and ultimately an excessive degree of muscle tonus in the animal.

Whatever the eventual interpretation of the research discussed so far in this chapter, there is one further facet to the problem, not yet considered, that deserves mention. I am referring to the possibility that the psychophysiological characteristics associated with schizophrenia and psychoticism may also include effects that are lateralized *across* the nervous system. Although the possibility has scarcely been looked at in normal subjects in relation to personality, there is certainly considerable evidence that schizophrenic patients show unusual patterns of lateralization on psychophysiological variables, including autonomic response measures and EEG (Gruzelier, 1983). It is not surprising that the results are so confused and contradictory as elsewhere in schizophrenia research, though the last mentioned author, one of the main exponents in the field, has claimed systematic relationships between the form of psychotic symptomatology and the direction of asymmetry for both skin conductance responding (Gruzelier & Manchanda, 1982) and EEG augmenting-reducing (Connolly, Gruzelier, Manchanda, & Hirsch, 1983). In contrast, another group of authors, reviewing several failures by themselves and others to find consistent laterality effects for the orienting response, tartly conclude that "perhaps the time has come to conclude that bilateral asymmetry of autonomic ORs does not differentiate schizophrenic patients from other persons" (Bernstein, Rieder, Pava, Schnur, & Lubowsky, 1985, p. 249). I am inclined to agree with them, though possibly for different reasons. In my view, the asymmetries observed on autonomic (and other psychophysiological) measures probably represent just another example of the dysregulation that characterizes the psychotic nervous system—occurring, in this case, across the brain and, like other parameters that have been examined in schizophrenia, showing immense variability, both within and across individuals. This, of course, does not diminish their importance, though it does perhaps direct us toward a new perspective on them: not as "test" indexes that by themselves can differentiate the psychotic from others but as an additional dimension along which to study the dynamics of the nervous system in relation to schizophrenia and psychoticism.

Hemisphere research is also important for other reasons, taking us back, in a perhaps unanticipated way, to Venables's early struggle to integrate psychophysiological and information-processing viewpoints on schizophrenia. Much of the work on hemisphere function in schizophrenia stems not from psychophysiology but from the quite separate research tradition of neuropsychology (Walker & McGuire, 1982). These two approaches have been guided by somewhat different theoretical models of brain function, a point articulated by Gruzelier (1983) when considering possible alternative interpretations of hemisphere asymmetries in schizophrenia. Are they due, he asks, to differences in neurological organization, possibly of a "fixed structure" kind and most likely to be revealed through neuropsychological examination of the higher nervous system? Or are they due to "dynamic process" variations, such as fluctuating arousal and attention, dependent on lower brain mechanisms such as the limbic system structures much beloved of theorizing psychophysiologists? Or, as is most likely, are both true?

Such questions have so far been confined to the clinical syndromes, but it is likely that they will also soon come to be asked about psychoticism, for there is already some evidence that one of its components, namely schizotypy, is associated in normal subjects with neuropsychological hemisphere asymmetries of a form similar to those observed in schizophrenia itself (Broks, 1984; Broks, Claridge, Matheson, & Hargreaves, 1984; Rawlings & Claridge, 1984). Future research, taking its cue from the clinical literature, may therefore have to consider whether nervous system explanations grounded solely in psychophysiological concepts like arousal can give an adequate account of the fascinating constellation of biological and psychological traits presently subsumed under the term *psychoticism*.

REFERENCES

Bentall, R. P., & Slade, P. D. Reliability of a scale measuring disposition towards hallucination: A brief report. *Personality and Individual Differences*, 1985, 6, 527–529.
Bernstein, A., Frith, C., Gruzelier, J., Patterson, P., Straube, E., Venables, P., & Zahn, T. An analysis of the skin conductance orienting response in samples of American, British, and German schizophrenics. *Biological Psychology*, 1982, 14, 155–211.

Bernstein, A., Rieder, J., Pava, J., Schnur, D., & Lubowsky, J. A limiting factor in the "normalization" of schizophrenic orienting response dysfunction. *Schizophrenia Bulletin*, 1985, *11*, 230–254.

Broks, P. Schizotypy and hemisphere function—II. Performance asymmetry on a verbal divided visual field task. *Personality and Individual Differences*, 1984, *5*, 649–656.

Broks, P., Claridge, G., Matheson, J., & Hargreaves, J. Schizotypy and hemisphere function—IV. Story comprehension under binaural and monaural listening conditions. *Personality and Individual Differences*, 1984, *5*, 665–670.

Chapman, L. J., Edell, W. S., & Chapman, J. P. Physical anhedonia, perceptual aberration, and psychosis proneness. *Schizophrenia Bulletin*, 1980, *6*, 639–653.

Claridge, G. *Personality and arousal*. Oxford: Pergamon Press, 1967.

Claridge, G. The schizophrenias as nervous types. *British Journal of Psychiatry*, 1972, *112*, 1–17.

Claridge, G. Psychoticism. In R. Lynn (Ed.), *Dimensions of personality. Papers in honour of H. J. Eysenck*. Oxford: Pergamon Press, 1981.

Claridge, G. The Eysenck Psychoticism Scale. In J. N. Butcher & C. Spielberger (Eds.), *Advances in personality assessment* (Vol. 2). Hillsdale, NJ: Erlbaum, 1983.

Claridge, G. *Origins of mental illness*. Oxford: Blackwell, 1985.

Claridge, G., & Birchall, P. M. A. Bishop, Eysenck, Block, and psychoticism. *Journal of Abnormal Psychology*, 1978, *87*, 664–668.

Claridge, G., & Broks, P. Schizotypy and hemisphere function—I. Theoretical considerations and the measurement of schizotypy. *Personality and Individual Differences*, 1984, *5*, 633–648.

Claridge, G., & Clark, K. Covariation between two-flash threshold and skin conductance level in first-breakdown schizophrenics: Relationships in drug-free patients and effects of treatment. *Psychiatry Research*, 1982, *6*, 371–380.

Claridge, G., Robinson, D. L., & Birchall, P. Characteristics of schizophrenics' and neurotics' relatives. *Personality and Individual Differences*, 1983, *4*, 651–664.

Claridge, G., Robinson, D. L., & Birchall, P. Psychophysiological evidence of "psychoticism" in schizophrenics' relatives. *Personality and Individual Differences*, 1985, *6*, 1–10.

Claridge, G., Stein, J., & Wingate, B. Psychophysiological effects of LSD-25 in the monkey similar to human psychosis (unpublished).

Connolly, J. F., Gruzelier, J. H., Manchanda, R., & Hirsch, S. R. Visual evoked potentials in schizophrenia: Intensity effects and hemisphere asymmetry. *British Journal of Psychiatry*, 1983, *142*, 152–155.

Dawson, M. E., & Nuechterlein, K. H. Psychophysiological dysfunctions in the developmental course of schizophrenic disorders. *Schizophrenia Bulletin*, 1984, *10*, 204–232.

Erlenmeyer-Kimling, L., Marcuse, Y., Cornblatt, B., Friedman, D., Rainer, J. D., & Rutschmann, J. The New York High-Risk Project. In N. F. Watt, E. J. Anthony, L. C. Wynne, and J. E. Rolf. (Eds.), *Children at risk for schizophrenia*. Cambridge: Cambridge University Press, 1984.

Eysenck, H. J. Schizothymia-cyclothymia as a dimension of personality—II. Experimental. *Journal of Personality*, 1952, *20*, 345–384.

Eysenck, H. J. *Dynamics of anxiety and hysteria*. London: Routledge & Kegan Paul, 1957.

Eysenck, H. J. *The biological basis of personality*. Springfield, Il.: Charles C Thomas, 1967.

Eysenck, H. J., & Eysenck, S. B. G. *Manual of the Eysenck Personality Questionnaire*. London: Hodder & Stoughton, 1975.

Eysenck, H. J., & Eysenck, S. B. G. *Psychoticism as a dimension of personality*. London: Hodder & Stoughton, 1976.

Eysenck, S. B. G., Eysenck, H. J., and Barrett, P. A revised version of the Psychoticism scale. *Personality and Individual Differences*, 1985, *6*, 21–29.

Gray, J. A. A critique of Eysenck's theory of personality. In H. J. Eysenck (Ed.), *A model for personality*. Berlin: Springer, 1981.

Gruzelier, J. H. A critical assessment and integration of lateral asymmetries in schizophrenia. In M. Myslobodsky (Ed.), *Hemisyndromes: Psychobiology, neurology, and psychiatry*. New York: Academic Press, 1983.

Gruzelier, J. H., & Manchanda, R. The syndrome of schizophrenia: Relations between electrodermal response, lateral asymmetries and clinical ratings. *British Journal of Psychiatry*, 1982, *141*, 488–495.

Gruzelier, J. H., & Venables, P. H. Skin conductance orienting in a heterogeneous sample of schizophrenics. *Journal of Nervous and Mental Disease*, 1972, *155*, 277–287.

Gruzelier, J. H., & Venables, P. H. Relations between two-flash threshold discrimination and electrodermal activity, re-examined in schizophrenics and normals. *Journal of Psychiatric Research*, 1975, *12*, 73–85.

Gruzelier, J. H., Lykken, D., & Venables, P. H. Schizophrenia and arousal revisited. *Archives of General Psychiatry*, 1972, *26*, 427–432.

Hare, R. D. Electrodermal and cardiovascular correlates of psychopathy. In R. D. Hare & D. Schalling (Eds.), *Psychopathic behaviour*. Chichester: Wiley, 1978.

Janes, C. L., Hesselbrock, V., & Stern, J. A. Parental psychopathology, age, and race as related to electrodermal activity of children. *Psychophysiology*, 1978, *15*, 24–34.

Kugelmass, S., Marcus, J., & Schmueli, J. Psychophysiological reactivity in high-risk children. *Schizophrenia Bulletin*, 1985, *11*, 66–73.

Lacey, J. I. Somatic response patterning and stress: Some revisions of activation theory. In N. H. Appley & R. Trumbell (Eds.), *Psychological stress: Issues in research*. New York: Appleton-Century-Crofts, 1967.

Lacey, B. C., & Lacey, J. I. Studies of heart rate and other bodily processes in sensorimotor behaviour. In P. Obrist, A. Black, J. Brener, & L. V. DiCara (Eds.), *Cardiovascular psychophysiology*. Chicago: Aldine, 1974.

Lykken, D. T., & Maley, M. Autonomic versus cortical arousal in schizophrenics and nonpsychotics. *Journal of Psychiatric Research*, 1968, *6*, 21–32.

Mednick, S. A., & Schulsinger, F. A learning theory of schizophrenia: Thirteen years later. In M. Hammer, K. Salzinger, & S. Sutton (Eds.), *Psychopathology*. New York: Wiley, 1973.

Mednick, S. A., Schulsinger, H., & Schulsinger, F. Schizophrenia in children of schizophrenic mothers. In A. Davids (Ed.), *Childhood personality and psychopathology: Current topics, 2*. New York: Wiley, 1975.

Muntaner, C., & Garcia-Sevilla, L. *Factorial structure of the Eysenck Personality Questionnaire in relation to other psychosis proneness scales*. Paper presented at the 2nd Conference of the International Society for the Study of Individual Differences, St. Feliu, Spain, June 1985.

Nielsen, T. C., & Petersen, N. E. Electrodermal correlates of extraversion, trait anxiety, and schizophrenism. *Scandinavian Journal of Psychology*, 1976, *17*, 73–80.

Ohman, A. Electrodermal activity and vulnerability to schizophrenia: A review. *Biological Psychology*, 1981, *12*, 87–145.

Prentky, R. A., Salzman, L. F., & Klein, R. H. Habituation and conditioning of skin conductance responses in children at risk. *Schizophrenia Bulletin*, 1981, *7*, 281–291.

Rawlings, D., & Claridge, G. Schizotypy and hemisphere function—III. Performance asymmetries on tasks of letter recognition and local-global processing. *Personality and Individual Differences*, 1984, *5*, 657–663.

Robinson, D. L. Properties of the diffuse thalamocortical system and human personality: A direct test of Pavlovian/Eysenckian theory. *Personality and Individual Differences*, 1982, *3*, 1–16.

Robinson, T. N., Jr., & Zahn, T. P. Covariation of two-flash threshold and autonomic arousal for high and low scores on a measure of psychoticism. *British Journal of Social and Clinical Psychology*, 1979, *18*, 431–441.

Robinson, T. N., Jr., & Zahn, T. P. Psychoticism and arousal: Possible evidence for a linkage of P and psychopathy. *Personality and Individual Differences*, 1985, *6*, 47–66.

Simons, R. F. Electrodermal and cardiac orienting in psychometrically defined high-risk subjects. *Psychiatry Research*, 1981, *4*, 347–356.

Spohn, H. E., & Patterson, T. Recent studies of psychophysiology in schizophrenia. *Schizophrenia Bulletin*, 1979, *5*, 581–611.

Stennett, R. G. The relationship of alpha amplitude to the level of palmar conductance. *Electroencephalography and Clinical Neurophysiology*, 1957, *9*, 131–138.

Van Dyke, J. L., Rosenthal, D., & Rasmussen, P. V. Electrodermal functioning in adopted-away offspring of schizophrenics. *Journal of Psychiatric Research*, 1974, *10*, 199–215.

Venables, P. H. The relationship between level of skin potential and fusion of paired light flashes in schizophrenic and normal subjects. *Journal of Psychiatric Research*, 1963, *1*, 279–287.

Venables, P. H. Input dysfunction in schizophrenia. In B. Maher (Ed.), *Progress in experimental personality research*. New York: Academic Press, 1964.

Venables, P. H. Input regulation and psychopathology. In M. Hammer, K. Salzinger, & S. Sutton (Eds.), *Psychopathology*. New York: Wiley, 1973.

Venables, P. H. Arousal: An examination of its status as a concept. In M. G. H. Coles, J. R. Jennings, & J. P. Stern (Eds.), *Psychophysiological perspectives*. New York: Van Nostrand, 1984.

Venables, P. H., & Wing, J. K. Level of arousal and the subclassification of schizophrenia. *Archives of General Psychiatry*, 1962, *7*, 114–119.

Venables, P. H., Mednick, S. A., Schulsinger, F., Raman, A. C., Bell, B., Dalais, J. C., & Fletcher, R. P. Screening for risk of mental illness. In G. Serban (Ed.), *Cognitive defects in the development of mental illness*. New York: Brunner/Mazel, 1978.

Walker, E., & McGuire, M. Intra- and interhemispheric information processing in schizophrenia. *Psychological Bulletin*, 1982, *92*, 701–725.

Watt, N. F., Anthony, E. J., Wynne, L. C., & Rolf, J. E. *Children at risk for schizophrenia*. Cambridge: Cambridge University Press, 1984.

PART III

Neo-Pavlovian Concepts of Temperament

A Neuropsychological Model of Personality and Individual Differences

DAVID L. ROBINSON

INTRODUCTION

From around 1900 until his death in 1936, the research carried on by Pavlov led to an empirically based theory of brain function and behavior. Unfortunately, this theory has never gained widespread acceptance among physiologists, although it has profoundly influenced the concepts developed by some psychologists. Two main reasons can be suggested to account for the limited impact of Pavlov's brain and behavior theory. The first of these arises because unfavorable comparisons can be made between his speculations concerning the actual mechanisms mediating *excitation* and *inhibition* and the knowledge of neuron physiology that has accumulated so rapidly in recent times. However, such comparisons only demonstrate a fundamental misconception of Pavlov's explicitly stated research aims, and they do not invalidate his theory. Because it is important to counter this misconception, I will let Pavlov (1927) speak in his own defense:

> A scientific investigation of biological phenomena can be conducted along several different lines each of which would treat the problem from a different point of view. For instance, one may have in view the purely physico-chem-

DAVID L. ROBINSON • Department of Psychology, University of Sydney, Sydney, Australia.

ical aspect, analyzing the elements of life by the methods of physics and chemistry. Again, keeping in view the fact of evolution of living matter one can try to elucidate the functions of complex biological structures by studying the functions of individual cells and of elementary organisms. Finally, one can make an attempt to elucidate the activities of complex structures in their fullest range directly, seeking for rigid laws governing this activity, or, in other words, trying to define all those conditions which determine the form this activity takes at every instant and in all its variations. The line of enquiry which has been adopted in the present investigation obviously belongs to the third point of view. In this research we were not concerned with the ultimate nature of excitation and inhibition as such. We took them as two fundamental properties, the two most important manifestations of activity, of living nervous elements. (pp. 377–378)

The second and more legitimate reason why Pavlov's brain and behavior theory has not gained general acceptance is that until recent times it has been difficult to perceive how it might be tested. Although this may have been so, direct tests of Pavlov's key hypotheses are now possible (Robinson, 1982a, 1982b, 1983a, 1985, 1986a). The results of such tests provide an empirical foundation for the theoretical developments described here. To furnish a basis for understanding these tests as well as the theoretical implications of the results, a brief outline of Pavlov's formulation will be necessary.

PAVLOV'S THEORY

Pavlov found initially that to account for the variability of learned salivary responses to specific stimuli he had to postulate the existence of two antagonistic mediating brain processes—one of these tending to excite and the other to inhibit responses. His experimental results led him to conclude, in the first instance, that the relative extent to which a particular stimulus engaged both processes depended in a lawful manner on the history and environmental context of stimulus presentations. These laws of learning are generally referred to as Pavlov's theory of classical conditioning. A lucid and parsimonious description of classical conditioning is provided by Gray (1979), and only one point requires special mention. Traditionally, classical conditioning has been conceived as involving the strengthening of stimulus-response connections, but recent developments in the field of animal learning indicate that it is a process that involves learning about the relationships between stimuli (Mackintosh, 1974). The latter view, which is accepted here, suggests that in classical conditioning, the neural representations of different stimuli become connected.

Pavlov's results ultimately demonstrated that the total variance of responses could not be explained by his laws of conditioning. In that part of his total conception that is neglected by learning theorists, he accounted for the unexplained variance by reference to the concept of *strength*.

Thus he claimed that the relative effectiveness of the excitatory and inhibitory processes depended on *intrinsic* differences in strength or working capacity as well as on the extent to which a stimulus could engage either process through conditioning. Despite the very great methodological problems, and albeit crudely, he was able to evaluate the relative strength of both processes across experimental animals by manipulating stimulus parameters, such as intensity, which produce response differences that cannot be explained by reference to associative learning or conditioning. He concluded that in some animals the excitatory and inhibitory processes had equal degrees of strength and hence were *balanced*, although both might be stronger or weaker than normal. In other cases, he concluded that the excitatory process was strong and the inhibitory process weak. The opposite combination was also conceived as a possibility, and such combinations were referred to as *unbalanced* with predominance of one or the other process. The fundamental postulate of his brain and behavior theory arose from the observation that some of these differences related systematically to differences in overall behavior that he classified as sanguine, melancholic, phlegmatic, or choleric, in accordance with the temperamental typology of antiquity. Although there are other important concepts associated with Pavlov's theory, and these will be considered in due course, it is to the manner of testing his central hypothesis that I now turn.

THE NEURAL BASES OF INTROVERSION-EXTRAVERSION AND NEUROTICISM

From the description just given it is clear that Pavlov's theoretical linking of brain function and human individuality can only be tested directly by first seeking to quantify in human subjects the temperamental traits that he recognized in the gross behavior of his experimental animals. In addition, the actual neurophysiological system that correspond to his excitatory and inhibitory processes must be suggested, and some way must be found to measure directly their relative transmission properties, or in Pavlov's terminology, their *strength*. If the trait variables relate systematically to the transmission properties of these systems, in the manner proposed by Pavlov, there is confirmation that they have been correctly identified and that his theory is valid.

In describing such a test, Robinson (1982a) points out that the first requirement is satisfied by analytical studies of human individual differences that suggest that the descriptions of temperamental types provided by Pavlov correspond to those associated with combinations of extremes on the introversion-extraversion and neuroticism dimensions of personality (Eysenck, 1964). The position of individuals on these dimensions can be quantified in human subjects using psychometric scales. This convergence and overlapping of two very different approaches to the study of individual differences is important of itself, but it has special significance in the present context because it provided the opportunity for a simultaneous test of the physiological underpinning of Eysenck's (1967) theory of personality.

With respect to the second requirement mentioned before, Robinson suggested that the identity of neurophysiological subsystems corresponding to Pavlov's hypothetical processes is indicated by findings that clarify the role of the reticular formation with respect to behavior. In an authoritative review of this work, Magoun (1963) concluded that:

> Many contributions point to the existence of a non-specific thalamocortical system, the low-frequency excitation of which evokes large slow waves, as well as recruiting responses and spindle bursts in the EEG . . . this system appears to manage all the Pavlovian categories of internal inhibition of higher nervous activity . . . it is now possible to identify a thalamocortical mechanism for internal inhibition, capable of modifying activity of the brain partially or globally. (pp. 173–174)

On consideration of the behavioral effects that Pavlov attributed to his processes of excitation and inhibition, Robinson concluded that the diffuse thalamocortical system (DTS) could also be suggested as the mediator of Pavlovian excitation. Doing very little violence to Pavlov's speculation that excitation and inhibition might be generated simultaneously but to varying degrees in the same cortical cells, the DTS model proposed by Robinson continues to identify the excitatory process with cortical cells but identifies the inhibitory process with distinct thalamic neurons.

Taking Pavlov's favored response as an example, the extent to which a specific CS generates more or less inhibition or excitation of the salivary nuclei of the brain stem depends first on the functional effectiveness of the cortical and thalamic elements that the CS activates and, secondly, on the proportion of exciting and inhibiting elements that it engages. The first-mentioned determinants of the excitation–inhibition balance are intrinsic neural properties that vary across subjects, and the second-mentioned determinant is the environmental experience of particular subjects. The suggestion here, that the DTS mediates associative learning, is in accord with the observation that it is only the diffuse thalamic projection system (DTPS) that has the capacity to produce

widespread but selective cortical activation. As Samuels (1959) pointed
out in an important review, the DTPS is

> functionally organised in a manner which would permit it to control the
> continuum of consciousness and to serve as a selective mechanism for the
> facilitation of certain perceptions, sensations, and memories, as well as the
> inhibition of others. (p. 5)

Of course, as already intimated, it is not enough to suggest the
identity of Pavlov's hypothetical processes. To test his theory and the
validity of implicating the DTS, some way had to be found to evaluate
directly the transmission characteristics of the cortical and thalamic cell
populations involved. The way to proceed is indicated in the passage
quoted from Magoun (1963) where there is reference to the EEG effects
of direct DTS stimulation. If it is possible to stimulate the DTS and
record a response, then the influence of the intrinsic transmission properties of the cerebral and thalamic elements will be manifest in the stimulus-response relationship. Robinson (1983a) describes how the DTS can
be preferentially excited in human subjects and a response detected in
the EEG. By recording the amplitude of sinusoidal EEG responses to
different frequencies of sinusoidally modulated diffuse light stimulation, it was possible to demonstrate the validity of the DTS model shown
in Figure 1; in effect, that the model could account for most of the within

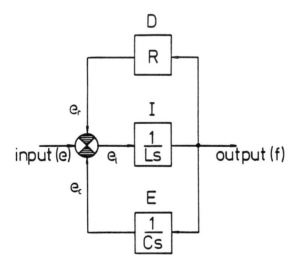

Figure 1. A model of the diffuse thalamocortical system. Elements I and E represent aggregates of thalamic and cerebral neurons, respectively. Element D has no specific locus and
represents dissipation of energy in the system as a whole (or *gain* in an *active* system). The
transfer functions of the elements are shown and the symbols f, e_r, e_c, and e_i denote inputs
and outputs of the system element.

and across subject variance of averaged EEG responses to stimulation in the alpha range of frequencies. Given such a model, mathematical procedures with great resolving power permitted the neurophysiologically meaningful analysis of DTS responses, manifest in the EEG, such that the relative values of constants shown in the model could be ascertained for different individuals. Element D in the model has no specific physical locus. It accounts for any loss of energy (or *gain* in an *active* system) and relates to the system as a whole. Of more immediate interest, neurons of the DTPS are represented in aggregate by Element I, and the cortical neurons to which they project are represented by Element E. The labeling of these elements refers to their effects on other systems of neurons, making the relationship with Pavlovian theory explicit, and not to the character of their interaction. The constants R, L, and C are only analogous to the resistance, inductance, and capacitance of electronics. They relate to a more general system-theory representation of the characteristics of the separate elements. Although the values of the constants are only relative, two summary systems-theory parameters can be calculated that completely describe the dynamic character of the system. First, damping ratio is defined as

$$\zeta = R/(2\sqrt{L/C}). \tag{1}$$

Second, natural frequency is defined as

$$\omega_n = 1/\sqrt{LC}. \tag{2}$$

The way in which these parameters relate to the three fundamental constants is of considerable significance, and the behavior of the system is best described by reference to them (Robinson, 1983a). However, the constants L and C are of more immediate interest because they are a formal representation of Pavlovian strength.

As already mentioned, Pavlov refers to four major types in his classification of individuals, and these have their counterpart in Eysenck's dimensional description of human personality when all four combinations of high and low extraversion (E) and neuroticism (N) are considered (Eysenck, 1964). In both cases, the four types are explicitly associated with the sanguine, melancholic, choleric, and phlegmatic temperaments. The sanguine description (high E/low N) was ultimately applied by Pavlov to lively, sociable, and confident animals. The melancholic description (low E/high N) was applied to those that were quiet and fearful. The results of the well-known experiments carried out by Pavlov and his colleagues over 30 years led him ultimately to conclude that the former had strong excitatory and strong inhibitory processes (Pavlov, 1955, pp. 315–344; Teplov, 1964, p. 35); that they were *strong balanced* types. The latter, he finally concluded, had both weak excitatory and weak inhibitory processes and hence were *weak balanced* types

(Pavlov, 1955, pp. 315–344; Teplov, 1964, p. 95). If there is a hypothetical dimension running from strong balanced to weak balanced, then this ought to be manifest in Eysenckian terms as running from high E/low N to low E/high N. If Pavlov's theory is correct, if his hypothetical inhibitory and excitatory processes do relate to the thalamic and cortical neurons of the DTS as suggested, and if there is substance to the physiological underpinning of Eysenck's theory, then those individuals who fall on the personality dimension just described ought to have a corresponding position on a dimension defined by the physicochemical constants that represent strength. That is, running from large C and large L to small C and small L values.

A test of the hypothesis just described yielded a correlation of .95. This and related findings, which are described in detail by Robinson (1982a), provide very strong support for the view that DTPS and associated cortical neurons, respectively, correspond to Pavlov's inhibitory and excitatory processes. There is also support for the hypothesis that the properties of strength and balance, which Pavlov inferred with respect to these processes, correspond to different values and combinations of values of the analytically determined physicochemical constants associated with DTS elements. Apart from confirmation for Pavlov's theory and identification of the neurophysiological systems involved, the results also support Pavlov's claim that the properties of the nervous system, which he described in terms of strength and balance, underlie individual differences in human personality.

Additionally, the neurophysiological underpinning of Eysenck's theory of personality has been tested directly and established with a very high level of confidence. That is to say, the major dimensions of Eysenck's personality theory, E and N, have been systematically related to differences in physicochemical properties of particular neurophysiological subsystems. Finally, it is noted that the results reported by Robinson establish a firm empirical basis for integrating the theories of Pavlov and Eysenck.

THE NEURAL BASES OF GROUP INTELLIGENCE FACTORS

Apart from the results referred to in the preceding paragraphs, relationships between the DTS constants and other psychological concepts are implied by reports that suggest that diffuse thalamic nuclei are capable of modifying activity of the brain partially or globally (Magoun, 1963). In the absence of *background activation*, inputs relayed to the cortex via the specific afferent systems do not reach conscious awareness (Mountcastle, 1980). Such considerations led Samuels (1959, p. 5) to conclude that the DTS could control the continuum of consciousness and serve as a selective mechanism for the facilitation of certain perceptions, sensations, and memories as well as the inhibition of others. Parameters that determine the mode of DTS function could, therefore, influence perception, memory and attention as well as the E and N dimensions of personality. However, as in Robinson's (1982a) paper, it is the linking of DTS parameters and Pavlovian concepts that leads to specific hypotheses.

From his experimental findings, Pavlov inferred that stimuli can produce either diffuse and general patterns of cortical activation or, alternatively, more selective and sharply defined patterns. This inference concerning the *irradiation* and *concentration* of cortical activity has since been confirmed by electrophysiological recordings (Magoun, 1961, p. 818). Concentration was associated with good performance on discrimination tasks, whereas irradiation was associated with poor performance. Such performance differences can be explained by suggesting that stimuli are perceived as different to the extent that they can preferentially activate well-defined subsets of cortical elements. This conception bears some resemblance to the ideas concerning DTS function that were discussed earlier. The parallel is all the more compelling because it is possible to relate concentration and irradiation to Pavlov's concept of strength and hence to the DTS parameters already associated with strength.

According to Pavlov (1941, p. 174), undue weakness or strength of either the excitatory or inhibitory processes results in irradiation rather than concentration of cortical activity. Thus we might expect that extremes of the overall strength dimension defined earlier would be associated with irradiation and inferior performance of certain cognitive tasks. However, it is possible to define an orthogonal continuum in terms of an inverse relationship between the constants associated with strength. Movement toward the extremes on this second dimension would correspond to what Pavlov referred to as lack of balance, and this condition also was held to be associated with irradiation and poor performance on discrimination tasks. In general, therefore, any deviation from the point where the overall strength and balance dimensions intersect can be associated with irradiation and poor performance on tasks similar to those employed by Pavlov.

The greatest insights concerning this less well-defined part of Pavlov's thesis emerged from a factor analysis that included Wechsler Adult Intelligence Scale (WAIS) subtest scores, scores on Witkin's Embedded Figures Test (EFT), and scores on the Psychoticism (P) and Lie (L) scales of the Eysenck Personality Questionnaire (EPQ). Values of a variable derived from the DTS parameters representing strength were also included in the analysis. This variable, denoted V, was obtained by regarding positions on the orthogonal overall strength and balance dimensions as Cartesian coordinates and then calculating one of the corresponding polar coordinates that indicates the magnitude of deviation from the intersection of the original dimensions. In Pavlovian terms, this derived variable should indicate a *predisposition* toward the concentration or irradiation of cortical activity, but for convenience it will hereafter be referred to as an index of concentration-irradiation.

The analysis yielded four factors, and three of these correspond to those normally associated with the WAIS. Although the EPQ E-scale was not included in this analysis, recent findings leave little doubt that the Verbal and Performance factors are related to introversion-extraversion and hence to the overall strength dimension discussed in the last section (Robinson, 1985, 1986a). The third WAIS factor, described as a Memory or Attention–Concentration factor, was loaded most highly, to the extent of .80, by the EEG concentration–irradiation index. The four highest loading WAIS subtests were Digit Span, Digit Symbol, Arithmetic, and Information, in that order. Needless to add, this psychological manifestation of concentration-irradiation has exactly the character suggested by Pavlovian theory and by the selective character of background cortical activity attributed to the DTPS. More specifically, the less diffuse and better defined patterns of background cortical activity, associated with greater concentration, would limit the content of consciousness and allow better resolution of the cortical representation, and hence perception, of specific stimuli (Mountcastle, 1980). Reduced *interference* and better resolution of the denotative representation of stimuli would be expected to favor short-term recall and the manipulation of *concrete* sensory inputs, albeit with special symbolic significance. By the same token, irradiation would impair short-term recall and *working memory*. It is also worth pointing out that concentration would not favor long-term recall because areas of the cortex not related to the denotative representation of current stimulus inputs would be less likely to contribute to the content of consciousness.

The fourth factor was loaded substantially by two of the WAIS performance subtests and by the EFT. It was also loaded by the P scale and, negatively, by the L scale of the EPQ. The L scale provided the highest loading. These last two loadings are not difficult to explain because individuals scoring high on P and low on L have the kind of personality traits that Witkin, Oltman, Raskin, and Karp (1971) considered a manifestation of the differentiated psychological functioning indicated by the high EFT scores. Although one of the reasons for selecting the EFT for hypothesis testing was the expectation that concentration-irradiation might relate to Witkin's concept of differentiation, the very high loading of *V* on the Attention–Concentration factor described previously suggested that the fourth factor, with a lower loading of V, could not be regarded as a primary manifestation of concentration-irradiation. In fact, the overall pattern of results could not be satisfactorily related to Pavlovian theory without reference to *mobility*. This additional concept of Pavlov's embraces the attributes of the fourth factor and suggests how it relates to concentration-irradiation while remaining distinct from the Attention–Concentration factor.

THE NEURAL BASES OF PSYCHOTICISM AND COGNITIVE STYLE

Teplov (1964, pp. 73–94) discusses the concept of mobility at length, and it is evident from his comments that it has to do with that aspect of nervous system function that relates to the formation of stereotypes. As to the nature of a stereotype, it is clear from Pavlov's works and from Teplov's discussion of mobility that it is believed to be a *system of conditioned connections that is elaborated in the nervous system by experience*. Animals with less extensive systems of conditioned connections responded more quickly to alteration of the significance of a specific stimulus because they were less influenced by context. Such animals were considered to have greater mobility than those forming more extensive systems of conditioned connections and, therefore, tended to be more influenced by context. That is to say, many features of the experimental context became conditioned stimuli, albeit inadvertently, in addition to the specific stimulus manipulated by the experimenter.

Thus mobility, in common with Witkin's concepts of field-independence and differentiation, is manifest as the "ability to overcome an embedding context" (Witkin *et al.*, 1971) and may, therefore, be associated with the fourth factor described earlier. As a result, new insights are provided concerning the nature of this factor, and principally it can be argued that it reflects differences in the *structural* changes produced in the nervous system by experience. In Pavlovian terms, these differences correspond to the formation of *more or less extensive* systems of conditioned connections. In effect, behavior at the low mobility pole is dominated by the generalization of CRs, whereas behavior at the high mobility pole is dominated by the differentiation of CRs. Because, in Pavlovian theory, irradiation is associated with the generalization of CRs, it must necessarily result in lesser mobility. Similarly, concentration is associated with the differentiation of CRs and must result in greater mobility. In this way, the fundamental neurophysiological differences associated with the phenomenon of concentration-irradiation, and indexed by V, may influence the manner in which experience is represented in the neural substrate that underlies the perceptual and conceptual matrix of each individual. This, of course, is in addition to the more immediate functional consequences that give rise to the WAIS Attention–Concentration factor.

One problem that arises with respect to this conception of mobility is that it would be expected to correlate highly with concentration-irradiation, yet the respective factors are uncorrelated. However, because mobility has been associated with the elaboration of more or less extensive systems of conditioned connections it can be suggested that high mobility must be a function of youth in association with the tendency toward concentration, whereas age-related experience and the resultant elaboration of conditioned connections will result in low mobility irrespective of differences in concentration-irradiation. In this way, mobility can be related to concentration-irradiation but yet emerge as an independent factor. Findings that bear on the relationship between these two factors are discussed in detail by Robinson (1983b, 1985, 1986a).

Having drawn additional parallels between Robinson's (1982a, 1982b) findings and Pavlovian theory as well as tracing out the interrelation of different concepts and putting some flesh on the bare bones of Pavlov's formulation, it is fitting that this part of the chapter should end with one of the rare statements concerning the interrelation of Pavlov's four major concepts concerning brain function. According to Teplov (1964):

> At one of the "Wednesdays," Pavlov observed that "concentration is to be understood as a result or product of strength". . . . Secondly, concentration is frequently regarded as an effect of equilibrium between the opposing processes. Thirdly, and finally, "concentration in time" is indissolubly connected with certain aspects of mobility. . . . In the phenomenon of concentration, all three basic properties of the nervous processes come together, as it were, at a point of focus. (p. 120)

In the next part of this account, these Pavlovian concepts are reformulated in terms of systems theory. This reformulation embraces new and more precise systems theory definitions for the contemporary concept of "arousability."

PAVLOVIAN CONCEPTS, SYSTEMS THEORY, AND AROUSABILITY

Up to this point, the analytically determined EEG parameters have necessarily been discussed with special reference to the concepts and terminology employed by Pavlov. However, the psychologically relevant dimension defined as running from large values of both constants to small values of both constants may also be conceived as relating to differences in arousability that are due to intrinsic differences in the sensitivity or reactivity of DTS neurons. Moreover, examination of Equation 1 shows that this dimension can be defined in terms of differences in DTS natural frequency. What this means is that it is now possible to define a sensitivity aspect of arousability in terms of a parameter that has a precise meaning in systems theory (Robinson, 1983a). One particularly relevant insight provided by systems theory is that natural frequency alone will not tell us all there is to know about the dynamic character or arousability of the DTS. We must also refer to the damping ratio parameter.

Equation 2 shows that, in general, damping ratio is determined by the values of all three analytically determined constants. That is, it is determined by the values of R, L and C. However, in the present context, it transpires that damping ratio is empirically related to the index of concentration-irradiation earlier represented by the symbol V. Moreover, this relationship is mediated by the constant R, rather than by L and C. This is particularly significant because the constant R can be associated with differences in the degree of synergistic activity that would result from the concentration–irradiation differences described by Pavlov. In this way, the second psychologically relevant dimension can also be associated with arousability. Here again, a precise systems theory definition is possible. Equally important, reference to damping ratio as well as to natural frequency provides a comprehensive description of DTS arousability.

In the following pages, a model will be outlined that embraces explanatory mechanisms that are conceived as providing the causal link between the sensitivity and synergism arousability dimensions and their psychological correlates. At the same time, it will be emphasized that distinct psychological types are determined as a result of the way in which the two arousability dimensions relate to each other. Psychological profiles of these types will be described.

AN INTEGRATED NEUROPSYCHOLOGICAL MODEL

The arousability dimensions described previously are conceived as having specific psychological correlates as well as having some correlates in common. It is suggested that common correlates exist because the arousability dimensions do both contribute to *overall* DTS arousability and to the resultant degree of BSRF (brain-stem reticular formation) inhibition. Hypothetical mechanisms that mediate the common correlates will be described before reference is made to mechanisms thought to mediate specific correlates.

First, it can be suggested that a chronically high level of DTS activity would enhance the functional effectiveness of neural connections that link the neural representations of stimuli. In this way, greater arousability would result in better associative learning. Second, individual differences in the degree of BSRF inhibition would influence the ability of this system to maintain the background cortical activation necessary for perception to occur. If it is assumed that DTS neurons are differentially influenced by learning or experience, then all BSRF neurons would not be inhibited equally. A logical consequence is that greater intrinsically determined DTS arousability and hence greater overall BSRF inhibition would narrow the span of attention. Third, it is noted that the BSRF is much involved in the acquisition and execution of complex automatic motor sequences. Thus differences in the degree of BSRF inhibition would influence execution of automatic involuntary responses as well as the ability to learn the complex motor sequences that underlie skilled performance.

In combination, it is suggested that the mechanisms described previously determine the fundamental differences between introverts and extraverts. At the same time, the proposed model reasserts Eysenck's claim that introversion-extraversion is determined fundamentally by thalamocortical arousability and by resultant inhibition of the BSRF (Eysenck, 1967). As we shall see, it is particularly significant that the motor differences attributed to differences in the degree of BSRF inhibition can easily be related to *both* the sociability and impulsivity traits embraced by measures of introversion-extraversion within the Eysenckian system of personality description (Eysenck & Eysenck, 1963).

Again referring to the neural mechanisms described previously, it is noteworthy that Jung (1923) gave great emphasis to the internal and external cognitive orientations signified by the terms *introvert* and *extravert*. This important distinction can be accounted for by the proposed model. For example, the introverted cognitive orientation would result from greater selective blocking of stimulus inputs in combination with enhanced associative learning. Together these attributes would determine that thalamocortical activity and conscious experience is more related to the imagery of associations than to representation of the immediate environment. This linking of introversion-extraversion with cognitive differences has been strongly reinforced by findings that demonstrate that introverts and extraverts have different WAIS profiles (Robinson, 1985, 1986a).

Up to this point, attention has been focused on effects that can be attributed to overall DTS arousability. Now it is appropriate to consider the mediation of psychological differences that are uniquely determined by one or other of the two arousability dimensions.

First, it is known that the intralaminar nuclei of the thalamus constitute the final terminus for the paleospinothalamic pathway for pain.
Because these nuclei form part of the DTS, it can be suggested that
neurophysiological sensitivity of the DTS is directly related to psychological sensitivity. In this way, the sensitivity dimension of arousability
can be related to anxiety and neuroticism, but the full expression of
these traits is thought to be dependent on better associative learning and
better generalization learning. The former has already been associated
with high overall DTS arousability, and momentarily it will be suggested
that the latter relates to high levels of synergistic activity.

The synergism dimension of arousability has been uniquely associated with the tendency of thalamocortical activity to spread laterally. In
the earlier part of this account, it was suggested that high synergism or
irradiation results in poor primary memory and better generalization
learning.[1] The converse would apply in the case of low synergism or
concentration. By virtue of poor generalization learning, low synergism
is especially associated with poor socialization and psychopathic tendency, and here again the converse would apply. With reference to the
Eysenckian system of personality description, low synergism is also
related to high P scores.

At this point it has become apparent that, although overall DTS
arousability can be linked to introversion-extraversion, the sensitivity
and synergism aspects of arousability can be associated with neuroticism and psychoticism, respectively. However, as indicated earlier, the
two arousability dimensions are known to relate to each other in a particular fashion. This interaction has an important bearing on the expression of personality traits and on the two major issues that have
dominated the field of personality description (Robinson, 1986b).

It will be recalled that, consistent with Pavlovian theory, the results
reviewed earlier indicate that less synergistic activity, or concentration,

---

[1]Where reference is made to generalization learning it should be understood as inductive
in character, with general laws inferred from particular instances. It is suggested that this
kind of generalization learning relates to what James (1961) referred to as association by
contiguity and that it allows a more integrated holistic conception of the world, as it is
directly experienced. More reactivity of cortical neurons and more irradiation of cortical
activity are both thought to facilitate the development of connections between concurrently active neuron pools. This, in turn, is conceived as the mechanism of greater
psychological integration and stronger association by contiguity. In contrast, less reactivity and less irradiation allows more differentiation of the neural representation of
experience. This is thought to facilitate what James referred to as association by similarity.
The reasoning here is that where the neural representation of experience is too tightly
bound together, it is difficult to abstract those features that are similar across situations
and across experiences. Following James, association by similarity is thought to favor a
cognitive style that is analytical and deductive in character.

occurs at the midpoint of the sensitivity dimension. More synergism occurs at both ends of the sensitivity continuum. These three points of coincidence yield three distinctive combinations of psychological manifestations or psychological types. The first and most distinct type can be attributed to the coincidence of high sensitivity and high synergism. The psychological attributes of this type have already been outlined in some detail. For present purposes, it will suffice to state that such individuals can be described most succinctly as neurotic introverts. It is particularly noteworthy that the coincidence of high sensitivity and high synergism can account for the psychometric coincidence of high neuroticism and introversion that has long bedeviled attempts to fully separate these dimensions (Robinson, 1986b).

The two remaining psychological types are extraverted by virtue of less overall DTS arousability. However, they differ in a way that relates to the relative influence of the sensitivity and synergism dimensions. One type derives from the coincidence of low sensitivity and high synergism. In this case also, a detailed profile can be constructed by reference to the earlier discussion. Here it is only necessary to point out that lower overall arousability determines extraversion and low sensitivity determines low neuroticism. There is, therefore, a contrast with the neurotic introvert on the dimension of sociability that has been defined in terms of a negative correlation between extraversion and neuroticism (Eysenck & Eysenck, 1963). It will be recalled that there is indeed a high correlation between this sociability dimension and the sensitivity aspect of DTS arousability (Robinson, 1982a).

The second extraverted type relates to the coincidence of moderate sensitivity and low synergism. This combination may determine lowest overall DTS arousability and thus a somewhat more pronounced expression of the purely extravert traits described earlier. However, the greatest distinction between this profile and the other two must relate to the traits especially linked to low synergism. It has already been noted that the poor generalization learning associated with low synergism relates to a psychopathic tendency. However, in the present context it is important to point out that poor generalization learning would have a more specific result. Poor generalization learning would result in less behavioral restraint or greater impulsivity. When it is recalled that this type may also have the lowest overall arousability, and, therefore, the least inhibition of BSRF motor systems, it is clear that the particular trait of impulsivity would be greatly accentuated. Thus the two extraverted types can be distinguished in terms of sociability and impulsivity. This feature of the model is particularly significant because it is possible to resolve the long-standing debate among psychometricians concerning the propriety of combining sociability and impulsivity traits to form an introversion–extraversion dimension (Robinson, 1986b). Apart from other considerations, the known interaction of the two arousability dimensions does determine distinct traits of sociability and impulsivity. However, these traits do both relate to a broader dimension of introversion-extraversion in the manner suggested by the Eysencks (Eysenck & Eysenck, 1963; Robinson, 1986b).

It remains to point out that the three profiles described previously are thought to be most manifest in young adult subjects. It will be recalled from the earlier discussion that, irrespective of intrinsic properties of the DTS, greater neural integration and generalization learning is considered a function of age and experience. This means that, with aging, there should be a shift away from those psychological attributes associated with low synergism toward those associated with high synergism. This hypothesis is supported by the results of two studies (Robinson, 1985, 1986a), and it is consistent with the reduction of psychoticism scores that occurs in older subject groups (Eysenck & Eysenck, 1975). The data provided by Eysenck and Eysenck also reveal that neuroticism and extraversion scores are lower in older subject groups. The most obvious explanation for lower neuroticism scores would be that, consistent with a general deterioration of nervous tissue, there is an age-related reduction in the sensitivity or reactivity of thalamocortical neurons. All else being equal, reduced sensitivity would reduce overall DTS arousability, but it can be argued that this would be compensated by more synergistic activity associated with greater age-related neural integration. This shift in the relative influence of sensitivity and synergism would not necessarily influence overall DTS arousability and hence does not provide an explanation for lower extraversion scores in older subject groups. However, it will be recalled that greater BSRF inhibition is considered an important determinant of extraversion. Like neural integration, such inhibition is conceived to be a function of learning as well as to relate to the intrinsic properties of the DTS. Thus it can be argued that a learning or experience-related increase in BSRF inhibition serves to reduce extraversion scores in older individuals. In general, it is suggested that aging and the cumulative effect of learning tends to facilitate the emergence of a fourth distinctive psychological profile. Within the Eysenckian system, this profile would correspond to that of the non-neurotic introvert, but low psychoticism scores and high lie scores would also be characteristic. Reference back to the material discussed earlier will suggest other attributes that can be related to this profile. In passing, it is also noted that the four profiles that have been described bear some resemblance to those associated with the classical sanguine, melancholic, choleric, and phlegmatic temperaments.

CONCLUSION

The most distinctive combinations of DTS-related motor, emotional, and cognitive attributes have been associated with the coincidence of two distinct continua of DTS arousability. Eysenck's dimensions of personality map onto these points of coincidence in a remarkably unambiguous fashion. Although the detail has not been elaborated here, the theoretical developments that have been suggested relate meaningfully to learning, and they have considerable relevance for those interested in perception, attention, and memory. With respect to individual differences, they embrace the concept of cognitive style and relate to intelligence. There are also developmental implications and, what is most important, hypotheses may be generated concerning DTS function and psychopathology. Notably, the syndromes associated with different diagnostic categories include motor, emotional, and cognitive symptoms that can be predicted for extreme modes of DTS function. In particular, it can be suggested that Freud's inductive thinking led him to identify the pathologically relevant combinations of DTS-related attributes as superego dominance and id dominance.

REFERENCES

Eysenck, H. J. *The structure of personality*. London: Methuen, 1958.

Eysenck, H. J. *The biological basis of personality*. Springfield, Il.: Charles C Thomas, 1967.

Eysenck, H. J., & Eysenck, S. B. G. *Manual of the Eysenck Personality Questionnaire*. London: Hodder & Stoughton, 1976.

Eysenck, S. B. G., & Eysenck, H. J. On the dual nature of extraversion. *British Journal of Social and Clinical Psychology*, 1963, *2*, 46–55.

Gray, J. A. *Pavlov*. London: Fontana, 1979.

James, W. *Psychology* (G. Allport, Ed.). New York: Harper & Row, 1961.

Jung, C. G. *Psychological types* (H. G. Baynes, Trans.). New York: Harcourt & Brace, 1923.

Mackintosh, N. J. *The psychology of animal learning*. New York: Academic Press, 1974.

Magoun, H. W. Electrophysiology of learning. *Annals of the New York Academy of Sciences*, 1961, *92*, 813–1198.

Magoun, H. W. *The waking brain* (2nd ed.). Springfield, Il.: Charles C Thomas, 1963.

Mountcastle, V. B. Sleep, wakefulness and the conscious state. In V. B. Mountcastle (Ed.), *Medical physiology* (14th ed.). St. Louis: Mosby, 1980.

Pavlov, I. P. *Conditioned reflexes* (G. V. Anrep, Trans.). London: Oxford University Press, 1927.

Pavlov, I. P. *Lectures on conditioned reflexes* (Vol. 2) (W. H. Gantt, Trans.). New York: International, 1941.

Pavlov, I. P. *Selected Works*. (S. Belsky, Trans.). Moscow: Foreign Languages Publishing House, 1955.

Robinson, D. L. Properties of the diffuse thalamocortical system and human personality: A direct test of Pavlovian/Eysenckian theory. *Personality and Individual Differences*, 1982, 3, 1–16. (a)

Robinson, D. L. Properties of the diffuse thalamocortical system, human intelligence and differentiated vs. integrated modes of learning. *Personality and Individual Differences*, 1982, 3, 393–405. (b)

Robinson, D. L. An analysis of human EEG responses in the alpha range of frequencies. *International Journal of Neuroscience*, 1983, 22, 81–98. (a)

Robinson, D. L. Structure of Witkin's Embedded Figures Test. *Perceptual and Motor Skills*, 1983, 57, 119–125. (b)

Robinson, D. L. How personality relates to intelligence test performance: Implications for a theory of intelligence, ageing research and personality assessment. *Personality and Individual Differences*, 1985, 6, 203–216.

Robinson, D. L. The Wechsler Adult Intelligence Scale and Personality Assessment: Towards a biologically based theory of intelligence and cognition. *Personality and Individual Differences*, 1986, 7, 153–159. (a)

Robinson, D. L. On the biological determination of personality structure. *Personality and Individual Differences*, 1986, 7, 435–438. (b)

Samuels, I. Reticular mechanisms and behaviour. *Psychological Bulletin*, 1959, 56, 1–25.

Teplov, B. M. Problems in the study of general types of higher nervous activity, in man and animals. In J. A. Gray (Ed.), *Pavlov's typology*. London: Pergamon Press, 1964.

Witkin, H. A., Oltman, P. K., Raskin, E., & Karp, S. *A manual for the Embedded Figures Tests*. Palo Alto: Consulting Psychologists Press, 1971.

CHAPTER 9

Basic Properties of the Nervous System and Arousal Model in the Light of Current Neuropsychophysiology

LUCIANO MECACCI

THE NOTION OF BASIC PROPERTIES

To approach the question of the basic properties of the nervous system and their relevance to current neurophysiology and psychophysiology, a preliminary reference to the notion of the "conceptual nervous system" is required. According o the interpretation formulated by Skinner (1938), Pavlov gave a "conceptual" description of the brain functions inferred from behavior, instead of a description founded on direct investigation of these functions. Indeed, Pavlov developed the theory of higher nervous activity through a long and insightful series of behavioral experiments, without trying to directly study the nervous activity involved in the dynamics of the conditioned reflex. This meant a clear rejection of contemporary physiological and neurological methods, like the ablations of brain tissue or electrophysiological recordings. However, that refusal was not simply a question of methodological choice. Pavlov maintained that the complexity of the nervous activity involved

LUCIANO MECACCI • Department of Psychology, 8 Via degli Apuli, 00185 Rome, Italy.

in behavior called for more appropriate methods than those used in brain research at that time. For a molecular investigation of single nervous units, current neurophysiological methods might be suitable. For the investigation of the brain in its behavioral functions, another methodology would be needed to meet such a complexity. The experiment had to be designed in order to exhibit the integrated activity of the brain during the dynamics of the conditioned reflex, and, correspondingly, an integrated behavioral process, just like the conditioned reflex, had to be investigated, rather than its single fragments. Needless to say, the Pavlovian approach implied a new terminology to illustrate the integrated brain dynamics that had not been previously investigated by other neurophysiologists. It is known that Pavlov used old terms for new concepts (for example, the term *inhibition* had a particular meaning in the Pavlovian theory, that was very different from the current meaning in neurophysiology). Undoubtedly, this renewed terminology often did not do justice to the innovation of Pavlov's concepts. In this sense, the theory of the four types of nervous systems might seem old hat (Hippocrates' four types of temperament) in the new form represented by the physiological framework. However, Pavlov expressed in very clear terms the idea that a theory of higher nervous activity involved in behavior should take into consideration the wide variety of individual differences observed. For this reason, a theory of brain activity at the behavioral level of complexity had to comprehend individual differences and to give a physiological explanation.

The two main aspects of Pavlov's heritage are, in our opinion: first, the idea of an integrative model of brain functions in order to investigate the physiological bases of behavior, an idea strongly opposed to the molecular approach dominant at the end of last century; and second, the strict and complementary link between general and individual characteristics of the physiological bases of behavior (for a further analysis of the Pavlovian theory see Mecacci, 1979).

With respect to these two main aspects of the Pavlovian theory, the following remarks may be made on contemporary neuropsychophysiological research. The notion of a conceptual nervous system was adopted by most of the neuroscientists interested in the physiological bases of behavior. Some psychologists (e.g., Hebb, 1949, 1955; Konorski, 1948, 1967) undertook to enrich the conceptual nervous system by means of the new physiological data on brain activity. Whereas we can still find references to Pavlov in the authors of the 1940s and 1950s, only the notion of a conceptual nervous system has survived in more recent years. Yet the great progress in the neurosciences since the 1960s, thanks to new research techniques, especially in the field of unicellular electrophysiology, has again shifted toward the molecular processes of single units in the brain. Although a deeper knowledge of the molecular activity was gained, the link between integrated brain activity and behavior has again been progressively lost, despite the suggestions made by Pavlov and other physiologists of behavior. The new models of brain activity began to consider only some special functional properties of single units (tone, wave length, orientation processing, etc.), without a sufficient attempt to explain how the psychological functions (like perception) arise from these molecular specializations. A kind of classification, or taxonomy, was proposed of neuronal functions, especially in vision research where there was both a wealth of new data on the functions of single neurons in the visual cortex and a poor heuristic value of the models of visual perception (Maffei & Mecacci, 1983).

The second feature of the Pavlovian theory, that is the link between the general and individual aspects of brain activity, received particular attention by psychologists who were interested in the biological dimension of the brain but were also directly engaged in the study of psychological individual differences. As it is generally known, the most significant example is Eysenck's work devoted to the integration of the Pavlovian concepts into modern neurophysiological data, in the general framework of a biological theory of psychological individual differences and personality (Eysenck, 1967). Also, in the field of clinical neuropsychology, especially in Luria's work on brain-injured patients (Luria, 1973), the problem of an individual organization (and disorganization) of the brain activity was thoroughly considered. Moreover, when the individual differentiation of brain functions are taken into consideration, a new question is opened up regarding the interaction between genetic and sociocultural factors (Mecacci, 1984). In the research trend closer to the Pavlovian theory and particularly devoted to the investigation of the psychological individual differences, it soon became clear that Pavlov's typology should be revised in accordance with both the new data of neurophysiology and the progress of the psychology of personality (Mangan, 1982; Strelau, 1983).

For neurophysiology, particular relevance was assigned to the role of the reticular formation in modulating the activation levels of behavior. The point was classically treated by Gray (1964). Moreover, Nebylitsyn devoted himself to a new formulation of the Pavlovian typology, both by introducing new electrophysiological techniques and by analyzing the conceptual principles of that typology (Nebylitsyn, 1972a). In particular, an important subject was considered by Nebylitsyn (1972b): the general and partial properties of the nervous system. On the one hand, there were the general and unitary neurophysiological dimensions of the brain as a whole; and on the other, the partial properties characterizing the functions of separate cortical regions. Nebylitsyn gave a neuroanatomical basis to this differentiation already introduced by Teplov (1961) at a conceptual level. He wrote that

> up-to-date neuropsychological data are becoming available concerning the functioning of the brain as a single, unified system, but one which is at the same time strictly differentiated, with a clear-cut division of functions. (Nebylitsyn, 1972b, p. 402)

In accordance with the brain functional organization proposed by Luria (1973), Nebylitsyn distinguished the role of the anterior regions of the brain and the role of the posterior regions; the two regions are anatomically divided by the central sulcus. The anterior regions (frontal lobes) have the functions of programming and regulating behavior and are strictly connected with subcortical regions involved in the "tone" (activation levels) of behavior, emotions, and motivation. Indeed an integrated behavioral act requires an "energy level" (according to Strelau's terminology) and a control system to be efficiently produced and developed. Brain structures—like the reticular formation, subcortical regions, and frontal lobes—would be directly involved in the production and modulation of behavior. For this function also the endocrine and autonomic nervous system should be considered (Strelau, 1972). Individual differences in the properties of this set of brain structures would be at the basis of the general individual differences and would correspond to the so-called general properties. In this set,

> the processes of general control over actions and states of the organism take place, and it is its structures that carry out the synthesis of integral, adaptive, and in Man, reasonable and creative behaviour as an indispensable attribute of *personality*. (Nebylitsyn, 1972b, p. 411)

In the posterior regions of the brain, the main function is the processing of the different modalities of information, multimodal integration, and memory. Individual differences may occur from the specific sensory modalities of information processed in these brain regions and probably from the other stages or levels of information processing, like the integration of multimodal information and memory. Differences in the functional properties of these structures would correspond to the partial properties of the nervous system and would indicate special individual abilities or skills. In Teplov and Nebylitsyn's opinions, the partial properties are relevant to an individual's ability or skill, but they would not reveal the whole dimension of her or his personality. In the light of current neuropsychophysiological research, the differentiation between the general and partial properties of the nervous system can no longer be stated in a rigid form. Strelau (1972) already remarked that partial differences may be observed in all the functional systems involved in behavior without concerning exclusively specific structures like the sensory areas of the cerebral cortex.

Another point to be examined regards the relationship between the *arousal* dimension (as we will call the phenomenon ascribed to the frontal and subcortical regions of the brain and investigated at the individual level with reference to the general properties of the nervous system) and *cognition* (as we will call the performance in cognitive tasks that in order to be carried out require the special activity of the posterior regions of the brain—an activity that involves a reference to the partial properties of the nervous system in Teplov's and Nebylitsyn's theoretical framework). Arousal and cognition are no longer considered as two separate dimensions of behavior: the "tone" and the "content" of behavior. Investigations in different research areas have shown that arousal and cognition are strictly interconnected, and the form of their relationship leads to relevant individual differentiations. The most notable research trends are in regard to the relationship between the extraversion–introversion dimensions (based on individual differences in the activation levels and arousal) and the performance in cognitive tasks. This kind of investigation has also been concerned with the role of individual differences in the circadian systems, and a more comprehensive relationship between personality (extraversion-introversion), circadian typology (morning vs. evening types; see the later discussion), cognition, and time of day in determining the individual differences has been described (Eysenck, 1982). This relationship may be investigated both with behavioral techniques and procedures, as it has been in most of the research, and with methods directly involving brain activity. In the following section, a review will be presented of the work carried out in our Laboratory of Neuropsychophysiology with respect to the question of the arousal–cognition relationship and its individual differentiation. Generally we have used evoked potentials as a physiological technique to obtain information on the brain processes that may be involved in the individual differences observed both in behavioral tasks and in subjective self-reports.

AROUSAL, COGNITION, AND PERSONALITY

One of the basic properties investigated by Pavlov and thoroughly analyzed, both theoretically and experimentally, by Soviet psychologists was the strength of the nervous system. If one considers, as Pavlov did, the strength (of excitation) as the functional capacity of single neurons and expresses, like Teplov and Nebylitsyn, its main features in terms of response threshold (sensitivity), it clearly appears, from research on the activating functions of the reticular formation, that the neuron sensitivity may be linked to the activation level (for the Pavlovian notion of strength and further developments, see Gray, 1964; Nebylitsyn, 1972a, 1972b; Strelau, 1983). Because the activation level changes throughout the day, according to a circadian sleep–wake cycle (Kleitman, 1963), a change throughout the day in neuron sensitivity may be postulated. Moreover, because the circadian cycles show remarkable individual differences, the diurnal change in sensitivity should be individually differentiated.

Early investigations on human sleep–wake cycles suggested the existence of the so-called morning and evening types, with an intermediate type between the two extremes. The differentiation was particularly evident comparing the early peak in body temperature of morning types and the late peak of the evening types. Also the performance curves over the day show a difference in the peak between the two circadian types. A Morningness–Eveningness Questionnaire (MEQ) was developed by Horne & Östberg (1976) to assess the circadian typology. One of the first results we obtained with the MEQ was a significant difference in the distribution of the MEQ scores when comparing samples that were different for age and profession. Previous studies on this distribution (Horne & Östberg, 1976; Posey & Ford, 1981) had investigated student samples and might not have noticed these differences. In a study of 435 subjects (age: 20–79 years), the distribution of MEQ scores in the different age groups showed a significant shifting toward a morningness typology with age and the disappearance of the eveningness (Mecacci, Zani, Rocchetti, & Lucioli, 1986). The findings agree with literature on elderly subjects, showing in particular an advance in their rising time (Tune, 1969; Webb, 1982). In another study comparing 175 students and 300 white-collar workers of the same age (20–30 years old), a significant difference was found in the MEQ distribution. The workers showed a shift toward the morningness typology, probably due to their regular daily work schedule (Mecacci & Zani, 1983). A stronger effect of profession (or rather of the habitual daily activity) was found in the MEQ distribution of a sample of athletes. In a first study, it was found that athletes practicing disciplines, normally performed at different times of the day, had corresponding MEQ scores (for example, golf players had morningness scores and water polo players had eveningness scores, in accordance with the fact that golf and water polo are usually played in the morning and evening, respectively). This difference was significant only in professional athletes, who were practicing their discipline with a regular schedule, and not in an amateur sample (Rossi, Zani, & Mecacci, 1983). In a further study, limited to top-level professional athletes (87 subjects practicing seven different disciplines), a significant relationship between the discipline and the distribution of MEQ scores was confirmed (Zani, Rossi, Borriello, & Mecacci, 1984). The whole set of data on the distribution of MEQ scores shows that the circadian typology is affected by at least two main factors—age and the daily habitual activity. Even if we have no direct evidence for samples of different ages and professions, we expect an interaction between age and habitual activity in determining the individual circadian typology. In the investigation of the diurnal variation in sensitivity as well as in motor and cognitive performance, one should consider that the diurnal variation differentiates both *within* a single sample (with a normal distribution of the MEQ scores) and *between* samples that are different for age and habitual activity. This point should be carefully taken in account when one plans an experiment at different times of the day. In this case, the circadian typology of the subject sample should be previously assessed.

The studies summarized here were a preliminary step in order to describe the circadian typology of some special samples to be physiologically investigated. Usually, in the case of previous physiological research, only one sample (students) had been considered. In our approach we studied the diurnal variation in sensitivity comparing samples of the same age but who were different in habitual activity. When evoked potentials are recorded over the day, a decrease in amplitude is observed from morning to night. This decrease is faster for the morning subjects than for the evening subjects (Kerkhof, Korving, Willemse, & Rietveld, 1981). We have compared students and top-level athletes, recording their visual-evoked potentials in the morning and in the evening. Athletes were chosen whose disciplines (pentathlon and fencing) might require competition to occur at different times of day. Indeed pentathlon and fencing athletes have an intermediate typology according to their MEQ scores, being neither extreme morning nor evening types (Zani *et al.*, 1984). In the experiment, the subjects had simply to look at a monitor generating checkerboards, and the evoked potentials were recorded. Whereas in the student sample (with an intermediate circadian typology) a decrease in evoked potential amplitude was observed, in the athletes such a decrease was not to be found. It is worth noting that the evoked potential morphology was more constant in athletes than in students over the repeated sessions both in the morning and in the evening (Rossi & Mecacci, 1985). Visual-evoked potentials represent the activity of the visual cortex (a region involved in the partial properties of the nervous types, according to Nebylitsyn's scheme), and their amplitude is an index of the sensitivity of the visual cells. The relationship between visual sensitivity and arousal (in its diurnal variation) turns out to depend on the sample taken into consideration. Whereas a "normal" effect of the diurnal variation in arousal on the sensitivity may be hypothesized for subjects with a "normal" diurnal activity, other patterns should be hypothesized for subjects with a special schedule of diurnal activity. A reorganization of the arousal–sensitivity relationship over the day seems to occur when the motor and cognitive tasks are habitually distributed at different times of the day.

The relationship between arousal and sensitivity becomes more complex if less elementary levels of information processing than the checkerboard processing are considered. We have approached the problem from two different angles. In the first approach, the diurnal variation in the performance for tasks of different complexity was investigated. In the second approach, the task remained very elementary, and it was studied, for reasons given later, when the processing depended on different diurnal variations of the two cerebral hemispheres.

Morning and evening types were compared in a reaction time experiment where the task consisted in judging, as same or different, several pairs of letters. Because the letters might be the same (e.g., AA) both in physical features and in meaning, or different (e.g., Aa) in physical features but not in meaning, or different (e.g., AB) both in physical features and in meaning, the processing might be purely physical or involve a linguistic level. Both circadian types showed a diurnal variation in reaction times; the morning types were faster in the morning, and the evening types were faster in the evening. In both types, the well-known phenomenon of delay in judging words different for linguistic features (Posner, 1978) was confirmed. However, an interaction between the time of day and the level of processing was not found. This result implies that the diurnal variation in arousal affects in a similar way the performance at different levels of information processing (Mecacci & Salmaso, 1985). However, because more complex cognitive tasks seem to require to be performed in the best way at a particular time of day (Folkard & Monk, 1983), a further systematic investigation should be devoted to assess the diurnal variation in cognitive performance in relation to the circadian typology.

In considering the diurnal variation in cognition, a reference to the hemispheric specialization is an obligatory requirement for the following reason. Because one may hypothesize, as, for example, Dimond and Beaumont (1973) did, that the relationship between each hemisphere and arousal is specific, the cognitive processing performed by each hemisphere might be related to a change in activation level throughout the day. The question was recently approached by Zani (1986) in our laboratory, taking into account, as a first step, an elementary kind of information whose processing should be equally represented in the two hemispheres. Visual-evoked potentials were recorded in morning and evening types who looked at a monitor generating gratings of different spatial frequencies. Recording sessions were made in the morning and in the evening. The known pattern of a decrease in the evoked potential amplitudes for the morning types in the evening session was confirmed, whereas the evening types showed a lesser amount of decrease. However a new phenomenon was observed: An asymmetry appeared between the two hemispheres, in the evening and in the morning for the morning and evening types, respectively. At the "best" time of day for each type, the two hemispheres would work in a more integrated fashion leading to a greater efficiency in the cognitive processing. With a behavioral method, like the reaction time measurement used in our experiment described previously, it was only possible to observe the general pattern of the diurnal variation in performance. With a physiological technique, like the evoked potentials recorded in the two hemispheres, the specific pattern of activity of each hemisphere and the hemispheric interaction might be studied. The results might suggest the different roles of each hemisphere, and correspondingly a different strategy, in performing cognitive tasks throughout the day.

An intriguing topic is represented by the role of the hemispheric specialization in the constitution of the *personality* of an individual (Gruzelier & Flor-Henry, 1980). In the context of the research area we have illustrated here, it should be evident that various physiological and psychological phenomena are implied in the relationship between personality and hemispheric specialization. However, they would all have a common point in their relation to individual differences in *arousal*. A recent study has pointed out that the individual differences in circadian typology are related to different personality profiles. The Eysenck Personality Questionnaire and the MEQ were administered to 233 subjects (20–29 years old). Evening subjects tended to have extraversion scores higher than the morning subjects (a phenomenon already described in literature; Horne & Östberg, 1977); moreover, morning types had higher neuroticism scores, and evening types had higher psychoticism scores (Mecacci *et al.*, 1986). Further research should investigate the personality profiles exhibited by the circadian types, in relation to the different diurnal patterns of activation of the two hemispheres and the different psychopathological syndromes that may arise depending on the injured hemisphere. Other investigations should be concerned with the relationship between the personality profiles of the diurnal types and their adjustment to the habitual activity and working schedule during the day. There is evidence that particularly in shift work, morning and evening types have different coping mechanisms (Colquhoun & Folkard, 1978). This phenomenon might be partly related to the different personality profiles of the two circadian types.

CONCLUSION

In respect to the Pavlovian conceptual framework where the basic properties of the nervous system represented a remarkably close link between a general description of brain functions and individual differences in behavior, current research has attempted to give direct evidence of the physiological bases of these properties. The differentiation between general and partial properties and their neuroanatomic-physiological description was a further step. In our opinion, in Nebylitsyn's revision of Pavlovian typology, there remained a rigid distinction between the role of brain structures involved in arousal control (directly concerning the individual personality) and the brain structures involved in information processing. Current research has shown that it is not possible to distinguish rigidly the arousal dimension from the cognitive processes. Beyond a "vertical" organization, where the arousal brain structures represent the basis (and the general modulation) of the cognitive processes, a "horizontal" organization appeared where the two cerebral hemispheres may have different activation patterns. As is known, both hemispheres are active in performing a cognitive task, each one with a special functional role. However, this functional integration and balance may change over the day, and cognitive performance may be affected. According to the habitual activity and the kind of profession, these changes may be an influential factor in the individual coping mechanisms. Forms of psychological maladjustment may arise from an inappropriate correspondence between the diurnal typology, the kind of cognitive task to be performed, and the time of day when the task has to be accomplished.

The individual personality emerges from a set of different (biological, temperamental, and cognitive factors) that are strictly related to each other. Social factors, like the habitual activity and the working schedule, are no less important in characterizing individual psychological differences.

REFERENCES

Colquhoun, P., & Folkard, S. Personality differences in body-temperature rhythm, and their relation to its adjustment to night work. *Ergonomics,* 1978, *21,* 811–817.

Dimond, S. J., & Beaumont, J. G. Differences in the vigilance performance of the right and left hemispheres. *Cortex,* 1973, *9,* 259–265.

Eysenck, H. J. *The biological basis of personality.* Springfield, Il.: Charles C Thomas, 1967.

Eysenck, M. *Attention and arousal: Cognition and performance.* New York: Springer, 1982.

Folkard, S., & Monk, T. H. Chronopsychology: Circadian rhythms and human performance. In A. Gale & J. A. Edwards (Eds.), *Physiological correlates of human behaviour: Attention and performance* (Vol. 2). London: Academic Press, 1983.

Gray, J. A. *Pavlov's typology*. Oxford: Pergamon Press, 1964.

Gruzelier, J. H., & Flor-Henry, P. (Eds.). *Hemisphere asymmetries of functions in psychopathology*. New York: Elsevier, 1980.

Hebb, D. O. *The organization of behavior: A neuropsychological theory*. New York: Wiley, 1949.

Hebb, D. O. Drives and the CNS (conceptual nervous system). *Psychological Review*, 1955, *62*, 243–254.

Horne, J. A., & Östberg, O. A self-assessment questionnaire to determine morningness-eveningness in human circadian rhythms. *International Journal of Chronobiology*, 1976, *4*, 97–110.

Horne, J. A., & Östberg, O. Individual differences in human circadian rhythms. *Biological Psychology*, 1977, *5*, 179–190.

Kerkhof, G. A., Korving, H. J., Willemse-V. D. Geest, H. M. M., & Rietveld, W. J. Diurnal differences between morning-type and evening-type subjects in some indices of central and autonomous nervous activity. In A. Reinberg, N. Vieux, & P. Andlauer (Eds.), *Night and shift work: Biological and social aspects*. Oxford: Pergamon Press, 1981.

Kleitman, N. *Sleep and wakefulness*. Chicago: University of Chicago Press, 1963.

Konorski, J. *Conditioned reflexes and neuron organization*. Cambridge: Cambridge University Press, 1948.

Konorski, J. *Integrative activity of the brain: An interdisciplinary approach*. Chicago: University of Chicago Press, 1967.

Luria, A. R. *The working brain*. Harmondsworth: Penguin, 1973.

Maffei, L., & Mecacci, L. Towards a neurophysiology of visual competence. *Journal of Social & Biological Structures*, 1983, *6*, 45–47.

Mangan, G. L. *The biology of human conduct: East–West models of temperament and personality*. Oxford: Pergamon Press, 1982.

Mecacci, L. *Brain and history: The relationship between neurophysiology and psychology in Soviet Union*. New York: Brunner/Mazel, 1979.

Mecacci, L. Looking for the social and cultural dimension of the human brain. *International Journal of Psychophysiology*, 1984, *1*, 293–299.

Mecacci, L., & Salmaso, D. *Time of day and levels of information processing in morning and evening types*. Roma: Istituto di Psicologia, CNR, 1985.

Mecacci, L., & Zani, A. Morningness–eveningness preferences and sleep–waking diary data of morning and evening types in student and worker samples. *Ergonomics*, 1983, *26*, 1147–1153.

Mecacci, L., Zani, A., Rocchetti, G., & Lucioli, R. The relationship between morningness-eveningness, aging and personality. *Personality and Individual Differences*, 1986, *7*, 911–913.

Nebylitsyn, V. D. *Fundamental properties of the human nervous system*. New York: Plenum Press, 1972. (a)

Nebylitsyn, V. D. The problem of general and partial properties of the nervous system. In V. D. Nebylitsyn & J. A. Gray (Eds.), *Biological bases of individual behavior*. New York: Academic Press, 1972. (b)

Posey, T. B., & Ford, J. A. The morningness–eveningness preference of college students as measured by the Horne–Östberg questionnaire. *International Journal of Chronobiology*, 1981, *7*, 141–144.

Posner, M. I. *Chronometric explorations of mind*. Hillsdale, NJ: Erlbaum, 1978.

Rossi, B., & Mecacci, L. *Visual information processing and time of day in top level athletes*. Roma: Istituto di Psicologia, CNR, 1985.

Rossi, B., Zani, A., & Mecacci, L. Diurnal individual differences and performance levels in some sport activities. *Perceptual and Motor Skills*, 1983, *57*, 27–30.

Skinner, B. F. *The behavior of organisms: An experimental analysis.* New York: Appleton-Century-Crofts, 1938.

Strelau, J. The general and partial nervous system types: Data and theory. In V. D. Nebylitsyn & J. A. Gray (Eds.), *Biological bases of individual behavior.* New York: Academic Press, 1972.

Strelau, J. *Temperament-personality-activity.* London: Academic Press, 1983.

Teplov, B. M. *Problems of individual differences.* Moscow: Akademia Pedagogicheskikh Nauk RSFSR, 1961 (in Russian).

Tune, G. S. The influence of age and temperament on the adult human sleep–wakefulness pattern. *British Journal of Psychology*, 1969, *60*, 431–441.

Webb, W. B. Sleep in older persons: Sleep structures of 50- to 60 years-old men and women. *Journal of Gerontology*, 1982, *37*, 581–586.

Zani, A. Time of day preference, pattern evoked potentials and hemispheric asymmetries: A preliminary statement. *Perceptual and Motor Skills*, 1986, *63*, 413–414.

Zani, A., Rossi, B., Borriello, A., & Mecacci, L. Diurnal interindividual differences in the habitual activity pattern of top level athletes. *Journal of Sport Medicine and Physical Fitness*, 1984, *24*, 307–310.

CHAPTER 10

Reactivity and the Control of Arousal

TATIANA KLONOWICZ

INTRODUCTION

Arousal or activation level is the central concept of many theories of personality and/or temperament (cf. Eysenck, 1967; Gray, 1964, 1981; Strelau, 1983; Zuckerman, 1979). Although Gray—not only wittily but also quite rightly—speaks of arousal theory as "a knight in shining armor . . . its banner bearing a strange device: the inverted U-shaped curve" (Gray, 1981, p. 254), his criticism is addressed not to the theory but against the interpretations that make a too liberal use of this concept.

The main postulates of the arousal or activation theories are too well known to present them here. Instead, I shall turn directly to the conceptualizations that seem most pertinent to the purposes of the present chapter. Hebb's (1961) theory with subsequent modifications put forward by different authors has had perhaps the greatest impact on our thinking in behavioral psychology and the study of individual differences. *Arousal* is here defined as a tonic level that extends from sleep to extreme emotional disorganization. It has been argued, too, that at low levels of arousal an increase in arousal may be rewarding, whereas at much higher levels of arousal a decrease is rewarding. This postulate implies that the process of self-regulation will occur because the orga-

TATIANA KLONOWICZ • Faculty of Psychology, University of Warsaw, Warsaw, Poland. This work has been financed by the Ministry of Science and Higher Education Grant RP. III. 25.

nism will tend to achieve and maintain an optimal level of arousal or activation. Our conclusion is that the optimal level of arousal or activation is the *standard of regulation* sought in every behavior.

Moving into the field of the psychology of individual differences, we find that this general postulate cannot account for the diversity of behaviors that we observe even within our limited range of interests, that is, when examining behavior and environment from the point of view of their nonspecific arousal properties. The generality of the inverted U-shaped curve makes it of little value in understanding systematic interindividual differences in behavior. A second postulate has been introduced to account for these differences, namely that there are stable differences in arousal between people. The regulative theory of temperament (RTT) (Strelau, 1983) explains this phenomenon by differences in stimulation processing coefficients (SPC). The notion of SPC is a direct derivation from the definition of reactivity considered as a basic temperamental feature.

There is considerable support for the claim that reactivity plays a pivotal role in mediating relations between the environmental factors and human respondent and operant behavior. Although it has been argued that the two other temperament dimensions—activity and mobility—partake in stimulation processing (Eliasz, 1981; Klonowicz, 1985; Strelau, 1983), unfortunately we have little to say about their exact role. This is primarily because most work has been done on reactivity, and the findings are therefore more numerous and more reliable here. In addition, however, there is both a theoretical and an empirical corroboration of the concept of reactivity considered as, in some ways, primary in the organization of behavior in that its physiological mechanism serves as a final common path on which the nonspecific stimulation terminates and on which the process of stimulation regulation relies.

Reactivity has been defined as a feature

> which determines a relatively stable intensity (magnitude) of reactions for a given individual . . . crucial of our understanding of reactivity is the fact that it co-determines the sensitivity (sensory and emotional) . . . and the organism's capacity to work. (Strelau, 1983, p. 177)

The two extremes of the reactivity dimension are high reactivity (high sensitivity, low endurance) and low reactivity (low sensitivity, high endurance). The physiological mechanism of reactivity is directly responsible for the stimulation processing: Its "program" either amplifies (high SPC, i.e., high reactivity) or suppresses (low SPC, i.e., low reactivity) the intensity of incoming stimuli. There is strong support, both direct and inferential, for the hypothesis that this mechanism is complex and multilevel (cf. Klonowicz, 1982).

The preceding theoretical assumptions concerning the nature of reactivity have had broad implications, for they have guided our research and permitted us to identify various focuses of the role of reactivity in the regulation of behavior. Research work in this area has largely been directed by two general paradigms defined by the following operations: (a) recording the occurrence, type, and temporal structure of behaviors in subjects with different reactivity levels performing a given task in a laboratory and/or carrying out various activities in a real-life situation; and (b) comparison of the psychophysiological and/or behavioral responses under different reactivity levels. An assessment of the data derived from these paradigms has led us to identify the basic regulatory processes accounted for by reactivity. The aim of this chapter is to attempt a survey of major research findings bearing upon the role of reactivity in the regulation of stimulation. Our discussion will be organized around four problems: (a) reactivity and the resting level of arousal; (b) reactivity and the stimulation impact; (c) reactivity and self-regulation; and (d) reactivity and anticipation. Space will not permit a thorough review of the literature. Rather, selected studies will be used to illustrate different points. For the same reason, no attempt will be made to discuss our data in a broader theoretical context, although a vast amount of interesting literature has emerged in this area. Hopefully, other chapters included in this volume will provide a necessary perspective.

REACTIVITY AND THE RESTING LEVEL OF AROUSAL

To examine this question, I turned to psychophysiological and physiological measures of arousal: EDA nonspecifics, pulmonary ventilation, oxygen consumption, respiratory quotient, and energy consumption (the latter index served to evaluate basic metabolic activity). All measures were taken at rest. As this experiment has been described in detail elsewhere (Klonowicz, in press), I shall turn directly to the main findings, presented in Table 1.

With $Fs \geq 7.831$ ($p < .002$, lower limit), it can be concluded that the level of arousal is considerably higher in high-reactive persons. Thus the experiment confirms that reactivity controls the level of arousal. These results have important implications because they prove our main theoretical assumption as to the nature of the reactivity dimension and its mechanism. It follows that the degree of nonspecific bombardment of the cortex by stimuli depends on the level of reactivity. A sufficiently high level of resting arousal helps toward a better and/or easier detection of stimuli because the cortex has an adequate tonus. The direct

Table 1. Level of Resting Arousal in High- and Low-Reactive
Persons: Mean Scores (x) and Standard Deviations (SD)

	Groups	
Measure	High-reactive	Low-reactive
EDA nonspecifics[a]		
x	27.00	15.00
SD	10.83	6.42
Ventilation (cm^3/min)[b]		
x	5857.00	4542.00
SD	794.25	922.67
Oxygen consumption[b] (ml/min)		
x	237.00	179.00
SD	56.03	47.46
Respiratory quotient[b]		
x	.94	.68
SD	.27	.22
Energy consumption[b]		
x	1.14	.88
SD	.36	.20

[a]$df = 1,28.$
[b]$df = 1,38.$

derivation from this conclusion is that the higher the reactivity, the greater the impact of stimulus intensity and—most probably—the impact of stimulus variability, novelty, and so forth. It should also be considered, however, that given sufficiently high levels of resting arousal and/or stimulus-induced increments in arousal, we are bound to find marked task- and situation-specific differences between low- and high-reactive persons. This issue will be more thoroughly discussed in what follows.

REACTIVITY AND THE IMPACT OF STIMULATION

We have reasoned that the environment serves as one of the principal sources of stimulation determining the level of arousal. Manipulations of the environmental influences should produce the general effect on arousal and, in consequence, on performance. Our general hypothesis is that reactivity accounts for quantitative and, perhaps, qualitative, differences in response to the environmental and/or task conditions that we describe in terms of the arousal potential of stimuli and that range from underload to overload.

The usual procedure for demonstrating the effect of reactivity on functioning under various stimulation conditions consists of two parts: selection of high- and low-reactive groups and a test of performance under various conditions, for example, stress versus no stress, the latter factor being manipulated in terms of anxiety-inducing instructions (Klonowicz, 1973; Strelau & Maciejczyk, 1977) or direct control of the stimulation condition (Klonowicz, 1973, 1984, 1985). Stated differently, we make use of agents that—whatever their specific effects—have a high degree of communality in their general effects: They either increase or reduce arousal and thus produce a shift in a person's position along the activation continuum. The impact of stimulation has been primarily assessed in terms of performance measures. In a number of studies, an additional index has been recorded as well: the cost of adaptation to a given condition.

The costs or aftereffects cover a wide variety of both objective and subjective work and/or environment-induced changes in functioning that—although not belonging to the category of direct task performance measures—originate from the same source. Just like changes in task performance, they are brought about by the real or imagined threat to the balance between demand and capacity. These effects occur either simultaneously with or after the termination of the task and/or environmental stress (cf. Cohen, 1980; Klonowicz, 1973, 1985). The two output measures—task performance and costs—are the means to assess the effort or capacity (cf. Kahnemann, 1973). I am also inclined toward the dynamic interpretation of costs that assumes that the costs originate from the environmental demands, appraisals of, and coping with, these demands, and—as they unfold over time—they affect appraisals of, and coping with, immediate and/or subsequent demands.

Consider, by way of illustration, my earlier experiment (Klonowicz, 1984). The stimulation load was varied in terms of intensity and type of stimulation imposed over the task (proofreading in quiet, white noise and street noise, the two latter conditions being equalized for the intensity of noise). The results are shown in Figure 1.

It can be seen that the two groups—low and high reactives—react very differently. Figure 1 shows the effect of reactivity and stimulation load on the quality of work in three experimental conditions. Quality of work was measured as the proportion of errors (misprints left uncorrected). The reactivity by stimulation interaction effect was significant (F /2,72/ = 14.500, $p < .001$), and the tests for simple effects indicated that low-reactive persons improved their performance as the stimulation load increased, whereas the reverse is observed in high-reactive persons. Moreover, these data show that low reactives apparently benefit from the fact that additional stimulation was imposed over a monoto-

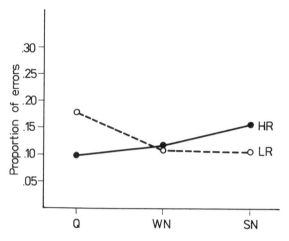

Figure 1. Proportion of errors as a function of reactivity and stimulation. Q: quiet (40–44 dBA); WN: white noise (82 dBA); and SN: street noise (85 dBA with the mode of 82 dBA).

nous task; high reactives were adversely affected by both the intensity of stimulation and its nature: Variable stimulation (street noise) produced more deficits in performance than invariant (white noise) stimulation (t = 2.28, $p < .02$).

The effect of the reactivity by stimulation interaction affects also the magnitude of costs. This issue is documented in the data presented in Figure 2.

The costs were assesed by means of the Activation–Deactivation Adjective Check List (AD ACL; Thayer, 1970). Our present discussion will be focused on two AD ACL scales: High Activation (as a measure of tension and anxiety) and General Deactivation (as a measure of non-specific changes in the level of arousal) that were shown to be the most powerful predictors of annoyance in response to noise (Thayer, 1978). The analyses of variance indicated significant reactivity by stimulation interaction effects on High Activation (F /2,72/ = 6,602, $p < .01$) and General Deactivation (F /2,72/ = 18.106, $p < .001$). Our data show that in high-reactive persons the levels of arousal and of anxiety/tension mount to a severe degree and that street noise induces significantly greater aftereffects than white noise. In low reactives, the level of arousal was significantly higher in quiet than in the two noise conditions (see later discussion), whereas the degree of anxiety/tension remained stable across the three experimental conditions. The covariance between the increase in stimulation load and the changes in both the task perfor-mance (Figure 1) and costs (Figure 2) seems rather remarkable.

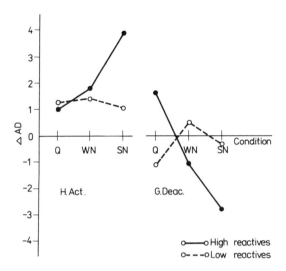

Figure 2. Changes in anxiety/tension (H. Act.) and activation (G. Deac.) as a function of reactivity and stimulation. Q: work in quiet; WN: work in white noise; and SN: work in street noise. Scores consist of changes from pre- to postwork level. The higher the G. Deac. score, the lower the level of activation.

In general, our findings in this area can be summarized as follows: the higher the reactivity, the bigger the changes in performance and the greater the costs with increase in stimulation load. However, a rather drastic reduction of stimulation inputs (e.g., vigilance task, Klonowicz, 1973) is required to produce the postulated reverse relation according to which the lower the reactivity, the bigger the changes with the decrease in stimulation load. It follows that the higher the reactivity, the more vulnerable is the demand/capacity ratio.

REACTIVITY AND SELF-REGULATION

Our previous discussion illustrated what happens when a person has no alternative but to endure a potentially noxious stimulation: overload or underload. A question arises how an individual can compensate for deficits from the inadequate environmental or task demands and his or her own capacity as determined by the level of reactivity. Stated otherwise, we ask here whether there are any means to control the stimulation in order to maintain the optimal level of stimulation and arousal. Eliasz (1981) distinguishes two types of self-regulation: self-regulation that occurs at the level of the physiological mechanism of reactivity and self-regulation at the behavioral level. The former relies on the modification of stimulation and can be further subdivided into transient and stable alternation in the mode of operation of the mechanism for stimulation processing. The empirical evidence concerning this issue is scarce, and the problem is debatable (cf. Strelau, 1983). Eliasz (1981) has demonstrated that prolonged exposure to environmental stimulation can change the program for stimulation processing: The level of reactivity in urban dwellers exposed to sociospatial density and noise is significantly lower than in their counterparts from the less dense and calm city areas. The transient changes are the task- or environment-induced sensory threshold shifts, that is, the functional sensitization/desensitization. This issue is documented with the data presented in Figure 2. Under the monotonous condition (work in quiet), low reactives have a higher level of arousal than under the two noise conditions. Most probably, they trigger some internal mechanisms instrumental in arousal and vigilance increase (similar phenomena have been demonstrated in the studies on sensory deprivation).

The possibility of behavioral control of stimulation has been studied more extensively, and several modes of control have been found. In its most elementary form, the behavioral control of stimulation is manifested by direct actions, for example, the "switch-on" and "switch-off" behaviors. Matysiak (1979) has reported that given a choice, deprived rats select a more stimulating environment (significantly more pressings of the "switch-on" key), whereas the reverse is true for overstimulated rats. The intensity of either of these two types of behavior is directly related to the need for stimulation that depends on reactivity: high-need-for-stimulation (or low-reactive) rats display more "on" behaviors than low-need-for-stimulation (or high-reactive) rats (cf. Klonowicz, 1982).

More elaborated modes of stimulation control rely on the use of the individually specific mode of performance (the so-called individual style of action), adjustment of behavior to the environmental and/or individual demands, and, finally, on the development of stable preferences for activities and environments that affect the development of personality. It is worth noting that although the modification of stimulation involves first and foremost the mechanism of reactivity, behavioral control of stimulation is apparently much more complex. Our recent studies show that an additional factor—experience with street noise—makes people disregard the task-irrelevant stimulation and thus increases the working capacity (Klonowicz, 1985).

Our next discussion will be focused on the role of reactivity in active coping with, and control of, stimulation. It will be useful to organize the presentation in terms of whether behavioral self-regulation is achieved by means of the individual style of action, adjustment of activity, and the development of personality traits.

INDIVIDUAL STYLE OF ACTION

The concept of the individual style of action (Strelau, 1983) emphasizes two facts: (a) There are individual differences in performing an action that are co-determined by reactivity, and (b) this individually specific mode of action has no effect on the excellence of performance. The hypotheses advanced by Strelau refer to the role of reactivity in the organization of goal-directed behavior and, in particular, in task performance. A detailed review of these problems is not attempted here.

Although the studies were originally concerned with various aspects of the individual style of action (see Strelau, 1983), for present purposes I shall concern myself only with the functional structure of performance; the main reason for this is that the results on gross parameters of behavior (its temporal structure and homogeneity/heterogeneity) are—at best—equivocal (Klonowicz, 1985), fortunately, the data on the functional structure of behavior (differentiation between the auxiliary and basic operations) are not. According to Strelau, in low reactives the auxiliary operations are in proportion with the basic ones, or the latter prevail over the former, whereas in high reactives this ratio is reversed. In the light of what has just been said about the role of reactivity in response to stimulation, the phychological significance of the postulated differences is quite clear: Auxiliary operations safeguard the course of performance, they protect from stress and help to avoid tensions.

The main research findings in this area can be summarized as follows.

1. Among the most reliable psychological phenomena that can be demonstrated both in the laboratory as well as in natural settings (Klonowicz, 1985; Strelau, 1983) is that in high-reactive persons, the so-called basic operations (which lead to the goal) are "padded" with auxiliary operations (which establish conditions of, and safeguard the target activity) and that the latter prevail over the former.

2. Individual differences in reactivity do not affect the excellence of the outcome, but even in this case, work may exact a bigger toll from high-reactive persons (Klonowicz, 1985).

3. The only statement that can be made with confidence about the low-reactives' style of action is that they make fewer attempts at

control and planning. Stated differently, it seems that—as predicted by Strelau—no distinct style of action can be associated
with the low level of reactivity.

ADJUSTMENT OF ACTIVITY

In the previous section, the main emphasis was on the impact of
stimulation supplied by the environment. Another important source of
stimulation is the individual's own behavior. According to our hypothesis, the preferences for, and frequency of, activities of a different stimulating value depend on the level of reactivity. Strelau's students,
Danielak and Popielarska, have corroborated this hypothesis in their
studies on the proportion of low- and high-reactive persons engaged in
more or less threatening sport and professional activities (see Strelau,
1983). Also of direct relevance here is Eliasz's 1981 study, for it both
substantiates the previously advanced general hypothesis and provides
new insights. Eliasz predicted that high-reactive persons differ from
low-reactive ones in that they have smaller capacity for behavioral regulation of stimulation according to the physical aspects of their environment. Several dependent variables associated with adolescents' daily
activities were assessed in groups from different (stimulating vs. calm)
environments. The data corroborate the hypothesis. Activity, which is a
source of stimulation, depends on both the physical aspects of environment and on reactivity. In a less stimulating environment, high reactives
more frequently engage in invigorating activities. The higher the stimulative value of the environment, the higher the proportion of invigorating activities in low reactives who seem to "tune" into the environment.
Eliasz concludes that the mechanism of reactivity determines both the
capacity for adequate stimulation regulation as well as the regulative
principle (positive vs. negative feedback).

REACTIVITY AND THE DEVELOPMENT OF PERSONALITY

Before presenting the studies on the relation of reactivity to personality dimensions, I would like to briefly draw attention to one theoretical
issue. The RTT differentiates between temperament and personality,
that is, between the formal and content features of behavior. However,
from the previously presented considerations, it follows that there is a
basic affinity between the RTT and those theories of personality that—
having abandoned the notion of temperament—are concerned with the
biological bases of personality. For one, all these theories make direct or
indirect claim to be concerned with individual differences in arousal.

Second, as argued by Strelau (1983), the reactivity-dependent stable preferences for activities and environments affect the development of personality.

The research in this area (see Strelau, 1983) yielded such illustrative findings as (a) conformity is associated with high reactivity; (b) the discrepancy between the real self and ideal self is smaller in high reactives; (c) strong Machiavellian tendencies are associated with low reactivity, whereas weak Machiavellian tendencies are related to high reactivity; and (d) a realistic level of aspiration is associated with low reactivity, whereas high reactives display either high or low levels of aspiration.

When analyzed from the point of view of their stimulative value, the four personality traits reveal a common "nucleus": Conformity helps to avoid tension; a good fit between the real self and ideal self serves to reduce emotional tension; weak Machiavellianism comprises, among other characteristics, susceptibility to social influence, whereas unrealistic aspiration helps to avoid strong emotional involvement and—perhaps not unlike the three other personality dimensions—responsibility that may result in having too much to do. The opposite personality traits would promote a more active behavior. Thus we can see that there is a correspondence between the personality traits that make a person engage in a situation of a given stimulative value and the physiological mechanism of reactivity that is directly responsible for stimulation-intensity processing and indirectly involved in the formation of those personality dimensions that would regulate the behavior according to the physiological capacity of an organism, that is, according to its stimulation-processing capacity. However, things are not always as simple as that and a conflict between the two regulators of behavior—personality and temperament—does occur. This issue is currently under investigation (e.g., Eliasz & Wrześniewski, 1986).

OVERVIEW

Before closing this section, I would like to consider briefly how the reported studies may be accomodated within the arousal framework. Essentially, what these findings tell us is that it is possible to distinguish behaviors that are aimed at increasing or decreasing stimulation supply. Thus it seems reasonable to use the notion of arousal as an explanatory construct. The aforementioned results make it evident that the mechanism of reactivity is either directly or indirectly involved in control of stimulation. The finding of greatest generality is that the control of stimulation serves the purposes of self-regulation and that individual differences in the modes of stimulation control are related to the level of reactivity.

REACTIVITY AND ANTICIPATION

This regulatory role of reactivity came into view only very recently (Klonowicz, in press). A reanalysis of data collected in earlier studies revealed an interesting peculiarity: High- and low-reactive persons differ not only with respect to the level of arousal but also with respect to the emotional tone of arousal that is negatively biased in high reactives. At first glance, it may seem that the negative emotional tone is the product of aversion to the discrepancy between the current and the optimal levels of arousal. The attractive simplicity of this explanation conceals a vital issue. For one, it does not identify the source of the discrepancy. Second, it precludes the possibility of self-regulation—a position that we can hardly accept having just demonstrated that the control of stimulation does take place. Taking into account the fact that the data on emotional tone of arousal were collected before the experimental manipulation and before the subjects were given detailed information on the experiment, another explanation seems more plausible here, namely that the differentiation of emotional tone is the product of specific person–environment transactions associated with uncertainty and that it may be interpreted in terms of anticipation (cf. Folkman, Schaefer, & Lazarus, 1979). This hypothesis has been tested both directly and indirectly. A direct test (Klonowicz, in press) used the manipulation of information: The subjects filled in Spielberger's STAI state forms either before or after being presented with detailed information on the subsequent experimental procedure. The results are shown in Figure 3.

It is immediately evident that the level of state anxiety depends on the knowledge (F /1,76/ = 13.658, p < .001). Although anxiety decreases with the decrease in uncertainty in both (high and low reactive) groups, the effect of information is significant for high reactives (F = 18.343, p < .001) and clearly insignificant for low reactives (F < 1).

A tentative explanation is that the results reflect high-reactive persons' preparedness for the worst: Potential stress is interpreted by them in terms of harm that may result from a small number of resources for coping. In keeping with the previously proposed dynamic interpretation of costs, we attempt now to evaluate the effect of these primary appraisals on task performance.

CONCLUDING OBSERVATIONS

At the beginning of this chapter, I identified a source of motivation that impels an organism to attend to stimuli irrespective of their "cue" value or, rather, that the instrumental value of stimuli is determined by the fact that after being processed by the physiological mechanism of

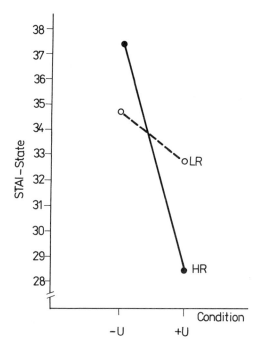

Figure 3. State anxiety as a function of reactivity and uncertainty. U: the uncertainty condition (no information about the experiment to follow); and -U: with information provided.

reactivity they maintain and/or alternate the level of arousal. This powerful motivator is the standard of regulation that depends on the level of reactivity.

From the foregoing review, it is evident that the reactivity mechanism controls reactions to nonspecific stimulation load that may be represented with a series of inverted-U curves along a stimulation dimension. The higher the reactivity, the closer the localization of the zone of comfort to the less stimulating pole of the stimulation dimension. Discomfort—impairment of performance and/or growing costs—becomes apparent when we move toward the opposite end of the stimulation dimension. These observations do not require much elaboration except to point out that reactivity has a great amount of control over stress-related reactions and coping with stress.

We have also demonstrated that reactivity is strongly implicated in various forms of self-regulation that make is possible to meet environmental demands. This analysis helped to identify reactivity as a functionally significant component of the system of stimulation regulation (Eliasz, 1981). Thus we have shown how reactivity and arousal may be involved, directly or indirectly, in the development of capacity.

By necessity, the review of the central findings on this problem was sketchy, and I have omitted what seems to be one of the most promising lines of research within the RTT framework, namely the conflict and/or interplay between reactivity and other regulators of behavior: We have good evidence on the relation of reactivity and arousal, but the research should be continued in order to understand the complexity of behavior.

REFERENCES

Cohen, S. Aftereffects of stress on human performance and social behavior: A review of research and theory. *Psychological Bulletin*, 1980, *88*, 82–108.

Eliasz, A. *Temperament a system regulacji stymulacji.* Warszawa: Państwowe Wydawnictwo Naukowe, 1981.

Eliasz, A., & Wrześniewski, K. Type A behavior resulting from internal or external reinforcements. *Polish Psychological Bulletin*, 1986, *17*, 39–53.

Eysenck, H. J. *The biological basis of personality.* Springfield, Ill.: Charles C Thomas, 1967.

Folkman, S., Schaefer, C., & Lazarus, R. S. Cognitive processes as mediators of stress and coping. In V. Hamilton & D. M. Warburton (Eds.), *Human stress and cognition: An information processing approach.* New York: Wiley, 1979.

Gray, J. A. *Pavlov's typology.* Oxford: Pergamon Press, 1964.

Gray, J. A. A critique of Eysenck's theory of personality. In H. J. Eysenck (Ed.), *A model for personality.* Berlin: Springer, 1981.

Hebb, D. O. *Organization of behavior.* New York: Science Editions, 1961.

Kahnemann, D. *Attention and effort.* Englewood Cliffs, NJ: Prentice-Hall, 1973.

Klonowicz, T. *Reaktywność a przydatność do zawodu operatora.* Unpublished doctoral dissertation, University of Warsaw, 1973.

Klonowicz, T. Potrzeba stymulacji. Analiza pojęcia. In J. Strelau (Ed.), *Regulacyjne funkcje temperamentu.* Wrocław: Ossolineum, 1982.

Klonowicz, T. *Reaktywność a funkcjonowanie człowieka w różnych warunkach stymulacyjnych.* Wrocław: Ossolineum, 1984.

Klonowicz, T. Temperament and performance. In J. Strelau (Ed.), *Temperamental bases of behavior: Warsaw studies on individual differences.* Lisse: Swets & Zeitlinger, 1985.

Klonowicz, T. Reactivity, level of activation, and anticipation: A scary world? *Polish Psychological Bulletin*, 1986, *17*, 15–26.

Matysiak, J. Activity motivated by the sensory drive. *Polish Psychological Bulletin*, 1979, *10*, 209–214.

Strelau, J. *Temperament—personality—activity.* London: Academic Press, 1983.

Strelau, J., & Maciejczyk, J. Reactivity and decision making in stress situations in pilots. In C. D. Spielberger & I. Sarason (Eds.), *Stress and anxiety* (Vol. 4). Washington: Hemisphere, 1977.

Thayer, R. E. Activation state as assessed by verbal report and four psychophysiological variables. *Psychophysiology*, 1970, *7*, 86–94.

Thayer, R. E. Toward a psychological theory of multidimensional activation (arousal). *Motivation and Emotion*, 1978, *2*, 1–34.

Zuckerman, M. *Sensation seeking: Beyond the optimal level of arousal.* Hillsdale, NJ: Erlbaum, 1979.

CHAPTER 11

Temperament-Contingent Cognitive Orientation toward Various Aspects of Reality

ANDRZEJ ELIASZ

INTRODUCTION

Temperament, in the most general terms, is a property that directly determines the dynamics of human behavior, regardless of its contents. The concept of temperament is described by the Warsaw research group on temperament along two dimensions: reactivity and mobility (Strelau, 1974, 1983, 1985a, 1985b). Reactivity, the main dimension of temperament, determines the intensity of reaction to stimuli. The main indices of reactivity are: sensitivity to stimuli, that is, the sensory threshold and the endurance threshold (endurance of strong stimuli). The greater the individual's sensitivity to weak stimuli, the lower is his or her endurance threshold. People with high sensitivity to weak stimuli and poor endurance of strong stimuli are called *highly reactive* and constitute one extremity of the continuum; the other pole groups people who are labeled *low reactive*. For clarity's sake, one can explain that these are individuals with low sensitivity to weak stimuli and high endurance of strong ones. Sensitivity to stimuli determines the quantum of stimulation indispensable for optimal activation. *Optimal activation* is a term used to describe a state of excitation of the central nervous system that

ANDRZEJ ELIASZ • Department of Psychology, Polish Academy of Sciences, Warsaw, Poland. This work has been financed by the Polish Academy of Sciences Grant 11.8.

favors (a) a state of well-being; and (b) the maximum utilization of possibilities while working on tasks of medium difficulty.

Of course, the more sensitive an individual is, the smaller the quantum of stimulation that suffices for attaining optimal activation. The quantum of stimulation indispensable for the attaining of optimal stimulation is called the *stimulation optimum*. People try to attain this stimulation optimum, therefore we may speak of a *stimulation need*. The higher an individual's reactivity, the lower is the stimulation need. This has been confirmed in a substantial number of studies. The compact description of these studies has been presented by several authors in the book edited by Strelau (1985a; see also Strelau, 1983). These studies have shown, moreover, that the stimulation need may be satisfied in a number of ways, that is, through different forms of activity and through preferring different situations. This is a need of a certain quantum of unspecific stimulation. Stimulation from different sources is mutually interchangeable.

Obviously, there are some exceptions to the rule that the higher the need for stimulation the more stimulation people provide themselves through their preference for more stimulative situations and actions. Proper satisfaction of needs, among others, need for stimulation, is only possible when skills for their fulfilment have been acquired (see for details: Eliasz, 1981, 1985b). The development of these skills depends on biological bases and environmental influences as well. The role of temperament on the one hand and the role of environment on the other in shaping the person–environment relations were presented in a transactional model of temperament (Eliasz, 1985a). Some specific premises of the line of research depicted later in this chapter were drawn from this model.

GENERAL AND SELECTIVE SENSITIVITY TO STIMULI

There are reasons to argue that temperament, which determines the magnitude of the need for stimulation, influences general relations of individuals with their environment manifested in specific orientation toward various aspects of reality, for example, the social and physical environments.

THEORETICAL PREMISES

A discrepancy between optimal and actual levels of activation and, in consequence, between optimal and actual levels of stimulation is an aversive state for individuals (Matysiak, 1985; cf. also Maslach, 1979). Thus susceptibility to aversive stimuli determines the resistance to changes of activation beyond the "band" of optimal activation. As a level of activation can be regulated by stimulation control, sensitivity to deviation of actual activation from the optimal level leads correspondingly to the same sensitivity to deviations of stimulation from the optimal level.

Susceptibility to stimuli determines susceptibility to punishment (cf. H. J. Eysenck, 1981a, 1981b; M. W. Eysenck, 1981). According to Gray (1981, 1982), general susceptibility to stimuli is correlated positively with the specific susceptibility to punishments and negatively with the specific susceptibility to rewards. The relations presented here are drawn from Gray's point of view on the relation between these susceptibilities and the extraversion–introversion dimension.

On this ground, it was assumed that high-reactive persons are more sensitive to any deviation of stimulation intensity from the optimal level (Eliasz, 1980, 1985a). The same hypothesis can be derived from other premises, too. Gray's analysis of differences between weak and strong nervous systems as regards the intensity of stimuli that induces the concentration process can lead to the same assumption (see Eliasz, 1985a for details). Robinson, too, (see Chapter 8 in this volume) came to a similar conclusion as regards the extraversion–introversion dimension. According to him, the extravert is attuned to a wider range of environmental stimuli than is the introvert. Robinson drew his hypothesis from very different assumptions from those presented here.

The findings presented by M. W. Eysenck (1981) are in line with the hypothesis. Extraverts are less affected than introverts by distraction in learning tasks. Also, the data collected by Klonowicz (1985) corroborate the hypothesis. The performance of high-reactive persons is more detrimentally affected than that of low-reactive by changes of stimulation load and the type of stimulation, that is, white noise and street noise.

The degree of sensitivity to deviation of stimulation from the optimal level probably determines the strength of motivation for precise stimulation control, that is, to maintain an actual level of stimulation that is very close to the optimal one. People with strong motivation to maintain changes of stimulation within a narrow range should concentrate their attention on those types of stimuli that could easily push them beyond the desired level of stimulation. We can expect that the greater the general susceptibility, and as a result, susceptibility to punishment (i.e., the higher the reactivity), the stronger is the motivation to maintain stimulation within a narrow optimal "band" of stimulation. Because, for humans, the social milieu is the main source of strong stimuli, this probably induces high-reactive people to focus their attention on the social aspects of their environment. This enables people to avoid too strong, or rarely, too weak stimuli from their social milieu.

One can suppose that the exaggeration of meaning of one type of stimulus leads to orientation mainly on these stimuli at the cost of others (cf. Skarżyńska, 1981). This means that the regulative role of one type of stimulus can be much stronger than of others; that is, one type of stimulus can have a stronger impact on people's behavior than others.

EMPIRICAL PREMISES

A selective attitude toward people and physical objects can already be observed in very small children (see the later discussion). The appearance of differences among children in the very early stages of life is considered very serious proof of the biological determination of these differences. Of course, one cannot absolutely rule out the influence of parents' and tutors' caring and educative activities on the further development of infants. The differentiation of small children's cognitive concentration on people versus physical objects goes hand in hand with differences in their behavior dynamics. This suggests a connection between temperament and children's selective attention, concentrated on stimuli from different sources.

In the psycholinguistic literature, Nelson (1973) presented the existence of important differences in assimilation of words by children. She analyzed lists of the first 50 words pronounced by children and stated:

> In terms of the function of the language, one child seems to be learning to talk about things and the other about self and other people; one is learning an object language, one a social interaction. (p. 22)

Nelson differentiated between a group of children labeled "referential" and another labeled *expressive.*

Escalona (cited by Schaffer, 1971) showed that active infants distinctly reacted fo even weak forms of social stimuli; that is, the mere appearance of a human being in their visual field was sufficient; but for inactive children it was not enough, and touch was indispensable. Objects, on the contrary, aroused greater activation in inactive infants than in active ones. Escalona found, moreover, that active infants show both greater reactivity to social stimulation and to hunger, as compared with inactive infants. On the basis of her data, one may suppose that concentration on internal stimuli goes together with concentration on social ones.

One may suppose here that active children are, in a given situation, more strongly aroused than inactive ones; they are generally more sensitive to stimuli. Further, in small children, we do not have yet to do with stimulation regulation on the basis of a negative feedback loop, which necessitates long learning (Eliasz 1981, 1985a). In this situation, the magnitude of the infants' arousal probably directly determines their level of activity on the basis of a positive feedback loop. The responsibility for the correction of the quantum of stimulation falls therefore on the infants' tutors. One may advance the suggestion that active children are characterized by a small stimulation need and inactive ones have large needs in this respect. Data obtained by Schaffer (1971) are in agreement with this point of view. Inactive children in situations of deprivation of social stimulation were found to develop more poorly than active ones.

Matczak (1973), on the basis of observation of 9-month-old infants, differentiated groups of "expressive," "exploring," "expressive-exploring," and generally inactive children. Exploring children established "objective," instrumental contacts with adults, whereas expressive children, in the presence of others, mainly exhibited their emotions, both positive and negative. Matczak made a follow-up study, after 6 months, on the cognitive, motor, and social developments of these children. Exploring children attained a high level of cognitive and motor development and a very low level of social development. The opposite was true of expressive children, who had high indexes of social development and average ones for the remaining developmental dimensions. Matczak did not measure temperamental indexes but did study reactions to frustration. Children labeled "exploring" showed much greater endurance of frustration than the other children. This result suggests a connection between the observed differences and reactivity because reactivity is very strongly correlated with stress endurance (Strelau, 1983).

In turn, Little (1976), on the basis of his study of constructs concerning various aspects of environment, divides people into the following categories: person specialist, thing specialist, generalist, and self-specialist. As in the case of all typologies, pure types are only found at the extremes of the population. In a dimensional approach to orientation toward the world, one may say that types of orientation toward the world are extremities of the dimension of meaning ascribed to physical and social stimuli. The extremities of this dimension are constituted by the dominance, for the subject, of the meaning of one kind of stimulus, whereas its central part is constituted by a relative equilibrium between the significance ascribed to physical and social stimuli. The data presented enable the formulation of a hypothesis of the influence of temperament on differential perception of stimuli from different spheres of reality. This hypothesis has been confirmed indirectly by data obtained by Białowąs and Strelau (Strelau 1985c) in a study based on the classical paradigm of Asch's research on conformism. They found that highly reactive people are more susceptible to social pressure than low-reactive ones and that this conformity among high-reactive people correlates with low state anxiety. High-reactive people who did not comply with social pressure manifested, however, high anxiety as a state.

Findings from other research (Eliasz, 1980) also testify that high-reactive persons adapt their behavior mainly to social influence, whereas low-reactive ones adapt their behavior mainly to the physical environment. The findings were obtained from a study of life-styles of high- and low-reactive individuals from habitats differing in stimulative value and spatial architectural characteristics, for example, old dense housing versus buildings scattered over a relatively large area. Low-reactive 14 and 15-year-old boys living in various urban areas (downtown and within the outskirts of the city) were found to differ considerably in respect to the ways of spending their leisure time and doing homework. On the other hand, there were no clear-cut differences between high-reactive boys from the city and suburban districts. These research findings suggest that low-reactive boys adjust their way of life to the environmental stimulation and space (to physical aspects of the environment), in contradistinction to high reactives. In other words, the ecological variables investigated in the study differentiated only the low-reactive subjects behavior. In the case of high-reactive subjects, internal and external factors directing their behavior were independent of both the stimulative and spatial characteristics of the habitat (on the macroscale). Besides, high-reactive subjects—as compared to low-reactive ones—were found to engage much more frequently in so-called "directed activities" (i.e., activities either inspired or imposed upon subjects by other people). The results permitted the conclusion that in high-reactive persons, the relatively large susceptibility to social influences is accompanied by lack of adaptation of their behavior to the stimulation provided by the physical environment.

Other results indicate that, on the analysis of the reactions of adolescents to social stimuli, one may speak of their selective sensitivity to the form and contents of social influence. This research dealt with the influence of parents' need for achievement and their fostering style on adolescents' need for achievement and with the specific side effect of social pressure on achievement maximization as constituted by the Type A behavior pattern as well as with nonspecific side effects, such as, among others, level of anxiety. The adolescents' temperament was also measured as the internal independent variable.

It was assumed that parents' need for achievement directed toward their children is related in content with these children's need for achievement and with their manifestation of the so-called Type A behavior pattern. An exaggerated form of need for achievement is considered—with some exceptions (e.g., Price, 1984, in manuscript; Hughes, Jacobs, Schucker, Chapman, Murrey, & Johnson, 1983)—commonly as a main content element of the Type A behavior pattern (Glass, 1977). Parental educative style (measured by Schaefer's The Child's Report of

Parent Behavior Inventory, in Kowalski's Polish adaptation) was treated as a form of social influence.

It was found that low-reactive subjects reacted mainly to the contents of social influence and, when parents' need for achievement was high, higher indexes of need for achievement and of Type A behavior pattern were found than when parents' need for achievement was low. High-reactive subjects, however, reacted mainly to the educative style, especially to two of its four differentiated types, that is, to severe control of children and to emotional distance of parents toward their children. The stricter the control or the greater the emotional distance between parents and the child, the greater were that child's need for achievement, Type A behavior pattern, and level of anxiety. These differences in sensitivity to contents and form of social influence are distinct in the boys' group; girls are more sensitive to the form of social influence than to its contents (Eliasz & Wrześniewski, 1986). This would mean that people react to stimuli in a highly selective way depending on their reactivity. This selectivity is manifested here in complying with various aspects of social stimuli.

The previously presented differences in sensitivity to contents and form of social stimuli are in agreement with data collected by Schwartz (cited by M. W. Eysenck, 1981). One of his experiments on paired-associate learning concerns the detrimental effect of semantic or phonemic similarities of response words on learning, depending on the subjects' level of arousal and anxiety.

In another experiment, a set of randomly placed categorized words was presented to subjects. They were to recall the list of words in a free order. The semantic organization of recalled words by subjects differing in their level of arousal and anxiety was assessed. It was found that "high arousal or anxiety reduces semantic processing but enhances physical processing" (M. W. Eysenck, 1981, p. 180). According to Eysenck, it is due to the fact that encodings depend on the number of potentially encodable attributes of a word; there are many more semantic attributes of a word than phonemic ones.

STUDIES ON COGNITIVE ORIENTATION TOWARD VARIOUS ASPECTS OF REALITY

Basing ourselves on the data presented here, we may assume that the selective exaggeration of stimuli from various sources is not limited to the behavioral level. The results presented, after M. W. Eysenck, suggest directly that it can be observed on the cognitive level as well. Studies of specialization in subjects' relations with their environment depending on temperament have only been undertaken relatively recently. By now, a few studies concerning this problem have been carried out by my collaborators.

The selective perception of messages relating to people was studied by Golińska (in press). She presented a fragment of a science fiction story with a hero within a very vivid plot, and she also presented a discussion between two female students who exchanged their opinions about a pending examination. Both materials were tape-recorded and contained appropriate information about either the main hero of the story or the women who were discussing the examination. The perception of social contents was studied in three situations.

First, subjects were asked to listen to part of the story in order to complete it. They were told that the experimenter was interested in creative thinking, but just after the story had been presented, they were asked to fill in an adjective checklist developed for assessing hero features.

Second, subjects were asked to listen to the female discussion in order to assess the women's features. Subjects could do this on the basis of messages relating to these women who exchanged this information incidentally to the main topic of their discussion.

Finally, the second task (listening to the discussion) was repeated just before an examination situation (test anxiety situation). Subjects participating in this stage of research also took part in the first one but did not participate in the second.

In all situations, subjects filled in the adjective checklists. The perception of features was assessed, taking into account the number of features correctly identified and the number of errors. These errors consisted in listing features that were not justified by the contents of the discussion and the story that the subjects had listened to. Reactivity was measured by the Strelau Temperament Inventory (STI). The study was carried out among university freshmen from various departments.

As may be seen in Table 1, in the first as well as in the second situation low reactives (Lr) made more errors (E) than medium reactives (Mr) and high reactives (Hr), but at the same time Lr were better than Hr and similar to Mr in the second situation as regards correctly identified features (C). This means that in the first situation in which a distractor was included (an experimenter drew the subjects' attention from the social contents of the story), there were no differences between the groups as regards correctly identified features. When subjects' attention was focused on social contents (the second situation), Lr were better than Hr subjects at the correct identification of features. Lr subjects, however, made many mistakes that impaired the general perception outcome (as measured by a complex indicator). In both situations, Lr

Table 1. *Difference between Groups of Subjects in Perception of Social Contents in Various Situations*[a]

Types of situations	Correctly identified features (C)	Errors (E)	Complex indicator of perception of social contents (P)
I Distractor and emotionally neutral situation	No differences	Lr[b] > Mr[b] ≈ Hr[b]	Lr < Mr ≈ Hr
II Focus of attention on social contents; neutral situation	Lr ≈ Mr > Hr	Lr > Mr ≈ Hr	Lr ≈ Hr < Mr
III Focus of attention on social contents; test anxiety situation	Lr < Mr ≈ Hr	Lr < Mr ≈ Hr	Lr < Mr ≈ Hr

[a]In Table 1 as well as in Table 2, only general dependencies are presented.
[b]Lr—low-reactive subjects; Mr—medium-reactive subjects; Hr—high-reactive subjects. All inequalities indicate statistically significant differences at least at .05 level. The groups were distinguished on the following bases using the Strelau Temperament Inventory: Lr: + 1 SD above the mean (boys: above 67 points, girls − 57); Hr: − 1 SD below the mean (boys: below 38, girls − 33); and Mr: within ± .5 SD from the mean (boys: 47–60, girls: 41–49).

subjects, in a carefree manner, ascribed various features to the "hero of the story of the women" that were not contained in the fictional story or in the women's discussion. In the test anxiety situation (the third situation), C indexes (see Table 1) are worse in Lr subjects than in Mr and Hr ones; but as regards E indexes, Lr are better than Mr and Hr subjects. It is important to note that this effect is not due to a lower number of errors made by the Lr group in Situation III (i.e., this number is the same as in Situation II). Rather, this result is attributable to the fact that the number of errors in the Mr and Hr groups in Situation III is very high (higher than in Situation II).

As mentioned before, the third situation of the study was identical to the second one, apart from the fact that it took place just before the students' exam, a few weeks after the first stage. As can be seen in Table 2, in this test anxiety situation (A) the number of correctly identified features (C) by Lr subjects is lower than in the emotionally neutral (N) situation, and at the same time there is no significant difference in the number of errors. In fact, the number of errors is slightly smaller. Hence there is no difference between the second situation (N) and the third

Table 2. Differences between Second and Third Situations within
Three Groups of Subjects

Groups	C[a]	E[b]	P[c]
Lr	N[d] > A[e]	No difference	No difference
Mr	N < A	N < A	N > A
Hr	N < A	N < A	N > A

Note: All inequalities indicate statistically significant differences.
[a]C—correctly identified features.
[b]E—errors.
[c]P—perception of social contents (complex indicator)
[d]N—the second situation emotionally neutral.
[e]A—the third test-anxiety situation.

situation (A) in the Lr group as regards the complex indicator of perception (P). An opposite effect is observed in the Hr group as regards C. In Situation A, the number of correctly identified features (C) is higher than in Situation N, but at the same time the number of errors (E) is higher in Situation A in comparison with N. Differences in the Mr group are similar to those in the Hr one, but they are slightly smaller.

Generally speaking, low-reactive individuals are worse in the perception of social contents than high-reactive ones as regards complex indicators of social contents consisting of erroneously and correctly identified features. The findings also imply that the situation type has a greater impact on the functioning of high- than on low-reactive subjects. Moreover, the data indicate that, generally, low-reactive subjects are more carefree in ascribing features to people (higher number of errors) than high-reactive subjects (Situations I and II).

In the test anxiety situation (Situation III), however, the number of errors made by high- as well as medium-reactive subjects is higher than in the low reactive-ones, but it is difficult to interpret this phenomenon in terms of lightheartedness regarding the social environment. It results from tension; this outcome was brought about by an increase in the number of mistakes made by medium- and high-reactive individuals, not by a decrease of errors in low-reactive ones.

These data show once again that differences in reactivity are not confined to general indiscriminate susceptibility to stimuli but that reactions to stimuli are selective. Data collected by Golińska are in agreement with outcomes testifying that high-reactive people are *person specialists* (Little's term) to a greater extent than low-reactive people.

Świętochowski (1986) assumed that the previously mentioned specialization ought to manifest itself in nonverbal communication. People who pay more attention to social stimuli are expected to understand messages transmitted nonverbally better. Subjects aged 18–19 (boys only) were asked to discuss in pairs (selected randomly) two problems for 10 minutes and to settle on two common opinions for the topics discussed. The discussions were recorded on videotape with hidden camera and microphone in the experimenter's absence. After the discussions, all subjects were asked to fill in a scale to assess their partners' behavior. Independent judges filled in the same scale after watching the video recording. The scale consisted of items pertaining to behavior usually expressed nonverbally, for example, the partner's attitudes toward the subject and the psychophysical and emotional state of the partner.

The discrepancy versus consistency between the subject's assessment of his or her partner and the average judge rating was an indicator of the accuracy of decoding (receiving) of nonverbal information. The accuracy of decoding informs us about the subject's functioning as a "receiver" of nonverbal information. Subjects were assessed as "senders" too. The discrepancy in the judges' ratings of a given subject was the indicator of his or her accuracy in encoding nonverbally transmitted messages.

It was found that the higher the reactivity, the better subjects are in both encoding (sending) and decoding (receiving) nonverbal messages. It is especially interesting that the correlation between reactivity and encoding, with mobility partialed out, is very high, much higher than in the case of decoding ($r = .78$ and $r = .27$, respectively).[1]

These data are apparently at variance with the findings described by Wilson (1981) concerning the relationship between extraversion/ introversion and the ability to receive and send messages in interpersonal relations. According to the studies presented by Wilson, introverts are better than extraverts in receiving information; inversely, extraverts are better than introverts as senders. This difference is enhanced by neuroticism; that is, the greatest difference is between stable extraverts and neurotic introverts. These findings testify to specialization in effective transmitting of nonverbal messages to others and effective decoding.

Because the physiological roots of extraversion/introversion and reactivity are similar (cf. Strelau, 1970, 1983; Strelau, Klonowicz, & Eliasz, 1972), one can expect low reactives to be better than high reactives in encoding, that is, in transmitting nonverbal messages, and high reactives to be better than low reactives in decoding, that is, receiving infor-

[1]The indicator of reactivity was the total score on the scale of Strength of Excitation (SE); the higher the SE (i.e., the higher the score) the lower the reactivity. This means that the negative correlation coefficient between SE and dependent variables can be reversed to a positive correlation coefficient as regards reactivity.

mation. The latter was confirmed, but the former was not supported by data collected by Świętochowski.

We cannot, however, easily generalize these data onto various situations. In fact, Świętochowski's study relates to nonverbal communications in a situation that was safe for subjects. In such situations, transmitting nonverbal messages does not depend on proneness to self-disclosure (cf. Cunningham's interpretation, cited by Wilson, 1981) but is contingent on the ability to learn nonverbal codes and the ability to acquire skills to transmit messages in everyday life. Obviously, understanding minute social feedback from the social milieu is conducive not only to "reading" nonverbal messages (accuracy of decoding) but also to sending such information in a readable way enabling its accurate perception (clarity of encoding). This leads us to the conclusion that in safe situations, the ability to encode is enhanced by the ability to decode social cues. It is very likely that in highly stimulative situations, low-reactive people are more "visible than high-reactive people." The significance of a situation type in which nonverbal communication succeeds in distinguishing good senders and receivers has been indicated by Wilson (1981).

STUDIES ON COGNITIVE DIFFERENTIATION (CD) OF PEOPLE, THINGS, AND INNER STATES

The data presented lead to the conclusion that specialization relative to the environment is manifested on the cognitive level. The question arises whether such specialization can also be manifested in the formal aspects of cognitive functioning that determine, in a most general way, people's relationships with their environment. One of the basic formal aspects of the cognitive functioning is so-called cognitive differentiation (CD). Data will be presented concerning CD pertaining to the social as well as the physical environments and inner subjective states.

The more frequently people communicate with others, the more information they have about others. This is obvious, but according to Crockett (1965), the more information people have about others, the more differentiated are their cognitions relating to others. On the grounds of the previously-presented studies, we can assume that the higher the reactivity, the more attention that is paid to others. This may bring about greater CD concerning others in high- rather than in low-reactive people. According to Bieri (1971), the CD of objects is the better the more important these objects are for a given person. In other words, a subject's CD depends on evaluation of objects for himself or herself. Departing from Crockett's and Bieri's points of view, various specific hypotheses can be formulated as regards CD. Both authors, however, pointed out that the level of CD of objects is commensurate with the degree of attention paid to them. Thus the data collected by now have suggested that the higher the reactivity is, the higher is the level of cognitive differentiation of others.

As motivation to perform tasks results mainly from social impact, we can assume that task orientations are proportional to a person's compliance with other people. As pointed out earlier, it has been found that high-reactive people are more submissive than low-reactive ones. On this ground, one can suppose that the higher the reactivity is, the higher is the level of cognitive differentiation of tasks.

It was found that the more independent of others people are, the more they take into account in their behavior the physical aspects of the environment. This suggests that the degree of cognitive differentiation of the physical environment is in line with the level of reactivity.

There are no clear premises concerning the link between people's reactivity and their orientation toward inner states of their own organism. On the one hand, we can expect general sensitivity to stimuli to determine susceptibility to inner stimuli. On the other hand, susceptibility to social pressure and development of a strong task motivation may confine attention to both social and task stimuli, drawing attention away from one's inner states.

A study was carried out in a large city by Ruszkiewicz (1985). Subjects, aged 17 to 18, were pupils at a large high school located in the central part of the city. Cognitive differentiation (CD) in the four previously mentioned aspects was assessed using four Rep-tests adapted for this purpose. These instruments contained lists of 15 social roles as well as real and ideal-self, physical objects, inner states or tasks (in the last case there were 24 tasks), and a set of 15 dimensions (i.e., constructs) imposed on the subjects and not—as in the classical procedure—revealed by the subjects themselves. The sum of similarities between poles of constructs chosen by a given subject divided by the number of compared constructs in all possible pairs was the indicator of CD. Temperament was measured with the STI and trait anxiety with Spielberger's STAI adapted to Polish conditions.

Baffling results were found about CD concerning people. No significant impact of reactivity, anxiety, or their interaction on cognitive differentiation in this respect was found.[2] On the basis of Rep-test data, an

---

[2]In fact many indexes of cognitive differentiation referring to part of the objects were included, for example, positively and negatively evaluated people (distinguished on the basis of similarity to the ideal-self), and positive and negative objects (distinguished on the basis of ascription to an object of one of the extremes of the "good-bad" construct).

index of articulation of social objects was also computed. It was found that the lower the reactivity, the higher the articulation of the social environment. These results are consistent with the previously presented data relating to low-reactive people's carefree manner of ascribing features to a fictional hero and the women in conversation. These outcomes are also in agreement with findings collected by Goulet and Mazzei (1969) in research on a paired-associate task. Goulet and Mazzei stated that

> high-anxiety subjects may withhold responding until fairly confident of the stimulus-response pairings, whereas low-anxiety subjects may require a lower degree of confidence. (p. 251)

Temperament-contingent differences in orientation toward people were not directly confirmed as regards cognitive differentiation. Indirectly, however, results concerning the CD of tasks are in agreement with the hypothesis; that is, the higher the reactivity, the higher the level of cognitive differentiation. What is more, high anxiety reduces the CD only in low-reactive subjects. Anxiety does not influence the CD of high-reactive subjects but enhances the CD of tasks in the intermediate range of reactivity. As regards inner states, the higher the reactivity is, the higher is the level of the CD. In this respect, the data layout is the same as for tasks.

Anxiety reduces CD not only in low-reactive subjects (as in the case of tasks) but in high-reactive ones as well. Among subjects characterized by an intermediate level of reactivity, anxiety leads to an increase of the CD of inner states of one's organism, as well as tasks. No significant results concerning the physical environment were found.

A study of CD was also carried out in a very small town by Budzińska (1985). The same versions of Rep-tests were used, and reactivity was measured in the same way by the STI. Subjects were of the same age, but they were pupils of much smaller high schools than in the previously discussed study. It was found that the higher the reactivity, the higher the level of CD is for people as well as physical objects. On the

---

Internal states and tasks were treated in the same way. Another index distinguished was environment articulation. Here the criterion was the number of zeros, with zero meaning the subject's inability to decide which construct extreme fits better to the given person, task, object, or internal state. An index of so-called positive bias was also included, that is, the number of similarities to the "ideal-self" divided by the number of all significant comparisons (excluding zeros). Analysis of these details is beyond the scope of this chapter. To summarize, we can say that in Ruszkiewicz's work most significant results were obtained for tasks. It was found, for instance, that the higher the reactivity the greater the predominance of differentiation of positive versus negative tasks. This is interesting because it enables analysis of the relationship between reactivity and orientation toward positive and negative reinforcement.

contrary, the higher the reactivity is, the lower is the level of the CD of inner states of one's organism. No significant differences were found for tasks.

It has thus been shown that the relation between temperament and cognitive differentiation of various aspects of reality depends to a great extent on the environment. In a quiet, peaceful environment, there is an agreement between environmental stimulation and the small need for stimulation of high-reactive people. In such an environment, high-reactive people can approach others as well as physical objects. Approaching a social as well as a physical environment is a precondition for development of CD with respect to these elements of the environment. Contrary to the situation in the small town, in a highly stimulative environment, such as is typical of a big city, high-reactive people probably withdraw or limit their contacts with both other people and the physical aspects of the environment. A highly stimulative environment is consistent with the needs of low-reactive people because of their high need for stimulation. Why, then, do they not develop a better CD of the environment than high-reactive people? Once again the hypothesis was indirectly confirmed that low-reactive people behave similarly in a broad range of stimulation intensities, in a much broader range than high-reactive ones do. The behavior and, in consequence, the development of high-reactive people depends to a much greater extent on intensity of stimulation than that of low reactives. High-reactive people's orientation toward external stimuli in low stimulative environments coincides with their low concern with inner states of their organism, which is manifested in their relatively poor inner state CD. High-reactive people's attention can be drawn away from inner states of their organism by external stimuli. Moreover, in a quiet environment, high-reactive people's inner states of their organism may be less frequently "pushed out" from the states of optimum activation levels, and hence the inner states of their organisms are rarely objects of self-attention.

The data obtained in our research on cognitive differentiation leads to the conclusion that the impact of temperament on subjects' orientation toward the environment depends on the fit between the need for stimulation and the stimulation provided by that environment.

FINAL REMARKS

The level of arousal has an impact on the selectivity of attention. This was stated on the basis of research on the capacity of working memory, depending on individual differences in arousal (M. W. Eysenck, 1981). The level of an individual's arousal depends, among other things, on reactivity—the dimension of temperament. The evaluation of stimuli, that is, assessing them as positive or negative and their importance depend among other things on their role in maintaining the optimal level of stimulation. Stimuli can facilitate the process of stimulation control or impair it, depending on people's temperament and their need for stimulation. This implies that, depending on temperament, the fundamental element of a stimulation system control, people approach or withdraw from contact with certain sources of stimuli. Focusing of attention on some stimuli is a prerequisite for the good development of cognitive representations of people and tasks, physical objects, and the inner states of one's organism.

The previously presented data on the relationship between temperament and selective orientation toward the environment are preliminary. The outcomes are promising and so further studies are planned in which the role of the environment in shaping the relation between temperament and cognitive orientation toward various realms of stimuli will be taken into account.

REFERENCES

Bieri, J. Cognitive structures in personality. In M. Schroeder & P. Suedfeld (Eds.), *Personality theory and information processing*. New York: Ronald, 1971.

Budzińska, E. *Temperament a wrażliwość na kary i nagrody*. Unpublished M.A. thesis, University of Łódź. 1985.

Crockett, W. H. Cognitive complexity and impression formation. In B. A. Maher (Ed.), *Progress in experimental psychology research* (Vol. 2). New York: Academic Press, 1965.

Eliasz, A. Temperament and trans-situational stability of behavior in the physical and social environment. *Polish Psychological Bulletin*, 1980, *11*, 143–153.

Eliasz, A. *Temperament a system regulacji stymulacji*. Warszawa: Państwowe Wydawnictwo Naukowe, 1981.

Eliasz, A. Transactional model of temperament. In J. Strelau (Ed.), *Temperamental bases of behavior: Warsaw studies on individual differences*. Lisse: Swets & Zeitlinger, 1985. (a)

Eliasz, A. Mechanisms of temperament: Basic functions. In J. Strelau, F. H. Farley, & A. Gale (Eds.), *The biological bases of personality and behavior: Theories, measurement techniques, and development* (Vol. 1). Washington: Hemisphere, 1985. (b)

Eliasz, A., & Wrześniewski, K., Type A behavior pattern resulting from internal and external reinforcements depending on temperament. *Polish Psychological Bulletin*, 1986, *17*, 39–53.

Eysenck, H. J. General features of the model. In H. J. Eysenck (Ed.), *A model for personality*. Berlin: Springer, 1981. (a)

Eysenck, H. J. Epilogue. In H. J. Eysenck (Ed.), *A model for personality*. Berlin: Springer, 1981. (b)

Eysenck, M. W. Learning, memory and personality. In H. J. Eysenck (Ed.), *A model for personality*. Berlin: Springer, 1981.

Glass, D. C. *Behavior pattern, stress, and coronary disease*. Hillsdale, NJ: Erlbaum, 1977.

Golińska, L. Wpływ reaktywności na percepcję przekazu społecznego, *Przegląd Psychologiczny*, in press.

Goulet, L. R., & Mazzei, J. Verbal learning and confidence thresholds as a function of test anxiety, intelligence, and stimulus stimilarity. *Journal of Experimental Research in Personality*, 1969, *3*, 247–252.

Gray, J. A. A critique of Eysenck's theory of personality. In H. J. Eysenck (Ed.), *A model for personality*. Berlin: Springer, 1981.

Gray, J. A. Précis of The neuropsychology of anxiety: An enquiry into the functions of the septo-hippocampal system. *The Behavioral and Brain Sciences*, 1982, *5*, 469–543.

Hughes, J. R., Jacobs, D. R., Schucker, B., Chapman, D. P., Murray, D. M., & Johnson, C. A. Nonverbal behavior of the Type A Individual. *Journal of Behavioral Medicine*, 1983, *6*, 279–289.

Klonowicz, T. Temperament and performance. In J. Strelau (Ed.), *Temperamental bases of behavior: Warsaw studies on individual differences*. Lisse: Swets & Zeitlinger, 1985.

Little, B. R. Specialization and varietes of environmental experience: Empirical studies within the personality paradigm. In S. Wapner, S. B. Cohen, & B. Kaplan (Eds.), *Experiencing the environment*. New York: Plenum Press, 1976.

Maslach, C. Negative emotional biasing of unexplained arousal. *Journal of Personality and Social Psychology*, 1979, *37*, 953–969.

Matczak, A. Early individual differences in needs and their significance for the child's development. *Polish Psychological Bulletin*, 1973, *4*, 115–124.

Matysiak, J. Need for sensory stimulation: Effects on activity. In J. Strelau (Ed.), *Temperamental bases of behavior: Warsaw studies on individual differences*. Lisse: Swets & Zeitlinger, 1985.

Nelson, K. Structure and strategy in learning to talk. *Monographs of the Society for Research in Child Development*, 1973, *38* (No. 149).

Price, V. *Conferring on Type A behavior and discussing future collaborative research*. Unpublished manuscript, 1984.

Ruszkiewicz, E. *Kategorie poznawcze odnoszące sie, do świata i do własnych stanów organizmu u ludzi o różnych cechach temperamentu*. Unpublished M.A. thesis, University of Warsaw, 1985.

Schaffer, H. R., *The growth of sociability*. Harmondsworth: Penguin Books, 1971.

Skarżyńska, K. *Spostrzeganie ludzi*. Warszawa: Państwowe Wydawnictwo Naukowe, 1981.

Strelau, J. Nervous system type and extraversion-introversion. A comparison of Eysenck's theory with Pavlov's typology. *Polish Psychological Bulletin*, 1970, *1*, 17–24.

Strelau, J. Temperament as an expression of energy level and temporal features of behavior. *Polish Psychological Bulletin*, 1974, *5*, 119–127.

Strelau, J. *Temperament—personality—activity*. London: Academic Press, 1983.

Strelau, J. (Ed.). *Temperamental bases of behavior: Warsaw studies on individual differences*. Lisse: Swets & Zeitlinger, 1985. (a)

Strelau, J. Pavlov's typology and the regulative theory of temperament. In J. Strelau (Ed.), *Temperamental bases of behavior: Warsaw studies on individual differences*, Lisse: Swets & Zeitlinger, 1985. (b)

Strelau, J. Temperament and personality: Pavlov and beyond. In J. Strelau, F. H. Farley, & A. Gale (Eds.), *The biological bases of personality and behavior: Theories, measurement techniques and development* (Vol. 1). Washington: Hemisphere, 1985. (c)

Strelau, J., Klonowicz, T., & Eliasz, A. Fizjologiczne mechanizmy cech temperamentalnych. *Przegląd Psychologiczny*, 1972, *15*, 25–51.

Świętochowski, W. Temperament as a determinant of nonverbal communication in face to face social interactions. *Polish Psychological Bulletin*, 1986, *17*, 63–69.

Wilson, G. D. Personality and social behavior. In H. J. Eysenck (Ed.), *A model for personality*. Berlin: Springer, 1981.

PART IV

Attempts at Integration Based on the Arousability Concept

A Critical Look at Three Arousal Constructs in Personality Theories

Optimal Levels of Arousal, Strength of the Nervous System, and Sensitivities to Signals of Reward and Punishment

MARVIN ZUCKERMAN

The first statement of an optimal level of arousal construct in personality theory was in Freud's constancy principle (Breuer & Freud, 1895/1937):

> There is a tendency to preserve at a constant level the intracerebral excitement. An excess of it becomes burdensome and annoying, and there arises an urge to consume it. . . . I believe we can also assume a level of the intracerebral tonic excitement, namely that it also has an optimum. On this level of tonic excitement, the brain is accessible to all external stimuli. (p. 143)

Freud's definition of the optimum level of arousal is remarkably appropriate to recent psychophysiological findings related to personality that will be described in the latter part of this chapter. He also suggested that there might be differences in temperament based on the "amount of energy set free by the functionally resting cerebral element," or a direct relationship between what he called "vivaciousness"

We gratefully acknowledge permission to reprint this article which originally appeared in J. T. Spence and C. E. Izard (Eds.), *Motivation, Emotion, and Personality* (selected-revised papers, vol. 5), 1985, 23rd International Congress of Psychology. Amsterdam: Elsevier.

MARVIN ZUCKERMAN • Department of Psychology, University of Delaware, Newark, Delaware 19716.

(behavioral activity) and arousability of the cerebral neurons. Freud's statements on optimal level theory seem to have been largely forgotten by later theorists for two reasons. One is the lack of interest of psycho-analysts and academic psychologists in Freud's insightful, if premature, neurophysiological theory of personality. The second is that Freud himself shifted to a simple arousal reduction theory that conceived of the nervous system as "an apparatus which has the function of reducing them [stimuli] to the lowest possible level . . . or maintaining itself in an altogether unstimulated condition" (Freud, 1920/1955, p. 120). Of course, our subsequent understanding of the central nervous system (CNS) and the regulation of cortical arousal by the reticular activating system supports Freud's earlier conception rather than the later one.

PAVLOV: STRENGTH OF THE NERVOUS SYSTEM

Pavlov's (1927/1960) classifications of temperament (largely in dogs) was also based on hypothetical properties of the CNS involving the strengths of general excitatory and inhibitory tendencies. Pavlov initially contrasted a "sanguine" temperament, identified with a strong nervous system, to a "melancholic" one related to a weak nervous system dominated by inhibition. One of the characteristics of the weak nervous system type is fearfulness or "cowardice." One system is used to explain both conditioning and emotional responsiveness.

As Strelau (1983) points out, the strong nervous system was further differentiated according to other properties. The sanguine temperament is finally described as strong (meaning strength of excitatory process), balanced (with regard to excitatory and inhibitory processes), and mobile (with regard to the capacity to shift from one process to the other). Strelau's definition of the behavioral characteristics of the temperament is: "This individual is lively and active when stimulated by the surroundings . . . [but] in non-stimulation conditions is prone to drowsiness and sleep" (p. 12). We all know students of this type. They are the gauge of our own liveliness during lectures. According to Strelau's interpretation of the Pavlovian classification, sanguine types are distinguished from the phlegmatic by the mobility of nervous processes rather than by strength because both types are assumed to have strong excitatory processes that are balanced with equally strong inhibitory processes.

NEO-PAVLOVIAN CONCEPTS

Pavlov's properties of the nervous system were hypothetical biological traits based on peripheral glandular and motor responses. In the

1950s and 1960s, Teplov and Nebylitsyn advocated the greater use of involuntary measures such as psychophysiological measures of autonomic and brain function. They also encouraged the use of modern experimental and statistical methods.

Strength of the nervous system as defined by Pavlov meant the ability of cortical cells to work under conditions of intense or prolonged stimulation. Teplov and Nebylitsyn also concluded that there was a dependence between the capacity of cells to work at high intensities and their sensitivity at low intensities. The weak nervous system type is sensitive to low intensity stimulation but at high intensities is likely to show a reduction of function labeled *transmarginal inhibition.* The strong nervous system type is relatively insensitive to weak intensities but responds well to high intensities of stimulation. According to this theory, one must specify the level of stimulation before one can predict the reactivity of different types.

Strelau (1983) translated the strength of the nervous system model into one for human personality. His "reactivity" dimension combines the characteristics of sensitivity and endurance in reaction to the range of stimulus intensity. Those familiar with the behavior genetics literature are liable to confuse the construct of "reactivity" with that used to contrast *emotionally* reactive and nonreactive strains of animals. Strelau's "reactivity" construct is a psychological (behavioral) one and deals primarily with nonemotional reaction phenomena and only secondarily with emotional responses. Strelau is a general arousal theorist and assumes that all "physiological systems responsible for the accumulation, as well as the release of, stored energy." (Strelau, 1983, p. 179) constitute the biological basis of reactivity. Given the typical lack of correlation between various physiological systems, one would not know where to start to investigate reactivity at the physiological level.

Strelau, to his great credit, is the first neo-Pavlovian to develop a questionnaire scale based on his rational translation of the reactivity temperament construct into behavioral terms appropriate to humans. The Strelau Temperament Inventory (STI) contains subscales for the assessment of strengths of excitation, inhibition, and mobility. The strength of excitation scale is regarded as inversely related to reactivity because "reactivity" refers to the sensitivity end of the dimension. Many of the items in the scale ask subjects about their capacity to work efficiently under difficult or distracting conditions. One problem with this test is that factor analyses of the items have not yielded the factors suggested by the rationally assembled subscales (Carlier, 1985; Stelmack, 1985). Indeed, the factors resemble the dimensions like extraversion and emotional instability described by Hans Eysenck and other Western investigators.

EYSENCK: EXTRAVERSION AND THE OPTIMAL LEVEL OF AROUSAL

There are obvious points of similarity between Eysenck's basic personality dimension of introversion-extraversion and the Pavlovian constructs "strength of nervous system" (Gray, 1967) and "reactivity" (Strelau, 1983). By comparing Pavlov's types with those formed by combinations of two of Eysenck's dimensions, we can equate the sanguine type with the stable extravert, the phlegmatic with the stable introvert, the choleric with the neurotic (emotionally unstable) extravert, and the melancholic with the neurotic introvert. As Gray (1981) has pointed out, Eysenck's earlier theory stressed the role of inhibitory processes in the extravert, whereas the later theory (Eysenck, 1967) shifted the emphasis to excitation or arousal. Eysenck adopted the optimal level of stimulation and arousal as the central construct of extraversion. The biological basis of these optimal levels was inherent sensitivity of the reticular activating system (RAS) to stimulation and the thresholds for the descending negative feedback control of stimulation and its arousal effects. This new formulation made stimulus intensity a critical variable in predicting results for introverts and extraverts. The introvert shows more sensitivity to stimuli at the low end of the intensity range, but the extravert has more capacity to respond to stimuli at the higher end. Hedonic tone or preference is maximally positive at the optimal level of stimulation, but it is lower and negative at both extreme low and high ends. The optimal level curves differ for introverts and extraverts; the introvert prefers lower intensities of stimulation and the extravert likes higher intensities. It is assumed that arousal varies directly and linearly with intensity of stimulation. We will see later that this assumption is not true for everyone. Note that this concept of arousal refers to phasic arousal in response to stimulation. However, the concept of a tonic cortical underarousal in extraverts and hyperarousal in introverts remained part of the theory and actually furnished the physiological explanation for the optimal level theory. Assuming that extreme states of arousal are intrinsically unpleasant (a dubious assumption if one considers arousal levels reached during sexual intercourse), aroused introverts do not enjoy stimuli that push them over their low optimal levels. Conversely, the underaroused extravert, who is likely to be in a dysphoric state in a waking, unstimulated condition, seeks and enjoys intense stimuli that raise his or her arousal level closer to the optimum.

In Eysenck's older theory, neuroticism or emotional instability was said to be based on the lability of the autonomic nervous system. The newer theory (Eysenck, 1967) is a little more specific, referring to differential thresholds in the limbic brain (hippocampus, amygdala, cingulum, septum, and hypothalamus) that regulates the autonomic system and furnishes the basis for specific emotional and motivational states. Although emotional instability is a general construct identified with neuroticism, in actual application the main emotion discussed is fear or anxiety. For some reason most of our theories do not account for positive emotions but focus entirely on the unhappy triad I have called the "FAD" (fear, anger, and depression) (Zuckerman, 1980). No optimal level of arousal construct was postulated for the limbic-autonomic system, although in principle there was every reason to do so. Hedonic responses are at least as much affective as cognitive and probably more so (Zajonc, 1980).

GRAY: SENSITIVITIES TO SIGNALS OF REWARD AND PUNISHMENT

Gray (1964) began his theoretical formulations with the optimal level of arousal construct as a bridge between neo-Pavlovian and Eysenkian concepts. However, beginning in the 1970s (Gray, 1973), the reticular activating system became relegated to the role of an amplifier of the other arousal systems underlying the basic dimensions of personality. On the basis of neurophysiological studies of animals (largely rodents), limbic systems were identified that were hypothesized to underlie the hypothetical functions of sensitivities to signals of reward and punishment. The conceptual model is that of an information-processing system that analyzes signals on the basis of prior associations and results in arousal as a secondary phenomenon rather than as a determinant of specific emotional response. Rather than a general conditionability factor, as in Eysenck's theory of extraversion, we have separate biological factors determining individual differences in response to signals of reward and punishment.

The biological bases and behavioral expressions of the systems are different. Sensitivity to signals of punishment depends on the frontal cortex and septohippocampal system and the Papez circuit that interact in a "behavioral inhibition system." This system responds to signals of punishment, nonreward, or just novel stimuli, with an inhibition of ongoing behavioral functions and an associated increase in sympathetic system autonomic arousal (Gray, 1982). Although the system is involved in functions other than anxiety, its sensitivity is considered the basis of the trait of "anxiety".

The trait characterized by sensitivity to signals of reward is called "impulsivity." In the 1970s, Gray (1973) identified the neural substrate of this trait with Old's reward system where high rates of self-stimulation are obtained from implanted electrodes. The system includes the part of the septum, lateral hypothalamus, and the medial forebrain bundle. More recently, Gray (1981) simply says that the neurophysiological basis for reward sensitivity is unknown. Part of the reason for this retreat may be the fact that Crow (1977) and Stein (1978) maintain that this reward system is neurochemically mediated by the catecholamine neurotransmitters, norepinephrine and dopamine. Gray has assigned another role for norepinephrine. He sees the dorsal ascending noradrenergic system as the triggering mechanism for the essentially serotonergic-mediated anxiety (behavioral inhibition) mechanism.

The role of the noradrenergic system in behavior and personality is widely debated (Zuckerman, 1984; Zuckerman, Ballenger, & Post, 1984). Recent evidence suggests that it functions as a "second arousal system" and is responsive to novel stimulation as well as stimuli with a signal value, with arousal in the locus coeruleus via the dorsal ascending noradrenergic bundle to the cortex. Wise (1982) has proposed that the dopaminergic system alone mediates reward motivation and pleasure.

The concept of biologically based sensitivities to signals of positive and negative reinforcement and Gray's approach in general differ from preceding models in several ways. Of foremost importance is the fact that the general trait of arousability is identified with the dimension of neuroticism rather than extraversion or strength of the nervous system. Actually, the interest is shifted from a concept of general arousal and conditionability to the specific types of arousal associated with signals of reward or punishment. The introversion–extraversion dimension reflects the balance between the two kinds of sensitivity or arousability. The intensity of stimulation and the idea of personality based on the regulation of stimulation plays little role in this theory.

Novelty is assumed to be an unconditioned stimulus for the anxiety system alone. This is one of my primary objections to the model. In my view, novelty is an unconditioned stimulus for exploration as well as fear. In fact, novel stimuli that have no association (cognitive or experiential) with aversive consequences rarely provoke fear, although such stimuli may elicit transient startle or even a mild but transient fear, if presented suddenly. Such stimuli are also attractive to many persons in the form of risk-taking behavior and enjoyment of vicarious fright experience, as when watching horror movies, or vicarious sexual experience when viewing erotic movies (Zuckerman & Litle, 1986). Differential physiological and affective responses to novel and intense stimuli constitute the basis of much of the research on sensation seeking (Zuckerman, 1979. 1983) to be discussed next. Because Gray's interest is in the limbic centers, not accessible to surface electrodes, he must work with nonhuman species in which such centers can be electrically or chemically lesioned. He has had little interest in psychophysiology, used in studies of arousal with humans, because these methods can tell us little about the status of the limbic systems believed to underlie the basic dimensions.

Gray has not developed a personality test to assess his translations of the model to the human level, borrowing instead from work with Eysenck's scales. The net result of this species and methodology "gap" is that the applicability of Gray's model to the other models is questionable. On the other side, Gray has been able to draw on the psychopharmacological literature on psychiatric patients and the experimental comparative literature to pursue the biological basis of personality to its more fundamental biochemical levels.

ZUCKERMAN: SENSATION SEEKING, OPTIMAL LEVEL OF AROUSAL OF CATECHOLAMINE SYSTEMS

The aim of the first sensation seeking scale (Form II, Zuckerman, Kolin, Price, & Zoob, 1964) was to measure a personality trait directly representing the seeking of stimulation that is highly arousing. The scale was developed to predict individual reactions to the experimental situation of sensory deprivation, but in the 1970s the use of the scale was extended into other areas like sexual experience, drug use, volunteering for unusual experiments or situations, and risk taking in general (Zuckerman, 1979). Sensation seeking has to do with positive emotions like joy as well as the positive feelings produced by novel experience. The first theory (Zuckerman, 1969) was oriented toward an explanation of reactions to situations of sensory deprivation and sensory overstimulation. The first biological basis hypothesized (Zuckerman, 1969) was broad, suggesting a constitutional factor of CNS and autonomic nervous system reactivity and "satiability" in response to specific arousal aspects of stimulation (intensity, novelty, complexity, and emotional associations). Later (Zuckerman, Murtaugh, & Siegel, 1974), the theory focused on the reticulocortical feedback system and its setpoints for arousal and inhibition. Finally, the theory turned to a biochemical basis in the limbic monoamine systems and their interactions (Zuckerman, 1979). After abandoning an optimal level of arousal theory based on the reticulocortical system, a new optimal level theory, based on activity of catecholamine systems related to intrinsic reward, was formulated (Zuckerman, 1984). Novel and intense stimuli have been shown to activate the noradrenergic system originating in the locus coeruleus that, in turn, activates the cortex through a diffuse projection system. Arousal of the cortex, however, is now seen as a secondary effect and not as the basis for the hedonic motivation of arousing stimulation. Still implicit in the theory, as in most of the other theories discussed, is an interaction of this personality dimension with stimulus intensity and novelty.

Problems in the Definitions of Arousal

Although Pavlov defined strength of the nervous system in terms of cortical cell arousal capacity, many of the experimental definitions have been in terms of behavioral responses like conditioned eye blinks or performance under intense or prolonged stimulation. There is no necessary one-to-one correspondence between physiological arousal and behavioral activity. Heightened activity may be a result of CNS arousal, or it may be compensatory to states of lowered arousal. The latter effect is the basis for Eysenck's concept of the extravert as a sensation seeker and Strelau's assumption that the low-reactive type shows a high degree of "positively oriented activity (stimulation seeking)." Arousal may produce activity, and activity produces arousal. States of lowered arousal lead to seeking of arousal by novel or intense stimuli. However, we would not expect sensation seekers or extraverts to have the endurance for prolonged stimulation if that stimulation is repetitive and therefore dearousing. Pavlov (1927) noted that the only way to condition sanguine types of dogs, who tended to fall asleep in the monotonous conditioning situation, was to vary the conditioned stimulus. Novelty has a disinhibiting effect. Because the sanguine type is also balanced and mobile, it shifts readily from excitation to inhibition when stimuli are weak and repetitive. In this regard, it is interesting that high sensation seekers are "sleep efficient" (Coursey, Buchsbaum, & Frankel, 1975), that is, they tend to go to sleep quickly after getting into bed. Low sensation seekers tend to be insomniac, probably because they are overreactive to low levels of internal and external stimuli at bedtime.

Given the uncertain relationship between physiological arousal and behavioral activity, many investigators have turned to the use of psychophysiological methods in order to assess the effects of stimulation or lack of stimulation (sensory deprivation) on arousal. The use of such methods has encountered a limitation in the lack of correlation between various physiological indexes of arousal and between the same measures in reaction to different stimulus modalities. Cardiovascular measures of arousal rarely correlate with electrodermal or EEG measures. Buchsbaum, Haier, and Johnson (1983) have not found cross-modality correlations for the "augmenting-reducing" evoked-potential measure. Strelau (1983) called the lack of correlations between various indexes of nervous system function in response to different sensory modalities the "partiality phenomenon." Although there may be sound physiological reasons for a dissociation between the reactivity of different sensory systems, the results raise doubts about the idea of a generalized arousal as the basis of personality traits.

Even when we look more closely at a single index like heart rate or evoked potentials, we find different kinds of response characteristics determined by specific characteristics of the stimulus and the task. Does heart rate acceleration or deceleration indicate "arousal" in immediate response to a stimulus? Which component of the EP measured from which electrode placement indicates the cortical "arousal" produced by the stimulus? The body has different patterns of reacting to stimuli depending on the factors of novelty, intensity, meaning, and the type of cognitive processing that is required. Generalized "arousal" is too gross a construct to encompass these differentiated modes of response. In my view, *arousal* should never be used without a specific referent term like *cardiovascular arousal, cortical arousal, electrodermal arousal, behavioral arousal, affective arousal,* and even this degree of specificity may not be sufficient.

A MULTIMODAL MULTIRESPONSE PSYCHOPHYSIOLOGICAL STUDY OF SENSATION SEEKING

Como, Simons, and Zuckerman (1984) did an experiment designed to examine the relationships among three psychophysiological correlates of sensation seeking across two stimulus modalities. The previously reported correlates were augmenting-reducing of cortical evoked potentials (EPs), acceleration and deceleration of heart rate (HR), and skin conductance (SC) response. A range of intensities for both the visual and auditory modalities was used. Another purpose was the replication of the relationships of these phenomena to sensation seeking, particularly to the Disinhibition subscale that has shown the strongest relationship to most of the measures.

Many measures have been used to define strength of the nervous system including conditioned responses, sensory thresholds, reaction time, and the photic driving of the EEG (Strelau, 1983). Strelau has summarized the correlations and found a general tendency toward a positive correlation, although the correlations are generally not high enough to justify substituting one method for another as a sole definition for the construct. If the choice of method must be made, it should be on some logical basis such as the fit to the theory. Because the construct involves cortical reactivity, the more direct EEG indexes would seem more appropriate. Strelau does report that the photic driving of the EEG is the currently popular method in the Soviet Union.

In Western countries, the cortical evoked potential (EP) has been recognized as the most effective way to measure cortical response to stimuli. Buchsbaum has used the N1-P1 component of the EP in response to a range of stimulus intensities to assess the trait of "augmenting-reducing" (Buchsbaum *et al.*, 1983). The trait may be defined by the slope of the correlation between stimulus intensity and EP amplitudes: Augmenters show high positive slopes and reducers show zero or negative slopes. The phenomena are largely determined by what happens to the EP at the higher intensities of stimulation where some individuals continue to show increasing cortical response (augmenters), whereas others show a reduced response (reducers). Reducing can be conceptually related to the Pavlovian construct of "transmarginal inhibition," a cardinal trait associated with the weak nervous system type. Although the name given to this biological trait is the same as that used by Petrie (1967) for an entirely different type of measurement, involving psychophysical judgments of width, the two constructs are actually opposite in their inferences for personality. This may be because Petrie's measure is a response to relatively low levels of stimulation, whereas Buchsbaum's augmenting-reducing occurs at the highest intensities. At any rate, Buchsbaum's measure gives reliable results, shows strong genetic determination, and is a direct measure of cortical reactivity rather than an inferred one.

Buchsbaum (1971) first suggested the direct relationship between EP augmenting and sensation seeking. Since then, studies by Como *et al.* (1984), Coursey *et al.* (1975), Lukas (1982), Lukas and Mullins (1985), Mullins and Lukas (1984), Orlebeke, Kok and Zeillemaker (1984), von Knorring (1981), and Zuckerman *et al.* (1974) have confirmed the relationship, particularly with the Disinhibition subscale. One study (Haier, Robinson, Braden, & William, 1984) could not confirm the finding on Disinhibition and, comparing extreme augmenters and reducers, claimed to find differences in the opposite direction on some of the other subscales. However, results on the full sample and analyses done separately for males and females simply reveal no differences. This failure to replicate may be due to the more limited range of stimulus intensity used by these investigators.

Coursey *et al.* (1975), Lukas and Mullins (1985), Mullins and Lukas (1984), and Orlebeke *et al.* (1984) used auditory EPs; Lukas (1982), von Knorring (1984), and Zuckerman *et al.* (1984) used the visual EP. Studies by Buchsbaum *et al.* (1983) and Raine, Mitchell, and Venables (1981) failed to find a correlation between EP augmenting and reducing across visual and auditory stimulus modalities. We decided to pursue the question of cross-modality generality further by testing visual and auditory EPs in the same subjects.

Como *et al.* (1984) selected subjects scoring in the upper and lower ranges on the Sensation Seeking Disinhibition subscale. Visual stimuli (light flashes) were used in one session and auditory stimuli (tones) in another. In the first series in each session, a long interstimulus interval (ISI) of 17 seconds was used in order to record the slower HR and SC responses simultaneously with EPs. In the second series in each session, measuring just the EPs, a short ISI of 2 seconds was used in order to sample more EPs at each stimulus intensity. The long ISI series had to be presented first in each session to avoid habituating the HR and SCR responses to the stimuli. Four intensities of stimulation were used for both auditory and visual modalities.

Evoked Potential (EP) Results

Significant interactions between stimulus intensity and sensation seeking were found for the short ISI series for auditory stimulation and for the long ISI series for visual stimulation. In accordance with previous results, the high disinhibitors showed augmenting, and the lows showed reducing at higher intensities for *both* the visual and auditory modalities. A significant correlation ($r = .39$, $p < .01$) was found between the visual and auditory slope measures of augmenting-reducing for the long ISI series, but the correlation was low and insignificant for the short ISI series.

Our results have shown replication of the sensation-seeking versus augmenting relationship for both sensory modalities and some evidence of cross-modality correlation of augmenting. The results varied for the two different ISI series for reasons that are not clear. Because the long ISI series always came first, the results for the short ISI visual condition may have been attenuated by habituation and a consequent lack of attention to the stimuli in the second series. This factor may have been more crucial for the visual than for the auditory stimuli, and the greater number of stimulus presentations in the second series may have resulted in clearer EP definitions.

Heart Rate (HR) and Skin Conductance (SC) Responses

Early findings (Neary & Zuckerman, 1976) of a direct relationship between the amplitude of the electrodermal (SC) orienting reflex (OR) to novel visual and auditory stimuli were replicated by Feij, Orlebeke, Gazendam, and van Zuilen (1985) but could not be replicated by Ridgeway and Hare (1981). More replicable results have been obtained using a beat-by-beat measure of HR. This method enables one to differentiate the OR (HR deceleration) from the startle or defensive reflexes (HR acceleration). Orlebeke and Feij (1979) and Ridgeway and Hare (1981) both found that at moderate intensities of auditory stimulation (60 to 80 dB), high disinhibitors tended to show a stronger deceleration of HR suggestive of an OR, whereas lows showed a stronger accelerative pattern, suggestive of startle or DR (Defensive Reflex). Both studies found that the differences were limited to the first one or two trials when the stimuli were relatively novel.

Stelmack, Plouffe, and Falkenberg (1983) have termed the finding of a stronger electrodermal OR in sensation seekers a "paradox" because the theory and results for the related trait of extraversion are in an opposite direction. Introverts tend to have stronger electrodermal ORs, presumably because of their greater sensitivity to stimulation. It should be noted that the correlation between sensation seeking and extraversion scales is significant but low (.3 to .4); so there is no statistical reason why they should have the same correlates. Actually, I do not believe the results are a paradox, but instead may reflect some basic distinction between sensation seeking and extraversion at the biological level. It is possible that sensation seekers are both more sensitive *and* show greater resistance to inhibition produced by high intensities of stimulation. The answers can only come from examining responses to a range of stimulus intensities as we did in this study using auditory intensities from 50 to 95 dB and visual intensities ranging from 5 to 370 footcandles.

In the Como *et al.* (1984) study, differences in heart rate change were found on the first trials at the extreme intensities of auditory stimulation but not at the middle ones. Although most subjects showed primarily deceleration of HR at 50 dB, the magnitude of the drop in HR was greater for the high than for the low disinhibitors, indicating a stronger OR for the highs. At the highest intensity of 95 dB, most responses were primarily accelerative, but the low disinhibitors showed a greater increase in heart rate than the highs, indicating a stronger startle or defensive reflex for the lows. If we examine the relationship between amplitudes of HR deceleration as a function of stimulus intensity, we find the expected negative linear slope for the high sensation seekers, indicating a shift from deceleration to acceleration as stimulus intensity increases. The low sensation seekers, however, show a curious inverted-U curve with weaker ORs at both the lowest and highest intensities.

No relationship between personality and HR response was found for the visual stimuli. Significant cross-modality correlations were found between HR deceleration ($r = .44$) and HR acceleration ($r = .35$) for the first three trials. Although these correlations are modest, it should be remembered that the stimuli in the two modalities were presented a week apart.

There were no significant findings relating sensation seeking and SCR. This constitutes the second failure of replication for the Neary and Zuckerman (1976) finding on the electrodermal OR. Stelmack *et al.*, (1983) did find some positive results limited to one of two types of visual stimulus. All we can say about this is that the finding is a weak one, if it does exist.

Our results show the difficulty in relating a simple generalized arousal construct to personality. Although augmenting-reducing is related to sensation seeking in both modalities and there is even some relationship between augmenting across modalities, the HR results relating to sensation seeking are confined to the auditory modality. There are significant relationships between HR accelerative and decelerative responses across modalities, but these are not impressively large. All of the HR findings represent an interaction of novelty and intensity because they are only found on the first one to three trials.

If we regard a strong OR to a relatively weak stimulus (50 dB) as a sign of "sensitivity," then high sensation seekers are more sensitive than lows, which is not what would be predicted from a strong nervous system interpretation of sensation seeking. However, the reducing of cortical reaction in the low sensation seekers and the augmenting of the highs is perfectly congruent with the construct, as is the stronger defensive accelerative HR in the lows at high intensities. Strelau (1983) has cited work by Eliasz hypothesizing differences in the width of the band of optimal arousal: Low-reactive types (high sensation seekers) have broader bands than high reactives. However, before we conclude that sensation seekers are more sensitive as well as have more endurance to high intensity stimulation, we must remember that we are speaking of a sensitivity to novel stimuli. The novelty may outweigh the low intensity in determining responses of sensation seekers.

Remembering Freud's definition of an optimum level of intracerebral excitement as the level at which the brain is "accessible to all external stimuli," we may say that the brain of the high sensation seeker has a high optimum level including a special cortical responsivity to novel and intense stimuli. The low sensation seeker seems to be equipped with a biological protection against novel or overarousing stimuli. The adaptive value of an "accessible" and alert brain or a "strong nervous system" is obvious. However, if such openness to stimulation is not modulated by biological protection (perhaps by enzymes like monoamine oxidase (MAO) or endogenous depressants like the endorphins) or a sensible appreciation of risk at the cognitive level, sensation seekers may end up in serious trouble with society (Zuckerman, 1978). Biology is not destiny, but in influencing our basic appetite for stimulation it takes us down some strange byways.

REFERENCES

Breuer, J., & Freud, S. *Studies in hysteria* (A. A. Brill, trans.) New York: Nervous and Mental Disease Publishing Company, 1937. (Originally published 1895.)

Buchsbaum, M. S. Neural events and the psychophysical law. *Science*, 1971, *172*, 502.

Buchsbaum, M. S., Haier, R. J., & Johnson, J. Augmenting and reducing: Individual differences in evoked potential. In A. Gale & J. A. Edwards (Eds.), *Physiological correlates of human behavior: Individual differences and psychopathology* (Vol. 3). London: Academic Press, 1983.

Carlier, M. Factor analysis of Strelau's questionnaire and an attempt to validate some of the factors. In J. Strelau, F. H. Farley, & A. Gale (Eds.), *The biological bases of personality and behavior: Theories, measurement techniques, and development* (Vol. 1). Washington: Hemisphere, 1985.

Como, P., Simons, R., & Zuckerman, M. Psychophysiological indices of sensation seeking as a function of stimulus intensity. *Psychophysiology*, 1984, *21*, 572–573. (Abstract)

Coursey, R. D., Buchsbaum, M. S., & Frankel, B. L. Personality measures and evoked responses in chronic insomniacs. *Journal of Abnormal Psychology*, 1975, *84*, 239–249.

Crow, T. J. Neurotransmitter-related pathways: The structure and function of central monoamine neurons. In A. N. Davison (Ed.), *Biochemical correlates of brain structure and function*. New York: Academic Press, 1977.

Eysenck, H. J. *The biological basis of personality.* Springfield, Il.: Charles Thomas, 1967.

Feij, J. A., Orlebeke, J. F., Gazendam, A., & van Zuilen, R. Sensation seeking: Measurement and psychophysiological correlates. In J. Strelau, F. Farley, & A. Gale (Eds.), *The biological bases of personality and behavior: Theories, measurement techniques, and development* (Vol. 1). Washington: Hemisphere, 1985.

Freud, S. Beyond the pleasure principle. In J. Strachey (Ed. and trans.), *The standard edition of the complete psychological works of Sigmund Freud* (Vol. 18). London: Hogarth, 1955. (Originally published 1920.)

Gray, J. A. Strength of the nervous system and levels of arousal: A reinterpretation. In J. A. Gray (Ed.), *Pavlov's typology*. New York: Macmillan, 1964.

Gray, J. A. Strength of the nervous system, introversion-extraversion, conditionability and arousal. *Behavior Research and Therapy*, 1967, *5*, 151–169.

Gray, J. A. Causal theories of personality and how to test them. In J. R. Royce (Ed.), *Multivariate analysis and psychological theory*, New York: Academic Press, 1973.

Gray, J. A. A critique of Eysenck's theory of personality. In H. J. Eysenck (Ed.), *A model for personality*. New York: Springer, 1981.

Gray, J. A. *The neuropsychology of anxiety: An inquiry into the functions of the septo-hippocampal system.* Oxford: Oxford University Press, 1982.

Haier, R. J., Robinson, D. L., Braden, W., & William, D. Evoked potential augmenting-reducing and personality differences. *Personality and Individual Differences*, 1984, *5*, 293–301.

Lukas, J. H. Human augmenting-reducing and sensation seeking. *Psychophysiology*, 1982, *19*, 333–334. (Abstract)

Lukas, J. H., & Mullins, L. F. Auditory augmenters are sensation seekers and perform better under high work-loads. *Psychophysiology*, 1985, *22*, 580–581. (Abstract)

Mullins, L. F., & Lukas, J. H. Auditory augmenters are sensation seekers—if they attend the stimuli. *Psychophysiology*, 1984, *21*, 589. (Abstract)

Neary, R. S., & Zuckerman, M. Sensation seeking, trait and state anxiety, and the electrodermal orienting reflex. *Psychophysiology*, 1976, *13*, 205–211.

Orlebeke, J. F., & Feij, J. A. The orienting reflex as a personality correlate. In H. D. Kimmel, E. H. van Olst, & J. F. Orlebeke (Eds.), *The orienting reflex in humans*. Hillsdale, NJ: Erlbaum, 1979.

Orlebeke, J. F., Kok, A., & Zeillemaker, C. W. Augmenting-reducing (disinhibition) and the processing of auditory stimulus intensity. *Psychophysiology*, 1984, *21*, 591. (Abstract)

Pavlov, I. P. *Conditioned reflexes, an investigation of the physiological activity of the cerebral cortex* (G. V. Anrep, Trans.). New York: Dover Publications, 1960. (Originally published 1927.)

Petrie, A. *Individuality in pain and suffering.* Chicago, Ill.: University of Chicago Press, 1967.

Raine, A., Mitchell, D. A., & Venables, P. H. Cortical augmenting-reducing-modality specific? *Psychophysiology*, 1981, *18*, 700–708.

Ridgeway, D., & Hare, R. D. Sensation seeking and psychophysiological responses to auditory stimulation. *Psychophysiology*, 1981, *18*, 613–618.

Stein, L. Reward transmitters, catecholamines and opioid peptides. In M. A. Lipton, A. DiMascio, & K. F. Killam (Eds.), *Psychopharmacology: A generation of process.* New York: Raven Press, 1978.

Stelmack, R. M. A factor analysis of the Eysenck Personality Inventory and the Strelau Temperament Inventory. *Personality and Individual Differences*, 1985, *6*, 657–659.

Stelmack, R. M., Plouffe, L., & Falkenberg, W. Extraversion, sensation seeking and electrodermal response: Probing a paradox. *Personality and Individual Differences*, 1983, *4*, 607–614.

Strelau, J. *Temperament, personality, activity.* London: Academic Press, 1983.

von Knorring, L. Visual evoked responses and platelet monoamine oxidase in patients suffering from alcoholism. In H. Begleiter (Ed.), *The biological effects of alcohol.* New York: Plenum Press, 1981.

Wise, R. A. Neuroleptics and operant behavior. The anhedonia hypothesis. *The Behavioral and Brain Sciences*, 1982, *5*, 39–87.

Zajonc, R. B. Feeling and thinking: Preferences need no inferences. *American Psychologist*, 1980, *35*, 151–175.

Zuckerman, M. Theoretical formulations: I. In J. P. Zubek (Ed.), *Sensory deprivation: Fifteen years of research.* New York: Appleton-Century, 1969.

Zuckerman, M. Sensation seeking and psychopathy. In R. D. Hare & D. Schalling (Eds.), *Psychopathic behavior: Approaches to research.* New York: Wiley, 1978.

Zuckerman, M. *Sensation seeking: Beyond the optimal level of arousal.* Hillsdale, NJ: Erlbaum, 1979.

Zuckerman, M. To risk or not to risk: Predicting behavior from negative and positive emotional states. In K. R. Blankstein, P. Pliner, & J. Polivy (Eds.), *Assessment and modification of emotional behavior.* New York: Plenum Press, 1980.

Zuckerman, M. A biological theory of sensation seeking. In M. Zuckerman (Ed.), *Biological bases of sensation seeking, impulsivity, and anxiety.* Hillsdale, NJ: Erlbaum, 1983.

Zuckerman, M. Sensation seeking: A comparative approach to a human trait. *The Behavioral and Brain Sciences*, 1984, *7*, 413–434.

Zuckerman, M., & Litle, P. Personality and curiosity about morbid and sexual events. *Personality and Individual Differences*, 1986, *7*, 49–56.

Zuckerman, M., Kolin, E. A., Price, L., & Zoob, I. Development of a sensation seeking scale. *Journal of Consulting Psychology*, 1964, *28*, 477–482.

Zuckerman, M., Murtaugh, T. M., & Siegel, J. Sensation seeking and cortical augmenting-reducing. *Psychophysiology*, 1974, *11*, 535–542.

Zuckerman, M., Ballenger, J. C., & Post, R. M. The neurobiology of some dimensions of personality. In J. R. Smythies & R. J. Bradley (Eds.), *International Review of Neurobiology* (Vol. 25). New York: Academic Press, 1984.

CHAPTER 13

Issues in the Measurement of Arousability

PAUL M. KOHN

AROUSABILITY AND SENSATION SEEKING

Some concept of arousability is central to several current theories of individual differences. Notable instances are the concepts of subjective augmentation versus reduction of stimulus intensities (Petrie, 1967), introversion-extraversion (Eysenck, 1967), reactivity (Strelau, 1983), and strength of the nervous system (Nebylistyn, 1972a). Several authors have noted the conceptual similarities among some or all of these theoretical constructs (e.g. Barnes, 1976; Davis, Cowles, & Kohn, 1983; Eysenck, 1981; Gray, 1967; Strelau, 1982). Accordingly, the term, *arousability*, will be used generically here when referring to common properties of these constructs or measures thereof.

THE INITIAL ISSUE

A significant feature of the theories cited is that they all assume a compensatory relationship between arousability, on the one hand, and arousal and sensation seeking, on the other. That is, extraverts, reducers, low reactives, and persons with strong nervous systems, being

PAUL M. KOHN • Department of Psychology, York University, Downsview, Ontario, Canada M3J 1P3. The author gratefully acknowledges the facilitation of his work by Research Grant No. 410-83-1270 and Leave Grant No. 451-85-0764 from the Social Sciences and Humanities Research Council of Canada.

relatively low in arousability, are, therefore, predisposed to pursue high stimulation and arousal; conversely, introverts, augmenters, high reactives, and persons with weak nervous systems are inclined, because of their high arousability, to avoid strong stimulation and arousal. It is as if we all strive to achieve or maintain an optimum level or range of arousal, one that may even be common to people generally (Sales, 1971, 1972). Given wide variations in arousability (which may be defined by tonic level of arousal), people vary in their probability of becoming either underaroused or overaroused and, therefore, differ also in how they typically pursue optimum arousal, that is, by sensation seeking or sensation avoiding, respectively.

Zuckerman and his associates have argued, to the contrary, that it is augmenters (highly arousable individuals) who are high and reducers (low arousable individuals) who are low in sensation seeking (Zuckerman, 1979; Zuckerman, Buchsbaum, & Murphy, 1980). They base this position on finding that high scorers on Zuckerman's (1971) Sensation-Seeking Scale (SSS) show increasing amplitudes of their cortical average evoked potentials (AEPs) to increasing intensities of visual and auditory stimulation, whereas low SSS scorers display decreasing amplitudes to the same variations (Buchsbaum, 1971; Zuckerman, Murtaugh, & Siegel, 1974). In Buchsbaum's (1971) terms—but not, as will be shown, in the original usage of Petrie (1967)—high sensation seekers are, therefore, augmenters, and low sensation seekers reducers, based on their AEP responses.

Furthermore, Zuckerman (1979) abandoned an earlier espousal of the concept of optimal level of arousal. His argument for so doing was the finding that a central nervous stimulant, d-amphetamine, improved both affect and cognitive performance for both high and low sensation seekers above the levels they showed under administration of a placebo or diazepam, a depressant drug (Carrol, Zuckerman, & Vogel, 1982). Presumably, optimum-level-of-arousal theories would predict better mood and performance for high sensation seekers on amphetamine and low sensation seekers on diazepam. Kohn and Coulas (1985) similarly found that both sensation seeking and stimulus intensity reducing correlated positively with the use of stimulant, depressant, and what Ray (1978) has called *phantasticant* drugs, specifically tobacco, alcohol, and marijuana, respectively. Furthermore, they observed that summed desirability ratings for stimulant effects and for depressant effects attributed to various drugs actually correlated positively, $r (76) = .47, p < .01$, and that high scorers on the Disinhibition (Dis) subscale of the SSS perceived *both* kinds of effects as more desirable than did low scorers. (A similar difference on the General subscale [Gen] of the SSS proved significant for males only.) Thus, it appears that the extent and variety of drug use rather than drug preference relate to sensation seeking (Zuckerman, 1983, p. 211); moreover, the specific attraction to drugs seems to be consciousness alteration as such, regardless of its direction in relation to one's optimum level of arousal (Kohn, Barnes, & Hoffman, 1979).

Rejection of the optimum-level-of-arousal theory merely on such grounds may well be premature. It seems to reflect an implicit assumption that liking versus disliking drug effects is a purely inherent matter. This overlooks the important role of learning, notably from cultural and subcultural sources, in forming such preferences (Becker, 1953) and in influencing the content of drug experience (Becker, 1967), possibly including even cognitive facilitation versus impairment.

A Suggested Theoretical Resolution

Regarding the relationship between augmenting-reducing and sensation seeking, Davis, Cowles, and Kohn (1983) have suggested that the disagreement between the Zuckerman and Petrie positions is semantic. There is equivocation in the use of the terms *augmenting* and *reducing*. Whereas Petrie applied them to subjective rather than physiological responses to increasing intensities of stimulation, Zuckerman defined them in terms of the amplitude of the cortical average evoked potential in response to such variations. Thus, Petrie's augmenter corresponds to Zuckerman's reducer, and her reducer to his augmenter.

The concept of transmarginal, or protective, inhibition (Nebylitsyn, 1972a) provides a possible explanation for the discrepancy. Theoretically, responses to stimulation, notably central nervous responses, increase with increasing stimulus intensity until a point is reached beyond which further response remains at the same level or diminishes for the protection of the nerve cells involved. This point is the threshold of transmarginal, or protective, inhibition, and it occurs at higher levels of stimulus intensity for individuals with strong nervous systems than for those with weak nervous systems. Stated differently, "strongs" have more "functional endurance," or capacity for continuing increased response to increasing intensity of stimulation than do "weaks."

The point in relation to studies concerning sensation seeking and average evoked potentials is that the visual and auditory stimuli used may be intense enough to exceed the thresholds of transmarginal inhibition for persons with weak, but not strong, nervous systems. Because Petrie's reducers, being rather nonarousable, correspond to the strong nervous system and her augmenters, being highly arousable, to the weak nervous system, her reducers should augment, and her augmenters reduce on the AEP. Davis *et al.* (1983) cite a study by von Knorring, Monakhov, and Perris (1978) in support of their position. The latter authors studied AEPs to wide intensity ranges of visual and auditory stimulation and reported that individuals with high sensitivity, that is, high magnitude of the first evoked response and low absolute sensory threshold, showed a reducing AEP amplitude to increasing stimulus intensity. Conversely, subjects with low sensitivity, that is, low magnitude of the first evoked response and high absolute sensory threshold, displayed an augmenting AEP amplitude to increasing stimulus intensity. Because strength-of-the-nervous-system theory claims that sensitivity to weak stimulation and functional endurance are inversely related (Nebylistyn, 1972a), these findings both fit that theory and explain why the usage of *augmenting* and *reducing* by Petrie and by Zuckerman has diametrically opposite meanings.

SOME INITIAL EMPIRICAL FINDINGS

The problematic relationship between sensation seeking and augmenting-reducing attracted the research attention of the present author and his associates. Unfortunately, Petrie's (1967) psychophysical measure of augmenting-reducing, the kinesthetic figural aftereffect (KFA), has had its reliability and validity severely questioned (e.g., Morgan & Hilgard, 1972; Weintraub, Green, & Herzog, 1973; Weintraub & Herzog, 1973). (One research team [Baker, Mishara, Kostin, & Parker, 1976; Mishara & Baker, 1978] rebutted such criticisms as follows: (a) There are consistent differential carryover effects from pretest to pretest that make retest reliability of KFA difference scores an inappropriate index of true reliability; (b) reliability of the KFA in terms of internal consistency is more than adequate; and (c) correspondingly, appropriate measures based on the first pretest only correlate predictably with validity criteria. Unfortunately, although the first two points are now generally conceded, recent studies have failed to demonstrate criterion validity for KFA measures based on the first pretest only [Davis, Cowles, & Kohn, 1984; Herzog & Weintraub, 1982].) Accordingly, we used a psychometric test, Vando's (1970) Reducer-Augmenter Scale (RAS) with fairly well-established reliability and validity (Barnes, 1985). Reducers on this measure, in line with theoretical expectation, are more pain-tolerant, less hypochondriacal, more extraverted, and more internal in locus of control, notably on Reid and Ware's (1974) Self-Control subscale, than are augmenters (Barnes, 1985).

We also found in several studies that reducers on the RAS score significantly higher on Zuckerman's (1971) Sensation-Seeking Scale than do augmenters (Davis *et al.*, 1984; Goldman, Kohn, & Hunt, 1983; Kohn & Coulas, 1985; Kohn, Hunt, & Hoffman, 1982; Kohn, Hunt, Cowles, & Davis, 1986). Correlations between the RAS and the General subscale of the SSS ranged from the .40s to the .60s. In any event, the relationship needs little further replication.

POSSIBLE PSYCHOMETRIC PROBLEMS

Although the issue of the relationship between arousability and sensation seeking would seem to have been closed, it was not. This is because of an unfortunate property of the Reducer-Augmenter Scale. The measure is based on the *assumption* that reducers are high and augmenters low in sensation seeking. Accordingly, it offers forced choices between high and low sensation-seeking alternatives (e.g., thrills vs. tranquility, too much exercise vs. too little exercise). The high sensation-seeking alternative always qualifies as the reducing response, and the low sensation-seeking alternative as the augmenting response. Thus, it could be claimed that a positive relationship with the SSS is "built into" the RAS, or, differently put, that the RAS is an alternative measure of sensation seeking.

The main argument against this position is that there is ample evidence for the validity of the RAS as a measure of augmenting-reducing, not sensation seeking. These validity data, therefore, support the attribution of stimulus-intensity reducing rather than augmenting to high sensation seekers, even if one does view the relationship between the SSS and the RAS as built in.

Recent research (Kohn *et al.*, 1986) points out some other difficulties with the Reducer-Augmenter Scale. It seems to consist of three moderately intercorrelated factors (.21 to .41), interpreted as Musical Augmenting-Reducing, General-Life-style Augmenting-Reducing, and Physical Thrill Seeking. These pertain, respectively, to preferences for loud, rhythmic, rock-type music versus quiet, melodic, nonrock music; very mixed aspects of high versus low sensation-seeking life-style, for example, preferences concerning pets, politics, people, occupations, leisure, and body odors; and physical thrill seeking, notably in the context of athletic activities. It is mainly the General-Life-style factor that contributes to relationships against measures of general arousal and sensation seeking, that is, the SSS, Mehrabian and Russell's (1973) Arousal-Seeking-Tendency Scale, and three of the four subscales of a revised version of Pearson's (1970) Novelty-Experiencing Scale (Kohn & Annis, 1975), although the Physical Thrill-Seeking factor also contributes substantially in this regard. The latter factor correlates primarily with other measures of physical thrill seeking, that is, the Thrill-and-Adventure-Seeking subscale of the SSS and the External Sensation-Seeking subscale of the Novelty-Experiencing Scale. The Musical factor, which correlates only slightly with most measures of general sensation and arousal seeking, and physical thrill seeking is a pretty good predictor of subjects' preferred volume for listening to popular music on stereo, whereas the other factors are not (Kohn, Cowles, & Lafreniere, in press; Kohn *et al.*, 1986). The Musical factor does not correlate with absolute auditory threshold (AAT). (Neither do the other two factors or the full-scale RAS.)

The conclusion was reached that problems with the RAS, notably its built-in sensation-seeking content and its overrepresentation of content parochially relevant to music, made it important to relate sensation seeking to other measures of arousability. Accordingly, the development and validation of our own measure, the Reactivity Scale, is detailed later following a brief discussion of why other, existing measures were not simply used instead.

FURTHER RESEARCH WITH AN ALTERNATIVE MEASURE

Two obvious alternative measures of arousability are the Extraversion subscales of either the Eysenck Personality Inventory (EPI-E; Eysenck & Eysenck, 1968) or the Eysenck Personality Questionnaire (EPQ-E; Eysenck & Eysenck, 1975) and the Strength of Excitation (SE) subscale of the Strelau (1972a) Temperament Inventory (STI). Eysenck's extraversion measures seem to have two main factorial constituents, impulsivity and sociability, the former of which is theoretically more relevant to arousability (Rocklin & Revelle, 1981). Thus, much of the contents of EPI-E and EPQ-E have limited relevance to arousability. Rocklin and Revelle (1981) hold this to be a more serious problem in the EPQ than the EPI. In any event, a decision was made not to rely on either Extraversion subscale as a sole measure of arousability.

With respect to Strelau's (1972a) Strength-of-Excitation measure, a number of studies have produced results that raise questions about its validity. Although reasonably high correlations of this measure against extraversion have been reported by Strelau (1983), Carlier (1985), Paisey and Mangan (1980), and by Gilliland (1985) for EPQ-E, no significant relationships were found in studies by Stelmack, Kruidenier, and Anthony (1985) and by Gilliland (1985) for EPI-E. Other problematic observations are as follows: Carlier (1985) found that SE did not predict the threshold of transmarginal inhibition in an eyelid-conditioning task. Similarly, Gilliland (1985) failed to find that low scorers on the SE subscale, presumably persons with weak nervous systems, showed a greater decline in alpha blocking on an EEG variant of the extinction-with-reinforcement procedure. Finally, Strelau and Terelak (1974) did not obtain the expected positive relationship between the EEG alpha index and SE. Although there are many positive results concerning the validity of the SE, the negative findings plus our sense that the STI's phrasing of items might not be congenial to North American subjects, even university students, made us decide not to rely on SE exclusively as a measure of arousability in our further research.

Accordingly, we decided to develop our own measure of arousability, calling the eventual product the Reactivity Scale (RS; Kohn, 1985). We generated an initial pool of 104 items (half procontent and half anticontent), each designed to reflect what we considered a defining property of reactivity, the obverse of strength of the nervous system. These properties were high sensitivity to weak stimulation, low functional endurance, low preferred level of stimulation, and high distractability. Items were also designed variously to reference the visual, auditory, other, and mixed modalities.

All items were administered in a 5-point Likert format to 231 undergraduates along with the Edwards (1957) Social Desirability Scale (ESDS). Initial item-selection criteria were a reasonably high item-other correlation within the finally selected set of items (minimum obtained value of .21) and a higher value for each item-other correlation than for the corresponding correlation against the ESDS. These criteria were applied not only overall but also within sex. However, it did prove necessary to relax the second criterion slightly in two cases out of 72 to retain a reasonable number of items. (The 72 cases reflect the responses to each of 24 items plus the ESDS of male subjects, female subjects, and the combined sample.) The product was a 24-item scale that appears elsewhere (Kohn, 1985). The alpha reliabilities were .83 for men ($N = 66$), .82 for women ($N = 165$), and .83 overall ($N = 231$). Correlations against the ESDS were $-.34$, $-.33$, and $-.34$ for these respective groups. Reliabilities were .79 and .74 overall in two other samples reported on in the same chapter and here (Ns of 212 and 60, respectively), and .79 and .80 in subsequently reported studies by Kohn et al. (in press) and Dubreuil and Kohn (in press), respectively. (Ns in these latter studies were 53 and 144, respectively.)

Initial validation efforts involved intercorrelating the Reactivity Scale with other psychometric tests with which it was either expected to correlate significantly (convergent validation) or not (discriminant validation). One college sample ($N = 212$) responded to the RS, the EPI, the RAS, and the SE subscale of the STI. Another ($N = 60$) did the RS, the Stimulus-Screening Questionnaire (SSQ; Mehrabian, 1977), the General subscale of the SSS, and the ESDS. The results for these two samples appear in Tables 1 and 2, respectively.

As Table 1 shows, all the supposed measures of arousability were significantly intercorrelated. RS, specifically, correlated substantially with SE ($-.45$) and RAS ($-.46$), but modestly, if significantly, with EPI-E

Table 1. *Intercorrelations among Measures of Reactivity, Extraversion, Neuroticism, Reducing-Augmenting, and Strength of Excitation*

Variable	1	2	3	4	5	6	7
1. Reactivity	—	—	—	—	—	—	—
2. Extraversion	$-.24^{**}$	—	—	—	—	—	—
3. Sociability	$-.23^{**}$	$.87^{**}$	—	—	—	—	—
4. Impulsivity	$-.14^{*}$	$.77^{**}$	$.42^{**}$	—	—	—	—
5. Neuroticism	$.26^{**}$	$-.13$	$-.13$	$.08$	—	—	—
6. Reducing-Augmenting	$-.46^{**}$	$.59^{**}$	$.46^{**}$	$.51^{**}$	$-.13$	—	—
7. Strength of Excitation	$-.45^{**}$	$.30^{**}$	$.27^{**}$	$.15^{*}$	$-.54^{**}$	$.29^{**}$	—
Mean	76.49	12.10	7.21	4.32	10.83	81.35	104.09
SD	11.59	4.22	2.53	1.88	4.76	8.40	11.19
Cronbach's Alpha (or KR-20)	.79	.75	.65	.53	.82	.85	.81

Note: $N = 212$.
$^{*}p < .05$, two-tailed.
$^{**}p < .01$, two-tailed.

($-.24$). (It should be noted that negative relationships with the other scales were expected for RS because it is conceptually opposite-keyed to them.) Surprisingly, RS correlated even slightly higher (.26) with EPI Neuroticism (EPI-N) than with EPI-E.

These results generally support the convergent validity of the RS.

Table 2. *Correlations among Measures of Reactivity, General Sensation Seeking, Desire for Novelty, Stimulus Screening, and Social Desirability*

Variable	1	2	3	4	5
1. Reactivity	—	—	—	—	—
2. General Sensation Seeking	$-.44^{**}$	—	—	—	—
3. Desire for Novelty	$.07$	$.09$	—	—	—
4. Stimulus Screening	$-.07$	$-.26^{*}$	$-.04$	—	—
5. Social Desirability	$-.32^{*}$	$.20$	$-.35^{**}$	$.30^{*}$	—
Mean	75.95	31.88	4.39	144.13	68.05
SD	10.71	4.49	2.99	31.67	5.06
Cronbach's Alpha (or KR-20)	.74	.81	.87	.90	.77

Note. $N = 60$.
$^{*}p < .05$, two-tailed.
$^{**}p < .01$, two-tailed.

However, the significant correlation of RS with Neuroticism seems to impugn its discriminant validity, notwithstanding the even stronger relationship of SE to EPI-N (−.54). It is entirely possible that significant correlations between measures of arousability and ones of neuroticism, trait anxiety, or autonomic lability reflect a conceptual reality, namely that the underlying traits are not altogether independent. It seems reasonable that people who often experience environmental stimulation as unduly intense should, over time, experience considerable anxiety as a result. The absence of a significant correlation between EPI-E and EPI-N may well simply reflect the fact that items were selected for both subscales to ensure that outcome (Eysenck, 1969).

As Table 2 shows, RS did not correlate significantly with the Stimulus-Screening Questionnaire. It showed a familiar degree of correlation with Social Desirability (−.32) and related substantially to the General subscale of the SSS (−.44). The nonsignificant relationship between RS and Desire for Novelty had been expected.

This last finding supports the discriminant validity of RS because DFN, a measure of boredom and desire for change, has been found unrelated to most major measures in the general domain of experience seeking (Kohn et al., 1982). The absence of correlation between RS and SSQ, however, is disturbing at first glance. We (Michael Cowles and I) found the SSQ to be correlationally "odd man out" in a previous, as yet unreported, study involving several measures of arousability, notably the RAS. Furthermore, Mehrabian (1977) himself found the SSQ to have a weak negative relationship to his own measure of Arousal-Seeking Tendency (Mehrabian & Russell, 1973).

The correlation of RS against Gen is entirely predictable if one assumes that people's dispositions to seek or avoid stimulation compensate for inherent levels of arousability. That is, highly arousable persons frequently avoid strong stimulation, and low arousable persons frequently seek it to compensate for states of overarousal and underarousal, respectively. The correlational results for RS are entirely consistent with what has been found previously with measures of Extraversion (Zuckerman, 1979, pp. 142–148), Strength of Excitation (Strelau, 1983), and the Reducer-Augmenter Scale (Davis et al., 1984; Goldman et al., 1983; Kohn & Coulas, 1985; Kohn et al., 1982; Kohn et al., 1986). Unless all these instruments, along with RS, can be impugned as measures of arousability, the evidence for the compensation hypothesis must be accepted as strong. It should further be noted with respect to RS that items were constructed to reflect the *experiencing* of sensation rather than its pursuit, specifically to avoid the criticism of a "built-in" relationship to sensation seeking.

THE REACTIVITY SCALE AS A PREDICTOR OF RESPONSE TO PAIN

Although data from correlations of the RS against other psychometric tests appeared generally reassuring, it seemed desirable to attempt
validation against experimental measures. The subjective perception and
tolerance of pain were considered ideal candidate measures because their
relationship to other measures of arousability, notably Extraversion
(Barnes, 1975) and the RAS (Barnes, 1985; Mahoney, Shumate, & Worthington, 1980; Vando, 1970), had already been established. Furthermore,
the prediction that highly arousable subjects (high RS scorers) would
experience pain as more intense and tolerate it less well than low arousable subjects (low RS scorers) seemed theoretically obvious.

Accordingly, Debora Dubreuil and I (Dubreuil & Kohn, in press)
administered the RS to 72 men and 72 women college volunteers who
afterward underwent testing for their perception and tolerance of pain.
Painful stimulation was applied via pressure to the index finger of the
dominant hand with Fiorgione and Barber's (1971) Strain-Gauge Stimulator. Two independent groups of subjects, each composed of 36 men
and 36 women, received two different intensities of stimulation: 1,150 g
(low intensity) and 2,300 g (high intensity). Subjects were asked to
endure stimulation for at least 1 minute and as long thereafter as they
could (up to a maximum of 5 minutes). Judgments of pain intensity were
made after 30 sec and 60 sec of stimulation on a predefined 11-point scale
where 0 represented "no pain", 5 "moderate pain," and 10 "severe
pain." Intercorrelations among pain responses, stimulus intensity, sex,
and reactivity appear in Table 3.

It should be noted that the two pain-intensity ratings intercorrelated
highly (.87) and, of course, related negatively to pain tolerance ($-.61$ and
$-.64$ for the 30-sec and 60-sec ratings, respectively). Although RS related
significantly to all three pain measures, stimulus intensity and sex proved
to be better predictors. Men, on average, rated pain as less intense, and
tolerated it longer than did women. Subjects, of course, found the pain
more intense and tolerated it less well under more intense stimulation.
Finally, as predicted, the higher subjects scored on RS, the more intense
they judged the pain to be and the more poorly they tolerated it.

Three hierarchical-entry stepwise multiple-regression analyses were
conducted, one for each pain measure. Main effects were entered first,
then two-way interactions, and finally the three-way interaction. All
three main effects but no interactions were significant predictors for all
three pain measures. (However, the alpha level for RS score as a predictor
of the 30-sec pain rating was relaxed to .06. There were two justifications
for this: The high intercorrelations among the pain measures and the
significant impact of RS score on rated pain at 60 sec [$p < .02$] and on pain

Table 3. Intercorrelations among Pain Responses, Stimulus Intensity, Sex, and Reactivity

Variable	1	2	3	4	5	6
1. Stimulus intensity	—	—	—	—	—	—
2. Sex	.00	—	—	—	—	—
3. Reactivity	−.10	.21*	—	—	—	—
4. Rated pain at 30 sec	.37**	.31**	.17*	—	—	—
5. Rated pain at 60 sec	.33**	.37**	.23**	.87**	—	—
6. Pain tolerance	−.37**	−.36**	−.25**	−.61**	−.64**	—
Mean	—	—	72.44	4.06	6.18	178.53
SD	—	—	12.48	2.35	2.54	93.76

Note. Means and standard deviations for sex and stimulus intensity are omitted because these statistics are meaningless for categorical variables. $N = 144$.
*$p < .05$, two-tailed.
**$p < .01$, two-tailed.

tolerance [$p < .01$].) Reactivity score accounted for 2% of the variance in the 30-sec rating, 3% in the 60-sec rating, and 5% in pain tolerance. Although these are clearly modest contributions in absolute terms, it should be noted that stimulus intensity accounted for only 14%, 11%, and 14% of the variance in these respective measures. In this light, the results for RS seem more respectable. Obviously, because the values of R^2 ranged from .26 to .32, a lot of variance in pain responses was not accounted for. Possibly, such unmeasured factors as the need for social approval (Milham & Jacobson, 1978) play an important role. Such variables would pertain to one's willingness to admit one's distress rather than the actual experience of pain.

The relationship of RS to pain tolerance is notably weaker than that reported by Vando (1970) for the RAS against his measure of pain tolerance. He observed an r value of .84! A possible reason for this was that he used a different measure of pain tolerance. Ours simply measured how long, up to 5 minutes, our subjects endured the experimentally induced pain. He, first of all, used a different pain stimulus, increasing pain pressure applied to the right shin; and second, he put it in the context of simulating a hypothetical medical procedure in which subjects reported when they were likely to flinch and thus impede the physician unless they received anesthetic. This hypothetical context seems likely to reduce the importance of impression managements for subjects and thereby the role of factors like the need for social approval. In any event, subsequent correlations between the RAS and pain measures have been much more modest and roughly comparable to the findings for RS as shown in Table 3 (Barnes, 1985, p. 172; Mahoney *et al.*, 1980).

AN ATTEMPT AT COMPARATIVE VALIDATION

It seemed desirable at this point, given several intercorrelated measures of arousability, to test their validity comparatively against experimental criteria. Accordingly, we (Kohn *et al.*, in press) administered to 53 college volunteers the RAS, the EPI-E, the STI-SE, and the RS. The subjects then performed visual and auditory magnitude estimation tasks plus simple visual and auditory reaction-time tasks. Stimulus intensities were 122, 224, and 740 lux for the visual tasks and 45dB, 70dB, and 85dB (all at 1 kHz) for the auditory tasks. Finally, subjects set the volume of a stereo tape-recorder to their preferred level while listening to a popular music selection. The five tasks produced nine experimental measures relevant to the concept of arousability, notably in strength-of-the-nervous-system terms: slopes and mean judgments for brightness and loudness magnitude estimation (Reason, 1968; Sales & Throop, 1972); slopes and means for reaction times to lights and tones of varying intensities (Keuss & Orlebeke, 1977; Nebylitsyn, 1972a; Reason, 1968; Sales & Throop, 1972; Strelau, 1983); and personally set volume for listening to popular music (Davis *et al.*, 1984; Kohn *et al.*, 1986).

Magnitude-estimation slopes were based on rise/run for the ratio of the difference in mean log estimate for the most and least intense stimuli to the difference in log values (e.g., decibels) of those intensities. For consistency, mean magnitude estimates were also based on log units. Reaction-time slopes were based on rise/run for the ratio of the difference between the logarithmically stabilized mean reaction times for the most and least intense stimuli to the difference (in lux or in decibels) between those intensities. (By "logarithmically stabilized," we mean that the antilogarithm was taken of each mean log reaction time so as to minimize the biasing effects of extremely slow responses.) Again, for consistency, mean reaction times were also expressed in log-stabilized terms.

Highly arousable subjects, whether so defined by RS, RAS, STI-SE, or EPI-E, were expected to show less steep slopes for reaction time, steeper slopes for magnitude estimation, and lower preferred volumes for musical listening. Mean values for magnitude estimation and reaction time are considered because mean reaction times have been considered in previous work (e.g., Reason, 1968) and because differences between introverts and extraverts have been found in overall level, rather than slope, of reaction time (Keuss & Orlebeke, 1977).

The four psychometric tests intercorrelated highly. Individual r values ranged from .45 to .66 in absolute value, taking the appropriate sign in all cases. This is impressive, given the variation in format, psychometric approach, and details of conceptualization. Although there were a few high intercorrelations among experimental measures, it was clear that, as a set, they were less univocal than the psychometric ones. Surprisingly, some fairly high correlations occurred across modalities, tasks, and types of measure (e.g., slopes vs. means). (Details appear in Kohn *et al.*, in press.)

Cross-correlations between single experimental and psychometric measures appear in Table 4. Few correlations proved significant. Two notable exceptions involve preferred stereo volume, on the one hand,

Table 4. *Correlations between Psychometric and Experimental Measures of Arousability*

	Extraversion scale	Reactivity Scale	Reducer-Augmenter Scale	Strength of Excitation
1. Stereo volume	.29*	−.13	.40**	.10
2. Slope of auditory magnitude estimation	−.03	.06	.09	.05
3. Slope of visual magnitude estimation	.20	.05	.04	−.01
4. Slope of auditory reaction time	.19	−.19	.23	.11
5. Slope of visual reaction time	.11	−.19	.09	.16
6. Mean log auditory magnitude estimation	−.11	.06	−.15	−.12
7. Mean log visual magnitude estimation	.10	−.35**	.20	.16
8. Log-stabilized mean auditory reaction time	.07	.08	−.10	.02
9. Log-stabilized mean visual reaction time	−.04	.18	−.21	−.16

Note: $N = 53$.
*$p < .05$, two-tailed.
**$p < .01$, two-tailed.

and EPI-E and RAS, on the other. The latter correlation was particularly high (.40).

It will be recalled that an earlier study (Kohn et al., 1986) revealed that the RAS consisted of three factors, Musical Augmenting-Reducing, General Life-style Augmenting-Reducing, and Physical Thrill Seeking. Furthermore, the significant relationships between RAS and stereo volume in that study ($r = .24$, $p < .05$) was accounted for solely by the Musical subscale ($r = .51$, $p < .01$). Here also stereo volume correlated substantially and significantly with the Musical subscale, r [51] $= .46$, $p < .01$, but not with the other two factor-based subscales.

The only other significant cross-correlation between single experimental and psychometric measures was a negative one between RS and mean log visual magnitude estimation. The latter correlation is theoretically counterintuitive, and its sign can only be justified by reference to the negative relationship between slope and mean level for visual magnitude estimation ($-.56$, $p < .01$).

Following the original rationale of this study as a comparative validation of alternative measures of arousability, one would have to declare RAS the clear winner with EPI-E second, RS a poor third, and STI-SE nowhere in sight. However, the original rationale seems to be somewhat beside the point because the psychometric tests on the one hand, and the experimental indexes on the other seem to be measuring two fairly independent things. To quote a previous presentation (Kohn et al., in press), "one might say that the tests and [experimental] indices used in this study essentially constitute two solitudes."

GENERAL VERSUS PARTIAL PROPERTIES REVISITED

A possible explanation for these findings may lie in the concept of "partial," as against "general," properties of the nervous system: that is, the notion that properties like strength of the nervous system or, in broader terms, arousability may differ somewhat by specific modality and task. Evidence for such partiality has been provided by Ippolitov (1972) and most notably Strelau (1972b, 1983), and the phenomenon was extensively discussed by Nebylitsyn (1972b). The latter identified general properties of the nervous system functionally with the regulation of behavior and adjustment to consequent feedback, and structurally with the anterocentral cortex; in contrast, partial properties were identified with the processing and integrating of sensory information, and with the retrocentral cortex as a structural locus.

The implication seems clear that strong relationships are hardly to be expected between measures of general properties, psychometric or otherwise, and indexes of partial properties. Yet this appears to be precisely what we tried in vain to find in the last study reported here.

Interpreting our findings in these terms raises some underexamined and not fully resolved issues: What kind of measures other than psychometric tests are appropriate to assess arousability as a general property of the nervous system? How should one validate psychometric tests of this property? One possibility that Nebylitsyn (1972b) proposed was to study the impact of temperamental differences on task performance, a challenge taken up with considerable success by Strelau (1983) and his associates. Another possibility would be to study what one might call pathologies of over- or understimulation, for example, Type A behavior, burnout, boredom, and dropping out. In general, one thing seems clear: If one seriously applies the distinction between general and partial properties to arousability, the would-be creator of psychometric measures in this area must pursue a course of construct validation, not criterion validation.

CONCLUSIONS

Our original objective was to provide unequivocal evidence that highly arousable persons tend to avoid strong stimulation and low arousable persons tend to pursue it. Psychometric evidence for this proposition from our own group (Davis *et al.*, 1984; Goldman *et al.*, 1983; Kohn, 1985; Kohn & Coulas, 1985; Kohn *et al.*, 1982; Kohn *et al.*, 1986) and others (Strelau, 1983) now seems overwhelming. For those dubious about the value of psychometric tests alone for testing such hypotheses, supportive behavioral data also exist (Sales, 1971, 1972).

The major issue resurrected by our research is that of general versus partial properties of the nervous system. If one takes this distinction seriously, it is clearly inappropriate to validate psychometric tests of general properties against experimental indexes of partial properties. Finding appropriate validational substitutes for the latter may be one of the great challenges facing contemporary researchers in this field.

REFERENCES

Baker, A. H., Mishara, B. L., Kostin, I. W., & Parker, L. Kinesthetic aftereffect and personality: A case study of issues involved in construct validation. *Journal of Personality and Social Psychology*, 1976, 34, 1–13.

Barnes, G. E. Extraversion and pain. *British Journal of Social and Clinical Psychology*, 1975, 14, 303–308.

Barnes, G. E. Individual differences in perceptual reactance: A review of the stimulus-intensity-modulation individual-difference dimension. *Canadian Psychological Review*, 1976, *17*, 29–52.

Barnes, G. E. The Vando R-A Scale as a measure of stimulus reducing-augmenting. In J. Strelau, F. H. Farley, & A. Gale (Eds.), *The biological bases of personality and behavior: Theories, measurement techniques, and development* (Vol. 1). Washington: Hemisphere, 1985.

Becker, H. S. Becoming a marihuana user. *American Journal of Sociology*, 1953, *59*, 235–242.

Becker, H. S. History, culture and subjective experience: An exploration of the social bases of drug-induced experiences. *Journal of Health and Social Behavior*, 1967, *8*, 163–176.

Buchsbaum, M. Neural events and psychophysical law. *Science*, 1971, *172*, 502.

Carlier, M. Factor analysis of Strelau's questionnaire and an attempt to validate some of the factors. In J. Strelau, F. H. Farley, & A. Gale (Eds.) *The biological bases of personality and behavior: Theories, measurement techniques, and development* (Vol. 1). Washington: Hemisphere, 1985.

Carrol, E. N., Zuckerman, M., & Vogel, W. H. A test of the optimal level of arousal theory of sensation seeking. *Journal of Personality and Social Psychology*, 1982, *42*, 572–575.

Davis, C. A., Cowles, M. P., & Kohn, P. M. Strength of the nervous system and augmenting-reducing: Paradox lost. *Personality and Individual Differences*, 1983, *4*, 491–498.

Davis., C. A., Cowles, M. P., & Kohn, P. M. Behavioural and physiological aspects of the augmenting–reducing dimension. *Personality and Individual Differences*, 1984, *5*, 683–691.

Dubreuil, D. L., & Kohn, P. M. Reactivity and response to pain. *Personality and Individual Differences*, in press.

Edwards, A. L. *The social desirability factor in personality assessment and research*. New York: Dryden, 1957.

Eysenck, H. J. *The biological basis of personality*. Springfield Il.: Charles C Thomas, 1967.

Eysenck, H. J. The origin and construction of the M.P.I. In H. J. Eysenck & S. B. G. Eysenck (Eds.), *Personality structure and measurement*. London: Routledge & Kegan Paul, 1969.

Eysenck, H. J. General features of the model. In H. J. Eysenck (Ed.), *A model for personality*. Berlin: Springer, 1981.

Eysenck, H. J., & Eysenck, S. B. G. *Manual of the Eysenck Personality Inventory*. San Diego: Educational and Industrial Testing Service, 1968.

Eysenck, H. J., & Eysenck, S. B. G. *Manual of the Eysenck Personality Questionnaire*. London: Holder & Stoughton, 1975.

Fiorgione, A., & Barber, T. X. A strain gauge pain stimulator. *Psychophysiology*, 1971, *8*, 102–106.

Gilliland, K. The Temperament Inventory: Relationship to theoretically similar Western personality dimensions and construct validity. In J. Strelau, F. H. Farley, & A. Gale (Eds.) *The biological bases of personality and behavior: Theories, measurement techniques, and development* (Vol. 1). Washington: Hemisphere, 1985.

Goldman, D., Kohn, P. M., & Hunt, R. W. Sensation seeking, augmenting-reducing and absolute auditory threshold: A strength-of-the-nervous-system perspective. *Journal of Personality and Social Psychology*, 1983, *45*, 405–419.

Gray, J. A. Strength of the nervous system, introversion-extraversion, conditionability and arousal. *Behavioral Research and Therapy*, 1967, *5*, 151–169.

Herzog, T. R., & Weintraub, D. J. Roundup time at personality ranch: Branding the elusive augmenters and reducers. *Journal of Personality and Social Psychology*, 1982, *42*, 729–737.

Ippolitov, F. V. Internalyzer differences in the sensitivity-strength parameter for vision, hearing and cutaneous modalities. In V. D. Nebylitsyn & J. A. Gray (Eds.), *Biological bases of individual behavior*. New York: Academic Press, 1972.

Keuss, P. J. G., & Orlebeke, J. F. Transmarginal inhibition in a reaction time task as a function of extraversion and neuroticism. *Acta Psychologica*, 1977, *41*, 139–150.

Kohn, P. M. Sensation seeking, augmenting-reducing, and strength of the nervous system. In J. T. Spence & C. Izard (Eds.), *Motivation, emotion, and personality: Proceedings of the XXIII International Congress of Psychology*. Amsterdam: North Holland-Elsevier, 1985.

Kohn, P. M., & Annis, H. M. Validity data on a modified version of Pearson's Novelty-Experiencing Scale. *Canadian Journal of Behavioural Science*, 1975, *7*, 274–278.

Kohn, P. M., & Coulas, J. T. Sensation seeking, augmenting-reducing, and the perceived and preferred effects of drugs. *Journal of Personality and Social Psychology*, 1985, *48*, 99–106.

Kohn, P. M., Barnes, G. E., & Hoffman, F. M. Drug-use history and experience seeking among adult male correctional inmates. *Journal of Consulting and Clinical Psychology*, 1979, *47*, 708–715.

Kohn, P. M., Hunt, R. W., Cowles, M. P., & Davis, C. A. Factor structure and construct validity of the Vando Reducer–Augmenter Scale. *Personality and Individual Differences*, 1986, *7*, 57–64.

Kohn, P. M., Hunt, R. W., & Hoffman, F. M. Aspects of experience seeking. *Canadian Journal of Behavioural Science*, 1982, *14*, 13–23.

Kohn, P. M., Cowles, M. P., & Lafreniere, K. Relationships between psychometric and experimental measures of arousability. *Personality and Individual Differences*, in press.

Mahoney, J., Shumate, M., & Worthington, E. L., Jr. Is the Vando Scale a valid measure of perceptual reactance? *Perceptual and Motor Skills*, 1980, *51*, 1035–1038.

Mehrabian, A. A questionnaire measure of individual differences in stimulus screening and associated differences in arousability. *Environmental Psychology and Nonverbal Behavior*, 1977, *1*, 89–103.

Mehrabian, A., & Russell, J. A. A measure of arousal seeking tendency. *Environment and Behavior*, 1973, *5*, 315–333.

Milham, J., & Jacobson, L. The need for approval. In H. London, & J. E. Exner (Eds.), *Dimensions of personality*. New York: Wiley, 1978.

Mishara, B. L., & Baker, A. H. Kinesthetic aftereffect scores are reliable. *Applied Psychological Measurement*, 1978, *2*, 239–247.

Morgan, A. H., & Hilgard, E. R. The lack of retest reliability in individual differences in the kinesthetic aftereffect. *Educational and Psychological Measurement*, 1972, *32*, 871–878.

Nebylitsyn, V. D. *Fundamental properties of the human nervous system*. New York: Plenum Press, 1972. (a)

Nebylitsyn, V. D. The problem of general and partial properties of the nervous system. In V. D. Nebylitsyn & J. A. Gray (Eds.), *Biological bases of individual behavior*. New York: Academic Press, 1972. (b)

Paisey, T. J. H., & Mangan, G. L. The relationship of extraversion, neuroticism and sensation seeking to questionnaire-derived measures of nervous-system properties. *Pavlovian Journal of Biological Science*, 1980, *15*, 123–130.

Pearson, P. H. Relationships between global and specified measures of novelty seeking. *Journal of Consulting and Clinical Psychology*, 1970, *37*, 23–30.

Petrie, A. *Individuality in pain and suffering*. Chicago: University of Chicago Press, 1967.

Ray, O. *Drugs, society and human behavior*. Saint Louis: Mosby, 1978.

Reason, J. T. Individual differences in auditory reaction time and loudness estimation. *Perceptual and Motor Skills*, 1968, *236*, 1089–1090.

Reid, D. W., & Ware, E. E. Multidimensionality of internal versus external locus of control: Addition of a third dimension and nondistinction of self versus others. *Canadian Journal of Behavioural Science*, 1974, *6*, 131–141.

Rocklin, T., & Revelle, W. The measurement of extraversion: A comparison of the Eysenck Personality Inventory and the Eysenck Personality Questionnaire. *British Journal of Social Psychology*, 1981, *20*, 279–284.

Sales, S. M. Need for stimulation as a factor in social behavior. *Journal of Personality and Social Psychology*, 1971, *19*, 124–134.

Sales, S. M. Need for stimulation as a factor in preference for different stimuli. *Journal of Personality Assessment*, 1972, *36*, 56–61.

Sales, S. M., & Throop, W. F. Relationship between kinesthetic aftereffect and "strength of the nervous system." *Psychophysiology*, 1972, *9*, 492–497.

Stelmack, R. M., Kruidenier, B. G., & Anthony, S. B. A factor analysis of the Eysenck Personality Questionnaire and the Strelau Temperament Inventory. *Personality and Individual Differences*, 1985, *6*, 657–659.

Strelau, J. A diagnosis of temperament by nonexperimental techniques. *Polish Psychological Bulletin*, 1972, *3*, 97–105. (a)

Strelau, J. The general and partial nervous system types—data and theory. In V. D. Nebylitsyn & J. A. Gray (Eds.), *Biological bases of individual behavior.* New York: Academic Press, 1972. (b)

Strelau, J. Biologically determined dimensions of personality or temperament. *Personality and Individual Differences*, 1982, *3*, 355–360.

Strelau, J. *Temperament, personality, activity.* New York: Academic Press, 1983.

Strelau, J., & Terelak, J. The alpha index in relation to temperamental traits. *Studia Psychologica*, 1974, *16*, 40–50.

Vando, A. A personality dimension related to pain tolerance. *Dissertation Abstracts International*, 1970, *31*, 2292B–2293B. (University Microfilms No. 70-18,865)

Von Knorring, L., Monakhov, K., & Perris, C. Augmenting/reducing: An adaptive switch mechanism to cope with incoming signals in normal and psychiatric subjects. *Neuropsychobiology*, 1978, *4*, 150–179.

Weintraub, D. J., Green, G. S., & Herzog, T. R. Kinesthetic aftereffects day by day: Trends, task features, individual differences. *American Journal of Psychology*, 1973, *86*, 827–844.

Weintraub, D. J., & Herzog, T. R. The kinesthetic aftereffect: Ritual versus requisites. *American Journal of Psychology*, 1973, *86*, 407–423.

Zuckerman, M. Dimensions of sensation seeking. *Journal of Consulting and Clinical Psychology*, 1971, *36*, 45–52.

Zuckerman, M. *Sensation seeking: Beyond the optimal level of arousal.* Hillsdale, NJ: Erlbaum, 1979.

Zuckerman, M. Sensation seeking: The initial motive for drug abuse. In E. Gotheil, K. A. Druley, T. E. Skoloda, & H. M. Waxman (Eds.), *Etiological aspects of alcohol and drug abuse.* Springfield, Il.: Charles C Thomas, 1983.

Zuckerman, M., Buchsbaum, M. S., & Murphy, D. L. Sensation seeking and its biological correlates. *Psychological Bulletin*, 1980, *88*, 187–214.

Zuckerman, M., Murtaugh, T., & Siegel, V. Sensation seeking and cortical augmenting-reducing. *Psychophysiology*, 1974, *11*, 535–542.

CHAPTER 14

The Study of Personality with Positron Emission Tomography

RICHARD J. HAIER, KEN SOKOLSKI, MARK KATZ, and MONTE S. BUCHSBAUM

INTRODUCTION

A number of researchers have proposed biologically based models of personality. The experimental testing of specific hypotheses concerning personality and brain structures, however, has not been attempted directly in humans because intrusive manipulations or assessments have not been possible without undue risk. The recent development of the technique of Positron Emission Tomography (PET) now allows direct, nonintrusive measures of brain function in specific areas and structures. Function is determined by the quantitative assessment of glucose metabolism.

The PET technique is conceptually simple. A special radioactive glucose analog (18F-2-deoxyglucose) is injected into the subject. The glucose is taken up by the brain during the next 35 minutes. During that time, those structures of the brain that are most active take up the most glucose. The injected glucose is special in that it is metabolically fixed after uptake so that those brain areas that use the most will be the most radioactive. The resulting distribution of glucose throughout the brain remains "frozen" for several hours. The radio-labeled glucose is positron-emitting. The positrons decay into gamma rays at 180° angles. When the subject's head rests in the PET scanner, a ring of crystals

RICHARD J. HAIER, KEN SOKOLSKI, MARK KATZ, and MONTE S. BUCHSBAUM • Department of Psychiatry and Human Behavior, Medical Science Building 1, University of California, Irvine, California 92717.

251

detects the gamma rays and the origin of the decaying positron can be calculated. After several hundred thousand such events, which occur in a matter of minutes, a high resolution picture of a plane of brain tissue can be computed much like a Computerized Axial Tomography (CAT) scan. The major difference is that a CAT scan shows only structure; a PET scan shows structure and how metabolically active the structure was during the 35-minute uptake period. Note that the uptake period need not occur while the subject is in the scanner because the glucose is metabolically fixed at the time of uptake. The scanning is performed after the uptake period.

There are three critical features of the PET technique for studying brain/personality relationships. The first is the condition, activity, or experiment performed during the 35-minute uptake period. Resting with the eyes closed, for example, is a relatively poor control condition for psychological study. An attention experiment like the Continuous Performance Test (CPT) is much better because it requires a specific cognitive activity. The second important consideration is the PET scan image resolution. With current technology, brain areas smaller than 7 mm cannot be imaged with clarity. Some of the brain structures hypothesized as important in personality theories are smaller than this. The third important consideration is cost. PET scanning requires a cyclotron to manufacture the glucose isotope in addition to the scanner itself. Capital costs of over $2 million and a large support staff result in a current per-scan cost of approximately $2,500. Undoubtedly, this will decrease in time as the technology becomes mass produced. For the time being, the high cost requires personality studies to be added on to other projects.

At this writing, in the fall of 1985, we have collected personality data on subjects who participated in a PET study of drug response in Generalized Anxiety Disorder. The data analyses are exploratory but demonstrate, we think, the potential of PET for testing brain/personality hypotheses. As our first effort, we examined part of Eysenck's theory, especially as to whether introversion/extraversion is related to cortical areas. We also were interested in whether the neuroticism dimension (i.e., stability) is related to limbic structures, as suggested by Eysenck (1967).

METHOD

SUBJECTS

Eighteen outpatients (8 male, 10 female; mean age = 40.2; SD = 13.3) meeting DSM-III criteria for Generalized Anxiety Disorder (GAD) and 9 normal controls (all male; mean age = 23.9; SD = 5.4) volunteered for a PET study of drug response. Each patient received two baseline scans during a drug-free period (minimum 2 weeks). Each of these scans had a different glucose uptake condition as is explained later. The patients had a third scan after drug treatment, but this scan is not analyzed for this chapter. Each normal control volunteer was screened for good physical health and the absence of psychiatric problems. All subjects were right-handed. All completed the Eysenck Personality Questionnaire (EPQ, Eysenck & Eysenck, 1976) and the Zuckerman Sensation Seeking Scale (SSS, Zuckerman, 1971) prior to their PET scan.

CPT PROCEDURE

The purpose of the anxiety study was to determine drug effects on attention. Therefore, the Continuous Performance Test (CPT) was used during the uptake period. The patients completed one baseline scan during which the CPT task was used and another baseline scan on a different day during which a control CPT was done. In the control task, subjects are exposed only to the CPT stimuli with no instructions or description of the task. This no-task condition controls for the brain's response to stimuli alone without a cognitive task. The 9 normal controls also completed the same no-task condition for their PET scan. A separate group of normals completed the same CPT task as the patients, but this group has not yet been analyzed. Specifically, the no-task condition required the subject to view random digits flashing for 50 msec each second on a rear projection screen 1 meter in front of them. The digits were 3 diopters out of focus. This blurring makes the number barely recognizable. The subject received no instructions other than to watch the flashes. Thus this no-task condition performed for 35 minutes is rather monotonous. In the task condition, the stimuli were the same, but subjects were instructed to press a button each time they viewed a zero. Moreover, irrespective of the subjects' performance, negative feedback was given during the task so that the subject thought his or her performance was poor. This was designed to increase anxiety during the task.

PET PROCEDURE

The exposure to the digit CPT stimuli took place in a darkened, quiet room for the entire 35-minute uptake period. Before the session began, an intravenous line of 0.9% saline drip was inserted into the subject's left arm for blood sampling and another one into the right arm for isotope injection. The left arm was wrapped in a hot pack for arteriolization of venous blood. The left arm was extended through a slit in a 6-foot-high black curtain, so as to screen blood-sampling activity. Intravenous lines were started well in advance of the glucose injection. At 2 to 3 minutes before the 18F-2-deoxyglucose (FDG) injection, room lights were extinguished and visual stimuli began; the stimuli continued for 30 to 35 minutes after isotope injection. Subjects were not spoken to during uptake, and all remained quiet and cooperative. Small, low-level penlights were kept on for blood sampling behind the curtain. Subjects received 4 to 5.2 millicuries of FDG. After 30 to 35 minutes, subjects were transferred to the scanning room. Nine planes (i.e., slices) parallel to the canthomeatal line (CM) were done between 45 and 100 minutes after FDG injection. The planes selected for this analysis were obtained with shadow shields in and septa shields out, a scanner configuration with measured in-plane resolution of 8 mm and axial resolution of 12. A calculated attenuation correction and smoothing filter were used. The scanner was calibrated each scan day, with a cylindrical phantom, and compared to well counter data.

QUANTIFICATION OF PET

Scans were transformed to the glucose metabolic rate according to the model of Sokoloff *et al.* (1977) using our adaptation of a program developed by Sokoloff. Kinetic constants and the lumped constant from Phelps *et al.* (1979) were used. Each pixel of each brain slice image was converted from raw counts to glucose use in micromoles/100 g tissue/minute. Thus glucose use for each whole slice is quantified. However, we were also interested in glucose use for specific areas and structures within a slice. To obtain these values, we used our region-of-interest method as follows. The image from a structural brain atlas (Matsui & Hirano, 1978) was photographed, digitized, and stored for reference. Atlas pictures for each brain slice scanned were stored. The digitized atlas picture was outlined by our boundary-finding algorithm. The vertical meridian was fitted by least squares regression to the midpoints of line segments joining the right and left edges for each pixel row of the image. This line was bisected and a horizontal 90° meridian was calculated. Then under cursor control, a 3 × 3 pixel box was placed in the center of each structure as identified in the atlas. This is illustrated in Figure 1. Using these standard templates, the proportional locations of these boxes were then transferred automatically to PET slices for each subject. Thus the area of interest was defined by the atlas, and the same area was automatically located in individual PET slices. The mean glucose metabolic rate, calculated by the Sokoloff equation, was calculated within each box. Statistical analyses were done both using the absolute glucose rate within a box and using the relative rate expressed

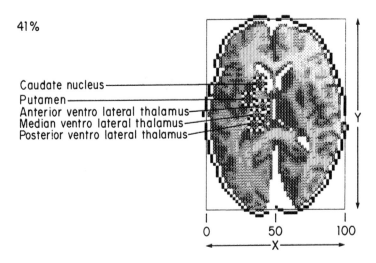

41%

Caudate nucleus
Putamen
Anterior ventro lateral thalamus
Median ventro lateral thalamus
Posterior ventro lateral thalamus

0   50   100
X

Figure 1. The Region-of-Interest Box Analysis. This is a digitized slice from the brain altas. The slice corresponds to the supraventricular level about 45 cm above the CM line. The boxes are placed over the areas of interest manually and their location with respect to horizontal and vertical meridians is calculated and stored. The same boxes are automatically located on the corresponding PET slice for each subject according to proportional meridians. Glucose use is determined within boxes and for the whole slice as described in the text.

as the mean rate within a box divided by the whole slice rate. This latter measure helps control for the large individual differences in brain glucose use.

We chose to use brain area names rather than arbitrary numbered boxes to represent the locations corresponding to the proportional coordinates because these were the likely average locations and were more convenient for discussion. Clearly, in individual subjects, variation in the position of actual areas could be large.

STATISTICAL ANALYSIS

This exploratory analysis is limited to correlating the personality measures with glucose use for the controls and the anxiety patients separately. Three brain slices were assessed for area glucose use as described previously. These slices, supra-, mid-, and infraventricular, are approximately 45, 35, and 25 cm above the canthomeatal (CM) line, respectively. Our atlas templates for these slices contain over 70 boxes of interest. We chose these 3 slices because they contain structures and areas of particular interest.

Table 1. Means, Standard Deviations, and Ranges for Personality Scales in Controls and Patients

Personality dimensions	Controls ($n = 9$)			Anxiety ($n = 18$)		
	Mean	SD	Range	Mean	SD	Range
Extraversion	14.1	4.2	8–20	10.3	5.2	2–19
Neuroticism	3.9	3.1	1–11	16.2	4.8	7–22
Psychoticism	4.6	2.0	1–7	3.3	1.9	0–7
Lie	4.9	3.1	0–8	7.3	2.9	2–12
Sensation seeking	55.8	3.8	49–60	42.6	11.4	22–59
Thrill and adventure	55.4	5.0	46–61	38.7	13.8	20–61
Experience seeking	53.4	6.3	43–59	45.3	7.5	31–62
Disinhibition	49.3	9.4	36–60	44.8	6.0	36–55
Boredom susceptibility	51.2	6.2	41–60	46.3	9.4	28–65

RESULTS

Table 1 shows the mean, standard deviation, and range for each personality scale for both controls and patients. All scales show ranges suitable for correlational analysis, although the ranges and variances tend to be greater for the anxiety group. Note the fourfold increase in mean N score in the anxiety group and the lower scores on the sensation-seeking scales.

Our primary data analysis was the correlating of glucose metabolism in a variety of areas with the personality scales during the active CPT task. We felt the correlations obtained during the active CPT were more likely to reflect any interactions between personality and cognition. The anxiety patients completed scans in both the active and the control CPT; only the normal controls who did the no-task CPT are analyzed. Therefore, in this report, we will compare the anxiety subjects doing the active CPT to themselves doing the no-task CPT and to the normals doing the no-task CPT. All correlations were computed using the absolute measure of glucose use within the template box and the relative measure (i.e., absolute rate within a box divided by the absolute rate for the whole slice).

EPQ

Table 2 shows the significant correlations (two-tailed tests are used for all analyses) between glucose use in cortical areas and the Eysenck scales in the anxiety group during the active CPT. The correlations in

Table 2. Correlations between Glucose Use[a] in Cortical Areas and the Eysenck Scales in the Anxiety Group during the Active CPT Condition (n = 14)

Cortical areas	Personality dimensions			
	E	N	P	L
Midventricular slice (0°–8)				
L. Sup. Frontal Gyrus	.72			
R. Sup. Frontal Gyrus	.65			
L. Mid. Frontal Gyrus				
R. Mid. Frontal Gyrus	.70 (.54)			
L. Inf. Frontal Gyrus	.58			
R. Inf. Frontal Gyrus	.62			
Infraventricular slice (0°–10)				
L. Frontal White Matter		(−.58)		
R. Frontal White Matter			−.56	
L. Sup. Temporal Gyrus	.77		−.55 (−.53)	
R. Sup. Temporal Gyrus	.59			
L. Post. Sup. Temporal Gyrus	.64			
R. Post. Sup. Temporal Gyrus	.64			
L. Mid. Temporal Gyrus	.70		−.54	
R. Mid. Temporal Gyrus				
L. Post. Occipital		(.56)		
R. Post. Occipital			−.55	
L. Sup. Occipital				
R. Sup. Occipital				
L. Mid. Occipital			−.66	
R. Mid. Occipital			−.64	
L. Post. Occipital			−.69 (−.58)	
R. Post. Occipital				
L. Mid. Occipital				
R. Mid. Occipital				
L. Mid. Post. Occipital		(.55)		
R. Mid. Post. Occipital				
L. Frontal	.61		−.55	−.73 (−.65)
R. Frontal	.62			
L. Temporal	.73			
R. Temporal		.53		

[a]Correlations based on relative glucose use are in parentheses.

parentheses are based on relative glucose use; the other correlations are based on absolute glucose use. Areas in the frontal and the temporal gyrus show many positive correlations between the E scale and absolute glucose use. There are no correlations between absolute glucose use and the N scale (and only one with the L scale). Absolute glucose correlations with the P scale are all negative with the highest ones in the mid-

Table 3. Correlations between Glucose Use[a] in Limbic and Basal Ganglia Areas and the Eysenck Scales in the Anxiety Group during the Active CPT Condition (n = 14)

Limbic and basal ganglia areas	Personality dimensions			
	E	N	P	L
Midventricular slice (0°–8)				
L. Caudate				
R. Caudate	.72			
L. Putamen	.74			−.57
R. Putamen	.69			
Infraventricular slice (0°–10)				
L. Putamen		.56 (.72)	−.57	
R. Putamen				
Midventricular slice (0°–8)				
L. AVL Thalamus				
R. AVL Thalamus			−.57	
L. MVL Thalamus	(−.56)			
R. MVL Thalamus			−.56	
L. PVL Thalamus				
R. PVL Thalamus				(.55)
L. Cingulate Gyrus				
R. Cingulate Gyrus			−.55	
Infraventricular slice (0°–10)				
L. Cingulate Gyrus			−.63	
R. Cingulate Gyrus	.55			
L. Hippocampal Gyrus				
R. Hippocampal Gyrus	.56			
L. Hippocampal Gyrus				
R. Hippocampal Gyrus	.59			
L. Parahippocampal Gyrus				
R. Parahippocampal Gyrus	.72			

[a]Correlations based on relative glucose use are in parentheses.

and posterior occiput areas. In contrast, only a sporadic few relative glucose correlations are significant in Table 2.

Table 3 shows the same analysis for limbic and basal ganglia areas. As in the cortical areas shown in Table 2, there are positive correlations between absolute glucose use and brain areas for the E scale. These are in caudate, putamen, cingulate gyrus, hippocampal gyrus, and parahippocampal areas. Negative correlations are found for the P scale in putamen, AVL and MVL thalamus, and cingulate gyrus areas. The N and the L scales show only one correlation each and, as in Table 2, correlations based on relative glucose are sporadically few.

Table 4 shows the same analyses in lower areas of the pons, vermis, and cerebellum. For these lower regions, the relative glucose rates show better correlations, especially with the L scale.

Table 4. Correlations between Glucose Use[a] in Pons, Vermis, and Cerebellum Areas and the Eysenck Scales in the Anxiety Group during the Active CPT Condition (n = 11)[b]

Pons, vermis, and cerebellum areas	EPQ			
	E	N	P	L
Temporal pole slice (0°–12)				
L. Ant. Pons		(−.67)		
R. Ant. Pons				(−.63)
L. Post. Pons		(−.64)		
R. Post. Pons				(−.72)
L. Vermis				(−.64)
R. Vermis				(−.81)
Infraventricular slice (0°–10)				
L. Ant. Cerebellum				
R. Ant. Cerebellum				(−.67)
L. Mid. Cerebellum				(−.68)
R. Mid. Cerebellum				
L. Post. Cerebellum				
R. Post. Cerebellum				
Temporal pole slice (0°–12)				
L. Ant. Cerebellum				
R. Ant. Cerebellum				
L. Post. Cerebellum	.64			
R. Post. Cerebellum				

[a]Correlations based on relative glucose use are in parentheses.
[b]Three subjects were not scanned for the lowest 0°–12 slice during the active CPT.

When the same glucose/personality correlations are computed for the anxiety group in the no-task CPT condition, only a very few correlations are statistically significant; all but one of these are based on relative glucose. No patterns of significant correlations are apparent for any brain areas or any slice. Similarly, very few glucose/personality correlations are significant in the normal control group with the same no-task CPT condition. No area or slice patterns are apparent in the normals. For comparison, all the significant correlations for the anxiety and normal no-task CPT groups are shown in Table 5.

SENSATION SEEKING

Whereas absolute glucose use within an area during the active CPT was more correlated with the Eysenck scales, relative glucose (i.e., box divided by slice) use during the no-task CPT is more correlated with sensation seeking. Table 6 shows the correlations of glucose use in cortical areas with sensation-seeking scales. The most correlations are

Table 5. Significant Correlations between Glucose Use[a] in all Brain Areas and the Eysenck Scales in the No-Task CPT Condition for Anxiety (AN)[b] and Control (C)[c] Groups

All brain areas	EPQ			
	E	N	P	L
Cortical areas (0°–8)				
R. Mid. Frontal Gyrus			C(.71)	AN(−.51)
L. Inf. Frontal Gyrus		AN(−.58)		
Infraventricular slice (0°–10)				
L. Frontal White Matter		AN −.48& AN(−.48)	C(−.79)	
R. Frontal White Matter		C −.79		
L. Sup. Temporal Gyrus				AN(−.61)
R. Sup. Temporal Gyrus			C −.90	C(.76)
L. Post. Sup. Temporal Gyrus				
R. Post. Sup. Temporal Gyrus			C −.68	
R. Mid. Temporal Gyrus	AN(.49)			
L. Post. Occipital	AN(−.54)		AN(−.56)& C(.69)	
L. Mid. Occipital				C(.68)
R. Mid. Occipital		C(−.81)	C −.76& C(−.73)	
L. Post. Occipital			C(−.68)	
L. Frontal			AN(.53)	
Limbic/basal ganglia (0°–10)				
R. Putamen		AN(.55)		
Midventricular slice (0°–8)				
L. AVL Thalamus				C(−.71)
L. MVL Thalamus			C −.75	C(−.79)
Infraventricular slice (0°–10)				
L. Cingulate Gyrus	AN(.48)			
Lower areas (0°–12)				
L. Vermis	AN(−.49)			
Infraventricular slice (0°–10)				
L. Ant. Cerebellum	AN(−.50)			
R. Ant. Cerebellum	AN(−.54)			

[a]Correlations based on relative glucose use are in parentheses.
[b]n = 18; the no-task condition was always first and four subjects were not scanned in the active CPT condition.
[c]n = 9.

found with relative glucose for the normal control group (no-task correlation). Positive and negative correlations are apparent with no strong patterns. The general scale seems most related to occipital areas. No correlations are found for the Boredom Susceptability (BS) subscale.

Table 7 shows the same analysis for limbic and basal ganglia areas. For the active CPT condition in the anxiety group, several relative

Table 6. *Correlations between Glucose Use[a] in Cortical Areas and Sensation-Seeking Scales for CPT Task and No-Task Conditions[b]*

Cortical areas	Sensation-Seeking Scale				
	SS	TA	ES	DIS	BS
Midventricular slice (0°–8°)					
L. Sup. Frontal Gyrus					
R. Sup. Frontal Gyrus				AT −.54	
L. Mid Frontal gyrus			AN −.50		
R. Mid Frontal Gyrus			AT −.57		
L. Inf. Frontal Gyrus				C −.70	
R. Inf. Frontal Gyrus					
Infraventricular slice (0°–10°)					
L. Frontal White Matter	AT .56	AT .57			
R. Frontal White Matter					
L. Sup. Temporal Gyrus					
L. Post. Sup. Temporal Gyrus					
R. Post. Sup. Temporal Gyrus					
L. Mid. Temporal Gyrus	C .73		C .69	C .69	
R. Mid. Temporal Gyrus				AN −.48	AN −.50
L. Post. Occipital					
R. Post. Occipital					
L. Sup. Occipital				C .71	
R. Sup. Occipital					
L. Mid. Occipital	C .75				
R. Mid. Occipital	C .81				
L. Post. Occipital			C −.67	C −.84	
R. Post. Occipital	C .73		C .71	C .79	
L. Mid. Occipital		AN −.53&		AN −.48	
		C −.64			
R. Mid. Occipital	C −.74				
L. Mid. Post. Occipital					
R. Mid. Post. Occipital					

[a] All correlations are based on relative glucose use (i.e., box divided by slice); no absolute correlations were significant.
[b] Correlations in the anxiety CPT task condition are labeled AT ($n = 14$); in the anxiety no-task condition AN ($n = 18$); in the normal controls no-task group, C.

Table 7. Correlations Between Glucose Use[a] in Limbic and Basal Ganglia Areas and Sensation-Seeking Scales for CPT Task and No-Task Conditions[b]

Limbic and basal ganglia areas	Sensation-Seeking Scale				
	SS	TA	ES	DIS	BS
Midventricular slice (0°–8)					
L. Caudate			AN .61	AN .50	
R. Caudate					C –.70
L. Putamen			AN .49	AN .57	
R. Putamen					
Infraventricular slice (0°–10)					
L. Putamen					
R. Putamen					
Midventricular slice (0°–8)					
L. AVL Thalamus	C –.86	AT –.59& AN –.52	AN –.65[c]		C –.78
R. AVL Thalamus	AT –.71	AT –.66& AN –.67			
L. MVL Thalamus			AT .57[d]		

Region				
R. MVL Thalamus	AN −.59			AN −.47
L. PVL Thalamus				
R. PVL Thalamus				
L. Cingulate Gyrus	AT .61& C −.74		AN −.51[e] C −.67	C −.68[f]
R. Cingulate Gyrus				C −.70
L. Cingulate Gyrus	AT .79	AT .61		
R. Cingulate Gyrus				
Infraventricular slice (0°–10)				
L. Hippocampal Gyrus				
R. Hippocampal Gyrus			AT .69	
L. Hippocampal Gyrus		AT .61		
R. Hippocampal Gyrus		AT .72		
L. Parahippocampal Gyrus				
R. Parahippocampal Gyrus				

[a] All correlations are based on relative glucose use (i.e., box divided by slice) unless otherwise identified.
[b] Correlations in the anxiety CPT task group are labeled AT (n = 14); in the anxiety no-task group, AN (n = 18); in the normal controls no-task group, C (n = 9).
[c] Absolute glucose, r = −.48.
[d] Absolute glucose in the AN group, r = −.49.
[e] Absolute glucose in the C group, r = −.68.
[f] Absolute value.

glucose correlations are apparent. The general scale (SS) is positively correlated with the cingulate gyrus; the Thrill and Adventure Seeking (TA) subscale is negatively correlated with areas in the thalamus and the Experience Seeking (ES) subscale is positively correlated with hippocampal gyrus areas.

These patterns are amplified when examined in the anxiety group and normal group no-task CPT condition. These correlations are also shown in Table 7. In the anxiety group no-task CPT condition (AN), the TA scale shows the same pattern as in the active CPT condition. That is, negative correlations with relative glucose use in thalamus areas. The ES pattern changes from hippocampal gyrus areas to caudate and putamen areas and adds negative correlations with thalamus areas. The Disinhibition (DIS) subscale also shows positive correlations with the same caudate and putamen areas as the ES scale, but the DIS scale also shows negative correlations in a different thalamus area and in the left cingulate gyrus. Again, no correlations are apparent for the Boredom Susceptibility subscale.

For the lower areas of pons, vermis, and cerebellum, only a few correlations are significant in all three groups (no table). In the active CPT condition, there are negative correlations between relative glucose use in the midcerebellum ($-.53, -.59$) and the DIS subscale. In the no-task CPT condition in the anxiety group, there are positive correlations between relative glucose in the pons and the BS subscale (.54, .52). In the normal control group, no correlations are significant.

DISCUSSION

There are marked individual differences in glucose metabolism throughout all brain areas. As this initial study demonstrates, the examination of glucose use and personality is quite complicated procedurally. In this project, we studied two groups (anxiety outpatients, drug free) and normal controls. There were two CPT conditions (task and no-task), and the data from one group/condition combination (i.e., normals/active task) were not available for this report. Moreover, we used two measures of glucose use—absolute within box and absolute within box divided by the absolute of the whole slice. Currently, there are no criteria for deciding a priori which measure is better. Boxes were studied from three different brain slices of the nine slices we obtained. Our statistical analyses here are limited to correlations without any multivariate analyses because of the relatively small sample sizes. Further complicating the picture is the necessary combining of males and females from a wide age range. Finally, the CPT itself may not be the best activity during the uptake period for highlighting personality/glucose relationships.

A major question bearing on the interpretation of results is the relationship between glucose use in the brain and constructs used in personality theories like arousal, excitation, and inhibition (to name only a few). For example, the process of inhibition may use more glucose than excitation. Any relationship between glucose use and brain activity may also change during the course of the 35 minutes we study. For all these reasons, we need to emphasize our strategy of reporting only two-tailed statistical tests and of interpreting only patterns of correlations, as discussed later.

Overall, the pattern of correlations with the EPQ was only partially expected. The E scale was positively correlated with absolute glucose use in the frontal cortical areas as well as the temporal gyrus areas during the active CPT. Eysenck has theorized that the E dimension is largely cortical. In our results, high E scores went with high glucose use. Eysenck's theory is that introverts (i.e., low scores on E) are over-aroused. Because we cannot say whether overarousal uses more or less glucose, the finding of positive correlations is not necessarily contradictory. We did, however, expect N scores to show correlations with glucose use in limbic areas because Eysenck has theorized that the N dimension is based largely on limbic system activity. We were surprised, therefore, that almost no N correlations were significant in limbic areas. In fact, the E scale showed several interesting positive correlations with putamen, caudate, cingulate gyrus, hippocampal gyrus, and parahip-pocampal gyrus areas. All but one of these correlations were in the right hemisphere. Only one additional correlation was negative in the left MVL thalamus. The strongest correlations for the N scale were actually in the left anterior and the left posterior pons in the low temporal pole slice. We had included this low slice for comparison because we had not expected any personality/glucose correlations in these low structures. We were also surprised that relative glucose use was negatively corre-lated with the L scale in areas of the pons, vermis, and cerebellum. We have no explanation for this fairly strong pattern. The last surprise came for the P scale that showed mostly negative correlations in both cortical and limbic areas, especially in the occiput, thalamus, and cingulate gyrus.

It appears that positive correlations with E and negative correlations with P are the general pattern in the anxiety group doing the CPT task. The no-task condition in both the anxiety group and the normals yielded the correlations shown in Table 5 for comparison with the correlations generated during the active task condition. In general, it appears to us that the task condition analyzed with absolute glucose yields a more interpretable pattern for the EPQ.

This is not the case, however, for the Sensation-Seeking scales. By far, the most correlations are found in the no-task condition, especially for the normals. Moreover, only the relative box divided bv the slice glucose measure seems to yield correlations. Although there are some strong correlations for certain areas, an overall pattern is not apparent to us.

We have deliberately included many tables and much data so that other researchers with expertise in personality/brain theories can argue their respective views. We hope our future analyses can be guided by specific hypotheses linking brain structures to personality/cognitive interactions that can be studied with PET. Our future studies will include the use of magnetic resonance imaging (MRI) to locate brain structures exactly in each subject before the PET scan. This will be a major improvement over our current automatic atlas template procedure. We are also developing computer programs for multivariate correlations. We are especially interested in correlating glucose use in each box with all other boxes within individuals. This will indicate which brain areas are working with other areas. The pattern of these area-to-area correlations may change between subject groups and uptake period task conditions. Finally, we plan to study samples selected for theoretically interesting personality combinations. For example, high neuroticism and low extraversion people compared to high neuroticism and high extraversion people during a stress or learning condition may be particularly revealing.

This report represents the first effort to use the powerful PET technology for studying individual differences in personality. We are quite encouraged by these initial results because they make direct links between brain function in specific areas and personality measures. It is now possible to design new experiments to extend the scientific investigation of personality from the realms of behavior and psychometrics to the deep recesses of the brain itself.

Acknowledgments

The authors wish to thank Erin Hazlett, Liz Praeger, and Heather Ceiley for technical assistance.

REFERENCES

Eysenck, H. J. *The biological basis of personality.* Springfield, Il.: Charles C. Thomas, 1967.
Eysenck, H. J., & Eysenck, S. B. G. *Manual of the Eysenck Personality Questionnaire.* San Diego and London: Hodder & Stoughton, 1976.
Matsui, T., & Hirano, A. *An atlas of the human brain for computerized tomography.* Tokyo: Igaku-Shoin, 1978.
Phelps, M. E., Huang, S. C., Hoffman, E. J., Selen, C., Sokoloff, L., & Kuhl, D. E.

Tomographic measurement of local cerebral glucose metabolic rate in humans with (F18) 2-fluro-2-deoxy-D-glucose: Validation of method. *Annals of Neurology,* 1979, *6,* 371–388.

Sokoloff, L., Reivich, M., Kennedy, C., Des Rosiers, M. S., Patlak, D. S., Pettigrew, K. D., Sakurada, O., & Shinohara, M. The [^{14}C] deoxyglucose method for the measurement of local cerebral glucose utilization: Theory, procedure, and normal values in the conscious and anesthetized albino rat. *Journal of Neurochemistry,* 1977, *28,* 897–916.

Zuckerman, M. Dimensions of sensation seeking. *Journal of Consulting and Clinical Psychology,* 1971, *36,* 45–52.

CHAPTER 15

Personality Dimensions Based on Arousal Theories

Search for Integration

JAN STRELAU

INTRODUCTION

The idea to interpret individual differences in behavior, treated as temperamental traits, in terms of relatively stable differences in cortical excitation and inhibition was introduced by Pavlov in the first quarter of our century. Strength of excitation and inhibition, the balance between the strength of both processes, and mobility of nervous processes are the main nervous system traits on which the well-known four nervous system types, regarded as physiological correlates of the four ancient temperaments, were distinguished by Pavlov (1951–52).

Especially important for the development of personality dimensions based on arousal theories was the Pavlovian concept of *strength of excitation*, or strength of the nervous system (NS). The two terms were used by Pavlov interchangeably. Strength of the nervous system, which explains individual differences in the level of excitation to stimuli of given intensity, has been studied by Pavlov and his students mainly from the functional point of view. Strength of the NS means the working capacity

This chapter is an expanded version of the paper presented at the 23rd International Congress of Psychology, Acapulco, Mexico, 1984, and published in the Proceedings: J. T. Spence & C. E. Izard (Eds.), *Motivation, Emotion, and Personality*. Amsterdam: North-Holland, Elsevier, 1985.

JAN STRELAU • Faculty of Psychology, University of Warsaw, Warsaw, Poland.

of the NS, and it is manifested in its withstanding strong and/or prolonged excitation without slipping into transmarginal (protective)
inhibition.

The appearance of *transmarginal inhibition*, manifested in the decrease or in the disappearance of reactions to stimuli of growing intensity and/or duration, has been used in Pavlov's laboratory as the main
index of strength of the NS. In individuals with a weak NS, transmarginal inhibition occurs to stimuli of a lower intensity as compared
with individuals with a strong NS. This is caused by the fact that the
strong type of NS, when compared with the weak type, has a higher
working capacity (endurance).

Many experiments conducted in Pavlov's laboratory, with the aim
of studying individual differences in working capacity revealed in behavior under conditions of varying stimulative value, should be regarded as prototypes of experiments in which the individual differences
in personality dimensions based on arousal theories have been related to
the level of performance under stimulation of different intensity.

The Pavlovian concepts of *excitation* and *inhibition* and that of *balance*
between the two processes were used at the turn of the 1940s and 1950s
by Eysenck (1947, 1957) as the main neurological constructs by means of
which, together with the Hullian notion of reactive inhibition, he explained the physiological basis of extraversion/introversion.

The idea of *conditionability*, developed by Eysenck (1957, 1970) within the framework of extraversion/introversion, may also be traced to the
Pavlovian theory of NS. Pavlov stated that in dogs with a strong type of
NS, the acquisition of conditioned reflexes (CRs) is quicker and easier as
compared with the weak type of NS. He used the speed of conditioning
as one of the main indexes of the strength of the NS. Nebylitsyn (1972a)
has suggested an opposite hypothesis. Evidence presented in one of my
reviews (Strelau, 1983) suggests that, unless strong or prolonged stimuli
are used, it is the weak type of NS in whom CRs develop easier and
quicker rather than in the strong type of NS.

> If a personality theory states that one group of subjects defined by a person-
> ality variable or variables conditions "better" than another group similarly
> defined, the implication is clear that an assumption is made that the theory is
> talking not about eyeblinks or SRR or finger withdrawal but about condi-
> tionability. (Levey & Martin, 1981, p. 158)

Taking Levey and Martin's argument into account, it has to be
stated that the concept of conditionability is implied in Pavlov's theory
of types of nervous system (temperaments).

On the basis of further studies conducted on animals and people,
the concepts of types of NS and NS properties have been developed,
and new evidence has been collected. For the purpose of our considera-

tion, it is important to note that Teplov (1985) and Nebylitsyn (1972a), on the basis of many studies, have stated that there exists a close dependence between the strength of the NS, which is understood as the capacity to work (endurance), and sensitivity. The endurance capacity of the nerve cells and their sensitivity (the latter measured by sensory thresholds) can be viewed as two facets of one nervous system property, namely, the strength of the NS. It means that the higher the endurance of the NS, the lower the sensitivity. Among other things, such an understanding of the concept of strength of the NS caused the development of new diagnostic methods, changed the way of thinking as regards the adaptability of the weak type of NS, and—crucial from our point of view—helped to link the concept of strength of the NS with dimensions of personality that referred to arousal theories in which the phenomenon of sensitivity is used as one of the indicators of these dimensions.

AROUSAL MECHANISMS AS A PHYSIOLOGICAL BASIS OF DIFFERENT PERSONALITY DIMENSIONS

The discovery that the reticular formation produces activation (Moruzzi & Magoun, 1949), that the level of performance depends on the level of activation (Duffy, 1951, 1962; Hebb, 1949; Malmo, 1959), and the development of theories of activation/arousal (Berlyne, 1960; Gray, 1964; Hebb, 1955; Lindsley, 1961) bolstered the Pavlovian idea of relating personality dimensions to relatively stable excitatory features of the central NS, which developed within a new theoretical framework based on neurophysiological evidence.

Of special importance for the development of biologically determined personality dimensions was the evidence relating to individual differences in the level of activation/arousal. Duffy (1962) characterized these differences within the concept of the *intensive dimension* of behavior. Gray (1964) introduced the concept of *arousability* by which he meant relatively stable individual differences in the level of arousal. This concept was probably most influential in the development of personality dimensions with respect to arousal theories. It also allowed the convergences between the concept of nervous system strength and the theory of activation/arousal to be pointed out.

> Individuals who are low on the dimension of arousability (i.e., who, in any given stimulus situation, show relatively low levels of arousal) correspond to individuals with a strong nervous system; individuals who are high on the dimension of arousability (i.e., who, in any given stimulus situation, show relatively high levels of arousal) correspond to individuals with a weak nervous system. (Gray, 1964, p. 306)

Hebb has stated that "any sensory event has two different effects: One is the *cue function*, guiding behaviour; the other, less obvious but no less important is the *arousal* or *vigilance function*" (1955, p. 249). Developing the idea regarding the arousal function of acting stimuli, it has to be said that this function refers to the level (intensity, magnitude, strength) of excitatory processes expressed in the energetic characteristics of the individual's activities. Whatever mechanisms are regulating the level of arousal, individual differences in their functioning occur, and they reveal themselves in the fact that in some individuals stimuli of given intensity (S_n) develop a higher level of arousal (A_{n+x}), whereas in others, the level of arousal to the same stimuli is lower (A_{n-x}). This might be expressed as follows:

$$S_n \rightarrow A_{n+x} = \text{high arousability}$$
$$S_n \rightarrow A_{n-x} = \text{low arousability}$$

As can be concluded from many studies (see Fahrenberg, Walschburger, Foerster, Myrtek, & Müller, 1983; Lacey, 1967; Myrtek, 1984; Zuckerman, 1983), it is highly probable that, depending on what types of indicators (stimuli, reactions, activities, situations) are used in order to measure individual differences in the level of arousal, different anatomophysiological mechanisms should be mentioned as regulators of arousal (e.g., cortex, reticular formation, limbic system, neurotransmitters, autonomic nervous system, and different interactions among them). As a consequence, the estimation of arousability varies significantly not only across individuals but also within individuals, depending on the measure of arousability under consideration. The fact that the level of arousal is, in essence, stimulus- and reaction-specific hinders the search for individual differences in this phenomenon.

Among causal theories of personality dimensions that concentrate on biological mechanisms when explaining the essential portions of variance, one may mention several personality constructs that refer to different physiological and anatomical as well as behavioral aspects of arousal/activation. Extraversion/introversion, sensation seeking, impulsivity, augmenting/reducing, anxiety, neuroticism, strength of the NS, and reactivity seem to be the most widely known. It is not the aim of this chapter to discuss the different meanings of the personality/temperament dimensions mentioned here. The assumption is made that they should be comprehended by referring to the authors whose views on the arousal/activation mechanisms underlying these dimensions are briefly presented later.

As mentioned, the balance between excitation and inhibition was regarded in Eysenck's (1957) earlier publications as the physiological basis of extraversion/introversion. In 1967, under the impact of studies on arousal, Eysenck changed his view. The reticulocortical arousal loop was hypothesized to be the physiological mechanism of extraversion/introversion (Eysenck, 1967, 1970).

Individual differences in sensation seeking that were primarily interpreted by Zuckerman (1974) in terms of the reticulocortical loop have recently been treated as being primarily determined by the activity of the monoamine neurotransmitters (dopamine, norepinephrine, and serotonin) that are most prominently located in the limbic brain systems. Zuckerman's statement that he moved away from the concept of optimal level of arousal as regards the biological foundations of sensation seeking in favor of biochemical mechanisms underlying this temperament trait seems to me to be illusive. What happened is that he changed his view on the mechanisms causing arousal.

> Generally speaking, MAO in conjunction with other biochemical factors determines the sensitivity of the neural systems it regulates. High levels of MAO would be expected to reduce sensitivity; low levels, by allowing high levels of neurotransmitters to accumulate in the neurons, would increase sensitivity. (Zuckerman, 1983, p. 55)

If we consider arousal rather broadly, as a state or trait that refers to the excitatory processes of the NS, Zuckerman's hypothesis as regards the function of the monoamine neurotransmitters in regulating sensation seeking is perfectly within the framework of the level-of-arousal concept.

Impulsivity, regarded by Gray (1981, 1982) in addition to anxiety, as one of the two primary personality dimensions, has its physiological basis in the lateral septal area, the medial forebrain bundle, and the lateral hypothalamus. Gray characterizes these centers from the functional point of view as the behavioral activation system (BAS). Barratt and Patton (1983) as well as Schalling, Edman, and Åsberg (1983; see also Schalling & Åsberg, 1985) perceive the physiological mechanism of impulsivity as lying in the limbic-frontal connections and that their sensitivity is modulated by the monoamine neurotransmitters.

Petrie (1967), who introduced the augmenting/reducing dimension, hypothesized that there exists a central stimulus intensity control mechanism; this is probably the general nonspecific arousal system (see also Barnes, 1976). Buchsbaum (1976), who also uses the concept of augmenting/reducing, however, interprets it in the opposite way as compared with Petrie's original view (see Davis, Cowles, & Kohn, 1984; Kohn, Hunt, Cowles, & Davis, 1986; Strelau, 1982), and he argues that three types of neural pathways may be responsible for the individual differences in augmenting/reducing: "descending inhibitory, nonspecific arousal, and cortical-cortical" (p. 110).

Gray (1981, 1982), who has conducted the most advanced studies devoted to physiological mechanisms underlying anxiety, concluded that the orbital frontal cortex, medial septal area, and hippocampus should be considered as the anatomical centers of this personality dimension. They constitute the behavioral inhibition system (BIS).

Neuroticism, treated by Eysenck (1967, 1970) as one of his three personality dimensions, has its physiological basis in the activation of the limbic system (visceral brain) that consists of the hypothalamus, septum, hippocampus, amygdala, and cingulum. The threshold of hypothalamic activity seems to be of special importance in determining individual differences in neuroticism.

Turning back to the concept of the strength of the NS, it is worth noting that neither Pavlov nor the Teplov–Nebylitsyn school identified the anatomical centers of this property. Nebylitsyn suggested that the morphological substrate of the general properties of the NS consists of the "anterocentral cortex together with the connected complex of paleocortex and subcortical nuclei" (1972a, p. 411), but he did not specify the anatomophysiological structures underlying the strength of the NS. Mecacci (1976) suggested that the neurophysiological processes that mediate the strength differentiation are related to arousal processes in the reticular formation, the septal area, hippocampus, and frontal areas. Robinson (1982) has argued that the Pavlovian excitatory and inhibitory processes, the properties of which constitute the types of NS, "correspond to cortical and thalamic neuron populations of the diffuse thalamocortical system (DTS)" (p. 1).

As regards the reactivity dimension that is primarily based on the concept of strength of excitation (see Strelau, 1983), the present author hypothesized that the physiological mechanism determining reactivity is a very complex one and includes all anatomical and physiological systems responsible for the accumulation as well as the release of stored energy. Which of the systems plays the dominant role in determining reactivity depends on the type of activity and situation. There exist not only inter- but also intra-individual differences in the physiological arousal mechanisms responsible for co-determining reactivity; thus the concept of *neuroendocrine individuality* seems to be most relevant.

DIFFERENT COMPONENTS OF AROUSAL USED AS MEASURES OF INTERRELATIONS AMONG PERSONALITY DIMENSIONS

The fact that all the previously mentioned dimensions refer to the neurophysiological mechanisms of arousal means that in spite of differences in their psychological content and interpretation they deal with common phenomena that reflect different aspects of arousal. This might

Table 1. Amplitude of AEPs and Personality
Dimensions

High amplitude	Low amplitude
Augmenters (Buchsbaum)	Reducers
Sensation seekers	Sensation avoiders
Weak type of NS	Strong type of NS
Introverts	Extraverts
High-impulsive	Low-impulsive

be shown at least on three different levels that refer to electrophysiological, psychophysiological, and behavioral components of
arousal.

The amplitude of the averaged evoked potentials (AEPs) may be
regarded as an example of electrophysiological phenomena related to
arousal. The individual differences in the amplitude of the AEPs to
stimuli of different modalities have been studied in relation to such
dimensions as augmenting/reducing (e.g., Buchsbaum, 1978; Buchsbaum, Haier, & Johnson, 1983), sensation seeking (Zuckerman, 1979,
1984; Zuckerman, Buchsbaum, & Murphy, 1980), strength of the nervous system (Bazylevich, 1974; Strelau, 1983), impulsivity (Barratt &
Patton, 1983) and extraversion (Haier, Robinson, Braden, & Williams,
1984; Shagass & Schwartz, 1965; Stelmack, 1981). The main outcomes of
these studies are presented in Table 1.

It may be seen that augmenters, as understood by Buchsbaum,
sensation seekers, the weak type of NS, high-impulsive individuals, and
introverts have a high amplitude of AEPs. No relation between this
electrophysiological component of arousal and neuroticism has been
found (see, e.g., Haier et al., 1984). I did not find any data in which the
amplitude of AEPs was related to anxiety, and no studies were conducted in relation to reactivity.

It has to be emphasized that the previously mentioned regularity
reflects rather a general tendency and does not mean that opposite
results may not be found, and we shall have this caution in mind when
presenting other regularities in respect to arousal phenomena and per-
sonality/temperament dimensions.

The sensory threshold used as a measure of arousal (see Duffy, 1962)
may serve as an example of a psychophysiological phenomenon to which
many of the biologically based personality (temperament) dimensions
refer. Generalizing, the data presented in the literature show (see Table 2)
that augmenters, as understood by Petrie (Barnes, 1976, 1985; Petrie,
1967), introverts (Eysenck, 1967, 1970), the weak type of NS (Nebylitsyn,
1972a), and high-reactive individuals (Strelau, 1983) have high sensory

Table 2. Sensory Threshold and Personality
Dimensions

High sensitivity	Low sensitivity
Augmenters (Petrie)	Reducers
Introverts	Extraverts
Weak type of NS	Strong type of NS
High-reactive	Low-reactive

sensitivity, whereas reducers, extraverts, the strong type of NS, and low-reactive individuals have a rather high sensory threshold.

The findings concerning the relation between sensory threshold and sensation seeking are inconsistent. Some data suggest that sensation seeking is related to a high sensory threshold (e.g., Davis, Cowles, & Kohn, 1983; Kohn, Hunt, & Hoffman, 1982), whereas other show that there is a lack of correlation between these phenomena (Zuckerman, 1979).

On the level of behavior, the efficiency of learning as well as general activity, which are known as phenomena related to arousal, are subject to examination within the framework of several biologically based personality dimensions. As regards learning efficiency in relation to personality, many studies refer to extraversion (Eysenck, 1970; Levey & Martin, 1981), anxiety (Gray, 1975, 1982; Spence, 1960), to impulsivity (Gray, 1981), and to the strength of the NS (Nebylitsyn, 1972a; Pavlov, 1951–1952; Strelau, 1983). As argued by Gray (1981, 1982), in the case of anxiety and impulsivity, the efficiency of learning is bound up with specific types of reinforcement. Anxious individuals are especially sensitive to punishment that is determined by the BIS, whereas impulsive individuals are sensitive to reward that is controlled by the BAS (see also Fowles, 1980). The regularity to be found in respect to the relation between these dimensions and the efficiency of learning is presented in Table 3.

The level of arousal is also expressed in general behavioral activity and the latter, having itself a given stimulative value, is considered to be one of the main regulators of the level of activation. This is especially emphasized within the concept of optimal level of activation (Berlyne, 1960; Fiske & Maddi, 1961; Hebb, 1955; Helson, 1964; Strelau, 1983). Most of the personality constructs under discussion and characterized as action-oriented personality dimensions (Barratt & Patton, 1983; Mangan, 1982; Zuckerman, Ballenger, Jimerson, Murphy, & Post, 1983) deal with the stimulative value of behavior revealed in different types of activities. From the data and theoretical considerations presented in the

Table 3. Efficiency of Learning and Personality
Dimensions

High efficiency	Low efficiency
Introverts	Extraverts
High-anxious (sensitive to punishment)	Low-anxious
High-impulsive (sensitive to reward)	Low-impulsive
Strong type of NS (early studies)	Weak type of NS
Weak type of NS (studies after 1950s)	Strong type of NS

literature, we see that behavioral activity of high stimulative value is typical of the strong type of NS (Nebylitsyn, 1972a; Rusalov, 1979; Strelau, 1983), extraverts (Brebner & Cooper, 1978; Eysenck, 1970, 1981), sensation seekers (Zuckerman, 1974, 1979, 1984), high-impulsive individuals (Barratt & Patton, 1983; Schalling et al., 1983), low-reactive individuals (Eliasz, 1981; Strelau, 1974, 1983), and reducers (Petrie, 1967; Kohn, Hunt, & Hoffman, 1982; Kohn et al., 1986). The general behavioral activity in the weak type of NS, introverts, sensation avoiders, low-impulsive individuals, high-reactive individuals, and augmenters is of low stimulative value (see Table 4).

The experimental data regarding the interrelation between personality dimensions and electrophysiological, psychophysiological, and behavioral components of arousal are far from being unequivocal. The research on nervous system properties (Nebylitsyn, 1972b; Strelau, 1972a), extraversion/introversion (Eysenck & Levey, 1972; Franks, 1956), and on the determinants of arousal (Fahrenberg et al., 1983; Foerster & Schneider, 1982; Lacey, 1967) shows beyond any doubt that the interre-

Table 4. Stimulative Value of Behavioral Activity and
Personality Dimensions

High stimulative value	Low stimulative value
Strong type of NS	Weak type of NS
Extraverts	Introverts
Sensation seekers	Sensation avoiders
High-impulsive	Low-impulsive
Low-reactive	High-reactive
Reducers (Petrie)	Augmenters

lations between personality dimensions and such phenomena as the AEPs, sensory thresholds, and conditioning depend on many variables. The specificity of stimuli used in the experiment, their modality and temporal structure, the type of reaction (response) under control, and the specificity of the experimental settings may be mentioned here as the variables that influence the results to a high degree. This causes laboratory data regarded as measures of personality to often be incoherent. Therefore the biologically determined personality dimensions can hardly be compared on the level of experimental indexes unless exactly the same experimental conditions are arranged, which is rather an exception in this kind of studies.

BIOLOGICALLY BASED PERSONALITY DIMENSIONS MEASURED BY PSYCHOMETRIC DATA

The most widely used way of studying personality dimensions, including those based on arousal theories, is the psychometric approach. In this case, the subject's self-report about different aspects of his or her own behavior and activity is the main subject of examination. In order to have a more complete presentation as regards the interrelations among the personality dimensions under discussion, an analysis of inventory data is needed. This is, however, difficult to do for several reasons, two of which seem to be of special significance. First, under the same term, different phenomena are meant, which is best expressed in the divergencies in defining separate personality dimensions. For example, when Petrie (1967) speaks about augmenters, it means reducers according to Buchsbaum's (1978, 1983) theory. This is no place to discuss the reasons for this divergence (for details see Barnes, 1976; Davis *et al.*, 1984; Goldman, Kohn, & Hunt, 1983; Strelau, 1982) that is a source of many misunderstandings. Second, the same or almost the same personality dimensions are often measured by different inventories. For example, Barratt and Patton (1983) describe more than 10 psychometric tools aimed at measuring impulsivity, and Eysenck himself developed several inventories in order to study extraversion/introversion.

Having these difficulties in mind, I will try to outline the main tendency of interrelations among biologically based personality dimensions measured by psychometric tools. Because the only inventory for measuring the basic NS properties as understood by Pavlov is the Strelau Temperament Inventory (STI) (Strelau, 1972b, 1983), the data concerned with strength of excitation are exclusively based on the STI. At the same time, the Strength of Excitation scale of the STI is used in our laboratory to measure reactivity, one of the main temperament dimensions included in the author's regulative theory of temperament (for explanation, see Strelau, 1983). The most typical relationships are presented in Table 5.

Extraversion, the most widely known dimension among those discussed in this chapter, correlates positively with strength of excitation (Carlier, 1985; Gilliland, 1985; Strelau, 1983, 1986), sensation seeking (e.g., Eysenck & Zuckerman, 1978; Morris, 1979), and impulsivity (Schalling & Åsberg, 1985; Schalling et al., 1983). Negative correlations have been found between extraversion and augmentation as measured by Vando's Reducing-Augmenting Scale (Barnes, 1976, 1985; Davis et al., 1984) and reactivity (Strelau, 1983). It seems that no correlation exists between this trait and anxiety (Bull & Strongman, 1971; Morris, 1979) or neuroticism (Amelang & Borkenau, 1982; Eysenck, 1970).

Sensation seeking correlates positively not only with extraversion but also with strength of the NS (Strelau, 1983) and with impulsivity (Barratt & Patton, 1983). Negative correlations have been found with augmentation (Barnes, 1985; Goldman et al., 1983; Kohn & Coulas, 1985; Kohn et al., 1982, 1986) and reactivity (Strelau, 1983). The data suggest that sensation seeking does not correlate with anxiety and neuroticism (Zuckerman, 1979, 1983).

No psychometric studies are known to me in which strength of the NS, which correlates positively with extraversion and sensation seeking, has been related to augmenting/reducing and to impulsivity. The correlations of this trait with neuroticism and anxiety are negative (Strelau, 1983). As regards reactivity, the relations are opposite to those described for strength of the NS. This follows from the fact that on the basis of indexes, strength of the NS is equivalent to low reactivity.

No data concerning the psychometrically measured augmenting/reducing dimension in relation to strength of excitation, reactivity, impulsivity, and anxiety, are known to me. As mentioned before augmentation correlates negatively with extraversion and sensation seeking. The only study known to me in which a psychometrically measured augmenting/reducing dimension has been related to neuroticism shows that there is no relation between these traits (Kohn et al., 1986).

Anxiety and neuroticism seem to share the same position with respect to their relation to other biologically determined personality dimensions. Mostly, no correlations with extraversion (Amelang & Borkenau, 1982; Bull & Strongman, 1971; Eysenck, 1970; Morris, 1979), sensation seeking (Zuckerman, 1979), and impulsivity (Barratt & Patton, 1983; Schalling et al., 1983) have been found. Both of these traits consequently correlate with strength of the NS (negatively) (Carlier, 1985; Gilliland, 1985; Strelau, 1983) that means that they are at the same time positively correlated with reactivity.

Table 5. Interrelations among Personality Dimensions: Psychometric Data[a]

Personality dimensions	Strength of NS	Sensation seeking	Augmenting	Impulsivity	Reactivity	Anxiety	Neuroticism
Extraversion	+	+	−	+	−	0	0
Strength of NS		+	×	×	×	−	−
Sensation seeking			−	+	−	0	0
Augmenting				×	×	×	0
Impulsivity					×	0	0
Reactivity						+	+
Anxiety							+

[a] + = positive correlation; − = negative correlation; 0 = no correlation; and × = data not available.

CONCLUSIONS AND METHODOLOGICAL REMARKS

The number of indexes on the basis of which the eight biologically based personality dimensions have been compared in this chapter varies from one to five (inventory data, sensory threshold, amplitude of AEPs, efficiency of conditioning, and general behavioral activity). Depending on which of these indexes is taken into account, the interrelations between given personality traits may differ. A positive correlation stated for one of the indexes can change into a negative one when another index is considered, as for example, when sensation seeking is compared with extraversion, strength of NS, and augmenting/reducing. It is remarkable that the highest consistency in the type of interrelations occurs when extraversion is compared with other dimensions. All of the indexes used show the same type of interrelations between extraversion, on the one hand, and strength of NS, augmenting/reducing, reactivity, and neuroticism, on the other. Table 6 illustrates the degree of consistency in interrelations among the eight personality dimensions when all the indexes being under examination are considered.

The analysis of data presented in this chapter leads to the conclusion that further progress in research aimed at mapping the interrelations between biologically based personality (temperament) dimensions that refer to arousal theories requires the fulfillment of several methodological demands (see e.g., Fahrenberg *et al.*, 1983; Gale & Edwards, 1983), some of which might be mentioned here. First, the specific aspects of the arousal system to which a given dimension refers have to be identified and functionally related to other physiological mechanisms of the arousal system. Second, because there exist individual-specific and stimulus-specific reaction patterns, it is necessary to study the personality dimensions on the same level of behavior (e.g., inventory vs. inventory, motor reaction vs. motor reaction) and by using stimuli of the same quality (e.g., visual vs. visual, auditory vs. auditory). Third, the estimation of personality dimensions that are based on the arousal system depends, among other things, on such variables as the intensity of stimuli used, the stimulative value of the situation, and the individual's current level of arousal. Therefore these variables have to be matched in order to draw any conclusion as regards the relation between dimensions being compared on the basis of the experimental data. Fourth, a consensus is needed in the terminology used to describe the basic phenomena to which different arousal-oriented personality concepts refer. It is my belief that bearing these proposals in mind would bring us closer to the understanding of similarities and differences among the dimensions in question.

Eysenck, H. J., & Levey, A. Conditioning, introversion-extraversion and the strength of the nervous system. In V. D. Nebylitsyn, & J. A. Gray (Eds.), *Biological bases of individual behavior.* New York: Academic Press, 1972.

Eysenck, S. B. G., & Zuckerman, M. The relationship between sensation seeking and Eysenck's dimension of personality. *British Journal of Psychology,* 1978, *69,* 483–487.

Fahrenberg, J., Walschburger, P., Foerster, F., Myrtek, M., & Müller, W. An evaluation of trait, state, and reaction aspects of activation processes. *Psychophysiology,* 1983, *20,* 188–195.

Fiske, D. W., & Maddi, S. R. (Eds.). *Functions of varied experience.* Homewood, IL.: Dorsey Press, 1961.

Foerster, F., & Schneider, H. J. Individualspezifische, stimulusspezifische und motivationsspezifische Reaktionsmuster im zweimal wiederholten Aktivierungsexperiment. *Zeitschrift für experimentelle und angewandte Psychologie,* 1982, *29,* 598–612.

Fowles, D. C. The three arousal model: Implications of Gray's two-factor learning theory for heart rate, electrodermal activity, and psychopathy. *Psychophysiology,* 1980, *17,* 87–104.

Franks, C. M. Conditioning and personaltiy: A study of normal and neurotic subjects. *Journal of Abnormal and Social Psychology,* 1956, *52,* 143–150.

Gale, A., & Edwards, J. A. A short critique of the psychophysiology of individual differences. *Personality and Individual Differences,* 1983, *4,* 429–435.

Gilliland, K. The Temperament Inventory: Relationship to theoretically similar Western personality dimensions and construct validity. In J. Strelau, F. H. Farley, & A. Gale (Eds.), *The biological bases of personality and behavior: Theories, measurement techniques, and development* (Vol. 1). Washington: Hemisphere, 1985.

Goldman, D., Kohn, P. M., & Hunt, R. W. Sensation seeking, augmenting-reducing, and absolute auditory threshold: A strength-of-the-nervous-system perspective. *Journal of Personality and Social Psychology,* 1983, *45,* 405–411.

Gray, J. A. (Ed.). *Pavlov's typology.* Oxford: Pergamon Press, 1964.

Gray, J. A. *Elements of a two-process theory of learning.* London: Academic Press, 1975.

Gray, J. A. A critique of Eysenck's theory of personality. In H. J. Eysenck (Ed.), *A model for personality.* Berlin: Springer, 1981.

Gray, J. A. Précis of The neuropsychology of anxiety: An enquiry into the functions of the septo-hippocampal system. *The Behavior and Brain Sciences,* 1982, *5,* 469–534.

Haier, J. R., Robinson, D. L., Braden, W., & Williams, D. Evoked potential augmenting-reducing and personality differences. *Personality and Individual Differences,* 1984, *5,* 293–301.

Hebb, D. O. *The organization of behavior.* New York: Wiley, 1949.

Hebb, D. O. Drives and the C.N.S. (conceptual nervous system). *Psychological Review,* 1955, *62,* 243–254.

Helson, H. *Adaptation-level theory. An experimental and systematic approach to behavior.* New York: Harper & Row, 1964.

Kohn, P. M., & Coulas J. T. Sensation seeking, augmenting-reducing, and the perceived and preferred effects of drugs. *Journal of Personality and Social Psychology,* 1985, *48,* 99–106.

Kohn, P. M., Hunt, R. W., Cowles, M. P., & Davis, C. A. Factor structure and construct validity of the Vando Reducer-Augmenter Scale. *Personality and Individual Differences,* 1986, *7,* 57–64.

Kohn, P. M., Hunt R. W., & Hoffman, F. M. Aspects of experience seeking. *Canadian Journal of Behavioural Science,* 1982, *14,* 13–23.

Lacey, J. I. Somatic response patterning and stress: Some revisions of activation theory. In M. H. Appley & R. Trumbull (Eds.), *Psychological stress. Issues in research.* New York: Appleton-Century-Crofts, 1967.

Levey, A. B., & Martin, I. Personality and conditioning. In H. J. Eysenck (Ed.), *A model for personality*. Berlin: Springer, 1981.

Lindsley, D. B. Common factors in sensory deprivation, sensory distortion and sensory overload. In P. Solomon, P. E. Kubzansky, P. H. Leiderman, J. H. Mendelson, R. Trumbull, & D. Wexler (Eds.). *Sensory deprivation*. Cambridge: Harvard University Press, 1961.

Malmo, R. B. Activation: A neuropsychological dimension. *Psychological Review*. 1959, *66*, 367–386.

Mangan, G. L. *The biology of human conduct. East–West models of temperament and personality*. Oxford: Pergamon Press, 1982.

Mecacci, L. Trends in the psychophysiology of individual differences. *Pavlovian Journal of Biological Science*, 1976, *11*, 93–104.

Morris, L. W. *Extraversion and introversion: An interactional perspective*. Washington: Hemisphere, 1979.

Moruzzi, G., & Magoun, H. W. Brain stem reticular formation and activation of the EEG. *Electroencephalography and Clinical Neurophysiology*, 1949, *1*, 455–473.

Myrtek, M. *Constitutional psychophysiology*. New York: Academic Press, 1984.

Nebylitsyn, V. D. *Fundamental properties of the human nervous system*. New York: Plenum Press, 1972 (a).

Nebylitsyn, V. D. The problem of general and partial properties of the nervous system. In V. D. Nebylitsyn & J. A. Gray (Eds.), *Biological bases of individual behavior*. New York: Academic Press, 1972 (b).

Pavlov, I. P. *Complete works* (2nd ed.). Moscow: USSR Academy of Sciences, 1951–1952 (in Russian).

Petrie, A. *Individuality in pain and suffering*. Chicago: University of Chicago Press, 1967.

Robinson, D. L. Properties of the diffuse thalamocortical system and human personality: A direct test of Pavlovian/Eysenckian theory. *Personality and Individual Differences*, 1982, *3*, 1–16.

Rusalov, V. M. *Biological bases of individual-psychological differences*. Moscow: Nauka, 1979 (in Russian).

Schalling, D., & Åsberg, M. Biological and psychological correlates of impulsiveness and monotony avoidance. In J. Strelau, F. H. Farley, & A. Gale (Eds.), *The biological bases of personality and behavior: Theories, measurement techniques, and development* (Vol. 1). Washington: Hemisphere, 1985.

Schalling, D., Edman, G., & Åsberg, M. Impulsive cognitive style and inability to tolerate boredom: Psychobiological studies of temperamental vulnerability. In M. Zuckerman (Ed.), *Biological bases of sensation seeking, impulsivity, and anxiety*. Hillsdale, NJ: Erlbaum, 1983.

Shagass, C., & Schwartz, M. Age, personality and somato-sensory evoked responses. *Science*, 1965, *148*, 1359–1361.

Spence, K. W. *Behavior theory and learning*. Englewood Cliffs, NJ: Prentice-Hall, 1960.

Stelmack, R. M. The psychophysiology of extraversion and neuroticism. In H. J. Eysenck (Ed.), *A model for personality*. Berlin: Springer, 1981.

Strelau, J. The general and partial nervous system types—data and theory. In V. D. Nebylitsyn, & J. A. Gray (Eds.), *Biological bases of individual behavior*. New York: Academic Press, 1972 (a).

Strelau, J. A diagnosis of temperament by nonexperimental techniques. *Polish Psychological Bulletin*, 1972, *3*, 97–105 (b).

Strelau, J. Temperament as an expression of energy level and temporal features of behavior. *Polish Psychological Bulletin*, 1974, *5*, 119–127.

Strelau, J. Biologically determined dimensions of personality or temperament. *Personality and Individual Differences*, 1982, *3*, 355–360.

Strelau, J. *Temperament—personality—activity.* London: Academic Press, 1983.

Strelau, J. Pavlovian properties of the nervous system and extraversion-introversion. *Psychologische Beiträge,* 1986. *28,* 192–205.

Teplov, B. M. *Selected works* (Vol. 2). Moscow: Pedagogika, 1985 (in Russian)

Zuckerman, M. The sensation seeking motive. In B. A. Maher (Ed.), *Progress in experimental personality research* (Vol. 7). New York: Academic Press, 1974.

Zuckerman, M. *Sensation seeking: Beyond the optimal level of arousal.* Hillsdale, NJ: Erlbaum, 1979.

Zuckerman, M. (Ed.). *Biological bases of sensation seeking, impulsivity, and anxiety.* Hillsdale NJ: Erlbaum, 1983.

Zuckerman, M. Sensation seeking: A comparative approach to a human trait. *The Behavioral and Brain Sciences,* 1984, *7,* 413–471.

Zuckerman, M., Ballenger, J. C., Jimerson, D. C., Murphy, D. L., & Post, R. M. A correlational test in humans of the biological models of sensation seeking, impulsivity, and anxiety. In M. Zuckerman (Ed.), *Biological bases of sensation seeking, impulsivity, and anxiety.* Hillsdale, NJ: Erlbaum, 1983.

Zuckerman, M., Buchsbaum, M. S., & Murphy, D. L. Sensation seeking and its biological correlates. *Psychological Bulletin,* 1980, *88,* 187–214.

Arousal, Control, Energetics, and Values

An Attempt at Review and Appraisal

ANTHONY GALE

INTRODUCTION

The purpose of this chapter is to review the key themes of earlier chapters and to identify potential growthpoints for future research into the biological bases of personality. Attention is paid to the concept of *arousal* because it is a construct that integrates many of the contributions. Many biological theories of personality see the individual as relatively passive, a victim of biological predisposition; however, when looked at as a *system seeking stable equilibrium*, attention must be paid to activity, feedback, and control. All living systems transmit energy, and possible mechanisms for acquisition, storage, and release are related to personality traits and psychopathological conditions. Lessons for personality research may be learned from theories of family behavior that necessarily deal with interacting and communicating systems. The concept of power and control over others appears to have been neglected in personality research, although in some fields it is seen as a primary source of motivation. Finally, the issue of values is briefly addressed because beliefs (themselves in part a function of biological determination) appear to be powerful mechanisms for determining the goals of behavior.

ANTHONY GALE • Department of Psychology, University of Southampton, Southampton, England.

COMMON FEATURES OF BIOLOGICAL THEORIES OF
PERSONALITY

Gale and Edwards (1983a, 1983b, 1986) and Gale, Strelau, and
Farley (1985) have set out the common assumptions of biological theories of personality. Such common features not only define the field of
enquiry but also have implications for methods of enquiry, experimental
procedures, and the interpretation of research findings. These features,
which are shared by many of the contributions to this volume, are as
follows:

1. Accounts of human behavior are incomplete if they focus on
general mechanisms at the expense of individual differences. Individual
differences are a source of systematic variation within psychological
dependent variables. A failure to consider individual differences leads to
an artificial enhancement of the error term in studies of behavior.

2. Biological factors, transmitted genetically, account for a significant proportion of observed individual variations. One aim of biological
theories of individual differences is to identify such factors by psychometric means and then to explore their functioning by means of behavioral, subjective, and physiological measurement.

3. These factors are expressed in complex ways in the structure of
the anatomy, biochemistry, and functional neurophysiology of the central and autonomic nervous systems; and both observable behavior and
subjective report reflect the operation and interactions between these
systems.

4. The observed variations in such factors within populations and
their consequences for individual and interpersonal behavior can be
seen to have adaptive significance for the species. It follows that the
same identified individual differences factors should emerge across
cultures and within cultures over time. Individual differences factors are
therefore biological universals, even though they may be conceptualized
or named in different ways by different theorists.

5. Factors of adaptive significance reflect, in part, environmental
constraints on the organism and the need to operate effectively within
the range of possible environmental conditions; such factors may, therefore, be observed in essential form, across several species. It follows that
individual differences factors may be observed in other species, as properties of nervous systems *as such*, and are not exclusively the property of
human nervous systems.

6. A basic property of living systems is the transmission of energy.
Energy is absorbed, stored, used to run the system, allocated to activity,
and discharged in a variety of ways. The concept of arousal is related to

energic properties in several ways: as a drive, as a set point for hedonic state, and as a consequence of stimulation or of action. But the logical bases and explanatory power of the concept of arousal are major topics for debate among theorists.

7. Living systems are not passive but develop active regulatory strategies to ensure adaptation between biological dispositions and environmental circumstances. Such strategies incorporate feedback both from the environment and from the consequences of action. Thus underlying predispositions are overlaid with adaptive mechanisms, and the relationship between dispositions and behavior is likely to be complex. Even those theories that have a limited set of specified traits will be unable to predict one-to-one relationships between predispositions and individual behaviors.

8. Adaptive strategies form an appropriate focus for the study of individual differences and imply systematic measurement of regulatory activity, the patterning of response, and the processes of adaptation considered over time. Such strategies will reveal the dynamic processes that emerge when structure and environment are in interaction and the ways in which energy is acquired and discharged.

9. The natural ecology in which human individuals live contains both physical and social stimuli, and adaptive processes include interaction with other human beings. Adaptive and regulatory processes are governed in part not only by predispositional and physical variables but by value structures that affect the cue value of both stimuli and actions.

Taken together, these general assumptions enable us to set out a program for research into the biological basis of personality: to identify those factors that are biological universals; to trace the genetic patterning of the transmission of traits; to describe the ways in which such genetic factors are expressed in the structure and function of the nervous system; to demonstrate how such structural features impose initial limits on individual capacity to adapt to the environment; and, finally, to explore the ways in which such limitations are overcome by learning and the development of appropriate strategies for successful living.

THE CONCEPT OF SYSTEMS

Principles derived from the work of Von Bertalanffy (e.g., 1968) are particularly salient to the present discussion. General system theory was seen by Von Bertalanffy and others to be appropriate for the description of biological systems. The emphasis is upon units within a system and their interrelationships. A system is seen as

a set of objects together with the relationships between the objects and their
attributes. The objects are the component parts of the system, the attributes
are the properties of objects and the relationships tie the system together.
(Hall & Fagen, 1956)

Such systems are characterized by *hierarchical structure, varying degrees of openness to external information, dynamic equilibrium* and/or *homeostasis* and *emergence*. Hierarchical structure implies that certain units
within the system have prior importance; openness to information implies adaptiveness; equilibrium implies that the system seeks to return
to a stable state; and emergence implies that units together with their
relationships will lead to more complex behaviors than those observed
when the units are considered separately. The relevance of the general
system approach to psychology and to individual differences has been
discussed by Miller (1978) and Crits-Christoph and Schwartz (1983). It
will be clear, however, from what has been said so far, that the contributors to this book are implicit or clandestine system theorists. Most of
the chapters presented describe personality characteristics in terms of
traits and/or mechanisms (units) with particular characteristics (attributes) with relative power to influence behavior (hierarchical structure) and that interact (relationships) in certain ways in order to achieve
a steady state by means of regulation (homeostasis/dynamic equilibrium) and whose interactions lead to a complex patterning of behavior
(emergence). The concepts of positive and negative feedback are also
incorporated (in implicit form) into several of the theoretical approaches,
as part of the thrust to dynamic equilibrium.

General system theory has not been free of criticism in its application to human behavior (Buckley, 1968; Vetere, 1984; Vetere & Gale,
1987); nevertheless, its key features are clearly represented in the present volume and therefore have heuristic value. The approach makes it
clear that criticisms of biological approaches based on the fact that they
do not yield simple main effects or neat physiology–behavior relationships, simply miss the point. Any observed behavior is an aggregate
of dispositions, interaction among dispositions, and regulatory strategies, reflecting also trait-situational interactions. In such circumstances,
and given the complexity of human systems, it is remarkable that certain
relationships *are* obtained. For example, the fact that answers to a paper-
and-pencil test (say the EPI or an IQ test) can be related to the electrical
activity of the brain (say the EEG or EP) is an astounding feat of science;
such findings are won *in spite* of the incredible complexity of the domains under investigation and in spite of the operational distance between psychometric and physiological measurement (see O'Gorman,
1977).

IMPLICATIONS OF A SYSTEMS APPROACH FOR INDIVIDUAL DIFFERENCES

Hierarchical Priority

Certain characteristics may be seen to have higher priority within a system and to be historically and/or functionally higher within the hierarchical structure. Thus Strelau (1983) sees *temperament* (an inborn characteristic) as having prior status to *personality*, which is a product of the interaction between temperamental traits and environmental demands and opportunities. Following Venables (1984) we may conceptualize such system units as relatively *active* and *invariant*. Within factor analytic studies (Kline, 1983), we expect to find such factors as principal organizing structures within cross-cultural studies of invariant attributes. Eysenck would identify extraversion-introversion, neuroticism-stability, and psychoticism-super ego at this level of organization, whereas Gray (1983a) focuses on his approach–avoidance factors (BAS and BIS). Strelau discusses the relationship between these characteristics and his own concepts of *reactivity* and *activity*. Within these latter two constructs, one gains the impression that Strelau sees reactivity as primary, with activity cast in the role of providing levels of adaptive response. Clarity about *level* within the hierarchical structure is essential; otherwise, one might be led to attempts to *correlate* factors that have surface similarity across theories (for example, extraversion, activity, sensation seeking), when in actuality they represent *different* levels of hierarchical priority.

Identifying Higher Order Factors

Because of the regulatory nature of systems, the factors at the highest level of organization are not easy to identify on the basis of simple physiological or behavioral indexes, derived in straightforward laboratory studies with unitary dependent variables. We have seen that systems are homeostatic and process information in order to maintain equilibrium. It follows that four optimal strategies for psychology are: (a) to study *developmental* processes (when regulatory patterns are not yet established); (b) focus on *processes* of adaptation rather than products (which might be equivalent for two disparate groups); (c) *stress* the organism so that it is obliged to respond and display adaptive mechanisms; and (d) study the adaptations consequent upon *natural* impositions of stress, such as continuous noise or environmental pressures (see, for example, Brebner & Cooper, 1978; Eliasz, 1985; Friedensberg, 1985;

Klonowicz, 1986). An important constraint on strategies involving stress is created by ethical considerations, which limit the range of stressors that can be used and/or undermine their plausibility for the experimental subject.

SUBSYSTEM SET POINTS

Zuckerman sees information seeking as a product of basic biological mechanisms that he has yet to characterize in psychological terms, although he is unable to identify them with the mechanisms or factors put forward by Eysenck, Gray, or Strelau. Zuckerman's notion of optimal level of stimulation may be seen to reflect *set points* for particular subsystems, within the overall system framework. The notion of set points, although clearly applicable to subsystems, cannot be applied to the system *as a whole*. This is the error made by *arousal* theorists. Within an overall system, different subsystems may have relatively higher influence on other systems, depending on the degree to which they are allowed to operate by systems higher up in the hierarchy than themselves. In more conventional terms, the level of *excitation* in one subsystem is in part a function of the degree to which it is *inhibited* by subsystems higher in the hierarchical structure.

It is likely, for example, that Revelle, Anderson, and Humphreys, in their elegant manipulations of state and trait, are actually tapping into *several* subsystems, each with different set points. Apart from the important problems they identify in setting up appropriate experimental designs and conditions for sound *ante hoc* prediction, they need also to determine (a) the limits within which subsystems (impulsivity, circadian variation, response to depressants) operate; (b) the means employed by each subsystem to return to equilibrium; (c) the interactive properties among subsystems; and (d) the extent to which the answers to (a) through (c) are *different* for different personality subgroups. Similarly, Werre's studies capture the physiological and behavioral consequences of complex aggregated effects. Robinson's quasi-mathematical modeling and identification of different neurophysiological substrates and EEG markers is a sound beginning on the path to explanation.

THE NEED FOR HIGHER ORDER CONTROL

Somewhere within the hierarchical structure of any system, there must be a *control* network that monitors the state of the system, inspects set points, compares subsystem states with a *comparator*, and then initiates regulatory activity. Traditionally, psychology has relegated such functions to concepts of *attention;* within the present volume the discussion by Eliasz of the notion of *cognitive orientation* and selective attention to stimuli having different meaning for high- and low-reactives is particularly refreshing. M. W. Eysenck considers *preattentive* and *attentional* process in relation to anxiety. His data show that high-anxiety subjects have an attentional bias to allocate more attention to the processing of threatening stimuli. We should note that neither Eliasz nor M. W. Eysenck seek to integrate their two viewpoints, although the conceptual similarity is considerable. Few authors within the biological traditions of individual differences theory have paid attention to concepts of *self-control* or the use of language and the *second-signaling* system to mediate regulatory processes. Such functional characteristics may be seen to be *complementary* to, rather than alternatives for, the energy-related construct of arousal. It is encouraging that there has been a revival of interest in the biological correlates of intelligence (Eysenck & Barrett, 1983; Gale & Edwards, 1983c); there is an urgent need for synthesis between conceptual analyses of intelligence and personality. In the case of children at risk for schizophrenia, for example, high intelligence can serve as a protective factor (Venables, 1986). Intelligence is a higher order factor that is implicated in the full description of regulatory mechanisms.

THE RELATIVE INVARIANCE OF SET POINTS

Some set points may be historically old and invariant for an individual; others may be established through repeated regulatory activity, whereas still others may be relatively less invariant and imposed on the overall system by transient cultural demands. Strelau (1983) clearly considers his *stimulation processing coefficient* to be associated with a higher level set point, whereas *style of action* is at the second level, and notions of *ideal self* are at the third level. Similarly, Gale and Edwards (1986) sought to distinguish between inherent optimal arousal levels, those learned through adaptive adjustments and those that are task-specific. The complex issue of trait-times-situational interaction may be resolved in part by partitioning set points to *inherent, learned, and task-specific* determinants. Again, there is a danger of confusion if such distinctions are ignored. Thus *optimal level of arousal* and *optimal level of stimulation* are not equivalent explanatory concepts because they refer to different levels of system functioning. *Value systems* (imposed by culture) are prime candidates for identification as transient set points that reflect contemporary role models and ideal templates that the individual uses as a comparator for his or her own behavior.

TRACKING CAUSAL RELATIONSHIPS

Because causal relationships within complex systems are seen to be *circular* and not *linear*, because of the concept of *emergence*, and because of the relative *activity* or *passivity* of subsystems vis-à-vis other subsystems, we cannot make confident assertions about the origins of particular behavioral patterns. It would require a very complex general model to enable us to predict the outcome of multiple interactions between subsystems. To take a simple example, extreme neuroticism is likely to play an important role in the development and invariance of value systems and the development of conscience. However, the developmental context within which the individual evolves (and the extent to which reward and/or punishment are emphasized) will interact with neuroticism.

We see, therefore, that a systems approach, taken together with the key assumptions of individual differences theory set out at the beginning of this chapter, can help us in several ways: It can direct us to future research strategies, can impose order on existing data, and can provide reassurances that existing failures to obtain expected outcomes might be the result of faulty reasoning and inappropriate experimentation.

PROBLEMS WITH THE CONCEPT OF AROUSAL

Claridge tells us that "arousal has many of the qualities of a difficult but persuasive lover, whom reason tells one to abandon yet who continues to satisfy an inescapable need." As Gale (1981) points out, the term *arousal* has been used in a variety of contexts: *as an individual differences trait* (extraversion-introversion, primary-secondary function, anxiety, gender); *as a characteristic of pathology* (psychopathy, schizophrenia); *as intrinsic fluctuation* (circadian rhythms, menstrual cycle); *as a result of stressors* (heat, light, noise, loss of sleep); *as a consequence of drug or food intake* (caffeine, nicotine, alcohol, stimulants, depressants, postprandial states); *as a social-psychological correlate* (social facilitation, evaluation apprehension, personal space, social intimacy, organizational climate); and *as a characteristic of tasks* (vigilance, memory, reaction time, stimulus deprivation, monotony). Thus we see that the term *arousal* does seem to fill a need. But it is hardly likely that the term when used in all these various contexts has the same logical structure or rules of relationship with other variables. After all, in the examples given, it is employed as a *drive, source of stimulation, consequence of stimulation, property of stimuli, quality of trait, state and mood, cyclic fluctuation,* and *property of tasks.* Moreover, in several of its uses, the *operational* definition employed ranges over a host of dependent variables, including paper-and-pencil tests, activity level, performance on tasks, sensory threshold, resistance to pain, preference for art forms, cold pressor test, sedation threshold, ERP, EEG, EDA, HR, variability in response, oxygen consumption, and so on.

Thus in both conceptualization and in measurement there seems to be an assumption concerning a central unitary state, which is reflected by different processes and performances. The concept seems able to act as an independent variable, dependent variable, intervening variable, and hypothetical construct, at one and the same time, while also having formal relationships with other constructs. There is a danger that an explanatory concept, if broadly used, can cease to have content. As with currency, inflation reduces value and purchasing power. However, as our discussion of systems has revealed, it is in fact possible to think of arousal as a property of different systems within an overall hierarchical structure; to a certain extent and apart from treating arousal as a drive, set point, and consequence of action, some reconciliation between uses is possible.

A very important paper by Venables (1984) is mentioned by several contributors to the present volume. Venables' examination of the status of the concept of arousal deserves a summary here.

Venables begins with two important quotations from Lacey (1967):

> There are many experimental results that sharply contradict activation theory. . . . I think the experiments show that electroencephalographic, autonomic, motor, and other behavioural systems are imperfectly coupled, complexly interacting systems. (p. 15)

> In lower animals, then, it seems that we may in truth speak of *different kinds* of arousal—autonomic, electrocortical and behavioral. They are functionally and anatomically separated by appropriate experimental means. Nature's experiments yield confirmatory data in human clinical subjects. (p. 18)

The following points are based on Venables' arguments:

1. At first glance, the concept of intelligence seems to provide a conceptual analog for arousal. Just as individuals vary along a continuum of academic ability, so do we observe a continuum of alertness in ourselves and others; individuals can be drowsy, awake but relaxed, alert, absorbed, angry, agitated, or on the point of psychological collapse. Thus the concept of an arousal continuum seems to make sense.

2. But although factor analysis offers evidence of a general factor of intelligence, the poor intercorrelations of purported measures of arousal hardly lead to a general factor solution. Nevertheless, we should note that mood studies (Mackay, 1980; Thayer, 1986) do seem to yield two arousal clusters, one relating to alertness (sleep/wakefulness) and the other to affect (positive/negative hedonic tone).

3. Apart from this, although intelligence is used to describe *interindividual* differences, arousal is treated as both a trait and a state measure and thus is also an *intraindividual* measure.

4. The status of the concept of arousal as an intervening variable becomes particularly strained when, within one design, it is used to describe trait (extraversion), circadian, drug (caffeine), and interactional effects. The implicit rules governing such disparate uses are not the same; yet the combination of uses in one context implies commonality.

5. When arousal is related to performance, and in particular, via the putative inverted-U relationship, then interpretation becomes even more difficult. Curvilinear relationships are difficult to demonstrate, and several data points are needed to provide convincing evidence of a fit to the curve. Such fitting often seems to come *post hoc* rather than *ante hoc*, as Revelle, Anderson, and Humphreys remind us in this volume. Moreover, when arousal is related to *activity*, it is sometimes seen as a *parallel* state and on other occasions as a *reciprocal* state causally related to activity, sensation seeking, and so on.

6. Venables presents a matrix of intercorrelations derived from some 640 subjects between the ages of 5 and 25 (for nonspecific SCR, SCL, SPI, and HR). The correlations are tiny. One group within the total sample, 20-year-old males, showed some modest intercorrelations but not all in the correct direction. (Perhaps the preponderance of this age/gender group within psychological research has helped to keep the concept alive!).

7. Even if we limit ourselves to intrastate correlations, given the possibility that trait times situation interactions yield complex effects, the *averaging* of intrastate correlations is likely to be misleading. Given several dependent variables, overall average group relationships can be strong, without there being consistent relationships across variables for individual subjects. Each subject contributes differentially to the average score for each variable.

8. Venables then traces the notion of complexly interacting systems back to Hughlings Jackson and to very early psychophysiology. Several of Lacey's key findings had already been demonstrated toward the beginning of this century, namely that under different conditions heart rate (HR) might accelerate or decelerate, even though the estimated level of arousal in both cases seemed equivalent.

9. Like other physiological variables, which reflect bodily maintenance and other functions *as well as the impact of psychological variables*, the relationship between HR and a putative arousal is indirect and affected by the heart's need to support vital functions. We may contrast the low correlations obtained between HR and felt arousal, anger, or fear and the very high correlations obtained between sexual arousal and penile activation (Zuckerman, 1983). In the latter case, the subject has more direct access to the mechanisms involved (including capacity to control activation), and the judgment made is more specific. Given that HR and oxygen uptake are correlated, one can measure oxygen intake and par-

tial out some of the vital function effects, treating the residual variation as the psychological consequences of task manipulation (the "additional HR" method). However, so far as I am aware, equivalent approaches are not available for other psychophysiological variables.

To Venables' list of criticisms, we might add the observation that even *within* a psychophysiological measure (say SCR) different objective indexes (tonic level, phasic level, recruitment, half-recovery, habituation, spontaneous responses) do not yield high intercorrelations (Gale & Edwards, 1986). Within psychometrics, this would amount to low inter-item consistency, poor reliability, and limited possibility for validity (i.e., correlation with external criterion measures).

But Venables concludes the chapter with a discussion of *control systems,* in which cortical and autonomic arousal may be seen as having mutual influence via a feedback control loop, in which active and passive control processes operate to achieve homeostasis. His discussion is of crucial importance to the issues raised in the present volume, and, as we have tried to demonstrate, the systems approach offers a possible way forward for future individual differences research.

Thus Venables (1964), Claridge (1967), and Hare (1978) have speculated about the temporal relationships between cortical and autonomic measures and between different autonomic measures, as possible indications of the operation of homeostatic mechanisms. For example, early acceleration in HR may operate to dampen SCR response. In an intriguing study of fluctuations in questionnaire and physiological measures over a working week, Venables and Christie (1974) showed neuroticism to correlate with the degree of fluctuation in T-wave amplitude (a component of the EKG) during the week. Because they speculate that the T-wave may reflect a vital control system that is active and thus requires invariance, instability in High N subjects may reflect an incapacity to remain stable when exposed to external stimulation. A clear implication of such an approach is that *processes* are more important than outcomes. Indeed, two subjects with very different personality scores may achieve identical performance but via completely different routes (this is the message of the Polish researchers; see the chapters by Strelau, Eliasz, and Klonowicz in this volume).

AROUSAL AND CONTEMPORARY STUDIES OF THE EXPRESSION OF EMOTION

Arousal theorists within the field of personality research would do well to draw upon the lessons learned in psychophysiological studies of emotion. Currently, two key theoretical positions are dominant and apparently contradictory. Following Darwin and the James-Lange theory of the emotions, Laird (for example, 1974) has pursued the "facial feed-back" hypothesis. This predicts high intercorrelation between modes of emotional expression; an early stage in the process is facial expression, which is antecedent to both autonomic responding and experienced emotion. His studies seem to provide some support for the notion of intercorrelation among measures of arousal. In contradiction, however, are the views of the "discharge" theorists, who following Freud, see emotion as some quantum of psychic energy that seeks external outlet; this view predicts a *reciprocal* relationship between modes of emotional expression (i.e., physiological response systems, behavior, subjective report; see, e.g., Buck, 1980). One particularly influential study, however, shows that the partialling out of *social desirability* effects can increase the correlation between trait anxiety and physiological responsiveness; the notion of *repression* has therefore been reintroduced to research on emotion (Weinberger, Schwartz, & Davidson, 1979). Finally, there are aspects of contemporary emotion research that have clear implications for biological studies of personality because they offer so many parallels in terms of the questions asked and the data obtained. Ekman (1984) has demonstrated pancultural homogeneity in key emotional expressions; these are overlaid by cultural display rules but are differentiated in terms of psychophysiological response and may be triggered by pancultural stimuli. Thus current research into emotion seems to share certain conceptual and empirical ambitions with personality research. Biological predispositions are seen to be accessible in spite of overlying effects of learning and cultural context; patterning of physiological response is a focus of interest; and the relationships between behavior, physiology, and subjective report are seen to be crucial to theory building. We should note that in individual differences research, anxiety appears to have been the only emotion to be investigated in any detail. And there are few studies of emotion within the contemporary paradigms, which have incorporated traditional psychometric measures of personality. Within traditional personality research, the emphasis has been upon *performance* rather than on *behavior* or upon modes of expression. Thus a marriage between individual differences and emotion researchers would seem to offer a useful way forward for the future. However, the degree of differentiation of responding demonstrated within research findings in the field of emotion indicates that we are unlikely to find evidence for a unitary concept of arousal. Moreover, the key idea in discharge theory approaches is that emotion (or arousal) may be discharged through *different* or *alternative* channels of expression. This implies an individual response stereotypy for emotional expression and the need to take multiple channel recordings (behavioral, physiological, and experiential), if the patterning of response is to be captured.

BIOENERGETICS AND INDIVIDUAL DIFFERENCE THEORY

Brener (1980) offers a succinct argument for the use in psychology of the energy concept, conceived of as the intake, storage, conversion, and expression of energy. He argues for a rapprochement (a) between bioenergetics (as seen in biological sciences) and psychological concepts and (b) between concepts of energy and concepts of information (as seen in human communication theory).

> In a physical system, entropy is a measure of the degree of organization of a system: The more disorganized and uniformly dispersed its elements are, the higher is its entropy value and the lower is the energy availability of the system. Thus entropy is identified with uncertainty. We might say that the less our knowledge about a question, the greater is the uncertainty or entropy. (1980, page 90)

Our skeletal musculature is the effector system through which we engage in energy exchange with the environment. Exposure to the environment and the process of learning reduce uncertainty, create efficiency, and conserve energy. Thus Brener offers a systems model of energy exchange, involving energy/information transmission, feedback, and control.

How can such notions be related to the individual differences concepts considered in this volume? Let us return to basic concepts and consider the elements necessary for an energy exchange system. Four components are required: an *acquisition* system, a *storage* system, an *expression* system, and a *control* or *monitoring* system that regulates and integrates the remaining three systems.

An *acquisition* system may take up energy slowly or quickly, spasmodically or rarely, and derive energy from few or several sources. If we translate such distinctions into observable behaviors, then extraverts may be seen to have an intense acquisition system, working at a high level of throughput; that is, activity is intense, stimulus sources are varied and are frequently sampled. The extravert (or the low-reactive) may be said to have a *high energy acquisition* style. In contrast, introverts engage in low-intensity activity, with less sampling of the environment, and more fixed patterns of acquisition (*low energy acquisition* style). Too much energy input is aversive and hedonically unsatisfactory for the introvert; therefore, considerable attention is paid to stimulation sources. So far as regulation is concerned, the *control* system of the introvert is biased towards the monitoring of input. Both introverts and extraverts have an efficient control system. But the set point for the introvert is low, and the set-point for the extravert is high.

The *energy expression* system of both extraverts and introverts is geared to dynamic equilibrium with the acquisition system. The motor expressivity of extraverts is vigorous. However, such vigorous activity itself involves energy conversion and is costly. The tendency to approach rewarding stimulation enables the cost of action to be minimised. Nevertheless, the *control* system of the extravert is focused upon expression to ensure that it is not so costly that energy output does not match input. In contrast, the introvert incurs less cost, in maintaining a low level of vigor in expression. Thus the control system of extraverts and introverts is efficient, but its focus differs (on output and input respectively). Input regulation is the focus for introverts, and output regulation is the focus for extraverts.

Storage systems may be efficient and conserve stored energy or be inefficient and leaky. In an *efficient* system, the control system is able to monitor the store and distribute its energy efficiently, allocating it to appropriate activities. The control system keeps stored energy within the confines of a set point and manipulates the rate of input, release, and output. At the same time, the control system needs to allocate energy to maintaining the overall system (vegetative functions). Thus energy is withdrawn from store as and when required in an orderly and organized fashion and distributed to appropriate functions. The suggestion here is that the neurotic individual has an inefficient and leaky energy store, which allows energy to run away in a disorganized and uncontrolled fashion. Thus, apart from uneconomic energy loss, additional energy is required for the control system to operate effectively because the control system utilizes more energy when required to exercise more control. The energy store for the neurotic is therefore set at a high set point. One control strategy is to operate a bias to the acquisition system because this allows monitoring of the stimulus field to ensure that aversive stimulation is avoided (because punishment is costly in energy terms). Unfortunately, avoiding the stimulus field means that there is reduced opportunity for learning and reduced opportunity to develop efficient energy conservation. In contrast, the stable individual has an efficient energy store, from which the control system may allocate energy resources as activity demands. In the case of attention, for example, the stable individual can sustain attention continuously and without disruption. It is suggested here that the bodily symptoms of anxiety (restlessness, difficulties of concentration, vegetative disorders) are a reflection of energy store disorganization. The control system of the neurotic individual is focused both in input and storage systems. The experience of anxiety may include an amalgam of correlates of both energy loss and the effort required to sustain the energy level of the system (by exercising control on the store system and the acquisition system).

It is possible to consider also certain forms of psychopathology in terms of this simplified energy exchange and regulation model. Depression may be seen to be a reflection of low acquisition and low expression, with a low set point for the store; depression is characterized by a very low metabolic rate. Agitated depression may include an anxiety component in the form of disorganized energy loss from store, combined with an inability in the control system to govern expression. Severe anxiety states may combine disruption of input and output mechanisms as well as energy storage mechanisms, so that the individual suffers not only from the consequences of uncontrolled energy loss but is unable to develop compensatory acquisition strategies or control further loss as a result of nonefficient output activity.

Venables has suggested that schizophrenia is characterized by an "openness to environmental input," and both he and Claridge suggest that there is disorganization and lack of integration among control systems. It is possible that the essential disorder in schizophrenia is the *control* system itself, which is unable to integrate *acquisition* and *storage* systems or even monitor their activities in a systematic fashion.

Thus, to review the key elements of this *energy-regulation conceptual nervous system:* There are four energic components (*acquisition, storage, expression,* and *control* systems); each may be in an efficient or nonefficient state; each may be have a high or low set point; in addition, the control system may have a bias or focus toward one of the three remaining systems. Thus extraverts have an efficient acquisition and expression system, both of which are run at a high level; introverts have an efficient acquisition and expression system, both of which are run at a low level. Thus extraverts and introverts run their input and output energy systems in dynamic equilibrium. In extraverts, an efficient control system is biased to expression (output) and in introverts to acquisition (input). What has not been considered so far is whether the set point for stored energy is different in extraverts and introverts, that is, whether the stable equilibrium for the two groups is different. In arousal terms, the concern is whether the *optimum level of arousal* is equivalent. At this state of the development of the energy regulation model, it is parsimonious to suggest that the set point is equivalent; there is little *direct* physiological evidence to sustain the optimum level construct. If the energy regulation approach can eschew this aspect of arousal theory, that is, can explain the available data, then it is best left in abeyance. However, it is clear that the notion of energy transmission within the four subsystems may be identified with "arousal" pertaining to different systems. In crude terms, the level of *work* (energy utilization required to maintain equilibrium) could be identified with the subsystem arousal state. For example, the Cooper and Brebner approach sees introverts and extraverts as showing excitation in input and output modes, respectively.

Neurotics have an inefficient energy store, with a high set point, and an inefficient control system biased to both input and energy store. Stables have an efficient energy store and an efficient control system that regulates input, storage, and output of energy without any particular bias or focus. Neurotics are inefficient in acquisition and storage and lose energy both through the leakiness of the store and through the need for the control system to use energy to sustain its effectiveness. These relationships may be represented schematically as in Table 1.

Does this scheme illuminate the problems associated with indi-

Table 1. A Conceptual Nervous System Based on Energy Transmission Mechanisms (Showing Possible Subsystem Combinations Underlying Key Personality Dimensions and Psychopathological States)

Individual difference dimension	Energy system component			
	Acquisition	Storage	Expression	Control state/focus
Extraversion	Efficient; high set point	Efficient	Efficient; high set point	Efficient; expression
Introversion	Efficient; low set point	Efficient	Efficient; low set point	Efficient; acquisition
Neuroticism		Nonefficient; high set point		Nonefficient; storage and acquisition
Stability		Efficient		Efficient
Depression	Nonefficient; low set point	Nonefficient; low set point	Nonefficient; low set point	Nonefficient; acquisition and expression
Anxiety	Nonefficient; high set point	Nonefficient; high set point		Nonefficient; acquisition and storage
Mania		Nonefficient; high set point	Nonefficient; high set point	Nonefficient; storage and expression
Schizophrenia	Nonefficient; high set point	Nonefficient; high set point	Nonefficient; low set point	Nonefficient; acquisition, storage, and expression

vidual differences theories and research or merely add further confusion? In Table 2, each of the contributions to this volume is summarized in terms of the key constructs employed, the variables of interest, the research strategy, and the main findings. In the final column is an attempt to relate findings that might seem discrepant in the light of the energy-regulation model.

So far as arousal is concerned, the energy-regulation model makes it clear that simple measures of bodily function will not yield high intercorrelations. Extraverts and introverts, in maintaining a stable equilibrium, are unlikely to yield differential data for autonomic measures. *Behavior* and the patterning of input and output activities are likely to provide superior differentiation. If cortical measures offer a reflection of the operation of control systems, then these might prove more fruitful because the control systems are geared to maintain high and low levels of input and output functions for extraverts and introverts respectively. In contrast, autonomic measures (both electrophysiological and biochemical) offer more promise for neuroticism and anxiety. However, the disorganization and lack of control within the energy store imply that variability and frequent fluctuation will underlie any observation; such lack of reliability within measures will reduce the chance of intermeasure correlation.

Venables suggests that active control systems will be relatively invariant because they require stability to maintain control over systems lower in the hierarchical structure. This implies that variability is a key parameter for measurement. Time-series analysis can enable the partitioning of serial effects so that an autocorrelation may be derived for each measure, followed by an estimate of the degree to which each measure is dependent on the variance due to other measures. Variability is rarely a focus of interest in personality research.

THE RELEVANCE OF FAMILY PROCESS THEORY TO INDIVIDUAL DIFFERENCES RESEARCH

Family process models are relevant to individual differences studies for several reasons. Some family process models have adopted a general system theory approach and the difficulties of applying a systems approach to human behavior have been well aired (Minuchin, 1974; Vetere & Gale, 1987). Second, because family members live within a confined environment over an extended period of time, *regulation* is a key feature in the account of family process. Exchange theory as applied to family process (Nye, 1983) states that such regulation has a *cost*; thus family theory has elements in common with the Polish approach. Third, sever-

Table 2. Key Approaches Adopted by Contributors to This Volume (Related Where Appropriate to an Energy Regulation Theory)

Authors	Typology and/or personality attributes	Explanatory constructs	Examples of scales and manipulations	Examples of independent and dependent variables	Comments (including similarity to energy model)
Claridge	Psychoticism and schizotypy	Dissociation of brain systems mediating arousal and attention; input dysfunction; information processing; hypo/hyper responsive; weakened regulation of Ex and Inh; defective laterality	High risk designs; study of relatives; perceptual sensitivity: two-flash threshold; EPQ P-scale; STQ; LSD-25	EDR; habituation; covariation of physiological indexes and perception; EEG augmenting response profiles	Shows similarities between issues in personality and psychopathology research and theory. Key issue is regulation/dysregulation of ANS/CNS. Focus on balance of Ex and Inh processes. AG: Nonefficient control system
Cooper & Brebner	Extraversion-introversion	Excitation (Ex); inhibition (Inh); stimulus analysis (S); response organization (RO); extraverts: SInh, ROEx; introverts: SEx, ROInh	Stimulus demands; response demands; crowding	Reaction time; inspection time; response patterning; EEG alpha	AG: Control system bias to acquisition (I) and expression (E); suggest focus on spatiotemporal patterning in motor cortex (EP, augmenting-reducing).
Eliasz	Reactivity	Person–environment fit; sensitivity; endurance; optimal activation; optimal stimulation;	Meaning of stimuli; avoidance; social pressure; environmental	Language acquisition; exploration; person/thing orientation; achievement motive;	Reviews the power and range of application of Strelau's theory. Emphasis on cognitive factors. AG: Control

susceptibility to punishment; cognitive orientation/concentration	stress; social/physical influence; semantic organization; Type A/B behavior	self-reported states; interpersonal communication		system bias to acquisition.
Eysenck, H. J.	Extraversion-introversion; neuroticism-stability	Cortical arousal; limbic activation; strength of NS; transmarginal/protective Inh; mobility		Full range of cognitive, performance, and social behaviors.	Recommends continued development of *progressive* research program; reviews historical development of arousal and related concepts.
Eysenck, M. W.	Extraversion-introversion; trait anxiety; neuroticism	Susceptibility to positive and negative affect; BIS/BAS; cognitive structures; limbic activation; pre-attentive and attentional bias; selective allocation of attention; general schemata; repression/sensitization; perceptual defense; mood-state-dependent-retrieval	Positive and negative content of verbal stimuli for perception and recall	Dichotic listening; attention to threatening and nonthreatening stimuli	High anxiety is associated with more thorough processing of threatening stimuli. AG: Control system bias to acquisition.

(Continued)

Table 2. (Continued)

Authors	Typology and/or personality attributes	Explanatory constructs	Examples of scales and manipulations	Examples of independent and dependent variables	Comments (including similarity to energy model)
Fahrenberg	Emotionality/ neuroticism	ANS activation; psychosomatic irritability; mood fluctuation; limbic system	Correlation of psychometric measures; psycho-physiology of anxiety; multi-parameter, multisituation stressors replication	Indexes of somatic dysfunction; state of health; nervousness; psychophysiological measures	Suggests semantic analysis of theory, hierarchical modeling, and multidimensional approach; AG: nonefficient energy storage and/or nonefficient control system.
Haier, Sokolski, Katz, & Buchs-baum	Extraversion-introversion; anxiety; psychoticism; sensation seeking	Glucose absorption/ uptake	Anxiety patients compared with normals; EPQ score; continuous performance; Positron Emission Tomography	Mean glucose metabolic rate in different brain areas; correlation of personality and brain area glucose concentration; hemisphere differences	Propose development of specific hypotheses following initial exploratory data; comment on cost of procedure and dependence of psychological studies on clinical requirements; AG: potential of technique for locating energy transfer.

Klonowicz	Reactivity; activity; mobility	Arousal, activation; optimal level of arousal; self-regulation; stimulation processing coefficient; cost of adaptation; style of action	Resting state; stress, nonstress; mood scales; active coping; Machiavellianism; sports preferences	Resting arousal levels; psychophysiological indexes; task performance; quality of work; mood, emotional tone; auxiliary operations	Comprehensive review of performance and physiological studies, with particular emphasis on regulatory mechanisms; AG: applies to all aspects of energy regulation model.
Kohn	Arousability; sensation seeking; reactivity; augmenters-reducers	Compensatory relations of arousability and sensation seeking; optimum level of arousal; endurance; transmarginal Inh	Vando scales; stimulant and depressant drugs; reactivity scale; interscale correlation; scale-behavior correlation	Pain tolerance; visual/auditory magnitude estimation; preferred level of stimulation	Proposes further construct validation of new reactivity scale; recommends revival of general/partial properties of NS distinction; AG: control system bias to acquisition.
Mecacci	Circadian types	Arousal-cognition relationships; interhemispheric integration	Morningness–eveningness scale; age differences; occupations; task complexity; cognitive tasks	Rising times; reaction time; EPs; levels of processing; hemisphere specialization scores	

(Continued)

Table 2. (*Continued*)

Authors	Typology and/or personality attributes	Explanatory constructs	Examples of scales and manipulations	Examples of independent and dependent variables	Comments (including similarity to energy model)
Revelle, Anderson, & Humphreys	Extraversion-introversion; impulsivity	Arousal; inverted-U; fatigue; transmarginal Inh; cue utilization; response competition	Environmental and task conditions; time of day; EPI, EPQ; cognitive processing; caffeine; multiple sessions; information transfer/STM	Cognitive performance; reasoning scores; perceptual scanning; memory load capacity	Important discussion of the different assumptions and interpretative constraints of factorial, additive, and multiple level designs; AG: could be manipulating all subsystems of energy model.
Robinson	Excitation-inhibition; arousability; strength; balance; attention; consciousness; intelligence	Diffuse thalamo cortical system; BSRF	Photic stimulation to provoke EEG changes; EPQ, IQ; mathematical modeling of EEG components	Fit of model to EEG data; natural frequency; damping ratio; wide range of performance and state variables	Danger of overgeneralization of model to account for too many aspects of behavior.
Simonov	Extraversion-introversion; strength; emotionality; mobility	Motivational and informational systems	Selective brain damage; shock/pain; rats tested in pairs	Disruption of motivational system; reordering of signal priorities (postlesion)	Hypothalamus is source of needs; amygdala determines need hierarchy; hippocampus responds to low

					probability signals; frontal cortex responds to low probability signals; extraversion is link between motivation/ information systems; emotionality reflected by neocortex– hypothalamus– hippocampus–amygdala system; mobility is hypothalamus– hippocampus system.
Strelau	Extraversion-introversion; sensation seeking; impulsivity; augmenting/ reducing; anxiety; neuroticism; strength; reactivity	Strength of Exc; transmarginal Inh; conditionability; arousal mechanisms; cue function; balance of nervous processes; neuroendocrine individuality	Correlation between scales; correlation between scales and physiological measures; sensory thresholds; learning efficiency; behavioral activation	Wide range of electrophysiological, and behavioral data	Seeks to integrate eight related personality dimensions.

(*Continued*)

Table 2. (Continued)

Authors	Typology and/or personality attributes	Explanatory constructs	Examples of scales and manipulations	Examples of independent and dependent variables	Comments (including similarity to energy model)
Werre	Extraversion-introversion	Excitation; inhibition; automatic processing; proportion of cortical cells available for work; inverted-U function	CNV paradigm; repeated sessions; drugs; noise; practice	Differential CNV-arousal relations for extraverts and introverts	Further testing of new model underway
Zuckerman	Reactivity; extraversion; anxiety; sensation seeking	Optimum level of arousal; strength of NS; sensitivity to reward and punishment (BAS & BIS); arousability; catecholamine systems and intrinsic reward	Psychometrics; drug manipulation; types of stimulation	Range of psychophysiological variables; augmenting-reducing EP; levels of MAO (and metabolites)	Far-reaching critical evaluation of status of key constructs and the problems of operationalization; recommends multimodal and multiresponse framework for exploring sensation-seeking subscales.

al family theories make the conceptual error of treating the family as an augmented individual (with needs, wishes, aims, habits, and so on); although this is misleading for family theory, it is convenient for individual differences theory because it makes the conceptual frameworks more portable to the individual case. Fourth, several family process theories are concerned with *power* or the capacity of individuals to maintain control over their environment, including other family members; such an emphasis enables us to think in *active* terms about the regulation process. Finally, because families serve the role of primary socialization agent in our culture, several theories emphasize the importance of *value systems* in determining aspects of interpersonal regulation and goal setting.

The *distance-regulation* theory of family process of Kantor and Lehr (1975) bears a remarkable resemblance to some of the conceptual frameworks presented in this volume. A detailed account and critical evaluation of the theory is given by Gale and Vetere (1987). We have room only to make a case for its consideration within the context of individual differences theory. The theory is a *systems* theory, in which the family is seen as being complex, open, adaptive, and constantly processing information. The information that is processed is information about *distance regulation*. All family activity occurs in a psychosocial space in which *distance, energy,* and *time* are manipulated in order to achieve *affect, power,* and *meaning.* Thus all activity can be classified in terms of six dimensions: positive and negative affect; control over others; realization of self within a system of values; regulation of space and distance; regulation of energy; and regulation of temporal patterning. Within the overall system they identify intrapersonal, interpersonal, and familial subsystems. These are ill-defined and need not concern us here, except to recognize that such subsystems are seen to operate at different levels within an overall hierarchical structure.

Kantor and Lehr (1975) describe the mechanisms that are deployed to regulate interpersonal behavior. In the case of energy, mechanisms are specified that relate to locating energy sources, tapping into them, charging up, storing, testing against comparator set points, investing for future uses, allocating to particular activities, withdrawing from particular activities, keeping track of requirements, prioritizing, and transforming from one form (physical, mental) or charge (positive, negative, neutral). Each of these mechanisms has a special name within the theory. The descriptions provided are reminiscent of Strelau's (1983) description of *styles of action* because the particular regulation strategies adopted depend on the mix of the six dimensions in any particular case. Similar mechanisms are described for spatial and temporal control. In the case of the latter, the actions of family members are described in terms of their synchrony or asynchrony.

Kantor and Lehr's categorization of three family types is very much like a personality-type theory. The styles of regulation used and the patterning of the six dimensions of family action lead to *types* whose typical behaviors are then described.

Finally, all actions by individual family members are described exhaustively by a fourfold classification: *moving (or proposing), opposing, following,* and *bystanding.* These describe the mechanisms deployed within the social space of "psychopolitics" whereby individuals negotiate power and control over resources such as affection, energy utilization, temporal planning, and so on. Throughout the theory, feedback systems are specified that sense incoming information, compare it against a comparator, act upon the environment, and store information about the consequences of action.

It is hoped that enough will have been said to tantalize the reader into further examination of the theory, which is dealt with quite inadequately at present. However, its relevance to personality theories that emphasize energy transfer, regulation, and styles of active engagement with the environment should be clear. If revived, the theory, which has been neglected in the family field until now, will undoubtedly yield a rich harvest in personality research.

WHY HAVE PSYCHOPHYSIOLOGICAL APPROACHES TO PERSONALITY FAILED?

At a symposium on the psychophysiology of individual differences, Gray (1983b) declared that "there is no psychophysiology of individual differences." Gale and Edwards (1983b, 1986) claim that such a judgment is premature and that many of the failures to produce satisfactory data could be attributable to faulty research. Gale and Edwards (1983b, 1986) attribute the existing untidy set of findings to what they call "the seven deadly sins of the psychophysiology of individual differences." Their seven sins are theoretical simplemindedness, obsession with correlation rather than process, poor psychometrics, poor physiology, trivial experimentation, procedural insensitivity, and low-level data handling and interpretation.

The majority of the faults considered by Gale and Edwards (1983b, 1986) are remediable. A variety of research strategies are also available for future work, so long as researchers pay attention to the cautions provided by Revelle, Anderson, and Humphreys (see Chapter 1 in this volume). Gale and Edwards (1983b, 1986) offer a variety of approaches to individual differences research, within a range of paradigmatic procedures.

CONCLUSION

The concept of arousal should be dead, given the assaults it has suffered over the last 20 years, but it simply will not lie down. Given the aggregational nature of psychological knowledge at large (in contrast with the incremental knowledge structure of the natural sciences), an integrative concept might seem welcome. However, it seems unlikely that evidence for a unitary concept of arousal will ever be produced, except in the most special circumstances, where the various bodily systems are somehow induced to all function in a common direction and at a shared intensity. The arousal systems (if they indeed exist) are like a group of soldiers; they are happier engaging in their own individual activities than marching in unison.

However, the concept of energy exchange and its identification with informational exchange (Brener, 1980) seems a more attractive proposition. Nevertheless, it will take considerable ingenuity to tease out the operation of the different components that have been specified in the *energy-regulation* model set out previously. The various contributors to this volume have offered a set of theoretical approaches that hopefully may be forced into a complementary framework. Gale and Edwards (1983b), in drawing together the various threads of theory, constructed a "patchwork model" in which all existing viewpoints were expressed. The "patchwork model" included approach/avoidance, sensory preparedness, modulation of sensory input, energy transmission, storage/retrieval, cognitive evaluation, response criterion, motor preparedness, and action. However, they did not go further than to set out the components of the model in diagrammatic form. The present chapter seeks to offer a dynamic integration of the various components. A future research program should seek to achieve the following objectives: (a) clarify the *level* at which each major variable (or subsystem) operates; (b) clarify the *nature of interaction* among subsystems; and (c) devise means whereby the operation of subsystems and their interactions may be measured and manipulated. The energy transmission model, cast within a systems framework, might assist in the process of elucidation.

However, regulation is not just about energic information. The control systems we have specified have a choice among a variety of strategies for maintaining energic equilibrium. Constraints are imposed upon strategy selection by the value systems that individuals acquire during development. The Polish theorists are the only contributors who seek to relate individual differences to concepts such as *the ideal self*. It is likely that temperamental traits interact with sociocultural norms in an elaborate fashion, both setting goals and inhibiting certain modes of action. It is possible that any biological theory of individual differences needs to take into account this interplay between values and regulatory behavior, namely to explore the third level of functional integration in greater detail. It comes as a shock to me as a lifelong empiricist that I must conclude this chapter by confessing my approach is in several respects indistinguishable from that of Sigmund Freud; for I have ended up with an energic system, a control system, and a hypothetical set of regulatory devices within which a value-based subsystem imposes operational constraints.

REFERENCES

Brebner, J., & Cooper, C. J. Stimulus- or response-induced excitation: A comparison of the behaviour of introverts and extraverts. *Journal of Research in Personality*, 1978, *12*, 306–311.

Brener, J. M. Energy, information and man. In A. J. Chapman & D. M. Jones (Eds.), *Models of man*. Leicester: The British Psychological Society, 1980.

Buck, R. Non-verbal behavior and the theory of emotion: The facial feedback hypothesis. *Journal of Personality and Social Psychology*, 1980, *38*, 811–824.

Buckley, W. (Ed.). *Modern systems research for the behavioral scientist*. Englewood Cliffs, NJ: Prentice-Hall, 1968.

Claridge, G. *Personality and arousal*. Oxford: Pergamon Press, 1967.

Crits-Christoph, P., & Schwartz, G. E. Psychophysiological contributions to psychotherapy research: A systems perspective. In A. Gale & J. A. Edwards (Eds.), *Physiological correlates of human behaviour: Individual differences and psychopathology* (Vol. 3). London: Academic Press, 1983.

Ekman, P. Expression and the nature of emotion. In K. Scherer & P. Ekman (Eds.), *Approaches to emotion*. Hillsdale, NJ: Erlbaum, 1984.

Eliasz, A. Mechanisms of temperament: Basic functions. In J. Strelau, F. Farley, & A. Gale (Eds.), *The biological bases of personality and behavior: Theories, measurement techniques, and development* (Vol. 1). Washington: Hemisphere, 1985.

Eysenck, H. J., & Barrett, P. Psychophysiology and the measurement of intelligence. In C. R. Reynolds & V. Willson (Eds.), *Methodological and statistical advances in the study of individual differences*. New York: Plenum Press, 1983.

Friedensberg, E. Reactivity and individual style of work exemplified by constructional-type task performance: A developmental study. In J. Strelau, F. Farley, & A. Gale (Eds.), *The biological bases of personality and behavior: Theories, measurement techniques, and development* (Vol. 1). Washington: Hemisphere, 1985.

Gale, A. EEG studies of extraversion-introversion: What's the next step? In R. Lynn (Ed.), *Dimensions of personality: Essays in honour of H. J. Eysenck*. Oxford: Pergamon Press, 1981.

Gale, A., & Edwards, J. A. A short critique of the psychophysiology of individual differences. *Personality and Individual Differences*, 1983, *4*, 429–435. (a)

Gale, A., & Edwards, J. A. Psychophysiology and individual differences: Theory, research procedures, and the interpretation of data. *Australian Journal of Psychology*, 1983, *35*, 361–379. (b)

Gale, A., & Edwards, J. A. Cortical correlates of intelligence. In A. Gale & J. A. Edwards (Eds.), *Physiological correlates of human behaviour: Individual differences and psychopathology* (Vol. 3). London: Academic Press, 1983. (c)

Gale, A., & Edwards, J. A. Individual differences. In M. G. H. Coles, E. Donchin, & S. W. Porges (Eds.), *Psychophysiology: Systems, processes and applications*. New York: Guilford, 1986.

Gale, A., Strelau, J., & Farley, F. Introduction: Overview and critique. In J. Strelau, F. Farley, & A. Gale (Eds.), *The biological bases of personality and behavior: Theories, measurement techniques, and development* (Vol. 1). Washington: Hemisphere, 1985.

Gale, A., & Vetere, A. Some theories of family behaviour. In A. Vetere & A. Gale (Eds.), *Ecological studies of family-life*, Chichester: Wiley, 1987.

Gray, J. A. Anxiety, personality and the brain. In A. Gale & J. A. Edwards (Eds.), *Physiological correlates of human behaviour: Individual differences and psychopathology* (Vol. 3). London: Academic Press, 1983. (a)

Gray, J. A. Discussion. Workshop on individual differences. 11th Annual Meeting of the British Psychophysiology Society, London, December 1983. (b)

Hall, A. D., & Fagen, R. E. Definition of system. *General Systems Yearbook*, 1956, *1*, 18–28.

Hare, R. D. Electrodermal and cardiovascular correlates of psychopathy. In R. D. Hare & D. Schalling (Eds.), *Psychopathic behavior: Approaches to research*. New York: Wiley, 1978.

Kantor, D., & Lehr, D. *Inside the family: Toward a theory of family process*, San Francisco: Jossey-Bass, 1975.

Kline, P. The factor structure. Workshop on individual differences. 11th Annual Meeting of the British Psychophysiology Society, London, December, 1983.

Klonowicz, T. Reactivity and performance: The third side of the coin. In J. Strelau, F. Farley, & A. Gale (Eds.), *The biological bases of personality and behavior: Psychophysiology, performance, and application* (Vol. 2). Washington: Hemisphere, 1986.

Lacey, J. I. Somatic response patterning and stress: Some revisions of activation theory. In M. G. Appley & R. Trumbell (Eds.), *Psychological stress: Issues in research*. New York: Appleton-Century-Crofts, 1967.

Laird, J. D. Self-attribution of emotion: The effects of expressive behaviour on the quality of emotional experience. *Journal of Personality and Social Psychology*, 1974, *29*, 475–486.

Mackay, C. J. The measurement of mood and psychophysiological activity using self-report techniques. In I. Martin & P. H. Venables (Eds.), *Techniques in psychophysiology*. Chichester: Wiley, 1980.

Miller, J. G. *Living systems*. New York: McGraw-Hill, 1978.

Minuchin, S. *Families and family therapy*. London: Tavistock, 1974.

Nye, I. F. (Ed.). *Family relationships: Rewards and costs*. Beverly Hills, CA.: Sage, 1983.

O'Gorman, J. Individual differences in habituation of human physiological responses: A review of theory, method and findings in the study of personality correlates in non-clinical populations. *Biological Psychology*, 1977, *5*, 257–318.

Strelau, J. *Temperament—personality—activity*. London: Academic Press, 1983.

Thayer, R. E. Activation (arousal): The shift from a single to a multidimensional perspective. In J. Strelau, F. Farley, & A. Gale (Eds.), *The biological bases of personality and behavior: Psychophysiology, performance and application* (Vol. 2). Washington: Hemisphere, 1986.

Venables, P. H. Input dysfunction in schizophrenia. In B. Maher (Ed.), *Progress in experimental personality research*. New York: Academic Press, 1964.

Venables, P. H. Arousal: An examination of its status as a concept. In M. G. H. Coles, J. R. Jennings, & J. P. Stern (Eds.), *Psychophysiological perspectives,* New York: Van Nostrand, 1984.

Venables, P. H. *What does high-risk research tell us about the nature of schizophrenia?* Paper presented at a symposium on contrasting models of schizophrenia. Annual Conference of the British Psychological Society, University of Sheffield, April 1986.

Venables, P. H., & Christie, M. J. Neuroticism, physiological state and mood: An exploratory study of Friday/Monday changes *Biological Psychology,* 1974, *1,* 201–211.

Vetere, A. *Participant observation in families with school-refusing children.* Unpublished doctoral dissertation, University of Southampton, 1984.

Vetere, A., & Gale, A. (Eds.), *Ecological studies of family life.* Chichester: Wiley, 1987.

Von Bertalanffy, L. *General system theory: Foundations, development, applications.* New York: Braziller, 1968.

Weinberger, D. A., Schwartz, G. E., & Davidson, R. J. Low-anxious, high-anxious, and repressive coping styles: Psychometric patterns and behavioral and physiological responses to stress. *Journal of Abnormal Psychology,* 1979, *88,* 369–380.

Zuckerman, M. Sexual arousal in the human: Love, chemistry or conditioning? In A. Gale & J. Edwards (Eds.), *Physiological correlates of human behaviour. Basic issues* (Vol. 1.). London: Academic Press, 1983.

Author Index

Achorn, E., 54
Aiello, J. R., 41
Althoff, M., 91–92
Amaral, P., 19
Amelang, M., 107, 279
Andersen, B., 106–107
Anderson, K. J., 17, 19, 24–26, 28–30
Anderson, P., 128
Annis, H. M., 237
Anthony, E. J., 134
Anthony, S. B., 238
Åsberg, M., 273, 279
Asch, S.E., 201
Ashton, H., 67
Averill, J. R., 115

Baker, A. H., 236
Ballenger, J. C., 222, 276
Bannister, D., 49
Barber, T. X., 242
Barnes, G. E., 233, 235–236, 242, 244, 273, 279
Barratt, E. S., 273, 276–279
Barrett, P., 79, 143, 293
Bartussek, D., 107
Bazylevich, T. F., 275
Bear, D. M., 54
Beaumont, J. G., 178
Becker, H. S., 235
Bell, B., 140
Bentall, R. P., 134
Benzuly, M., 26, 29
Berger, H., 45
Berlyne, D. E., 271, 276

Bernal, J. D., 9
Bernstein, A., 138, 146
Berquist, W. H., 87
Berretty, E. W., 74–75
Białowąs, D., 201
Bieri, J., 208
Bingham, E., 412
Birchall, P. M., 142, 144, 146
Blake, M. J. F., 22, 26
Blaylock, B. A., 90
Blinkhorn, S., 80
Borkenau, P., 279
Borkovec, T. D., 84
Borriello, 174
Bower, G. H., 84
Bowyer, P. A., 31
Braden, W., 45, 275
Brand, C. R., 41
Brebner, J., 37–38, 40–41, 46, 277, 291, 306
Brelje, T., 87
Breuer, J., 217, 299, 312
Broadbent, D. E., 29
Broadhurst, P. L., 18, 23
Brocke, B., 108–109
Broen, W. E., 29
Broks, P., 134, 147
Buchsbaum, M. S., 224, 226, 234, 251, 273, 275, 278
Buckley, W., 290
Budzińska, E., 210
Bull, R. H., 279
Buse, L., 116
Butler, G., 84, 88
Byrne, D., 86, 88, 91

Campbell, K. B., 45–47, 55
Caelier, M., 219, 238, 279
Carr, S. M., 39
Carrol, E. N., 234
Carrol, D., 87
Cattell, R. B., 79
Cattanach, L., 60
Chapman, D. P., 202
Chapman, L. J., 134
Churchland, P. S., 49
Claridge, G., 6–7, 18, 133–136, 141–142, 144–147, 294, 297
Clark, G. M., 50
Clark, K., 142, 145
Clark, L. A., 80, 86, 89
Cohen, S., 187
Cole, J. O., 68
Coles, M. G. H., 82
Colquhoun, P., 179
Como, P., 225–228
Conley, J. J., 85
Connolly, J. F., 146
Connor, W. H., 79
Cooper, C., 37–41, 277, 291, 306
Corcoran, D. W. J., 75
Cornblatt, B., 139
Coulas, J. T., 234, 236, 241, 247, 279
Coursey, R. D., 224, 226
Cowles, M. P., 233, 235–237, 241, 273, 276
Craig, K. D., 93
Craske, M. G., 93
Crits-Christoph, P., 290

Crockett, W. H., 208
Cronbach, L. J., 11
Crow, T. J., 222

Dalais, J. C., 140
Davidson, R. J., 92, 298
Davis, C. A., 233, 235–236, 241, 244, 247, 273, 276, 278–279
Dawson, M. E., 138
Deary, I. J., 41
Deecke, L., 60
DePree, J. A., 84
DeRisi, D. T., 41
Dimond, S. J., 178
Dixon, N. F., 86
Dodson, J. D., 18, 23
Dubreuil, D. L., 242
Duffy, E., 18, 271
Dumas, J. B., 10

Easterbrook, J. A., 29
Eber, H. W., 79
Eccles, J., 129
Edell, W. S., 134
Edman, G., 273
Edwards, J. A., 105, 281, 288, 293, 311–312
Ehrhardt, K. J., 106
Ekman, P., 298
Eliasz, A., 184, 189–195, 197–200, 202–203, 207, 229, 277, 291, 297
Emanuel, G., 92
Endler, N., 17, 85–86
Epstein, Y. M., 41
Erlenmeyer-Kimling, L., 139
Ervin, F. R., 54
Evans, G. W., 41
Eysenck, H. J., 1–2, 4, 7–8, 11, 18–20, 22, 33, 37–39, 59, 66, 68, 79–80, 83, 91, 100, 102–106, 108, 113, 121, 126, 133, 136, 143, 156, 158, 165–168, 173, 183, 199, 219, 220, 233, 238, 241, 252, 270, 272–276, 279, 291–293
Eysenck, M. C., 25

Eysenck, M. W., 1–2, 7–8, 11, 18–20, 22, 25, 29, 33, 79, 100, 102–103, 105–106, 113, 133, 143, 165, 167, 177, 199, 203, 211, 238, 293,

Fagen, R. E., 290
Fahrenberg, J., 99, 101, 103–105, 109–112, 114–116, 272, 277, 281,
Faily, 134
Falkenberg, W., 228
Farley, F., 288
Faverey, H. A., 61
Feij, J. A., 227–228
Fifkova, E., 124
Fiorgione, A., 242
Fiske, D. W., 276
Flavel, R., 40, 46
Fletcher, R. P., 140
Flor-Henry, P., 179
Foerster, F., 104, 110, 114, 272, 277
Folkard, S., 22, 24–26, 28, 30, 178–179
Folkman, S., 194
Ford, J. A., 174
Fortgens, C., 74
Fowles, D. C., 106, 276
Frankel, B. L., 224
Franks, C. M., 277
Freud, S., 217–218, 313
Friedensberg, E., 291
Friedman, D., 139
Frith, C., 138

Galambos, R., 46–47
Gale, A., 8, 63, 82, 105–106, 281, 287, 289–290, 293, 294, 307, 310–312
Garcia-Sevilla, L., 126
Gazendam, A., 227
Gilligan, S. G., 84
Gilliland, K., 19–20, 24, 26, 238, 279
Glaser, R., 26
Glass, D. C., 202
Glow, P., 123
Goldman, D., 236, 247, 278–279

Golińska, L., 206
Goulet, L. R., 210
Gray, J. A., 6, 18, 22, 33, 80–83, 106, 122, 136, 154, 173–174, 183, 199, 220–222, 233, 271, 273, 276, 292, 311
Green, G. S., 236
Greenaway, F., 10
Gross, O., 3–6
Gruzelier, J., 138, 141, 146–147, 179
Gupta, B. S., 19, 26

Haier, R. J., 45, 224, 251, 275
Halkiopoulos, C., 87–88
Hall, A. D., 290
Hall, J. W., 32
Hamilton, P., 24
Hamilton, V., 83–84
Hampel, R., 101
Haney, J. N., 90
Hare, R. D., 140, 227–228, 297
Hargreaves, J., 147
Hebb, D. O., 18, 172, 183, 271, 276
Helson, H., 276
Herzog, T. R., 236
Heshka, S., 41
Hesselbrook, V., 139
Heymans, G., 4
Hilgard, E. R., 236
Hillyard, S. A., 46–47
Hirano, A., 254
Hirsch, R. S., 146
Hobson, J. A., 51–52
Hockey, G. R. J., 24, 30
Hoffman, F. M., 235–236, 276–277
Horne, J. A., 174, 179
Howarth, E. A., 113
Hughes, J. R., 202
Hull, C. L., 28, 37
Humphreys, M. S., 17, 19, 24, 29–32, 292
Hundleby, J. D., 79
Hunt, R. W., 236, 273, 276, 278

Irmis, F., 128
Isaacson, R., 122

Jacobs, D. R., 202
Janes, C. L., 139
Janssen, R. H. C., 61, 63, 65, 68
Jimerson, D. C., 276
Johnson, C. A., 202
Johnson, J., 224, 275
Jung, C. G., 4, 165

Kahnemann, D., 187
Kant, I., 2
Kantor, D., 310–311
Karlin, R. A., 41
Karp, S., 161
Katsikitis, M., 41
Kelly, D., 82
Keuss, P. J. G., 244
Khew, K., 41, 43–45
Klein, R. H., 139
Kline, P., 79, 82
Klonowicz, T., 183–184, 187, 189–191, 194, 199, 207, 292, 297
Knauth, P., 25
Kohn, P. M., 233–239, 241–242, 244–247, 273, 276–279
Kok, A., 226
Kolin, E. A., 223
Konorski, J., 172
Kornhuber, H. H., 60
Kostin, I. W., 236
Kotz, M., 251
Krausz, H. J., 47
Krekule, I., 128
Krohne, H. W., 89
Kruidenier, B. G., 238
Kugelmass, S., 139
Kuhn, T. S., 12
Kuypers, H. G. J. M., 51

Lacey, B. C., 82, 135, 140
Lacey, J. I., 8, 82, 140, 272, 277, 295
Lader, M., 82
Lafreniere, K., 238
Laird, J. D., 298
Lakatos, T., 10, 12

Lally, M., 41
Lang, P., 93
Lat, J., 128
Lawrence, D. G., 51
Lazarus, R. S., 194
Lehr, D., 310–311
Levey, J., 270, 276–277
Levey, A., 22
Lewinsohn, P. M., 87
Lindsley, D. B., 51, 271
Litle, P., 222
Little, B. R., 201
Loo, R., 22, 113
Lubowsky, J., 146
Lucioli, R., 174
Lukas, J. H., 226
Luria, A. R., 173
Lynch, M. J., 25, 32
Lyons, W., 81–82

Maciejczyk, J., 187
Mackay, C. J., 295
Mackenzie, B., 42
Mackintosh, N. J., 154
MacLead, C., 87–89
Madoli, S. R., 276
Magnusson, D., 17
Magoun, H. W., 49–50, 156–159, 271
Mahoney, J., 242, 244
Maley, M., 136, 141
Malmo, R. B., 271
Manehanda, R., 146
Mangan, G. L., 173, 238
Marcus, J., 139
Marcuse, Y., 139
Marsh, V. R., 67
Marshall, J., 124
Martin, I., 82, 270, 276
Maslach, C., 198
Matczak, A., 201
Matheson, J., 147
Mathews, A., 84, 87–88
Matsui, I., 254
Mattie, H., 63, 65, 74–75
Matysiak, J., 190, 198
Mayer, J. D., 84
Mazzei, J., 210
McClearn, G., 122
McDougall, W., 4–6
McGuiness, D., 106

McGuire, M., 147
Mecacci, L., 171–175, 178–179, 274
Mednick, S. A., 139–140
Mehrabian, A., 237, 239, 241
Michaud, A., 54
Miller, J. G., 290
Millman, J. E., 67
Minuchin, S., 307
Mishara, B. L., 236
Mitchell, D. A., 226
Monakhov, K., 235
Monk, T. W., 25, 178
Monteiro, K. P., 84
Morgan, A. H., 236
Morris, L. W., 279
Moruzzi, G., 49–50, 271
Mountcastle, V. B., 159, 161
Mulholland, T. M., 26
Müller, W., 104, 114, 272
Mullins, L. F., 226
Murphy, D. L., 234, 275–276
Murray, D. M., 202
Murtaugh, T. M., 223, 234
Musgrave, A., 10
Myrtek, M., 103–106, 112, 114–115, 272

Nauta, W. H. J., 50
Neary, R. S., 227
Nebylitsyn, V. D., 6, 121, 173–176, 219, 233, 235–236, 244, 246–247, 270–271, 274, 276–277
Nelsen, J. M., 67
Nelson, K., 200
Nettelbeck, T., 41
Nielsen, T. C., 82, 134
Niemela, P., 94
Noldy-Cullum, N., 45–47, 55
Nuechterlein, K. H., 138
Nye, I. F., 307

Oakeshott, J., 123
O'Connor, K. P., 66–67, 73

O'Gorman, J. G., 82
Ohman, A., 138
Oltman, P. K., 161
Opton, E. M., 115
Orlebeke, J. F., 226–228, 244
Ostberg, O., 174, 179
Ostwald, 10

Paisey, T. J. H., 238
Parker, L., 236
Patterson, P., 138
Patterson, T., 138
Patton, J. H., 273, 276–279
Paunonen, S. V., 114
Pava, J., 146
Pavlov, I. P., 6–7, 121, 153–156, 158, 160, 163, 172, 218, 224, 269, 276
Pawlik, K., 116
Pearson, P. H., 237
Pedersen, V., 92
Pellegrine, R. J., 92
Pellegrino, J. W., 26
Pennebaker, J. W., 116
Perris, C., 235
Petersen, K. E., 82
Petersen, N. E., 134, 139
Petrie, A., 233, 236, 273, 277–278
Phelps, M. E., 254
Phillips, C. G., 53
Picton, T. W., 47
Pigareva, M. L., 123, 126
Plooij-van Gorsel, P. C., 63, 65
Plouffe, L., 82, 228
Porter, R., 53
Posey, T. B., 174
Posner, M. J., 178
Post, R. M., 222, 276
Prentky, R. A., 139
Preobrazhenskaya, L. A., 126–127
Pribram, K. H., 106
Price, L., 223
Price, V., 202
Pruzinsky, T., 84
Pylypuk, A., 41

Radil-Weiss, T., 128
Raine, A., 226
Rainer, J. D., 139
Raman, A. C., 140
Ramon-Moliner, E., 50
Rasmussen, P. V., 139
Raskin, E., 161
Rawlings, D., 147
Rawlins, M. D., 67
Ray, O., 234
Reason, J. T., 244
Reid, D. W., 236
Revelle, W., 17, 19–21, 23–26, 28–32, 238, 292
Ridgeway, D., 227–228
Rieder, J., 146
Roback, A. A., 2
Robinson, D. L., 45, 72–74, 136, 144, 146, 153, 157, 159–163, 165–167, 274–275
Robinson, E., 84
Robinson, T. N., 142
Rocchetti, G., 74
Rocklin, T., 238
Roderick, T. H., 122
Rogner, J., 89
Rolf, J. E., 134
Rosenthal, D., 139
Rosler, F., 105
Rossi, B., 174–175
Routenberg, A., 2
Rusalov, V. M., 277
Russell, J. A., 237, 241
Ruszkiewicz, E., 209
Rutenfranz, J., 25
Rutschmann, J., 139

Saegart, S., 41
Saito, Y., 54
Sales, S. M., 234, 244, 247
Salmaso, D., 178
Salzman, L. F., 139
Samuels, I., 74, 157, 159
Sasaki, H., 54
Saville, P., 80
Schaefer, C., 194, 202
Schaffer, H. R., 200–201
Schalling, D., 273, 277, 279
Scheibel, A. B., 50–52

Scheibel, M. E., 50
Schill, T., 91–92
Schmidt, J., 115
Schmueli, J., 139
Schneider, H. J., 104, 110, 115, 272
Schneider, L., 92
Schnur, D., 146
Schucker, B., 202
Schulsinger, F., 139
Schulsinger, H., 139–140
Schwartz, G., 92, 203, 290, 298
Schwartz, M., 275
Schweizer, K., 115
Schwent, Y. L., 46
Selg, H., 101
Shagas, C., 275
Shumate, M., 242
Siegel, J., 223, 234
Simon, L., 19
Simonov, P. V., 121–122, 129
Simons, R. F., 140, 144, 225
Singer, C., 9
Singer, W., 50
Simpson, G. B., 90
Skarżyńska, K., 200
Skinner, B. F., 171
Skinner, J. E., 51
Slade, P. D., 134
Sokoloff, I., 254
Sokolski, K., 251
Spence, J. T., 28
Spence, K. W., 28, 276
Spohn, H. E., 138
Stassen, H. G., 75
Stein, L., 222
Stelmack, R. M., 54, 82, 103, 106, 219, 228, 238, 275
Stemmler, G., 114, 116
Sternet, R. G., 136
Stern, J. A., 139
Stepney, R., 67
Storms, L. H., 29
Straube, E., 138
Strelau, J., 6–7, 38, 74, 173–176, 183–184, 187, 190–193, 197–198, 201,

Strelau (*Cont.*)
207, 218, 220, 224–225,
229, 233, 238, 241, 244,
246, 269, 271, 273–279,
288, 291–293, 297, 310
Strongman, K. T., 279
Suppe, F., 10
Świętochowski, W., 206,
208

Tata, P., 87
Tatsouka, M. M., 79
Tecce, J. J., 60, 66, 68
Telford, R., 67
Tellegen, A., 80, 107
Teplov, B. M., 6, 121, 158,
162–163, 176, 219, 271,
274
Terelak, J., 238
Thayer, R. E., 188, 295
Thompson, J. W., 67
Thomson, J. J., 10
Throop, W. F., 244
Tune, G. S., 174
Turriff, S., 19

Ullmann, L. P., 87
Uttal, W. R., 48

Vando, A., 236, 242, 243
Van Dyke, J. L., 139
Van Egeren, L., 87
Van Zuilen, R., 227
Venables, P. H., 7, 134–
135, 137–141, 226, 291,
293, 295–297, 307
Vetere, A., 290, 307, 310
Vogel, W. H., 234
Von Bertalanffy, L., 289
Von Knorring, L., 226,
235

Wachowiak, D., 92
Wagstaff, G. F., 87
Walker, E., 147
Walter, W. G., 59
Walschburger, P., 104, 110
Ware, E. E., 236
Watson, D., 80, 86, 89
Watt, N. F., 134
Webb, W. B., 174
Weinberger, D. A., 92–
93, 298
Weinstein, N. D., 24
Weinstraub, D. J., 236
Werre, P. F., 59, 61, 63,
65, 67, 74
Whytt, R., 100–101

Wiersma, E., 4
Williams, D., 45, 84, 275
Wilson, G. D., 12, 207
Wimer, R. E., 122
Wimer, C. C., 122
Wine, J., 30
Wing, J. K., 137
Wing, L., 82
Wise, R. A., 222
Witkin, H. A., 161–162
Wittman, W. W., 114
Worthington, E. L., 242
Wrześniewski, K., 193,
203
Wundt, W., 2–3
Wynne, L. C., 134

Yerkes, R. M., 18, 23

Zahn, T. P., 138, 142
Zajonc, R. B., 221
Zani, A., 174, 175
Zeillemaker, C. W., 226
Zoob, I., 223
Zuckerman, M., 183, 217,
221–223, 226–227, 229,
234–236, 241, 253, 272–
273, 275–277, 279, 292,
296

Subject Index

Activation, 106–111
  activation processes, 109–111
  See also Arousal
  autonomic and cortical arousal, 102–107, 136
    measures of, 103
  behavioral activity
    and personality dimensions, 276–277
  cortical activity
    concentration/irradiation, 160
Activity, 121
  active/inactive children, 200–201
  of catecholamine systems, 223
  nervous, 171–173
  and personality dimensions, 277
  and reactivity, 192
  as a source of stimulation, 192
Anxiety, 79–94, 303
  BIS, 81
  and long-term memory (LTM), 84–86
  physiological basis of, 80–83
  repression and sensitization, 86–88
    and behavioral differences, 91–92
    and performance, 92
Arousal, 7–8, 29–30, 59, 134–35, 183, 224, 288–289, 294–296
  and anxiety, 221
  arousability, 135, 163–164, 233, 270, 273, 304–305
    measures of, 244–245
  and cognition, 177–180
  and emotional expression, 298
  and impulsivity, 23–24, 221
  optimal level of, 184, 197–198, 217, 234, 293
  and personality dimensions, 179–180, 275, 278–279

Arousal (*Cont.*)
  and personality dimensions (*Cont.*)
    measured by different indexes, 282
  and reactivity, 185–186, 188–190
  sensory threshold
    and personality dimensions, 276
  and task difficulty, 23
    substained information transfer (SIT), 24, 27
    short-term memory (STM), 24, 27
    memory-scanning task, 25
  task performance
    information transfer and memory availability, 30–32
    range of cue utilization, 29–30
    response competition, 28–29
    transmarginal inhibition, 28
  and stimulus-analysis and response organization, 45–54
Augmenting/reducing dimension, 270–271, 278, 304
  and efficiency of learning, 277
  and extraversion, 279
  and sensation-seeking, 226, 229, 234–238, 279

Circadian types, 174
  diurnal variation in cognitive performance, 178–179
  hemispheric specialization, 178–179
  measured by MEQ
    and age, 174–175
    and habitual activity, 175
    and profession, 174
  and personality profiles, 179
Cognitive orientation, 203, 292
  and reactivity, 204–206
Conditioning, 154

Diffuse thalamocortical
    system (DTS), 156–161,
    164–169
  and arousability, 164
  and concentration/irradiation, 160–161
  DTPS, 156–161
  and EEG effects, 157–159
  as a mediator of excitation, 156–159
  neural bases of intelligence, 159–162
  and selective cortical activation, 156–
    157
  and sensitivity, 166

Emotionality, 121, 303
  and autonomic arousal, 100, 102–108
  determinants of emotions, 122
  See also Neuroticism
Energy system components
  acquisition system, 299, 306
  and anxiety, 300, 303, 306
  control system, 299, 306
  expression system, 299–300, 306
  and extraversion, 299–307
  and individual difference dimension,
    306–307
  and neuroticism, 300, 303, 306
  and personality attributes, 302–309
  and reactivity, 302–306
  and sensation seeking, 303–304
  storage system, 299, 300–301, 306
Excitatory/inhibitory processes, 136–137,
    156, 272
  balance between, 6–7, 39, 136, 155,
    272
  and DTS, 159, 274
  reactive inhibition, 37–38
  strength of, 155, 177, 269–270
    and concentration/irradiation, 160–
      162
    scale of, 244–245
  transmarginal inhibition, 7, 219, 235,
    272
Extraversion-introversion, 2–5, 37–45,
    155–159, 302–305
  and arousal, 22, 45–55, 220–221
  and cognitive performance, 18–20
    stimulus–analysis and response–or-
      ganization, 38, 42–45
  and conditionability, 272
  and contingent negative variation
    (CNV), 60–73

Extraversion-introversion (Cont.)
  and cortical areas, 257–259
  and inhibition of BSRF, 165
  and reactivity, 199, 207, 279–280
  scale, 244–246
  and susceptibility to stimuli, 199
  and temperamental types, 2, 7, 158,
    272
  and thalamocortical arousability, 165–
    168

General system theory, 289–290

Impulsivity, 271, 278
  effect of caffeine
    on complex analogies, 26
    on performance, 26
  and time of day, 21–23
  See also Circadian types
Intelligence
  neural base, 159–162
Individual differences, 288
  in activation/arousal, 273
  in augmenting/reducing, 271
  in circadian typology, 179
  dimension, 306
  and family processes, 307–311
  in glucose metabolism, 264
  in sensation-seeking, 271
  style of action, 191

Limbic structures
  and sensation seeking scale, 262
  and motivational and informational
    system, 122–126

Neuroticism, 100–101, 113, 155–159, 274,
    303
  See also Anxiety
  contingent negative variation (CNV),
    61–62
  limbic structures, 102, 258
  and nervous system strength, 126
  and personality dimensions, 279
  personality inventory FPI, 101
  psychophysiology of, 103–105
Nervous system
  brain functional organization, 176
  mobility of, 7, 162
    and concentration/irradiation, 162–
      163

Nervous system (*Cont.*)
  and hippocampal theta rhythm,
    128–130
  properties, 171–177, 246–247
  strength of, 6, 177, 218
    measure of, 225–227
    and sensitivity, 273
  type of, 6, 218

Positron Emission Tomography (PET),
    251–252
  and personality dimensions, 256–259
  quantification of, 254–255
  and sensation-seeking, 259–264
Psychoticism, 133–134, 302–303
  biological basis of, 138–147
  electrodermal activity, 138–140, 142
  EPQ P-scale, 133, 141–144
    and arousal, 138, 141–142, 145
    and performance, 141–142
    and STQ scale, 143
  hyperresponsiveness, 139–140, 144–145
  schizophrenia, 137–138

Reactivity, 184–185, 197, 219, 274, 291,
    302, 304
  and anticipation of stress, 194
  and anxiety, 201
  and cognitive differentiation (CD),
    208–211
  endurance and sensory threshold, 197
  and life-styles, 202
  and nonverbal communication, 206–
    207
  and pain, 242–243
  and perception, 204
  and performance, 186–188, 203–206
  and personality dimensions, 192–193

Reactivity (*Cont.*)
  scale, 239–244
    and social/physical stimuli, 200–202
    and stimulation, 186–189, 198–203
    and style of action, 191–192

Sensation-seeking, 225, 234, 271, 303–
    304
  and arousability, 233–234
  and arousal, 223–225
  and cortical areas, 259–264
  and deceleration of heart rate, 227–
    228
  and efficency of learning, 277
  and evoked potentials, 227, 235, 275
  and extraversion, 279–280
  and heart rate, 227–229
  measures of, 236–238
  and skin conductance, 229
Sensory threshold
  and personality dimensions, 276
Stimulation
  actual and optimal level of, 198–199,
    293
  control, 189, 199
  sensitivity to social influence, 203
  susceptibility to stimuli, 199
  type of stimulus, 199–200

Temperament, 184, 197, 218, 291
  and perception, 201
  and personality, 270
  See also Reactivity
  temperamental traits, 269
  temperamental types
    and extraversion-introversion, 2–4,
      156
    and properties of CNS, 218